American Democracy

American Democracy

Representation, Participation, and the Future of the Republic

Anthony J. Eksterowicz
Paul C. Cline
Scott J. Hammond

James Madison University

Prentice Hall, Englewood Cliffs, New Jersey 07632

Library of Congress Cataloging-in-Publication Data

Eksterowicz, Anthony J.
American democracy : representation, participation, and the future of the Republic / Anthony J. Eksterowicz, Paul C. Cline, Scott J. Hammond.
p. cm.
ISBN 0–13–336546–8 (pbk.)
1. Democracy—United States. 2. Representative government and representation—United States. 3. Political participation—United States. 4. United States—Politics and government. I. Cline, Paul C. II. Hammond, Scott J. III. Title.
JK271.E27 1995
320.473—dc20 94–27997
CIP

Acquisitions editor: Charlyce Jones Owen
Editorial/production supervision
and interior design: Scott Pass
Cover design: DeLuca Design
Buyer: Bob Anderson
Editorial assistant: Nicole Signoretti

Printed in the United States of America
10 9 8 7 6 5 4 3 2 1

ISBN 0-13-336546-8

Prentice-Hall International (UK) Limited, *London*
Prentice-Hall of Australia Pty. Limited, *Sydney*
Prentice-Hall Canada Inc., *Toronto*
Prentice-Hall Hispanoamericana, S.A., *Mexico*
Prentice-Hall of India Private Limited, *New Delhi*
Prentice-Hall of Japan, Inc., *Tokyo*
Prentice-Hall of Southeast Asia Pte. Ltd., *Singapore*
Editora Prentice-Hall do Brasil, Ltda., *Rio de Janeiro*

To Nancy, Diane, and Chereé

Contents

American Democracy

Introduction

Every year, thousands of government instructors and their students struggle to explain and understand the theoretical foundations of the United States Constitution. This is not an easy task, for these foundations can be quite confusing. How, for example, does one explain the seemingly contradictory political ideas of liberty and equality, rugged individualism and commonwealth, private property rights and faith in community, government by the best and government by the people, republican democracy and participatory democracy?

One way of explaining these ideas is to explore the "great debate" by Federalists and Antifederalists over the ratification of the Constitution. Both camps presented arguments that have had profound and lasting effects upon American government structures and processes. The problem, however, is in the presentation of this debate. Most American government textbooks concentrate upon Federalist positions or arguments to the point of losing much of the debate occurring between the two camps.[1] The same is true for many American history textbooks.[2] To fully appreciate this debate, students must understand not only what was being asserted by the pro-Constitution Federalist forces but also what was being denied by them, mainly the arguments of the Antifederalists.

This presentation problem is not as great as it once was, owing to the appearance of Herbert Storing's volumes on Antifederalist writings[3] and Ralph Ketchum's work, *The Antifederalist Papers and the Constitutional Convention Debates.* Still, what is missing is a juxtaposition of Antifederalist and Federalist arguments on the various constitutional issues. This volume seeks to fill that void.

Each chapter covers a central idea or constitutional structure that was de-

---

[1]Anthony J. Eksterowicz and Paul C. Cline, "Ratification of the Constitution; The Great Debate as Portrayed in American Government Textbooks," *Political Science and Politics*, Vol. 24, No. 2 (1991): 211–215.

[2]Paul C. Cline and Anthony J. Eksterowicz, "Textbooks and the Ratification of the Constitution: A Review Essay," *The Magazine of History*, Vol. 6, No. 4 (1992): 67–72.

[3]Indeed, without Storing's massive seven-volume compilation of Antifederalist writings, subsequent efforts on Antifederalism and the ratification debate might not be possible. For further information, see Herbert Storing, ed., *The Complete Anti-Federalist* (Chicago: University of Chicago Press, 1981), *passim.*

bated by both Federalists and Antifederalists. Our aim is to provide the student with a sense of debate that is missing in many textbooks and readers covering the theoretical foundations of the Constitution. Key sections of the Constitution debated by both camps are reprinted at the beginning of each chapter. The Bill of Rights appears at the end of Chapter 1. In addition, each chapter includes modern writings and thoughts that are still influenced by the arguments made during the ratification debate. Our purpose here is to illustrate the ongoing importance of this debate to our modern government's structures and processes. Ralph Ketchum has wisely noted, " . . . Anti-federal ideas have also surfaced again and again in various guises among later generations of Americans. Those ideas, as well as the enticing prospects held out by Publius, are a vital element in the American political tradition and are properly viewed as the philosophy of the Constitution." [4]

In fact, the struggle between the Federalists and Antifederalists has defined us as a people. Ever since this great debate the citizens of this nation have been struggling with the contradictory ideas of government for versus government by the people. Clearly, Federalist ideas emphasized the former, whereas Antifederalist ideas stressed the latter. A large part of our nation's history has been devoted to democratizing our republican structure inherited from the Federalists. One can note, for example, the Jacksonian, Populist, and Progressive eras, the struggle for civil rights, the environmental and women's movements, and modern interest group activity. This democratization is much broader than simply increasing the access to suffrage rights for previously restricted groups. The Equal Opportunity Act of 1964, for example, mobilized the poor and involved them in policy-making decisions. Other acts like the Coastal Zone Act and the Housing and Community Development Act required citizen participation by either legislation or regulation. This trend has also increased at the state and local levels. The Advisory Commission on Intergovernmental Relations gathered data in 1978 and found that 155 federal grant programs had citizen participation requirements mandated by either legislation or regulation. Many federal legislative programs have also been amended to include citizen participation provisions.[5] As a result, citizens have been incorporated into many planning bodies across diverse fields like health, education, transportation, and the environment. The debate over how big a role citizens would play in their government defined the differences between Federalists and Antifederalists during the Constitutional ratification debate.

Historical Background and Antifederalist and Federalist Beliefs

For nearly a decade prior to the Philadelphia Convention that produced the Constitution, the emerging American nation had been operating under a confederal scheme of government that can be accurately designated the First American Republic. Framed by the Articles of Confederation and Perpetual Union and forged

[4]Ralph Ketcham, ed. *The Anti-Federalist Papers and the Constitutional Convention Debates* (New York: Mentor Books, 1986), p. 20.

[5]Stuart Langton, *Citizen Participation in America* (Boston, MA: D.C. Heath & Co., 1978), p. 3.

during the revolution against British autocracy, the First American Republic embraced the principles of self-government that drove the Colonies into war. By clearly locating the center of sovereignty within the several states, providing for the representational equality of the states as sovereign entities, and characterizing the confederacy as a "firm league of friendship," the framers of the Articles of Confederation, who represented a mix of "conservatives" such as John Dickinson and "radicals" such as Samuel Adams, affirmed their desire to ensure the strength of republican government within the states while simultaneously guarding against the return of the autocratic, centralized form against which they were risking everything in rebellion. Some of the elements of the Articles would be incorporated into the Constitution, but the approach to union was very different in the First and Second Republics. In addition to the specifically drawn sovereignty of the participating states, the confederal organ was deliberately diluted, left with no enforcement power to administer its enactments, and dependent upon the generosity of the states for its effective operation. Hard upon the signing of the Declaration of Independence, the Articles were drafted and instituted in 1777 and served as the foundation for the new government that would successfully achieve independence and work toward the establishment of a North American union of states.

In 1786, after several years of economic stress along the colonial seaboard, the leadership of the new republic was alerted to a turbulent series of events in Massachusetts, wherein angry farmers from the western quarter of the state rose in insurrection against the political and economic elite of the east. The Confederation stood by idly while the state of Massachusetts was left alone to deal with the situation. Although this insurrection, known as Shay's rebellion, was eventually contained, the more conservatively inclined among the Confederation's leadership were shaken and appalled by the apparent disorder that menaced the union. Convincing the leadership that the Articles of Confederation needed revision in order to deal more energetically with economic decay and political discord, prominent dissenters against the First Republic formed and participated in conventions located in Annapolis and Philadelphia which amounted to the creation of a Second American Republic. At Philadelphia in 1787, the delegates were granted the authority by the states to propose amendments and revisions to the new Constitution. Before the convention began, members such as James Madison and Edmund Randolph drafted proposals that would lead to the composition of an entirely new Constitutional document and the construction of a significantly different breed of government.

Opposition to the proposed Constitution immediately appeared. While notables such as Washington, Franklin, Dickinson, Madison, Randolph, Wilson, Morris, Hamilton, Marshall, Iredell, Noah Webster, Sherman, and Jay all rallied to its support, individuals of like prominence such as George Mason, George Clinton, Patrick Henry, Richard Henry Lee, James Monroe, Luther Martin, James Withrop, Melancton Smith, Robert Yates, Mercy Otis Warren, Elbridge Gerry, John Francis Mercer, and Samuel Bryan were among those who represented dissent. Although the names of the opponents do not evoke the same significance in the American *mythos* as Washington and Franklin, they were, in their time, held in nearly equal esteem. In an interesting twist of fate, the young republic's two most athletic minds, Thomas Jefferson and John Adams, were in diplomatic service and therefore not present to lend their peerless talents to the Convention or the ratification debates. Nonetheless, their views regarding the new document did enter the general debate from a distance, with Adams lending enthusiastic support for ratification and Jefferson giving qualified, conditional support for the new instrument. Throughout the latter part of 1787 and into 1788 the new Constitution was debated throughout the states. This debate not only involved the approval or disapproval of a new government but also provided a fertile medium for the cultivation of political and secular moral principles.

Often employing pseudonyms drawn from political heroes of antiquity or, in the case of names such as "John DeWitt," "Sydney," and "William Penn," pseudonyms drawn from more "modern" inspiration, the participants returned to familiar methods of advocacy and rhetoric: pamphlets, newspaper articles, and speeches. Hamilton, Madison, and Jay wrote what we now call the *Federalist* Papers under the pseudonym of Publius, drawn from one of the heroes involved in the formation of republican Rome after the demise of the early Roman monarchy. Antifederalists, after a fashion truly indicative of their diversity, drew upon a number of heroic names to add to the supply of pseudonyms. The name Brutus served to indicate that the author was a fierce opponent of despotism. The use of the name Centinel informed the reader that the author assumed the role of a defender of the republic. Cato, a name used by two separate authors, was unusual in that it not only drew upon Cato the Younger, a Stoic philosopher, statesman, and champion of republican Rome, but also evoked memories of the "Cato Letters" composed by the libertarian pamphleteers Gordon and Trenchard, whose indictment of centralized, intrusive government in early 18th-century Britain provided considerable inspiration for American pamphleteers in the years preceding the Revolution and continued to have relevance for the opponents of the newly proposed Constitution. Names of skeptics, republican heroes, and friends of the people such as Agrippa, Cincinattus, and Vox Populi (voice of the people) were further indications of the political positions of the various Antifederalists. Once attributed to Hamilton but now linked to an authorship cast in doubt, the "Caesar Letters" employed a pseudonym that clearly conveyed the deeper sympathies of their anonymous Federalist author. (See Chapter 6 for a further discussion of this elusive authorship.)

Soon divisions between the participants were cast in relief, and one could see the forensic lines of battle drawn. The opponents of the Constitution were characterized by considerable diversity, challenging the Constitution on numerous grounds but not always for consistent reasons. Agrarians, merchants, and mechanics alike raised hard resistance against the new proposed framework of government. Although their general dissent was not always unified, many consistent themes did emerge from within this heterogeneous Antifederalist opposition. However, one of the themes that the Antifederalist held in common was the belief that they were not "anti" Federalist. Indeed, they saw themselves as the true Federalists resisting the resurrection of the very same form of centralized national government that they had just recently joined in war to escape. The Antifederalists considered the Federalists to be true centralists and nationalists, interested in power and empire first and republican government and individual liberty second, if at all. Stemming from this basic emphasis in the essential form of the federation, the opposition developed several critiques against the Constitution that, when considered together, represent a political philosophy. The tenets of individual liberty, equality, limited government, consent of the governed, and individual rights are consistent throughout most of the Antifederalist essays and speeches. Additionally, many Antifederalists were critical of the Madisonian scheme of separation of powers, although not always for the same reason.

Finally, the opposition appeared quite perplexed at the supporters' arguments regarding the dire condition of the Confederacy. In their view, reports of chaos and disarray were hyperbolic to say the least, a blatant scare tactic invented to panic the citizenry into hasty ratification. The Articles of Confederation were scarcely ten years old and their peacetime operation had been quite brief. If given a chance to work, the confederal form that respected the sovereignty and mild governments of the republican states could succeed and could do so in favor of liberty for individual citizens rather than for the sake of empire and power. These latter purposes seemed to many Antifederalists to be the real goals of the "pseudo-Federalists." These goals could not, by any stretch of the imagination, be defended as compatible with the principles of the American Revolution and its Declaration of Independence.

Federalist response to the opponents of the Constitution was quick and formidable. By and large, the Federalists were a more homogeneous group than their opponents, and they enjoyed the advantage of greater preparation owing to their experiences just before and during the Constitutional Convention proceedings. Madison's background in and talent for political theory were considerable, and Hamilton's rhetorical style and keen facility for logic exceeded those of most individuals on either side of the controversy. Furthermore, the Federalists deftly cloaked themselves in the role of active framers and leaders politically affirming necessary changes to save an unstable republic and its vulnerable states. Both Washington and Franklin, the pre-eminent statesmen of their day, supported the Constitution, thus lending considerable political strength to the Federalist side. Had Jefferson withdrawn his qualified support and joined the opposition, the debate might have turned, but in any event, the character of Washington and the intellectual reputation of Franklin provided an invaluable service to the Federalist cause.

The Federalists, like their opposition, also argued for the continuation of many of the ideals of the American Revolution, hence deflecting at every turn the accusations of incipient and insidious autocracy leveled by the Antifederalists. In spite of this, within the debate one can discern at least two distinct political theories, both embracing to some extent and in some form the ideals of the American Revolution. However, both sides in the debate cast these ideals differently and in so doing established disparate and competing visions for the American polity. The Federalist position essentially emphasized a basic and inherent distrust of popular democracy, preferring representative schemes that contained the populist elements in democracy, allowing only a limited amount of participation from the general citizenry. Government was seen as an energetic and forthright champion of "ordered liberty," and the institutions of government must be crafted so as to prevent the abuses of democratic and popular politics. Most Antifederalists inclined toward more popular forms of government, recognizing that democracy must be more than simply representative but participatory as well. Hence, the ideals of the Revolution—rights of individuals, limited government, consent of the governed, and equality before the law—could be secured and promoted only if the people were involved in the act of governance to a fairly high degree. To the Antifederalists, participatory forms of government were not possible under a Constitution that promised to centralize power at the expense of state and local governments. Only a bill of rights could placate the opposition, and even that was not enough for some who remained categorically opposed to the Constitution. Under the old Articles of Confederation, a bill of rights did not seem necessary; protections of individual liberties in state constitutions sufficed. Power under the new Constitution was of a different order, and it was in response to this that the combined efforts of Antifederalists and sympathetic Federalists worked toward the production of the federal Bill of Rights, perhaps the only true and pure link between Jefferson's Declaration of Independence and Madison's Constitution.

Organization of the Book

As previously indicated, each chapter contains Antifederalist and Federalist writings covering a major topic in American government. The goal is to convey to students a sense of argument and debate between the two sides sorely missing in most textbook accounts of the ratification debate. Each chapter also contains modern writings that reflect Antifederalist and Federalist sentiments noted at the time of the ratification debate. In addition, a series of discussion questions precedes each writing, not only to guide students in understanding the main arguments of the authors but also to relate these writings to one another in thematic fashion.

Chapter 1 covers Antifederalist and Federalist sentiments concerning the role of government power and the Constitutional inclusion of a bill of rights. This chapter notes the Antifederalist apprehension over such Constitutional phrases as "necessary and proper," the "commerce clause," and the "supremacy clause." Federalists like Madison responded that there was a need for "ordered liberty" in the new republic. Washington and Hamilton were alarmed by the people's tendencies toward insurrection and championed the need for a stronger central government. Antifederalists agreed with the need for a rule of law, but they almost universally agreed that liberty was a function of some level of power and that power could be retained by the people only through participation. The chapter ends with the debate over the inclusion of the Bill of Rights in the Constitution.

Chapter 2 covers the conflicting views toward property and commerce. Although both Federalists and Antifederalists agreed that private ownership of property was an inalienable right, consensus yielded to controversy over the specific kind of economic system that was to be developed. Many Antifederalists favored an agrarian economic system, whereas Federalists favored movement toward new forms of enterprise through sophisticated, urban commerce and incipient industrialism. Several Antifederalists sided with Thomas Jefferson's view of an agrarian-based society, whereas most Federalists believed in Hamilton's vision of urban commerce and international manufacturing with its alliance between the public and private sectors. It is this alliance that Antifederalists feared. The more modern writings in this chapter trace the relationship between property and democracy and note the tension between the struggle for political equality so necessary to participatory democracy and the realities of economic inequality that is often the disturbing result of capitalism.

Chapter 3 describes the debate over the federal relationship of nation to states. Patrick Henry notes the threat to the autonomy of the states posed by the Constitution and favors reliance upon the Articles of Confederation. From the Federalist perspective, Alexander Hamilton discusses the shortcomings of the Articles of Confederation as they apply to the nation and states. Modern writings trace the relationship and various stages of evolution between the federal government and the states. Finally, excerpts from the inaugural addresses of President's Reagan and Clinton offer some insight into the two conflicting views concerning Federalism evidenced during the ratification debate.

Although no specific argument concerning political parties arose during the ratification debate, considerable discussion concerned the different classes of people in the nation. Antifederalists feared a dominant, elite faction of people in the new republic. Richard Henry Lee (The Federal Farmer) argued that freedom depended upon the existence of parties and that public liberty was harmed by the existence of a single party. James Madison, in his famous *Federalist* Paper 10, answers that having a majority included in a faction permits citizens to protect their liberties. He contends that the Antifederalists' preference for societies of smaller groups of citizens is no guarantee of liberty or "cure for the mischiefs of faction." Madison sets the stage for the problems associated with what modern political scientist Theodore Lowi has termed "interest group liberalism."

This problem, along with the long-term decline in political parties, has, according to James MacGregor Burns, left the nation with little to counteract the divisive tendencies of interest groups. Finally, Eksterowicz and Cline present a plan to fuse increased citizen participation to strong political parties in the hope of preserving the best of Antifederalist and Federalist thought.

Chapter 5 underscores the Antifederalist fear concerning federal control of elections under Article 1, Section 4 of the Constitution. Brutus argues that national elections set by the federal government could subvert the people's elections in the states, resulting in a government farther removed from the people. Cato and John DeWitt call for annual elections for the House of Representatives in order to keep the government closer to and more representative of the people. In a subtle way, Antifederalists seemed to be arguing that voting procedures matter because those procedures may facilitate the election of representatives who might be divorced from the middle and poor classes. Therefore, the policies that these representatives might advocate could also differ from the interests of the poor and middle classes. In the Antifederalist mind, voting is linked to substantive policies rather than to mere procedures. Federalists disagreed and generally rebuked the Antifederalists for relying on annual elections for representatives. Both Madison and Hamilton were concerned that the federal union would not last long under such a scheme. Madison also argued against frequent change in the Constitution.

Modern writings trace the evolution and enlargement of the franchise. Voting rights in this nation were well on their way to being democratized when Alexis de Tocqueville visited America in 1831. Finally, William Riker demonstrates that the modern liberal interpretation of voting was heavily influenced by Madison, whereas the populistic, more participatory, interpretation of voting was influenced by Rousseau. Antifederalists exhibited traits of this latter thinking.

Chapter 6 illustrates the wide differences in Antifederalist and Federalist positions concerning the public's opinions. Generally, Antifederalist literature displays a greater trust in the capacity of people to know and understand the constitutional issues affecting them. Federalist literature, on the other hand, generally displays skepticism concerning the public's capacity to make informed and intelligent decisions on constitutional issues. These attitudes surface in discussions concerning the influence of the aristocracy, representation in the House and Senate, term limits and frequency of elections, and the Constitutional scheme for the judicial branch of government. In a modern excerpt, public opinion pollster Daniel Yankelovich shares his thoughts about the expert's views of the public's opinions. He then presents a vision for the future which seems to draw upon Antifederalist confidence in the public and Jeffersonian ideals of civic education.

Chapter 7 covers Antifederalist and Federalist arguments concerning the Congress. Antifederalist arguments can be characterized as an effort to ensure greater representation of and participation by the people. Antifederalists objected to the small membership in the House of Representatives because it would be unlikely for common people from various professions to hold office in this body. Rotation of office provisions were championed by many Antifederalists.

Federalists disagreed. Madison argues that the small membership in the House will only be temporary because the membership will be adjusted with each census. In addition, checks and balances would protect the people from the usurpation of government by a few individuals.

Perhaps nowhere is the debate between Antifederalists and Federalists better mirrored than in the current debate over term limits. Both Charles R. Kessler and John H. Fund provide arguments that are heavily influenced by those heard during the ratification debate.

Chapter 8 investigates the discontinuity and division of Antifederalist thought concerning the national executive. Some critics of the newly proposed Constitution either accepted the need for an independent executive as conceived by the Philadelphia convention or simply remained silent on the issue. Others accepted the idea of an independent executive but chose to argue against certain details of the office or feared that the President might become the minion of an aristocratic Senate. Still others desired to re-examine the process of Presidential selection, with some advocating direct election and others favoring investing the power of direct selection in the several states.

The *Federalist* Papers provided a much more detailed and cohesive argument in favor of a single, independent executive in contrast to the arguments of the scattered opposition. Alexander Hamilton was particularly convinced that the executive should combine unity and strength, and he devoted a considerable amount of his own energies to this notion.

Hamilton's ideas have led to the modern view of the Presidency as the embodiment of the national will. This Hamiltonian idea is echoed in the modern writings of Richard Neustadt and caught most persuasively by President Kennedy in one of his campaign speeches. Modern critics of the executive branch are capable of answering those supporters who treat the office as the lodestar of American politics and government. This is particularly evident in the criticisms of Theodore Lowi and Francis Hutchins.

Chapter 9 details the strong opposition of the Antifederalists to the judicial branch. They viewed this branch as the least democratic of the three. They were uncomfortable with the lifetime tenure afforded judges by the Constitution. In addition, the Constitutional provision for the removal of judges was viewed as inadequate. Antifederalists were concerned that the use of judicial power, especially as proscribed by Hamilton, would impinge upon state legislative and judicial power.

The Federalists and specifically Alexander Hamilton viewed the judicial branch as the least dangerous. Hamilton argued against temporary commissions for judges because he believed that the political expediency of the legislators would affect judicial appointments. He believed that the legislators' knowledge of the law was inferior to the knowledge of judges.

Modern writings by Dolbeare and Medcalf illustrate that Hamilton's thoughts launched our modern legal and economic system. Richard A. Brisbin, Jr., traces the conservative ideology of Supreme Court Justice Anton Scalia, which can in turn be traced to the traditions of former Supreme Court Justice Felix Frankfurter. This tradition possesses ties to both Federalist Alexander Hamilton and Antifederalist Brutus.

Chapter 10 attempts to make some sense of the ratification debate and how it has affected the evolution of democracy in our nation. The authors argue that the United States has been slowly moving away from purely representative democracy and toward participatory democracy ever since the ratification of the Constitution. The enlargement of the franchise and the civil rights and women's movements are indicators of this. Perhaps the greatest indicator of a new course for American democracy after the ratification of the Constitution was the Civil War and Lincoln's Gettysburg Address. With this address, President Lincoln rededicated this nation to the goals ensconced in the Declaration of Independence, virtually guaranteeing the movement toward greater participation in political affairs and a continuing journey toward participatory democracy.

1

Governmental Power and Democratic Citizenry

Nothing is more certain than the indispensable necessity of government, and it is equally undeniable that whenever and however it is instituted, the people must cede to it some of their natural rights, in order to vest it with requisite powers.

—John Jay, *Federalist* Paper 2

Government, like dress, is the badge of lost innocence; the palaces of kings are built on the ruins of the bowers of paradise.

—Thomas Paine, *Common Sense*

American political thought has, throughout its short history, developed a variety of properties, coexisting and competing within a field of conflict and tension and yet orbiting around an axis of essential consensus and fundamental principle. American political culture, at least within the mainstream and even including positions at the margins, is basically settled on certain first principles, an ideological core that provides the substance of the balance of American political thought and action. Within this core we can discern the positing of such notions, among others, as consent of the governed, dispersion of power, written compacts, the Lockean notion of majority rule combined with a respect for minority interest, and perhaps even more importantly, the ideas of individual liberty, equality, and limited government. The latter three might be considered the most critical of the core ideals, yet it is within the development and attempted application of these ideals that we are drawn into an awareness of the interpenetrating tensions that strain within the soul of American political culture. Disagreements regarding the nature of dispersed power have appeared, as evinced in the antagonistic ideas of John Adams and Thomas Paine,[1] and different notions formed around the ideal of "majority rule," as forwarded by such disparate

[1]Adams was a champion of separation of powers combined with an intricate system of checks and balances. Paine was a critic of such complicated schemes of governing, arguing that they were fundamentally undemocratic.

thinkers as David Buel, Jr., and John C. Calhoun[2] do indeed present examples of conflict within these areas of thought as well. If one considers the issues closely, however, one might find that the path of discourse leads back to the philosophic foundations as they are constructed upon the first principles of liberty, equality, and minimal government. It is here that most of the debate within American politics and political thought is joined.

Both supporters and opponents of the newly proposed Constitution in 1787 affirmed the need to impose limitations upon government in general. However, the more ardent supporters of the Constitution also emphasized in almost the same breath the notion that government must be imbued with the requisite powers to accomplish the ends of "ordered liberty." Owing to tendencies within "human nature" toward abuse of power and corruption, according to the Federalists, checks must be provided within the scheme of institutions to prevent any one segment of government from wielding excessive power at the expense of the others. Regarding this issue, Antifederalists did not speak with the same consensual voice. Some Antifederalists, agreeing that checks and balances are indeed needed to limit government, argued that the proposed Constitution actually failed to provide enough safeguards against the extensive powers granted therein, whereas others argued against the very premise of checks and balances itself, claiming that the future success of any republic is a function of a virtuous and active citizenry rather than the automatic mechanisms of state institutions and complicated restraints imposed upon governance. In any event, Antifederalists did agree in almost every instance that the proposed federal structure endowed the central government with too much power and excluded the general citizenry from genuine participation. Within the Constitution, fragments such as the "necessary and proper clause," the "commerce clause," the various clauses dealing with martial concerns, clauses granting Congress extensive enumerated powers of the purse, and particularly the "supremacy clause" all filled the opponents of the Constitution with a sense of dread. Thus it was clear to all of the Antifederalists, regardless of their numerous differences, that this new instrument invested considerable power in the new government at the expense of the states and the people as a whole. Furthermore, the admitted distrust on the part of the Federalists regarding participatory forms of democracy was readily evident in the structure of the document. Many Antifederalists bristled at the manner in which the Constitution apparently provided too many "checks" against the people, a charge to which the Federalists responded with arguments against the feasibility of more direct forms of democracy, combined with a celebration of the representative form, deemed by Madison to be the only way to involve the people in a practical fashion while continuing to safeguard against the possible tyranny of the masses. Most Antifederalists rejected the notion that more participatory forms were impractical, and some mocked the Federalists' "more practical" solution through the representative form. Upon considering the numbers involved, some Antifederalists argued against the scheme of representation as Madison designed it with great indignation. Brutus quite unequivocally considered the plan for representation included within the proposed Constitution to be "merely nominal" and a "mere burlesque," not even worthy of Madison's own notion of representation, let alone demo-

---

[2]David Buel, Jr., of New York, was an early and eloquent advocate of universal suffrage, following the Lockean notion of majority rule. John C. Calhoun, of South Carolina, was a severe critic of universal suffrage and the dependence of the polity on the will of the numerical majority; in its stead, Calhoun offered a theory of "concurrent majorities," based upon region and interest, and established as an antipodal alternative to the rule of what John Randolph referred to as "King Numbers."

cratic participation. In addition to this, the basic attitudes toward the people as harbored by the opponents are quite indicative of their respective attitudes toward representation and participation. Federalists such as Washington and Hamilton had been alarmed by the people's tendencies toward "insurrection" and believed that stronger central government was needed not only as a check against power from above, but also, and perhaps more importantly, as a check against power from "below"—against the people as active participants. Thomas Jefferson was more sanguine, confidently stating that a "little rebellion" now and again is beneficial, as the "tree of liberty is nourished by the blood of patriots and tyrants." For Jefferson, the active participating citizenry served as the first and best defense of liberty; for Hamilton, the institutions and laws were the only sure guarantees against the abridgment of liberty.

Madison and Hamilton both argued that liberty was critical, and perhaps the most essential dimension of government. Antifederalists also sounded liberty's trumpet; hence, one finds both Madison and Patrick Henry delivering stirring declarations on behalf of liberty. Once again, the difference between these positions seems to develop from the disparate attitudes regarding the people's role in securing their own liberty. Madison borrowed extensively from Montesquieu, arguing that the only liberty possible or worthy of republican citizens was the "ordered liberty" framed within law and secured through institutional mechanisms. Most Antifederalists seemed to follow Jefferson's line of reasoning, eschewing institutional complexity in favor of citizen responsibility and government accountability. The Antifederalists generally did agree with the principles behind the necessity for the rule of law and the recognition that good institutions were salubrious to the polity, but they almost universally agreed that liberty is a function of some level of power and that power could be retained by the people only through participation.

Collateral with this tendency toward expanded participation, we find the general consensus from the opposition for the inclusion of a bill of rights into any governmental compact. Jefferson lent his qualified support to the new Constitution, but only on the condition that the executive article be revised and, more importantly, that a bill of rights be appended to the document. Others such as Henry, George Mason, Richard Henry Lee, and "John DeWitt" opposed the document, in part because of the absence of a "bill of rights." Federalists Hamilton, James Wilson, and James Iredell remained unmoved, even arguing that affixing a bill of rights to the Constitution could actually result in greater danger to the liberties of citizens. Hamilton's argument against a bill of rights was the most corrosive, as he agreed to the fundamental notion of the natural rights of humankind but remained skeptical regarding their codification.[3] In one sense Hamilton argued that the Constitution is itself a "bill of rights," for it protects individual liberty by providing, in numerous passages, against the abuses of power in government. More provocatively and persuasively, Hamilton argued that any document enumerating specific rights is in itself a restriction upon civil liberties, for through enumeration of rights, the rights themselves are limited to those that the government possesses the largesse to concede and sustain. A bill of rights would, according to Hamilton," . . . contain various exceptions to powers which are not

[3]Hamilton wrote in an uncharacteristically metaphysical passage that " . . . the sacred rights of mankind are not to be rummaged for among old parchments or musty records. They are written, as with a sunbeam, in the whole volume of human nature by the hand of divinity itself, and can never be erased or obscured by mortal power." Quoted in Bernard Bailyn, *The Ideological Origins of the American Revolution* (Cambridge: The Belknap Press of Harvard University Press, 1967), p. 188.

granted, and, on this very account, would afford a colorable pretext to claim more than were granted. . . ."[4]

Regardless of Hamilton's true motivations, which he himself admitted were forever concealed within his own breast, the argument was formidable. Nonetheless, through the efforts of both opponents and conditional supporters of the Constitution, the sentiment for a bill of rights securing the liberty of the citizenry eventually waxed and, with the support and promise of Madison, the federal Bill of Rights was amended to the Constitution. Hamilton's arguments against enumerating rights was deflated by Madison's own Ninth Amendment,[5] and the Antifederalists succeeded in contributing to the ratification process perhaps the most democratic aspect of the new Constitution, a contribution that is rooted in the political first principle advancing the notion that governments can never grant or even secure rights but can only protect liberties that already exist by virtue of our humanity.

Upon the consideration of the principle of equality, the Federalists were far more reserved, as a rule, than the Antifederalists. The Constitution, as it was originally drafted, contains elements of institutionalized inequality, including the infamous "3/5 of a person" clause, which in effect, and in a rather insidious fashion, legitimized the worst instance of inequality and oppression in American history. The framers of the Constitution, while sharing sentiments with the Antifederalists regarding limited government and liberty (albeit with notable differences, as mentioned above), were less eager to advance the cause of equality throughout the American polity. Their emphasis was primarily directed toward equality before the law, as well as the extension of some degree of political equality across the new republic. Although the framers of the Constitution were critical of the kind of static inequality that pervaded Europe as a result of the feudal legacy, as critical as any Antifederalist, they considered the role of equality within the republican frame of governing askance, and thus remained aloof to more progressive arguments toward equality of condition as well as equality of opportunity and equality before the law. The latter two aspects of equality were conceded by the Federalists sometimes with reservation. The former, equality of condition, seems to be a characteristic of the egalitarian impulse within the Antifederalists. Again, the Antifederalists did not speak with one voice, for some Antifederalists immediately focused upon the need for equality of opportunity and thus the need for minimal government. However, most Antifederalists recognized that a broader expansion of real social and economic equality must accompany any political and legal reforms if democracy is to become successfully participatory. Arguments against the "highborn" Federalist and the use of such appellations as "John Humble" and "A Citizen Who Has Catched a Cold" indicate the tenor of the Antifederalist position. Antifederalists were certainly not levelers, and they recognized that some degree of inequality will exist in even the most democratic state, but their egalitarian bent toward popular democracy and a desire for a less hierarchical distribution of property, which in many instances of Antifederalist thought resembles the Jeffersonian model of the citizen-farmer,[6] represent the most visible lines of demarcation that separate the Federalist from the Antifederalist mind. This is accompanied by a general tendency toward more trust in the people on behalf of many (but certainly not all) Antifederalists, in contrast to the Federalist tendency to

---

[4]Cf. Hamilton, *Federalist* Paper 84, excerpted below.

[5] "The enumeration in the Constitution, of certain rights, shall not be construed to deny or disparage others retained by the people," Ninth Amendment, *The Constitution of the United States.*

[6]See Chapter 2.

gravitate toward different levels of distrust (mild distrust in Madison's case; considerable and unabashed distrust in the arguments of Hamilton and Fisher Ames). Finally, many Federalist arguments seem to work toward ways in which government can militate against both autocracy and ochlocracy and "mitigate against the violence of faction." Although many Antifederalists were not above using similar language, instances of the benefits of mild government for the sake of advancing human goodness are more noticeable in the arguments of the Antifederalists. One example of this can be found in the writer who uses the *nom de plume* of "William Penn" in the selections below.

In the excerpts presented in this chapter, these issues and others are brought forward. The nature of power and its relationship to a democratic citizenry, and the debate over the necessity of a bill of rights, are addressed throughout the selections from the Antifederalists and the Federalists. Modern commentaries from Leonard Levy and Martin Diamond defend the democratic and revolutionary properties of the Constitution, while in the excerpts from J. Allen Smith and Gordon Wood, the Constitution as well as its sponsors are decidedly revalued. Regardless of the position one chooses to assume in this debate, the tensions between the nature of governmental power and the essence of a free and active citizenry are continually drawn and formed anew.

ANTIFEDERALIST ARGUMENTS

"Centinel" *(Probably Samuel Bryan)* *Essay I*

DISCUSSION QUESTIONS

1. Compare Centinel's emphasis on a virtuous citizenry with Madison's comments in *Federalist* Paper 51 below. What are the important issues raised in this comparison?
2. Which theory produces the groundwork for participatory government?

I have been anxiously expecting that some enlightened patriot would, ere this, have taken up the pen to expose the futility, and counteract the baneful tendency of such principles. Mr. Adams's[1] *sine qua non* of a good government is three balanc-

[1]Centinel is responding directly to the theory of mixed government as advanced by John Adams. Central to Adams' political philosophy, the balancing of three disparate powers within the structure of government would achieve equilibrium between mutually antagonistic elements within the mixed government as a whole. Adams argued that "the passion for distinction" will ever inspire individuals to promote their private interest above all concerns and that, rather than extinguish this passion, a well-crafted government and set of institutions could appropriately channel these energies for the good of the whole. Although not entirely the same as Madison's arguments in *Federalist* Paper 10 or Montesquieu's theory as discussed in *The Spirit of the Laws*, Adams' position remains an excellent example of Federalist thought, particularly regarding the emphasis on the quest for the perfection of political and governmental institutions failing the perfection of "human nature." [Eds.]

ing powers, whose repelling qualities are to produce an equilibrium of interests, and thereby promote the happiness of the whole community. He asserts that the administrators of every government, will ever be actuated by views of private interest and ambition, to the prejudice of the public good; that therefore the only effectual method to secure the rights of the people and promote their welfare, is to create an opposition of interests between the members of two distinct bodies, in the exercise of the powers of government, and balanced by those of a third. This hypothesis supposes human wisdom competent to the task of instituting three coequal orders in government, and a corresponding weight in the community to enable them respectively to exercise their several parts, and whose views and interests should be so distinct as to prevent a coalition of any two of them for the destruction of the third. Mr. Adams, although he has traced the constitution of every form of government that ever existed, as far as history affords materials, has not been able to adduce a single instance of such a government; he indeed says that the British constitution is such in theory, but this is rather a confirmation that his principles are chimerical and not to be reduced to practice. If such an organization of power were practicable, how long would it continue? not a day—for there is so great a disparity in the talents, wisdom and industry of mankind, that the scale would presently preponderate to one or the other body, and with every accession of power the means of further increase would be greatly extended. The state of society in England is much more favorable to such a scheme of government than that of America. There they have a powerful hereditary nobility, and real distinctions of rank and interests; but even there, for want of that perfect equality of power and distinction of interests, in the three orders of government, they exist but in name; the only operative and efficient check, upon the conduct of administration, is the sense of the people at large.

Suppose a government could be formed and supported on such principles, would it answer the great purposes of civil society; if the administrators of every government are actuated by views of private interest and ambition, how is the welfare and happiness of the community to be the result of such jarring adverse interests?

Therefore, as different orders in government will not produce the good of the whole, we must recur to other principles. I believe it will be found that the form of government, which holds those entrusted with power, in the greatest responsibility to their constitutents, the best calculated for freemen. A republican, or free government, can only exist where the body of the people are virtuous, and where property is pretty equally divided[;] in such a government the people are the sovereign and their sense or opinion is the criterion of every public measure; for when this ceases to be the case, the nature of the government is changed, and an aristocracy, monarchy or despotism will rise on its ruin. The highest responsibility is to be attained, in a simple structure of government, for the great body of the people never steadily attend to the operations of government, and for want of due information are liable to be imposed on—If you complicate the plan by various orders, the people will be perplexed and divided in their sentiments about the source of abuses or misconduct, some will impute it to the senate, others to the house of representatives, and so on, that the interposition of the people may be rendered imperfect or perhaps wholly abortive. But if, imitating the constitution of Pennsylvania, you vest all the legislative power in one body of men (separating the executive and judicial) elected for a short period, and necessarily excluded by rotation from permanency, and guarded from precipitancy and surprise by delays imposed on its proceedings, you will create the most perfect responsibility for then, whenever the people feel a grievance they cannot mistake the authors, and will apply the remedy with certainty and effect, discarding them at the next election. This tie of responsibility will obviate all the dangers apprehended from a single legislature, and will the best secure the rights of the people.[2]

Having premised this much, I shall now proceed to the examination of the proposed plan of government, and I trust, shall make it appear to the meanest capacity, that it has none of the essential requisites of a free government; that it is neither founded on those balancing restraining powers, recommended by Mr. Adams and attempted in the British constitution, or possessed of that responsibility to its constituents, which, in my opinion, is the only effectual security for the liberties and happiness of the people; but on the contrary, that it is a most daring attempt to establish a despotic aristocracy among freemen, that the world has ever witnessed. . . .

From this investigation into the organization of this government, it appears that it is devoid of all responsibility or accountability to the great body of the people, and that so far from being a regular balanced government, it would be in practice a *permanent* ARISTOCRACY.

Who's here so vile, that will not love his country?
Who's here so base, that would a bondman be?
If any, speak; for him have I offended.
Who's here so vile, that will not love his country?
If any, speak; for him have I offended.

CENTINEL

[2]For an even more impassioned argument against the Federalist approach to power, virtue, and complicated schemes of governing, refer to the excerpt from Patrick Henry provided in Chapter 3. Particularly this passage: " . . . When the American spirit was in its youth, the language of America was different. Liberty . . . was then the primary object . . . now . . . the American spirit . . . is about to convert this country to a powerful and mighty empire. . . . Such a government is incompatible with the genius of republicanism: There will be no checks, no real balances, in this Government. What can avail your specious imaginary balances, your rope-dancing, chain rattling, ridiculous ideal checks and contrivances?" and *passim.* Another critic of complicated government was Thomas Paine, who argued that schemes of governing along the order of those proposed by the likes of Adams are, through root and branch, undemocratic. Paine was among the most ardent champions of minimalism in government. [Eds.]

Melancton Smith
June 20, 1788
(Excerpt)

DISCUSSION QUESTIONS

1. What does Smith mean by the statement " . . . if this government is to become oppressive, it will be by degrees"? Are there any examples, historical or current, that might verify this proposition?
2. What elements of the Constitution could Smith be referring to when he states that the persons and pocketbooks of the citizenry are in jeopardy? Was he right?

I believe were we to create a despot, he would not immediately dare to act the tyrant; but it would not be long before he would destroy the spirit of the people, or the people would destroy him. If our people have a high sense of liberty, the government should be congenial to this spirit—calculated to cherish the love of liberty, while yet it had sufficient force to restrain licentiousness. Government operates upon the spirit of the people, as well as the spirit of the people operates upon it—and if they are not conformable to each other, the one or the other will prevail. In a less time than 25 years, the government will receive its tone. What the spirit of the country may be at the end of that period, it is impossible to foretell: Our duty is to frame a government friendly to liberty and the rights of mankind, which will tend to cherish and cultivate a love of liberty among our citizens. If this government becomes oppressive it will be by degrees: It will aim at its end by disseminating sentiments of government opposite to republicanism; and proceed from step to step in depriving the people of a share in the government. A recollection of the change that has taken place in the minds of many in this country in the course of a few years, ought to put us upon our guard. Many who are ardent advocates for the new system, reprobate republican principles as chimerical and such as ought to be expelled from society. Who would have thought ten years ago, that the very men who risqued their lives and fortunes in support of republican principles, would now treat them as the fictions of fancy?—A few years ago we fought for liberty—We framed a general government on free principles—We placed the state legislatures, in whom the people have a full and fair representation, between Congress and the people. We were then, it is true, too cautious; and too much restricted the powers of the general government. But now it is proposed to go into the contrary, and a more dangerous extreme; to remove all barriers; to give the New Government free access to our pockets, and ample command of our persons; and that without providing for a genuine and fair representation of the people. No one can say what the progress of the change of sentiment may be in 25 years. The same men who now cry up the necessity of an energetic government, to induce a compliance with this system, may in much less time reprobate this in as severe terms as they now do the confederation, and may as strongly urge the necessity of going as far beyond this, as this is beyond the Confederation.—Men of this class are increasing—they have influence, talents and industry—It is time to form a barrier against them. And while we are willing to establish a government adequate to the purposes of the union, let us be careful to establish it on the broad basis of equal liberty.

"William Penn"
(Unknown)
Essay I

DISCUSSION QUESTIONS

1. What is the author's definition of government? Is this definition appropriate to a democratic society? Is it served by the Constitution as originally written? As amended? Why or why not?
2. What is the author's definition of liberty? What does this definition reveal about the author's views regarding "human nature"? Contrast this view of liberty with references to liberty in *Federalist* Paper 10 (below).

Fellow Citizens,

At this important moment which is to decide on your future happiness or misery by the adoption or rejection of the *new proposed form of government*, a cool and dispassionate investigation of that system becomes indispensably necessary—I have waited for a considerable time, hoping that the subject would be taken up by some abler pen than mine—I have been disappointed in my expectation—a great many pieces have indeed appeared, which have thrown a considerable light on this interesting subject, but they have been mostly of the desultory kind, and no person (at least that I know of) has as yet attempted a methodical examination of the proposed constitution, or a comparative view of its principles with the principles of a government in general, and of a *federal* government in particular—Although I am greatly deficient in the necessary abilities, I have however undertaken the arduous task; and I propose, in this and the ensuing papers, to go through it in the best manner I am able, and without attempting to display any ornament or elegance of style, I shall endeavour to explain my ideas with clearness and simplicity—my sole object is to be understood, and to render (if possible) these observations as useful, as their subject is interesting.

I shall in the first place lay down general principles, and proceed afterwards to their applications. I shall make very few quotations, from political writers, and take very few examples from the government of other countries whether ancient or modern—truth needs nothing but itself to enforce conviction on unprejudiced minds, and principles are a thousand times above precedents.

I shall therefore begin with examining into the nature of government in general.

Government in its general sense may be defined *a human institution by which certain powers are delegated by the people to one or more citizens to preserve their national ex-*

istence, and secure to each individual, the enjoyment of his natural rights: otherwise, in the words of the constitution of Massachusetts, It is *a social compact by which the whole people covenants with each citizen, and each citizen with the whole people, that all shall be governed by certain laws for the common good.*

Government was originally instituted for the benefit of mankind—The welfare of the community is the great end which, under every form, it is intended to obtain—but what is the best form of government has long been an object of dispute among the learned and speculative. It is not true that that government is best which is best administered—it is a sophism invented by tyranny to quiet the inquisitive mind; a good administration is at best but a temporary palliative to a bad government, but it does not alter its nature, any more than a bad man by doing one good action in the course of his life, ceases to be a bad man. The best government is certainly that which is the least liable to be ill administered, in which the rulers have the most power to do good and the least to do evil. In other words it is that in which the natural rights of mankind are the most inviolably secured.

And of consequence as liberty is the most essential of those rights, which man holds by inheritance from all-bountiful nature, that which takes from him the least share of that liberty ought to be the best—for the same principle holds in the political as in the mechanical science, and that machine in either must be allowed to be the most perfect, which with the least *strength* performs the greatest *execution.*

But here a long agitated question will occur: *What is liberty?* What is that supreme good which every one feels, and so very few can define?—I would call it *the unlimited power of doing good,* and without very critically examining into this definition, I know not what internal voice tells me that I am not mistaken. But again, What is good?—When that is fully known and understood, men will no longer differ about forms of government; it is the tree of knowledge which we have as yet only tasted; it is that we have for thousands of years, with various successes, been eagerly seeking after; it is the ultimate end of the painful researches of the human mind, and the object of these disquisitions.

Without going too deep into metaphysical investigations, that are no part of our present design, let us go back to the leading principle already established, that the best government is that which secures to the citizens the greatest share of their natural rights: their full extent unfortunately is not yet known to us; it is by slow, and often interrupted, steps that we have discovered those we now enjoy. That discovery is owing partly to our own sad experience, and partly to the philanthrophic researches of those chosen few to whom the Almighty has in his mercy bestowed a larger portion of the ethereal fire than usually falls to the lot of the common race of men. Those men, whom we call *philosophers* or *lovers of wisdom,* have generally been persecuted while they lived, and have had altars erected to them after their death. Because prejudice, supported by private interest, has always stood in the way of useful truths, which however have in the end seldom failed to prevail. And wherever a sufficient number of those truths has been established and generally diffused, liberty and happiness have become the portion of every nation so enlightened—liberty is the fair offspring of knowledge, as tyranny is the grim-child of ignorance.

In this respect America is of all other nations the most favored of Heaven—

The book of the constitutions of the different states reflects such a mass of light as would have dazzled the greatest philosophers of antiquity. After the holy scriptures, it is certainly of all books that which contains the greatest store of eternal truths. I never open that sacred volume without feeling a kind of awful reverence, mixed with gratitude to the Almighty giver of all good gifts, who has been pleased to enlighten the minds of the legislators of this favored nation.

The truths which those great men have thus declared and established, are not (GOD be thanked) solely consigned to books made of perishable materials; they are deeply engraved in the hearts of every American. This nation may boast of enjoying the greatest collective store of political knowledge of any people on earth. Maxims of the utmost importance to the happiness of mankind, are familiar to our meanest citizens, which many eminent Philosophers in other parts of the world, have perhaps never had an idea of—hence it must be inferred, that if we are ever brought into slavery, we shall never be allowed the easy plea of ignorance: the nations that now envy us, will despise our meaness, and see our miseries without pity.

Let us therefore try this new federal constitution that is now offered to us by the light of our own knowledge—Let us recur to those original principles upon which our present constitutions have been established. These guides never can mislead us; they are a sure touchstone to try any form of government by. If we find that the federal plan conformable to those principles, let us by all means adopt it, and thereby secure perpetual happiness to ourselves and our posterity—If, on the contrary, we find that it is built on a different foundation, we must not hesitate a moment, but with a manly firmness, worthy of ourselves, unanimously reject it.

WILLIAM PENN

Richard Henry Lee
Letter to Edmund Randolph
December 22, 1787
(Excerpt)

DISCUSSION QUESTIONS

1. Why is a declaration or bill of rights necessary? What fears did the proponents of a bill of rights wish to allay?
2. Examine the items discussed by Lee as worthy of inclusion in a bill of rights. What reasons can you develop to support these separate proposals? What proposals would you argue against, and why?

It having been found from universal experience, that the most express declarations and reservations are necessary to protect the just rights and liberty of mankind from the silent powerful and ever active conspiracy of those who govern; and it appearing to be the sense of the good people of America, by the various bills or declarations of rights whereon the government of the greater number of states are founded. That such precautions are necessary to restrain and regulate the exercise of the great powers given to rulers. In conformity with these principles, and from respect for the public sentiment on this subject, it is submitted,—That the new constitution proposed for the government of the United States be bottomed upon a declaration or bill of rights, clearly and precisely stating the principles upon which this social compact is founded, to wit: That the rights of conscience in matters of religion ought not to be violated—That the freedom of the press shall be secured—That the trial by jury in criminal and civil cases, and the modes prescribed by the commonlaw for the safety of life in criminal prosecutions shall be held sacred—That standing armies in times of peace are dangerous to liberty, and ought not to be permitted unless assented to by two thirds of the members composing each house of the legislature under the new constitution—That the elections should be free and frequent—That the right administration of justice should be secured by the independency of the judges—that excessive bail, excessive fines, or cruel and unusual punishments should not be demanded or inflicted—That the right of the people to assemble peaceably for the purpose of petitioning the legislature shall not be prevented—That the citizens shall not be exposed to unreasonable searches, seizure of their persons, houses, papers or property; and it is necessary for the good of society, that the administration of government be conducted with all possible maturity of judgment, for which reason it hath been the practice of civilized nations and so determined by every state in the Union.—That a council of state or privy council should be appointed to advise and assist in the arduous business assigned to the executive power. Therefore let the new constitution be so amended as to admit the appointment of a privy council to consist of eleven members chosen by the president, but responsible for the advice they may give. For which purpose the advice given shall be entered in a council book, and signed by the giver in all affairs of great moment, and that the counsellors act under an oath of office. In order to prevent the dangerous blending of the legislative and executive powers, and to secure responsibility—The privy, and not the senate, shall be joined with the president in the appointment of all officers civil and military under the new constitution—That the constitution be so altered as not to admit the creation of a vice president, when duties as assigned may be discharged by the privy council, except in the instance of proceding [presiding?] in the senate, which may be supplied by a speaker chosen from the body of senators by themselves as usual, that so may be avoided the establishment of a great officer of state, who is sometimes to be joined with the legislature, and sometimes administer the government, rendering responsibility difficult, besides giving unjust and needless pre-eminence to that state from whence this officer may have come.—That such parts of the new constitution be amended as provide imperfectly for the trial of criminals by a jury of the vicinage, and so supply the omission of a jury trial in civil causes or disputes about property between individuals, whereby the common law is directed, and as generally it is secured by the several state constitutions. That such parts of the new constitution be amended as permit the vexatious and oppressive callings of citizens from their own country, and all controversies between citizens of different states and between citizens and foreigners, to be tried in a far distant court, and as it may be without a jury, whereby in a multitude of cases, the circumstances of distance and expence, may compel numbers to submit to the most unjust and ill founded demand. That in order to secure the rights of the people more effectually from violation, the power and respectability of the house of representatives be increased, by increasing the number of delegates to that house where the popular interest must chiefly depend for protection—That the constitution be so amended as to increase the number of votes necessary to determine questions in cases where a bare majority may be seduced by strong motives of interest to injure and oppress the minority of the community as in commercial regulations, where advantage may be taken of circumstances to ordain rigid and premature laws that will in effect amount to monopolies, to the great impoverishment of those states whose peculiar situation expose them to such injuries.

"An Old Whig"
(Unknown)
Essays IV and V
(Excerpts)

DISCUSSION QUESTIONS

1. According to "An Old Whig," what is the purpose of a bill of rights?
2. What is meant by the term "unalienable rights"? Why does the author argue that a document declaring certain rights is necessary?
3. Why is "liberty of conscience" considered of "utmost importance" to "An Old Whig"? Is this a fair assessment? What other rights would be considered of critical import? Explain.
4. Given what "An Old Whig" has stated in his essays, what can we conclude about his views regarding the duties of government and an active citizenry?

IV

The science of politics has very seldom had fair play. So much of passion, interest and temporary prospects of gain are mixed in the pursuit, that a government has been much oftener established[,] with a view to the particular advantages or necessities of a few individuals, than to the permanent good of society. If the men, who, at different times, have been entrusted to form plans of government for the world, had been really actuated by no other views than a regard to the public good, the condition of human nature in all ages would have been widely different, from that which has been exhibited to us in history. In this country perhaps we are possessed of more than our share of political virtue. If we will exercise a little patience, and bestow our best endeavours on the business, I do not think it impossible, that we may yet form a federal constitution, much superior to any form of government, which has ever existed in the world;—but, whenever this important work shall be accomplished, I venture to pronounce, that it will not be done without a *careful attention to the framing of a bill of rights.*

Much has been said and written, on the subject of a bill of rights;—possibly without sufficient attention to the necessity of conveying distinct and precise ideas of the true meaning of a bill of rights. Your readers, I hope, will excuse me, if I conclude this letter with an attempt to throw some light on this subject.

Men when they enter into society, yield up a part of their natural liberty, for the sake of being protected by government. If they yield up all their natural rights they are absolute slaves to their governors. If they yield up less than is necessary, the government is so feeble, that it cannot protect them.—To yield up so much, as is necessary for the purposes of government; and to retain all beyond what is necessary, is the great point, which ought, if possible, to be attained in the formation of a constitution. At the same time that by these means, the liberty of the subject is secured, the government is really strengthened; because wherever the subject is convinced that nothing more is required from him, than what is necessary for the good of the community, he yields a chearful obedience, which is more useful than the constrained service of slaves.—To define what portion of his natural liberty, the subject shall at all times be entitled to retain, is one great end of a bill of rights. To these may be added in a bill of rights some particular engagements of protection, on the part of government[;] without such a bill of rights, firmly securing the privileges of the subject, the government is always in danger of degenerating into tyranny; for it is certainly true, that "in establishing the powers of government, the rulers are invested with every right and authority, which is not in explicit terms reserved." —Hence it is, that we find the rulers so often lording over the people at their will and pleasure. Hence it is that we find the patriots, in all ages of the world, so very solicitous to obtain explicit engagements from their rulers, stipulating, expressly, for the preservation of particular rights and privileges.

In different nations, we find different grants or reservations of privileges appealed to in the struggles between the rulers and the people, many of which in the different nations of Europe, have long since been swallowed up and lost by time, or destroyed by the arbitrary hand of power. In England we find the people, with the Barons at their head, exacting a solemn resignation of their rights from king John, in their celebrated *magna charta*, which was many times renewed in Parliament, during the reigns of his successors. The *petition of rights* was afterwards consented to by Charles the first, and contained a declaration of the liberties of the people. The *habeas corpus act*, after the restoration of Charles the Second, *the bill of rights*, which was obtained from the Prince and Princess of Orange on their accession to the throne[,] and the act of settlement, at the accession of the Hanover family, are other instances to shew the care and watchfulness of that nation, to improve every opportunity, of the reign of a weak prince, or the revolution in their government, to obtain the most explicit declarations in favor of their liberties. In like manner the people of the country, at the revolution, having all power in their own hands, in forming the constitutions of the several states, took care to secure themselves by bills of rights, so as to prevent, as far as possible, the encroachments of their future rulers upon the rights of the people. Some of these rights are said to be *unalienable*, such as the rights of conscience: yet even these have been often invaded, where they have not been carefully secured by express and solemn bills and declarations in their favor.

Before we establish a government, whose acts will be THE SUPREME LAW OF THE LAND, and whose power will extend to almost every case without exception, we ought carefully to guard ourselves by a BILL OF RIGHTS, against the invasion of those liberties which it is essential for us to retain, which it is of no real use to government to strip us of; but which in the course of human events have been too often insulted with all the wantonness of an idle barbarity.

Your's,
AN OLD WHIG

V

Mr. Printer,

In order that people may be sufficiently impressed, with the necessity of establishing a BILL OF RIGHTS in the forming of a new constitution, it is very proper to take a short view of some of those liberties, which it is of the greatest importance for Freemen to retain to themselves, when they surrender up a part of their natural rights for the good of society.

The first of these, which it is of the utmost importance for the people to retain to themselves, which indeed they have not even the right to surrender, and which at the same time it is of no kind of advantage to government to strip them of, is the liberty of conscience. I know that a ready answer is at hand, to any objections upon this head. We shall be told that in this enlightened age, the rights of conscience are perfectly secure: There is no necessity of guarding them; for no man has the remotest thoughts of invading them. If this be the case, I beg leave to reply that now is the very time to secure them.—Wise and prudent men always take care to guard against danger beforehand, and to make themselves safe whilst it is yet in their power to do it without inconvenience or risk.—[W]ho shall answer for the ebbings and flowings of opinion, or be able to say what will be the fashionable frenzy of the next generation? It would have been treated as a very ridiculous supposition, a year ago, that the charge of witchcraft would cost a person her life in the city of Philadelphia; yet the fate of the unhappy old woman called Corbmaker, who was beaten—repeatedly wounded with knives—mangled and at last killed in our streets, in obedience to the commandment which requires "that we shall not suffer a witch to live," without a possibility of punishing or even of detecting the authors of this inhuman folly, should be an example to warn us how little we ought to trust to the unrestrained discretion of human nature.

Uniformity of opinion in science, morality, politics or religion, is undoubtedly a very great happiness to mankind; and there have not been wanting zealous champions in every age, to promote the means of securing so invaluable a blessing. If in America we have not lighted up fires to consume Heretics in religion, if we have not persecuted unbelievers to promote the unity of the faith, in matters which pertain to our final salvation in a future world, I think we have all of us been witness to something very like the same spirit, in matters which are supposed to regard our political salvation in this world. In Boston it seems at this very moment, that no man is permitted to publish a doubt of the infalibility of the late convention, without giving up his name to the people, that he may be delivered over to speedy destruction; and it is but a short time since the case was little better in this city. Now this is a portion of the very same spirit, which has so often kindled the fires of the inquisition: and the same Zealot who would hunt a man down for a difference of opinion upon a political question which is the subject of public enquiry, if he should happen to be fired with zeal for a particular species of religion, would be equally intolerant. The fact is, that human nature is still the same that ever it was: the fashion indeed changes; but the seeds of superstition, bigotry and enthusiasm, are too deeply implanted in our minds, ever to be eradicated; and fifty years hence, the French may renew the persecution of the Huguenots, whilst the Spaniards in their turn may become indifferent to their forms of religion. They are idiots who trust their future security to the whim of the present hour. One extreme is always apt to produce the contrary, and those countries, which are now the most lax in their religious notions, may in a few years become the most rigid, just as the people of this country from not being able to bear any continental government at all, are now flying into the opposite extreme of surrendering up all the powers of the different states, to one continental government.

The more I reflect upon the history of mankind, the more I am disposed to think that it is our duty to secure the essential rights of the people, by every precaution; for not an avenue has been left unguarded, through which oppression could possibly enter in any government[,] without some enemy of the public peace and happiness improving the opportunity to break in upon the liberties of the people; and none have been more frequently successful in the attempt, than those who have covered their ambitious designs under the garb of a fiery zeal for religious orthodoxy. What has happened in other countries and in other ages, may very possibly happen again in our own country, and for aught we know, before the present generation quits the stage of life. We ought therefore in a bill of rights to secure, in the first place, by the most express stipulations, the sacred rights of conscience. Has this been done in the constitution, which is now proposed for the consideration of the people of this country?—Not a word on this subject has been mentioned in any part of it; but we are left in this important article, as well as many others, entirely to the mercy of our future rulers.

FEDERALIST ARGUMENTS

Alexander Hamilton
Federalist *Paper 1*
(Excerpts)

DISCUSSION QUESTIONS

1. What are rights? What does Hamilton mean by the "overscrupulous jealousy of danger to the rights of the people"? What are the implications of this? Are there any contemporary debates that might sustain this concern?

2. What kind of government would be "efficient" and "energetic"? What does Hamilton mean by "enlightened zeal"? Has the Constitution promoted efficient and energetic government? Should it do so? Why or why not?

To the People of the State of New York:

After an unequivocal experience of the inefficiency of the subsisting federal government, you are called upon to deliberate on a new Constitution for the United States of America. The subject speaks its own importance; comprehending in its consequences nothing less than the existence of the UNION, the safety and welfare of the parts of which it is composed, the fate of an empire in many respects the most interesting in the world. It has been frequently remarked that it seems to have been reserved to the people of this country, by their conduct and example, to decide the important question, whether societies of men are really capable or not of establishing good government from reflection and choice, or whether they are forever destined to depend for their political constitutions on accident and force. If there be any truth in the remark, the crisis at which we are arrived may with propriety be regarded as the era in which that decision is to be made; and a wrong election of the part we shall act may, in this view, deserve to be considered as the general misfortune of mankind.

Among the most formidable of the obstacles which the new Constitution will have to encounter may readily be distinguished the obvious interest of a certain class of men in every State to resist all changes which may hazard a diminution of the power, emolument, and consequence of the offices they hold under the State establishments; and the perverted ambition of another class of men, who will either hope to aggrandize themselves by the confusions of their country, or will flatter themselves with fairer prospects of elevation from the subdivision of the empire into several partial confederacies than from its union under one government.

A torrent of angry and malignant passions will be let loose. To judge from the conduct of the opposite parties, we shall be led to conclude that they will mutually hope to evince the justness of their opinions, and to increase the number of their converts by the loudness of their declamations and the bitterness of their invectives. An enlightened zeal for the energy and efficiency of government will be stigmatized as the offspring of a temper fond of despotic power and hostile to the principles of liberty. An over-scrupulous jealousy of danger to the rights of the people, which is more commonly the fault of the head than of the heart, will be represented as mere pretence and artifice, the stale bait for popularity at the expense of the public good. It will be forgotten, on the one hand, that jealousy is the usual concomitant of love, and that the noble enthusiasm of liberty is apt to be infected with a spirit of narrow and illiberal distrust. On the other hand, it will be equally forgotten that the vigor of government is essential to the security of liberty; that, in the contemplation of a sound and well-informed judgment, their interest can never be separated; and that a dangerous ambition more often lurks behind the specious mask of zeal for the rights of the people than under the forbidding appearance of zeal for the firmness and efficiency of government. History will teach us that the former has been found a much more certain road to the introduction of despotism than the latter, and that of those men who have overturned the liberties of republics, the greatest number have begun their career by paying an obsequious court to the people; commencing demagogues, and ending tyrants.

Alexander Hamilton
Federalist ***Paper 27***
(Excerpts)

DISCUSSION QUESTIONS

1. Why is it important, in Hamilton's view, for government to operate upon the citizenry with such frequency? Are there institutions in today's government that are commonly and repeatedly "intermingled in the ordinary exercise of government"?
2. Is this type of intimacy between government and the citizenry, as Hamilton envisioned it, compatible with democratic principles? Why or why not?

To the People of the State of New York:

It has been urged, in different shapes, that a Constitution of the kind proposed by the convention cannot operate without the aid of a military force to execute its laws. This, however, like most other things that have been alleged on that side, rests on mere general assertion, unsupported by any precise or intelligible designation of the reasons upon which it is founded. As far as I have been able to divine the latent meaning of the objectors, it seems to originate in a presupposition that the people will be disinclined to the exercise of federal authority in any matter of an internal nature. . . .

I will, in this place, hazard an observation, which will not be the less just because to some it may appear new; which is, that the more the operations of the national authority are intermingled in the ordinary exercise of government, the more the citizens are accustomed to meet with it in the common occurrences of their political life, the more it is familiarized to their sight and to their feelings, the further it enters into those objects which touch the most sensible chords and put in motion the most active springs of the human heart, the greater will be the probability that it will conciliate the respect and attachment of the community. Man is very much a creature of habit. A thing that rarely strikes his senses will generally have but little influence upon his mind. A government continually at a distance and out of sight can hardly be expected to interest the sensations of the people. The inference is, that the authority of the Union, and the affections of the citizens towards it, will be strengthened, rather than weakened, by its extension to what are called matters of internal concern; and will have less occasion to recur to force, in proportion to the familiarity and comprehensiveness of its agency. The more it circulates through those channels and currents in which the passions of mankind naturally flow, the less will it require the aid of the violent and perilous expedients of compulsion.

One thing, at all events, must be evident, that a government like the one proposed would bid much fairer to avoid the necessity of using force, than that species of league contended for by most of its opponents; the authority of which should only operate upon the States in their political or collective capacities. It has been shown that in such a Confederacy there can be no sanction for the laws but force; that frequent delinquencies in the members are the natural offspring of the very frame of the government; and that as often as these happen, they can only be redressed, if at all, by war and violence.

James Wilson
Speech
October 6, 1787

DISCUSSION QUESTIONS

1. Identify the major points of controversy regarding the Constitution, and determine the manner in which Wilson responds to each one. What are the strengths and weaknesses of his arguments?
2. How does Wilson deflect the proposal calling for immediate amendments to produce a bill of rights? Is there anything to be said for this argument? Why or why not?
3. What is an impost? How would Wilson respond to the system of taxation as it now exists in the United States?
4. Analyze the statement: "It is the nature of man to pursue his own interest, in preference to the public good. . . ." Is this statement a fair assessment of human essence? What theory of human nature underlies this statement? What other essays in this anthology exhibit similar reflections?

Mr. Chairman and Fellow Citizens,

Having received the honour of an appointment to represent you in the late convention, it is, perhaps, my duty to comply with the request of many gentlemen, whose characters and judgments I sincerely respect, and who have urged that this would be a proper occasion to lay before you any information, which will serve to elucidate and explain the principles and arrangements of the constitution that has been submitted to the consideration of the United States. I confess that I am unprepared for so extensive and so important a disquisition: but the insidious attempts, which are clandestinely and industriously made to pervert and destroy the new plan, induce me the more readily to engage in its defence: and the impressions of four months constant attendance to the subject, have not been so easily effaced, as to leave me without an answer to the objections which have been raised.

It will be proper, however, before I enter into the refutation of the charges that are alleged, to mark the leading discrimination between the state constitutions, and the constitution of the United States. When the people established the powers of legislation under their separate governments, they invested their representatives with every right and authority which they did not in explicit terms reserve: and therefore upon every question, respecting the jurisdiction of the house of assembly, if the frame of government is silent, the jurisdiction is efficient and complete. But in delegating fœderal powers, another criterion was necessarily introduced: and the congressional authority is to be collected, not from tacit implication, but from the positive grant, expressed in the instrument of union. Hence, it is evident, that in the former case, everything which is not reserved, is given: but in the latter, the reverse of the proposition prevails, and every thing which is not given, is reserved. This distinction being recognized, will furnish an answer to those who think the omission of a bill of rights, a defect in the proposed constitution: for it would have been superfluous and absurd, to have stipulated with a fœderal body of our own creation, that we should enjoy those privileges, of which we are not divested either by the intention or the act that has brought that body into existence. For instance, the liberty of the press, which has been a copious subject of declamation and opposition: what controul can proceed from the fœderal government, to shackle or destroy that sacred palladium of national freedom? If, indeed, a power similar to that which has been granted for the regulation of commerce, had been granted to regulate literary publications, it would have been as necessary to stipulate that the liberty of the press should be preserved inviolate, as that the impost should be general in its operation. With respect, likewise, to the particular district of ten miles, which is to be the seat of government, it will undoubtedly be proper to observe this salutary precaution, as there the legislative power will be vested in the president, senate, and house of representatives of the United States. But this could not be an object with the convention: for it must naturally depend upon a future compact; to which the citizens immediately interested, will, and ought to be parties: and there is no reason to suspect, that so popular a privilege will in that case be neglected. In truth, then, the proposed system possesses no influence whatever upon the press; and it would have been merely nugatory, to have introduced a formal declaration upon the subject; nay, that very declaration might have been construed to imply that some degree of power was given, since we undertook to define its extent.

Another objection that has been fabricated against the new constitution, is expressed in this disingenuous form— "the trial by jury is abolished in civil cases." I must be excused, my fellow citizens, if, upon this point, I take advantage of my professional experience, to detect the futility of the assertion. Let it be remembered, then, that the business of the fœderal constitution was not local, but general—not limited to the views and establishments of a single state, but co-extensive with the continent, and comprehending the views and establishments of thirteen independent sovereignties. When, therefore, this subject was in discussion, we were involved in difficulties, which pressed on all sides, and no precedent could be discovered to direct our course. The cases open to a jury, differed in the different states; it was therefore impracticable, on that ground, to have made a general rule. The want of uniformity would have rendered any reference to the practice of the states idle and useless: and it could not, with any propriety, be said, that "the trial by jury shall be as heretofore:" since there has never existed any fœderal system of jurisprudence, to which the declaration could relate. Besides, it is not in all cases that the trial by jury is adopted in civil questions: for causes depending in courts of admiralty, such as relate to maritime captures, and such as are agitated in the courts of equity, do not require the intervention of that tribunal. How, then, was the line of discrimination to be drawn? The convention found the task too difficult for them: and they left the business as it stands—in the fullest confidence, that no danger could possibly ensue, since the proceedings of the supreme court are to be regulated by the congress, which is a faithful representation of the people: and the oppression of government is effectually barred, by declaring that in all criminal cases, the trial by jury shall be preserved.

This constitution, it has been further urged, is of a pernicious tendency, because it tolerates a standing army in the time of peace. This has always been a popular topic of declamation: and yet I do not know a nation in the world, which has not found it necessary and useful to maintain the appearance of strength in a season of the most profound tranquility. Nor is it a novelty with us; for under the present articles of confederation, congress certainly possesses this reprobated power: and the exercise of it is proved at this moment by the cantonments along the banks of the Ohio. But what would be our national situation, were it otherwise? Every principle of policy must be subverted, and the government must declare war before they are prepared to carry it on. Whatever may be the provocation, however important the object in view, and however necessary dispatch and secrecy may be, still the declaration must precede the preparation, and the enemy will be informed of your intention, not only before you are equipped for an attack, but even before you are fortified for a defence. The consequence is too obvious to require any further delineation; and no man, who regards the dignity and safety of his country, can deny the necessity of a military force, under the controul, and with the restrictions which the new constitution provides.

Perhaps there never was a charge made with less reason, than that which predicts the institution of a baneful aristocracy in the fœderal senate. This body branches into two characters, the one legislative, and the other executive. In its legislative character, it can effect no purpose without the co-operation of the house of representatives: and in its executive character, it can accomplish no object, without the concurrence of the president. Thus fettered, I do not know any act which the senate can of itself perform: and such dependence necessarily precludes every idea of influence and superiority. But I will confess, that in the organization of this body, a compromise between contending interests is discernible: and when we reflect how various are the laws, commerce, habits, population, and extent of the confederated states, this evidence of mutual concession and accommodation ought rather to command a generous applause, than to excite jealousy and reproach. For my part, my admiration can only be equalled by my astonishment, in beholding so perfect a system formed from such heterogenous materials.

The next accusation I shall consider, is that which represents the fœderal constitution as not only calculated, but designedly framed, to reduce the state governments to mere corporations, and eventually to annihilate them. Those who have employed the term corporation, upon this occasion, are not perhaps aware of its extent. In common parlance, indeed, it is generally applied to petty associations for the ease and conveniency of a few individuals; but in its enlarged sense, it will comprehend the government of Pennsylvania, the existing union of the states, and even this projected system is nothing more than a formal act of incorporation. But upon what pretence can it be alleged that it was designed to annihilate the state governments? For, I will undertake to prove that upon their existence depends the existence of the fœderal plan. For this purpose, permit me to call your attention to the manner in which the president, senate, and house of representatives, are proposed to be appointed. The president is to be chosen by electors, nominated in such manner as the legislature of each state may direct; so that if there is no legislature, there can be no senate. The house of representatives is to be composed of members chosen every second year by the people of the several states, and the electors in each state shall have the qualifications requisite to electors of the most numerous branch of the state legislature—unless, therefore, there is a state legislature, that qualification cannot be ascertained, and the popular branch of the fœderal constitution must likewise be extinct. From this view, then, it is evidently absurd to suppose, that the annihilation of the seaprate governments will result from their union; or, that, having that intention, the authors of the new system would have bound their connection with such indissoluble ties. Let me here advert to an arrangement highly advantageous; for you will perceive, without prejudice to the powe:s of the legislature in the election of senators, the people at large will acquire an additional privilege in returning members to the house of representatives—whereas, by the present confederation, it is the legislature alone that appoints the delegates to congress.

The power of direct taxation has likewise been treated as an improper delegation to the fœderal government; but when we consider it as the duty of that body to provide for the national safety, to support the dignity of the union, and to discharge the debts contracted upon the collective faith of the states, for their common benefit, it must be acknowledged that those, upon whom such important obligations are imposed, ought, in justice and in policy, to possess every means requisite for a faithful performance of their trust. But why should we be alarmed with visionary evils? I will venture to predict, that the great revenue of the United States must, and always will, be raised by impost; for, being at once less obnoxious, and more productive, the interest of the government will be best promoted by the accommodation of the people. Still, however, the object of direct taxation should be within reach in all cases of emergency; and there is no more reason to apprehend oppression in the mode of collecting a revenue from this resource, than in the form of impost, which, by universal assent, is left to the authority of the fœderal government. In either case, the force of civil constitutions will be adequate to the purpose; and the dread of military violence, which has been assiduously disseminated, must eventually prove the mere effusion of a wild imagination, or a factious spirit. But the salutary consequences that must flow from thus enabling the government to relieve and support the credit of the union, will afford another answer to the objections upon this ground. The state of Pennsylvania, particularly, which has encumbered itself with the assumption of a great proportion of the public debt, will derive considerable relief and advantage; for, as it was the imbecility of the present confederation, which gave rise to the funding law, that law must naturally expire, when a complete and energetic fœderal system shall be substituted—the state will then be discharged from an extraordinary burden, and the national creditor will find it to be to his interest to return to his original security.

After all, my fellow-citizens, it is neither extraordinary nor unexpected, that the constitution offered to your consideration, should meet with opposition. It is the nature of man to pursue his own interest, in preference to the public good; and I do not mean to make any personal reflection, when I add, that it is the interest of a very numerous, powerful, and respectable body, to counteract and destroy the excellent work produced by the late convention. All the officers of government, and all the appointments for the administration of justice and the collection of the public revenue, which are transferred from the individual to the aggregate sovereignty of the states, will necessarily turn the stream of influence and emolument into a new channel. Every person, therefore, who either enjoys, or expects to enjoy a place of profit under the present establishment, will object to the proposed innovation? not, in truth, because it is injurious to the liberties of his country, but because it effects his schemes of wealth and consequence. I will confess, indeed, that I am not a blind admirer of this plan of government, and that there are some parts of it, which, if my wish had prevailed, would certainly have been altered. But, when I reflect how widely men differ in their opinions, and that every man (and the observation applies likewise to every state) has an equal pretension to assert his own, I am satisfied that any thing nearer to perfection could not have been accomplished. If there are errors, it should be remembered, that the seeds of reformation are sown in the work itself, and the concurrence of two thirds of the congress may at any time introduce alterations and amendments. Regarding it, then, in every point of view, with a candid and disinterested mind, I am bold to assert, that it is the BEST FORM OF GOVERNMENT WHICH HAS EVER BEEN OFFERED TO THE WORLD.*

Alexander Hamilton
Federalist *Paper 84*
(Excerpts)

DISCUSSION QUESTIONS

1. Hamilton is clearly opposed to affixing a "bill of rights" to the proposed federalist Constitution. How many arguments against a "bill of rights" does Hamilton use in *Federalist* Paper 84? What are the merits of these various arguments? How would you answer these arguments in support of a "bill of rights"? How would you expand upon these arguments against a "bill of rights"?
2. One of the arguments that Hamilton raises against a "bill of rights" is addressed through one of the amendments? Which argument and which amendment?

---

*The candid Reader will suppose Mr. Wilson here means, that it is the best form of fœderal government, which has ever been offered to the world—and it is surely true that the foederal constitution, considered in due connexion with the state constitutions, is the best form of government that has ever been communicated to mankind.

The most considerable of the remaining objections is that the plan of the convention contains no bill of rights. Among other answers given to this, it has been upon different occasions remarked that the constitutions of several of the States are in a similar predicament. I add that New York is of the number. And yet the opposers of the new system, in this State, who profess an unlimited admiration for its constitution, are among the most intemperate partisans of a bill of rights. To justify their zeal in this matter, they allege two things: one is that, though the constitution of New York has no bill of rights prefixed to it, yet it contains, in the body of it, various provisions in favor of particular privileges and rights, which, in substance, amount to the same thing; the other is, that the Constitution adopts, in their full extent, the common and statute law of Great Britain, by which many other rights, not expressed in it, are equally secured.

To the first I answer, that the Constitution proposed by the convention contains, as well as the constitution of this State, a number of such provisions. . . .

To the second—that is, to the pretended establishment of the common and statute law by the Constitution, I answer, that they are expressly made subject "to such alterations and provisions as the legislature shall from time to time make concerning the same." They are therefore at any moment liable to repeal by the ordinary legislative power, and of course have no constitutional sanction. The only use of the declaration was to recognize the ancient law, and to remove doubts which might have been occasioned by the Revolution. This consequently can be considered as no part of a declaration of rights, which under our constitutions must be intended as limitations of the power of the government itself.

It has been several times truly remarked that bills of rights are, in their origin, stipulations between kings and their subjects, abridgments of prerogative in favor of privilege, reservations of rights not surrendered to the prince. Such was MAGNA CHARTA, obtained by the barons, sword in hand, from King John. Such were the subsequent confirmations of that charter by succeeding princes. Such was the *Petition of Right* assented to by Charles I., in the beginning of his reign. Such, also, was the Declaration of Right presented by the Lords and Commons to the Prince of Orange in 1688, and afterwards thrown into the form of an act of parliament called the Bill of Rights. It is evident, therefore, that, according to their primitive signification, they have no application to constitutions professedly founded upon the power of the people, and executed by their immediate representatives and servants. Here, in strictness, the people surrender nothing; and as they retain every thing they have no need of particular reservations.

"WE, THE PEOPLE of the United States, to secure the blessings of liberty to ourselves and our posterity, do *ordain* and *establish* this Constitution for the United States of America." Here is a better recognition of popular rights, than volumes of those aphorisms which make the principal figure in several of our State bills of rights, and which would sound much better in a treatise of ethics than in a constitution of government.

But a minute detail of particular rights is certainly far less applicable to a Constitution like that under consideration, which is merely intended to regulate the general political interests of the nation, than to a constitution which has the regulation of every species of personal and private concerns. If, therefore, the loud clamors against the plan of the convention, on this score, are well founded, no epithets of reprobation will be too strong for the constitution of this State. But the truth is, that both of them contain all which, in relation to their objects, is reasonably to be desired.

I go further, and affirm that bills of rights, in the sense and to the extent in which they are contended for, are not only unnecessary in the proposed Constitution, but would even be dangerous. They would contain various exceptions to powers not granted; and, on this very account, would afford a colorable pretext to claim more than were granted. For why declare that things shall not be done which there is no power to do? Why, for instance, should it be said that the liberty of the press shall not be restrained, when no power is given by which restrictions may be imposed? I will not contend that such a provision would confer a regulating power; but it is evident that it would furnish, to men disposed to usurp, a plausible pretence for claiming that power. They might urge with a semblance of reason, that the Constitution ought not to be charged with the absurdity of providing against the abuse of an authority which was not given, and that the provision against restraining the liberty of the press afforded a clear implication, that a power to prescribe proper regulations concerning it was intended to be vested in the national government. This may serve as a specimen of the numerous handles which would be given to the doctrine of constructive powers, by the indulgence of an injudicious zeal for bills of rights.

On the subject of the liberty of the press, as much as has been said, I cannot forbear adding a remark or two: in the first place, I observe, that there is not a syllable concerning it in the constitution of this State; in the next, I contend, that whatever has been said about it in that of any other State, amounts to nothing. What signifies a declaration, that "the liberty of the press shall be inviolably preserved"? What is the liberty of the press? Who can give it any definition which would not leave the utmost latitude for evasion? I hold it to be impracticable; and from this I infer, that its security, whatever fine declarations may be inserted in any constitution respecting it, must altogether depend on public opinion, and on the general spirit of the people and of the government.* And here, after all, as is intimated upon another occasion, must we seek for the only solid basis of all our rights.

There remains but one other view of this matter to conclude the point. The

---

*To show that there is a power in the Constitution by which the liberty of the press may be affected, recourse has been had to the power of taxation. It is said that duties may be laid upon the publications so high as to amount to a prohibition. I know not by what logic it could be maintained, that the declarations in the State constitutions, in favor of the freedom of the press, would be a constitutional impediment to the imposition of duties upon publications by the State legislatures. It cannot certainly be pretended that any degree of duties, however low, would be an abridgment of the liberty of the press. We know that newspapers are taxed in Great Britain, and yet it is notorious that the press nowhere enjoys greater liberty than in that country. And if duties of any kind may be laid without a violation of that liberty, it is evident that the extent must depend on legislative discretion, regulated by public opinion; so that, after all, general declarations respecting the liberty of the press, will give it no greater security than it will have without them. The same invasions of it may be effected under the State constitutions which contain those declarations through the means of taxation, as under the proposed Constitution, which has nothing of the kind. It would be quite as significant to declare that government ought to be free, that taxes ought not to be excessive, etc., as that the liberty of the press ought not to be restrained.—PUBLIUS.

truth is, after all the declamations we have heard, that the Constitution is itself, in every rational sense, and to every useful purpose, A BILL OF RIGHTS. The several bills of rights in Great Britain form its Constitution, and conversely the constitution of each State is its bill of rights. And the proposed Constitution, if adopted, will be the bill of rights of the Union. Is it one object of a bill of rights to declare and specify the political privileges of the citizens in the structure and administration of the government? This is done in the most ample and precise manner in the plan of the convention; comprehending various precautions for the public security, which are not to be found in any of the State constitutions. Is another object of a bill of rights to define certain immunities and modes of proceeding, which are relative to personal and private concerns? This we have seen has also been attended to, in a variety of cases, in the same plan. Adverting therefore to the substantial meaning of a bill of rights, it is absurd to allege that it is not to be found in the work of the convention. It may be said that it does not go far enough, though it will not be easy to make this appear; but it can with no propriety be contended that there is no such thing. It certainly must be immaterial what mode is observed as to the order of declaring the rights of the citizens, if they are to be found in any part of the instrument which establishes the government. And hence it must be apparent, that much of what has been said on this subject rests merely on verbal and nominal distinctions, entirely foreign from the substance of the thing.

CONTEMPORARY INFLUENCES

Leonard W. Levy
"American Consitutional History, 1776–1789"

DISCUSSION QUESTIONS

1. How does the author view the relationship between the Declaration of Independence and subsequent Constitutional developments?
2. How does the author answer claims that the Constitution was the undemocratic product of a *coup d'état*?
3. What are the Constitution's democratic elements as emphasized by the author?
4. How does the author answer the claims about the Constitution as developed by Charles Beard (see below)?

Excerpted with permission of The Macmillan Publishing Company from *The Framing and Ratification of the Constitution,* by Leonard W. Levy and Dennis J. Mahoney, eds. Copyright © 1987 by The Macmillan Publishing Company.

On July 4, 1776, King George III wrote in his diary, "Nothing of importance this day." When the news of the Declaration of Independence reached him, he still could not know how wrong he had been. The political philosophy of social compact, natural rights, and limited government that generated the Declaration of Independence also spurred the most important, creative, and dynamic constitutuional achievements in history; the Declaration itself was merely the beginning. Within a mere thirteen years Americans invented or first institutionalized a bill of rights against all branches of government, the written constitution, the constitutional convention, federalism, judicial review, and a solution to the colonial problem (admitting territories to the Union as states fully equal to the original thirteen). Religious liberty, the separation of church and state, political parties, separation of powers, an acceptance of the principle of equality, and the conscious creation of a new nation were also among American institutional "firsts,'' although not all these initially appeared between 1776 and 1789. In that brief span of time, Americans created what are today the oldest major republic, political democracy, state consitutuion, and national constitution. These unparalleled American achievements derived not from originality in speculative theory but from the constructive application of old idea, which Americans took so seriously that they constitutionally based their institutions of government on them.

If the United States was to survive and flourish, a strong national goverment had to be established. The Framers of the Constitution were accountable to public opinion; the convention was a representative body. That its members were prosperous, well-educated political leaders made them no less representative than Congress. The state legislatures, which elected the members of the convention, were the most unlikely instruments for thwarting the popular will. The Framers, far from being able to do as they pleased, were not free to promulgate the Constitution. Although they adroitly arranged for its ratification by nine state ratifying conventions rather than by all state legislatures, they could not present a plan that the people of the states would not tolerate. They could not control the membership of those state ratifying conventions. They could not even be sure that the existing Congress would submit the Constitution to the states for ratification, let alone for ratification by state conventions that had to be specially elected. If the Framers had strayed too far from public opinion, their work would have been wasted. The consensus in the convention coincided with an emerging concensus in the country that recaptured the nationalist spirit of '76. That the Union had to be strengthened was an almost universal American belief.

For its time the Constitution was a remarkably democratic document framed by democratic methods. Some historians have contended that the convention's scrapping of the Articles and the ratification process were revolutionary acts which if performed by a Napolean would be pronounced a coup d'état. But the procedure of the Articles for constitutional amendment was not democratic, because it allowed Rhode Island, with one-sixtieth of the Nation's population, to exercise a veto power. The convention sent its Constitution to the lawfully existing government, the Congress of the Confederation, for submission to the states, and Congress, which could have censured the convention for exceeding its authority, freely complied—and thereby exceeded its own authority under the Articles! A coup d'état ordinarily lacks the deliberation and consent that marked the making of the Constitution and is characterized by a miliary element that was wholly lacking in 1787. A convention elected by the state legislatures and consisting of many of the foremost leaders of their time deliberated for almost four months. Its members included many opponenents of the finished scheme. The nation knew the convention was considering changes in the government. The proposed Constitution was made public, and voters in every state were asked to choose delegates to vote for or against it after open debate. The use of state ratifying conventions fit the theory that a new fundamental law was being adopted and, therefore, conventions were proper for the task.

The Constitution guaranteed to each state a republican or representative form of government and fixed no property or religious qualifications on the right to vote or hold office, at a time when such qualifications were common in the states. By leaving voting qualifications to the states the Constitution implicitly accepted such qualifications but imposed none. The convention, like the Albany Congress of 1754, the Stamp Act Congress, the Continental Congresses, and Congresses of the Confederation, had been chosen by state (or colonial) legislatures, but the Constitution created a Congress whose lower house was popularly elected. When only three states directly elected their chief executive officer, the Constitution provided for the indirect election of the President by an Electoral College that originated in the people and is still operative. The Constitution's system of separation of powers and elaborate checks and balances was not intended to refine out popular influence on government but to protect liberty; the Framers divided, distributed, and limited powers to prevent one branch, faction, interest, or section from becoming too powerful. Checks and balances were not undemocratic, and the Federalists were hard pressed not to apologize for checks and balances but to convince the Anti-Federalists, who wanted far more checks and balances, that the Constitution had enough. Although the Framers were not democrats in a modern sense, their opponents were even less democratic. Those opponents sought to capitalize on the lack of a bill of rights, and ratification of the Constitution became possible only because leading Federalists committed themselves to amendments as soon as the new government went into operation. At that time, however, Anti-Federalists opposed a bill of rights because it would allay popular fears of the new government, lending the chance for state sovereignty amendments.

Although the Framers self-consciously refrained from referring to slavery in the Constitution, it recognized slavery, the most undemocratic of all institutions. That recognition was a grudging but necessary price of union. The three-fifths clause of Article I provided for counting three-fifths of the total number of slaves as part of the population of a state in the apportionment of representation and direct taxation. Article IV, section 2, provided for rendition of fugitive slaves to the slaveholder upon his claim. On the other hand, Article I, section 9, permitted Congress to abolish the slaves trade in twenty eyars. Most delegates, including many from slaveholding states, would have preferred a Contitution untainted by slavery; but southern votes for ratification required recognition of slavery. By choosing a union with slavery, the Convention deferred the day of reckoning.

The Constitution is basically a political document. Modern scholarship has completely discredited the once popular view, associated with Charles Beard, that the Constitution was undemocratically made to advance the economic interest of personalty groups, chiefly creditors. The largest public creditor at the convention was Elbridge Gerry, who refused to sign the Constitution and opposed its ratification, and the largest private creditor was George Mason, who did likewise. Indeed, seven men who either quit the convention in disgust or refused to sign the Constitution held public securities that were worth over twice the holdings of the thirty-nine men who signed the Constitution. The most influential Framers, among them Madison, Wilson, Paterson, Dickinson, and Gouverneur Morris, owned no securities. Others, like Washington, who acted out of patriotism, not profit, held trifling amounts. Eighteen members of the convention were either debtors or held property that depreciated after the new government became operative. On crucial issues at the convention, as in the state ratifying conventions, the dividing line between groups for and against the Constitution was not economic, not between realty and personalty, or debtors and creditors, or town and frontier. The restrictions of Article I, section 10, on the economic powers of the states were calculated to protect creditor interests and promote business stability, but those restrictions were not undemocratic; if impairing the obligations of contracts or emitting bills of credit and paper money were democratic hallmarks, the Constitution left Congress free to be democratic. The interest groups for and against the Constitution were substantially similar. Economic interests did influence the voting on ratification, but no simple explanation that ignores differences between states and even within states will suffice, and many noneconomic influences were also at work. In the end the Constitution was framed and ratified because most voters came to share the vision held by Franklin in 1775 and Dickinson in 1776; those two, although antagonists in Pennsylvania politics, understood for quite different reasons that a strong central government was indispensable for nationhood.

Martin Diamond
"The Revolution of Sober Expectations"
(Excerpts)

DISCUSSION QUESTIONS

1. What is meant by "consent of the governed"? How does the author treat this concept in respect to the Declaration of Independence? Do you agree?
2. Why does the author contrast the "American truth" to "Robespierre's truth" and "Lenin's truth"? What does he mean by this, and why could it be relevant?
3. What does the author mean by a "revolution in sober expectations"? Do the author's arguments adequately explain the American founding?

What wants understanding is precisely how our institutions of government sprang from the principle of the Declaration of Independence. How and to what extent were they generated by the Declaration of Independence? And what more had to be added actually to frame those institutions? . . .

Mary Polingue, ed., *Readings in American Government* (Dubuque, IA: Kendall/Hunt, 1976), pp. 23–25.

We must read the Declaration closely to free ourselves from two centuries of obscuring usage. We have transformed the Declaration in our minds by reading the phrase "consent of the governed" as meaning rule by majorities, that is, democratic government. Indeed we think of the Declaration as our great democratic document, as the clarion call to and the guide to our democratic nature. But the Declaration does *not* say that consent is the means by which government is to operate. Rather, it says that consent is necessary only to institute the government, that is, to establish it.

The people need not, then, *establish* a government which *operates* by means of their consent. In fact, the Declaration says that they may organize government on "such principles" as they choose, and they may choose "any form of government" they deem appropriate to secure their rights. That is, the Declaration was not prescribing any particular form of government at all, but rather was following John Locke's contract theory, which taught the right of the people, in seeking to secure their liberties, to establish *any* form of government. And by any form of government the Declaration emphatically includes—as any literate eighteenth century reader would have understood—not only the democratic form of government but also aristocratic and monarchical government as well. That is why, for example, the Declaration has to submit facts to a "candid world" to prove the British king guilty of a "long train of abuses." Tom Paine, by way of contrast, could dispose of King George more simply. Paine deemed George III unfit to rule simply because he was a *king* and kingly rule was illegitimate as such. The fact that George was a "Royal Brute" was only frosting on the cake; for Paine his being royal was sufficient warrant for deposing him. But the Declaration, on the contrary, is obliged to prove that George was indeed a brute. That is, the Declaration holds George III "unfit to be the ruler of a free people" not because he was a king, but because he was a *tyrannical* king. Had the British monarchy continued to secure to the colonists their rights, as it had prior to the long train of abuses, the colonists would not have been entitled to rebel. It was only the fact, according to the Declaration, that George had become a tyrannical king that supplied the warrant for revolution.

Thus the Declaration, strictly speaking, is neutral on the question of forms of government: *any* form is legitimate provided it secures equal freedom and is instituted by popular consent. . . .

It is to the constitution that we must ultimately turn as the completion of the American Revolution. As to those democratic institutions, the Declaration says no more than this: If you choose the democratic form of government, rather than the aristocratic or monarchic or any mixture thereof, it must be a democratic government which secures to all people their unalienable rights. But how to do that? The Declaration is silent. . . .

What was truly revolutionary in the American Revolution and its Declaration of Independence was that liberty, civil liberty—the doctrine of certain unalienable rights—was made the end of government. Not, as had been the case for millennia, whatever end power haphazardly imposed upon government; nor any longer the familiar variety of ends—not virtue, not piety, not privilege or wealth, not merely protection, and not empire and dominion; but now deliberately the principle of liberty. . . .

While modern followers of Edmund Burke may warn of the dangers of devotion to abstract principles, they cannot blink aside the revolutionary American devotion to precisely such an abstract principle. The American truth was undeniably as abstract as, say, Robespierre's tyrannizing truth or Lenin's tyrannizing truth. And yet there is indeed something moderate and nonutopian in the American devotion to liberty which warrants Burkean celebration. Whence then the difference? Wherein was the American Revolution one of sober expectations while the Jacobin and Leninist were revolutions of unbridled expectations? The answer lies not in degrees of devotion to abstractness, but in the substantive nature of the principle each was abstractly devoted to. It is one thing to be abstractly devoted to the Reign of Virtue or to unlimited equality in all respects or to mass fraternity or to classless society or to the transformation of the human condition itself, and quite another to be devoted to the abstract principle of civil liberty. Civil liberty as a goal constrains its followers to moderation, legality, and rootedness in regular institutions. Moreover, moderate civil liberty does not require terror and tyranny for its fulfillment. Liberty is an abstract principle capable of achievement; Jacobin or Leninist equality or mass fraternity are not. Moderate civil liberty is a possible dream, utopian equality and fraternity are impossible dreams. And the recent popular song to the contrary notwithstanding, the political pursuit of impossible dreams leads to terror and tyranny in the vain effort to actualize what cannot be. . . .

[S]obriety also lies in the Founding Fathers' coolheaded and cautious acceptance of democracy. Perhaps not a single American voice was raised in unqualified, doctrinaire praise of democracy. On the contrary, there was universal recognition of the problematic character of democracy, a concern for its weaknesses and a fear of its dangers. The debate in American life during the founding decade gradually became a debate over how to create a decent democratic regime. Contrary to our too complacent modern perspective regarding democracy, which assumes that a government cannot be decent unless democratic, our Founding Fathers more skeptically, sensibly, and soberly, were concerned how to make this new government *decent even though democratic.* All the American revolutionaries, whether they were partisans of the theory that democratic republics had to be small or agrarian or only loosely confederated in order to remain free, or whether they retained the traditional idea that democracy had to be counterbalanced by nobility or wealth, or whether they subscribed to the large-republic theory implicit in the new Constitution—all the American revolutionaries knew that democracy was a problem in need of constant solution, in constant need of moderation, in constant need of institutions and measures to mitigate its defects and guard against its dangers. . . .

The half-revolution begun in 1776 reached its completion only when the peculiar American posture toward democracy received its definitive form in the framing and ratification of the Constitution a decade later. . . . [I]n contemplating that convention we would find the answer to our earlier question: how did our institutions spring from the Declaration and what had to be added to bring those institutions into being? They sprang on the one hand from the love of free government inspired by the noble *sentiments* of Jefferson's Declaration, and on the other hand from the theoretic *wisdom* of James Madison whose sober clarity regarding democracy gave the shape and thrust to our unique democratic form of government and way of life.

J. Allen Smith
"The Constitution as Counter-Revolution"

DISCUSSION QUESTIONS

1. What is the essence of "democratic philosophy"? In your judgment, does the United States Constitution fall within the measure of democratic ideals? Explain.
2. According to the author, how did the framers of the Constitution regard democracy? What were their attitudes regarding the people?
3. The author mentions the absence from the federal convention of such notables as Thomas Jefferson, Samuel Adams, Thomas Paine, and Patrick Henry. What might have been produced from the Philadelphia convention had these individuals been present and actively involved?
4. Compare the arguments in this article with the ones advanced by Martin Diamond. In your judgment, is the Constitution progressive or conservative? Revolutionary or reactionary? Explain.

The sweeping changes made in our form of government after the Declaration of Independence were clearly revolutionary in character. The English system of checks and balances was discarded for the more democratic one under which all the important powers of government were vested in the legislature. This new scheme of government was not, however, truly representative of the political thought of the colonies. The conservative classes who in ordinary times are a powerful factor in the politics of every community had, by reason of their Loyalist views, no voice in this political reorganization; and these, as we have seen, not only on account of their wealth and intelligence, but on the basis of their numerical strength as well, were entitled to considerable influence.

With the return of peace these classes which so largely represented the wealth and culture of the colonies, regained in a measure the influence which they had lost. This tended strongly to bring about a conservative reaction. There was besides another large class which supported the Revolutionary movement without being in sympathy with its democratic tendencies. This also used its influence to undo the work of the Revolutionary radicals. Moreover, many of those who had espoused democratic doctrines during the Revolution became conservatives after the war was over.[1] These classes were naturally opposed to the new political doctrines which the Revolutionary movement had incorpo-

---

J. Allen Smith, *The Spirit of American Government,* copyright © 1907 by The Macmillan Company. Reprinted in *Problems in American Civilization* (Boston: D. C. Heath and Company, 1949), pp. 29–34. Reprinted with permission.

[1] "Who would have thought, ten years ago, that the very men who risked their lives and fortunes in support of republican principles, would now treat them as the fictions of fancy?" M. Smith in the New York Convention held to ratify the Constitution, *Elliot's Debates,* Second Edition, Vol. II, p. 250.

rated in the American government. The "hard times" and general discontent which followed the war also contributed to the reactionary movement; since many were led to believe that evils which were the natural result of other causes were due to an excess of democracy. Consequently we find the democratic tendency which manifested itself with the outbreak of the Revolution giving place a few years later to the political reaction which found expression in our present Constitution.

The United States are the offspring of a long-past age. A hundred years, it is true, have scarcely passed since the eighteenth century came to its end, but no hundred years in the history of the world has ever before hurried it along so far over new paths and into unknown fields. The French Revolution and the First Empire were the bridge between two periods that nothing less than the remarking of European society, the recasting of European politics, could have brought so near.

But back to this eighteenth century must we go to learn the forces, the national ideas, the political theories, under the domination of which the Constitution of the United States was framed and adopted.[2]

It is the general belief, nevertheless, that the Constitution of the United States is the very embodiment of democratic philosophy. The people take it for granted that the framers of that document were imbued with the spirit of political equality and sought to establish a government by the people themselves. Widely as this view is entertained, it is, however, at variance with the facts.

"Scarcely any of these men [the framers of the Constitution] entertained," says Fiske, "what we should now call extreme democratic views. Scarcely any, perhaps, had that intense faith in the ultimate good sense of the people which was the most powerful characteristic of Jefferson."[3]

Democracy—government by the people, or directly responsible to them—was not the object which the framers of the American Constitution had in view, but the very thing which they wished to avoid. In the convention which drafted that instrument it was recognized that democratic ideas had made sufficient progress among the masses to put an insurmountable obstacle in the way of any plan of government which did not confer at least the form of political power upon the people. Accordingly the efforts of the Constitutional Convention were directed to the task of devising a system of government which was just popular enough not to excite general opposition and which at the same time gave to the people as little as possible of the substance of political power.

It is somewhat strange that the American people know so little of the fundamental nature of their system of government. Their acquaintance with it extends only to its outward form and rarely includes a knowledge of the political philosophy upon which it rests. The sources of information upon which the average man relies do not furnish the data for a correct understanding of the Constitution. The ordinary text-books and popular works upon this subject leave the reader with an entirely erroneous impression. Even the writings of our constitutional lawyers deal with the outward form rather than the spirit of our government. The vital ques-

---

[2]Simeon E. Baldwin, *Modern Political Institutions*, pp. 83 and 84.

[3]*Critical Period of American History*, p. 226.

tion—the extent to which, under our constitutional arrangements, the people were expected to, and as a matter of fact do, control legislation and public policy, is either not referred to, or else discussed in a superficial and unsatisfactory manner. That this feature of our Constitution should receive more attention than it does is evident when we reflect that a government works well in practice in proportion as its underlying philosophy and constitutional forms are comprehended by those who wield political power.

"It has been common," says a late Justice of the United States Supreme Court, "to designate our form of government as a democracy, but in the true sense in which that term is properly used, as defining a government in which all its acts are performed by the people, it is about as far from it as any other of which we are aware."[4]

In the United States at the present time we are trying to make an undemocratic Constitution the vehicle of democratic rule. Our Constitution embodies the political philosophy of the eighteenth century, not that of to-day. It was framed for one purpose while we are trying to use it for another. Is free government, then, being tried here under the conditions most favorable to its success? This question we can answer only when we have considered our Constitution as a means to the attainment of democratic rule.

It is difficult to understand how anyone who has read the proceedings of the Federal Convention can believe that it was the intention of that body to establish a democratic government. The evidence is overwhelming that the men who sat in that convention had no faith in the wisdom or political capacity of the people. Their aim and purpose was not to secure a larger measure of democracy, but to eliminate as far as possible the direct influence of the people on legislation and public policy. That body, it is true, contained many illustrious men who were actuated by a desire to further what they conceived to be the welfare of the country. They represented, however, the wealthy and conservative classes, and had for the most part but little sympathy with the popular theory of government.

> Hardly one among them but had sat in some famous assembly, had signed some famous document, had filled some high place, or had made himself conspicuous for learning, for scholarship, or for signal services rendered in the cause of liberty. One had framed the Albany plan of union; some had been members of the Stamp Act Congress of 1765; some had signed the Declaration of Rights in 1774; the names of others appear at the foot of the Declaration of Independence and at the foot of the Articles of Confederation; two had been presidents of Congress; seven had been, or were then, governors of states; twenty-eight had been members of Congress; one had commanded the armies of the United States; another had been Superintendent of Finance; a third had repeatedly been sent on important missions to England, and had long been Minister to France.
>
> Nor were the future careers of many of them to be less interesting than their past. Washington and Madison became Presidents of the United States; Elbridge Gerry became Vice-President; Charles Cotesworth Pinckney and Rufus King became candidates for the Presidency, and Jared Ingersoll, Rufus King, and John Langdon candidates for the Vice-Presidency; Hamilton be-

[4]S. F. Miller, *Lectures on the Constitution of the United States*, pp. 84–85.

came Secretary of the Treasury; Madison, Secretary of State; Randolph, Attorney-General and Secretary of State, and James McHenry, a Secretary of War; Ellsworth and Rutledge became Chief-Justices; Wilson and John Blair rose to the Supreme bench; Gouverneur Morris, and Ellsworth, and Charles C. Pinckney, and Gerry, and William Davie became Ministers abroad.[5]

The long list of distinguished men who took part in the deliberations of that body is noteworthy, however, for the absence of such names as Samuel Adams, Thomas Jefferson, Thomas Paine, Patrick Henry and other democratic leaders of that time. The Federal Convention assembled in Philadelphia only eleven years after the Declaration of Independence was signed, yet only six of the fifty-six men who signed that document were among its members.[6] Conservatism and thorough distrust of popular government characterized throughout the proceedings of that convention. Democracy, Elbridge Gerry thought, was the worst of all political evils.[7] Edmund Randolph observed that in tracing the political evils of this country to their origin, "every man [in the Convention] had found it in the turbulence and follies of democracy."[8] These views appear to reflect the general opinion of that body. Still they realized that it was not the part of wisdom to give public expression to this contempt for democracy. The doors were closed to the public and the utmost secrecy maintained with regard to the proceedings. Members were not allowed to communicate with any one outside of that body concerning the matters therein discussed, nor were they permitted, except by a vote of the Convention, to copy anything from the journals.[9]

It must be borne in mind that the Convention was called for the purpose of proposing amendments to the Articles of Confederation. The delegates were not authorized to frame a new constitution. Their appointment contemplated changes which were to perfect the Articles of Confederation without destroying the general form of government which they established. The resolution of Congress of February 21, 1787, which authorized the Federal Convention, limited its business to "the sole and express purpose of revising the Articles of Confederation," and the states

---

[5]McMaster, *With the Fathers*, pp. 112–113.

[6] "They [the framers of the Constitution] represented the conservative intelligence of the country very exactly; from this class there is hardly a name, except that of Jay, which could be suggested to complete the list." Article by Alexander Johnston on the Convention of 1787 in *Lalor's Cyclopaedia of Pol. Science, Pol. Econ. and U. S. Hist.*

[7]*Elliot's Debates*, Vol. V, p. 557.

[8]*Ibid.*, p. 138.

[9] "By another [rule] the doors were to be shut, and the whole proceedings were to be kept secret; and so far did this rule extend, that we were thereby prevented from corresponding with gentlemen in the different states upon the subjects under our discussion. . . . So extremely solicitous were they that their proceedings should not transpire, that the members were prohibited even from taking copies of resolutions, on which the Convention were deliberating, or extracts of any kind from the Journals without formally moving for and obtaining permission, by a vote of the Convention for that purpose." Luther Martin's Address to the Maryland House of Delegates. Ibid., Vol. I, p. 345.

"The doors were locked, and an injunction of strict secrecy was put upon everyone. The results of their work were known in the following September, when the draft of the Federal Constitution was published. But just what was said and done in this secret conclave was not revealed until fifty years had passed, and the aged James Madison, the last survivor of those who sat there, had been gathered to his fathers." Fiske, *The Critical Period of American History*, p. 229. McMaster, *With the Fathers*, p. 112.

of New York, Massachusetts, and Connecticut copied this in the instructions to their delegates.[10] The aim of the Convention, however, from the very start was not amendment, but a complete rejection of the system itself, which was regarded as incurably defective.

This view was well expressed by James Wilson in his speech made in favor of the ratification of the Constitution before the Pennsylvania convention.

> The business, we are told, which was entrusted to the late Convention [he said] was merely to amend the present Articles of Confederation. This observation has been frequently made, and has often brought to my mind a story that is related by Mr. Pope, who, it is well known, was not a little deformed. It was customary with him to use this phrase, "God mend me!" when any little accident happened. One evening a link-boy was lighting him along, and, coming to a gutter, the boy jumped nimbly over it. Mr. Pope called to him in turn, adding, "God mend me!" The arch rogue, turning to light him, looked at him, and repeated, "God mend you! He would sooner make half-a-dozen new ones." This would apply to the present Confederation; for it would be easier to make another than to amend this.[11]

The popular notion that this Convention in framing the Constitution was actuated solely by a desire to impart more vigor and efficiency to the general government is but a part of the truth. The Convention desired to establish not only a strong and vigorous central government, but one which would at the same time possess great stability or freedom from change. This last reason is seldom mentioned in our constitutional literature, yet it had a most important bearing on the work of the Convention. This desired stability the government under the Confederation did not possess, since it was, in the opinion of the members of the Convention, dangerously responsive to public opinion; hence their desire to supplant it with an elaborate system of constitutional checks. The adoption of this system was the triumph of a skillfully directed reactionary movement.

Of course the spirit and intention of the Convention must be gathered not from the statements and arguments addressed to the general public in favor of the ratification of the Constitution, but from what occurred in the Convention itself. The discussions which took place in that body indicate the real motives and purposes of those who framed the Constitution. These were carefully withheld from the people and it was not until long afterward that they were accessible to students of the American Constitution. The preamble began with, "We, the people," but it was the almost unanimous sentiment of the Convention that the less the people had to do with the government the better. Hamilton wanted to give the rich and well born "a distinct, permanent share in the government."[12] Madison thought the government in ought "to protect the minority of the opulent against the majority."[13] The prevalence of such views in this Convention reminds one of Adam Smith's state-

---

[10] *Elliot's Debates*, Vol. I, pp. 119–127.

[11] *Elliot's Debates*, Vol. II, p. 470.

[12] *Elliot's Debates*, Vol. I, p. 422.

[13] *Ibid.*, p. 450.

ment in his "Wealth of Nations," that "civil government, so far as it is instituted for the security of property, is in reality instituted for the defence of the rich against the poor, or of those who have some property against those who have none at all."[14] The solicitude shown by the members of this convention for the interests of the well-to-do certainly tends to justify Adam Smith's observation.

The framers of the Constitution realized, however, that it would not do to carry this system of checks upon the people too far. It was necessary that the government should retain something of the form of democracy, if it was to command the respect and confidence of the people. For this reason Gerry thought that "the people should appoint one branch of the government in order to inspire them with the necessary confidence."[15] Madison also saw that the necessary sympathy between the people and their rulers and officers must be maintained and that "the policy of refining popular appointments by successive filtrations" might be pushed too far.[16] These discussions, which took place behind closed doors and under pledge of secrecy, may be taken as fairly representing what the framers of our Constitution really thought of popular government. Their public utterances, on the other hand, influenced as they necessarily were, by considerations of public policy, are of little value. From all the evidence which we have, the conclusion is irresistible that they sought to establish a form of government which would effectually curb and restrain democracy. They engrafted upon the Constitution just so much of the features of popular government as was, in their opinion, necessary to ensure its adoption.

Gordon S. Wood
The Radicalism of the American Revolution
(Excerpts)

DISCUSSION QUESTIONS

1. Was there a class element to the American Revolution and the framing of the Constitution?
2. How does Wood characterize the political disposition of the framers? Specifically how does Wood describe the Hamiltonian conception of government?
3. What is the difference between "patrician" and "populist"? Are there elements of these in American society today?
4. What does Wood mean by the following statement: "The Anti-Federalists lost the battle over the Constitution. But they did not lose the war over the kind of national government the United States would have for a good part, at least, of the next century"? Is he correct? Why or why not?

---

[14]Book 5, Ch. I, Part II.

[15]*Elliot's Debates*, Vol. V, p. 160.

[16]*Ibid.*, p. 137.

Gordon S. Wood, *The Radicalism of the American Revolution* (New York: Alfred A. Knopf, Inc., 1992) pp. 254–263.

The new federal Constitution was designed to ensure that governmental leadership would be entrusted as much as possible to just those kinds of disinterested gentlemen who had neither occupations nor narrow mercantile interests to promote, "men who," in Madison's words, "possess most wisdom to discern and most virtue to pursue the common good of the society." In an interest-ridden society the secret of good government was to enlarge and elevate the national government, in the manner projected by the new federal Constitution of 1787, and thus screen out the kind of interested men who had dominated the state legislatures in the 1780s— "men of factious tempers, of local prejudices, or of sinister designs" —and replace them with classically educated gentlemen "whose enlightened views and virtuous sentiments render them superior to local prejudices, and to schemes of injustice."[1]

With "the purest and noblest characters" of the society in power, Madison expected the new national government to play the same suprapolitical neutral role that the British king had been supposed to play in the empire. In fact, Madison hoped that the new federal government might restore some aspect of monarchy that had been lost in the Revolution. In monarchies, he said, the king was sufficiently neutral toward his subjects, but often he sacrificed their happiness for his avarice or ambition. In small republics the government had no selfish will of its own, but it was never sufficiently neutral toward the various interests of the society. The new extended republic, said Madison, was designed to combine the good qualities of each. The new government would be "sufficiently neutral between the different interests and factions, to control one part of the society from invading the rights of another, and at the same time sufficiently controlled itself, from setting up an interest adverse to that of the whole society." That someone as moderate and as committed to republicanism as Madison should speak even privately of the benefits of monarchy adhering in the Constitution of 1787 is a measure of how disillusioned many of the revolutionary gentry had become with the democratic consequences of the Revolution.[2]

Given this Federalist reasoning and these Federalist aims, it is not surprising that the opponents of the Constitution in 1787–88, or the Anti-Federalists, as they were called, charged that the new federal system was aristocratically designed to

---

[1]*The Federalist*, No. 57, No. 10. Madison and other Federalists were willing to allow ordinary people to pursue their partial selfish interests in the expectation that such interests would be so diverse and clashing that they would rarely be able to combine to create tyrannical majorities in the new federal government in the ways they had in the state legislatures. In an enlarged society, wrote Madison, "the people are broken into so many interests and parties, that a common sentiment is less likely to be felt, and requisite concert less likely to be formed, by a majority of the whole." This competitive situation would then allow those educated gentlemen "who possess the most attractive merit, and the most diffusive and established characters" to dominate the national government and promote the common good in a disinterested manner. Madison understood that it had worked that way in American religion; the multiplicity of religious sects in America prevented any one of them from dominating the state and permitted the enlightened reason of liberal gentlemen like Jefferson and himself to shape public policy and church-state relations and protect the rights of minorities. "In a free government," wrote Madison in *The Federalist*, No. 51, "the security for civil rights must be the same as that for religious rights. It consists in the one case in the multiplicity of interests, and in the other in the multiplicity of sects."

[2]Madison, Vices of the Political System of the United States (1787), in Rutland et al., eds., *Papers of Madison*, IX, 352, 357.

"raise the fortunes and respectability of the well-born few, and oppress the plebeians."[3] Because the Constitution seemed to be perpetuating the classical tradition of virtuous patrician leadership in government, the Anti-Federalists felt compelled to challenge that tradition. There was, the Anti-Federalists said repeatedly, no disinterested gentlemanly elite that could feel "sympathetically the wants of the people" and speak for their "feelings, circumstances, and interests." That elite had its own particular interests to promote. However educated and elevated such gentry might be, they were no more free of the lures and interests of the marketplace than anyone else.[4]

The consequences of such thinking were immense and indeed devastating for republican government. If gentlemen were involved in the marketplace and had interests just like everyone else, they were really no different from all those common people—artisans, shopkeepers, traders, and others—who had traditionally been denied a role in political leadership because of their overriding absorption in their private occupational interests. In short, the Anti-Federalists were saying that liberally educated gentlemen were no more capable than ordinary people of classical republican disinterestedness and virtue and that consequently there was no one in the society equipped to promote an exclusive public interest that was distinguishable from the private interests of people. . . .

Without realizing the full implications of what they were doing, in the ratification debates over the Constitution they also called into question all the time-honored conceptions of society known to the revolutionary leaders. To be sure, there were a number of Anti-Federalist aristocrats like George Mason and Richard Henry Lee who had a whiggish fear of centralized power but no desire to undermine the traditional order of society. Such Anti-Federalist southern gentry could not emotionally speak for all the entrepreneurial and debtor forces of ordinary people that were emerging, particularly in the northern parts of America. But common Anti-Federalists like Melancton Smith and William Petrikin could; they shared a whiggish fear of power with aristocrats like Lee and Mason, but they also had a desire to challenge both aristocratic leadership and the social order. To these plebeian Anti-Federalists, pulling together at least two decades of intense polemics and developing reality, American society could no longer be thought of as either a hierarchy of ranks or a homogeneous republican whole. Many of them, in fact, saw a society more pluralistic, more diverse, and more fragmented with interests than even someone as hardheaded and realistic as James Madison had. Society, they said, was not a unitary entity with a single common interest but a heterogeneous mixture of "many different classes or orders of people, Merchants, Farmers, Planters, Mechanics, and Gentry or wealthy Men," all equal to one another. In such a pluralistic egalitarian society there was no possibility of a liberal enlightened elite speaking for the whole; men from one class or interest could never be acquainted with the "Situation and Wants" of those from another. "Lawyers and planters," whatever their genteel pretensions, could never be "adequate judges of tradesmen's concerns." The occupations and interests of the society were so diverse and discrete that only individuals

---

[3]*Providence Gazette*, 5 Jan. 1788.

[4]Elliot, ed., *Debates of the State Conventions*, II, 260, 13.

sharing a particular occupation or interest could speak for that occupation or interest. It was foolish to tell people that they ought to overlook their local interests when local interests were all there really were. "No man when he enters into society, does it from a view to promote the good of others, but he does it for his own good." Since all individuals and groups in the society were equally self-interested, the only "fair representation" in government, wrote the "Federal Farmer," ought to be one where "every order of men in the community . . . can have a share in it." Consequently any American government ought "to allow professional men, merchants, traders, farmers, mechanics, etc. to bring a just proportion of their best informed men respectively into the legislature." Only an explicit form of representation that allowed Germans, Baptists, artisans, farmers, and so on each to send delegates of its own kind into the political arena could embody the democratic particularism of the emerging society of the early Republic.[5]

Momentous consequences eventually flowed from these Anti- Federalist arguments. In these populist Anti-Federalist calls for the most explicit form of representation possible, and not in Madison's *Federalist* Paper 10, lay the real origins of American pluralism and American interest-group politics. The grass-roots Anti-Federalists concluded that, given the variety of competing interests and the fact that all people had interests, the only way for a person to be fairly and accurately represented in government was to have someone like himself with his same interests speak for him; no one else could be trusted to do so.

Ultimately, the logic of this conception of actual representation determined that no one could be represented in government unless he had the right to vote. The interests of a person were so particular, so personal, that only by exercising the ballot could he protect and promote his interests. Election in America became the sole criterion of representation. Insofar as American politics became localist and dominated by interest groups and calls for extending the suffrage, the Anti-Federalists prepared the way.

The Anti-Federalists lost the battle over the Constitution. But they did not lose the war over the kind of national government the United States would have for a good part, at least, of the next century. Their popular understanding of American society and politics in the early Republic was too accurate and too powerful to be put down—as the Federalists themselves soon came to appreciate. Even the elections for the First Congress in 1788 revealed the practical realities of American democratic life that contradicted the Federalists' classical republican dreams of establishing a government led by disinterested educated gentlemen. . . .

Madison's remedy of an elevated and extended republic in 1787 seemed much too mild and insufficient for many Federalists in the 1790s worried about the spread of what Alexander Hamilton called "the amazing violence & turbulence of the democratic spirit."[6] So deeply pessimistic over the interest-ridden and unvirtu-

---

[5]Philip A. Crowl, "Anti-Federalism in Maryland, 1787—88," *WMQ* 3rd Ser., IV (1947), 464; Walsh, *Charleston's Sons of Liberty*, 132; [James Winthrop], "Letters of Agrippa," *Massachusetts Gazette*, 14 Dec. 1787, in Storing, ed., *Complete Anti-Federalist*, IV, 80; Walter Hartwell Bennett, ed., *Letters from the Federal Farmer to the Republican* (University, Ala., 1978), 10.

[6]Farrand, ed., *Records of the Federal Convention*, I, 289.

ous reality of American society were many of the Federalists of the 1790s—who clung to the name used by the supporters of the Constitution in 1787–88—that in filling out the new national government they went way beyond Madison's "strictly republican" remedy and sought to bring back some of the basic characteristics and adhesives of monarchical society that many revolutionaries had thought they had gotten rid of in 1776 once and for all.

Despite their fears of democracy, however, the Federalists and even their leader Hamilton were not monarchists. Although in the Philadelphia Convention Hamilton had "acknowledged himself not to think favorably of Republican Government," he had no stake in claims of blood and had no intention of returning to the monarchical and patriarchal politics of the *ancien régime* in which government was treated as a source of personal and family aggrandizement. Still, he and the other Federalists did believe that some monarchical surrogates had to be found to strengthen government in order to keep the unvirtuous American people from flying apart in licentious pursuits of happiness. "The mass of men," observed John Jay, "are neither wise nor good, and virtue, like the other resources of a country, can only be drawn to a point and exerted by strong circumstances ably managed, or a strong government ably administered."[7]

By the 1790s the Federalists had no confidence left in the radical enlightened hope that governmental power was, in Hamilton's derisive words, a mere "consequence of the bad habits which have been produced by the errors of ancient systems" and therefore not ultimately necessary for holding society together. Although many of the artisan and plebeian followers of the Republicans were quite willing, like the Federalists, to recognize the prevalence of interests, most of their leaders, and Jefferson especially, still held out hopes that virtue and the natural sociability of people were the best social adhesives. In Hamilton's view, however, these hopes were nothing but delusions. The idea that, "as human nature shall refine and ameliorate by the operation of a more enlightened plan" based on a common moral sense and the spread of affection and benevolence, government eventually "will become useless, and Society will subsist and flourish free from its shackles," was a "wild and fatal . . . scheme," even if its Republican "votaries" like Jefferson did not push such a scheme to its fullest.[8]

The Federalists thus repudiated the emerging Jeffersonian Republican view that the best government was the least government. Hamilton believed deeply in the "need" for "a common directing power" in government, and had only contempt for those who thought trade and other private interests could regulate themselves. "This is one of those wild speculative paradoxes," he said, "which have grown into credit among us, contrary to the uniform practice and sense of the most enlightened nations. . . . It must be rejected by every man acquainted with commercial history."[9]

[7]Hamilton, in Farrand, ed., *Records of the Federal Convention*, I, 424; Jay, quoted in David Hackett Fischer, *The Revolution of American Conservatism: The Federalist Party in the Era of Jeffersonian Democracy* (New York, 1965), 7.

[8]Hamilton (1794), in Morton J. Frisch, ed., *Selected Writings and Speeches of Alexander Hamilton* (Washington, D.C., 1985), 415.

[9]Hamilton, "The Continentalist, No. V," (1782), in Syrett et al., eds., *Papers of Hamilton*, III, 76.

In place of the impotent confederation of separate states that had existed in the 1780s, the Federalists aimed to build a strong, consolidated, and prosperous "fiscal-military" state in emulation of eighteenth-century England, united "for the accomplishment of great purposes" by an energetic government composed of the best men in the society. Like Madison, Hamilton recognized and accepted the prevalence of economic and commercial interests in the society, but he sought to use the national government to harness these interest for the creation of a European-like great power of a sort that Madison had never anticipated.[10] As Secretary of the Treasury, he was undoubtedly concerned with the commercial prosperity of the country—with promoting "the great interests of a great people" —but we make a mistake to see him as a capitalist promoter of America's emerging business culture.[11] He had as much contempt for the vulgarity and selfishness of that popular business culture as did Madison. Hamilton was very much the aristocratic eighteenth-century statesman—willing to allow ordinary people their profits and property, their interests and their pursuits of happiness, but wanting honor and glory for himself and for the United States.

To achieve that honor and glory Hamilton deliberately set out to "corrupt" American society, to use monarch-like governmental influence to tie existing commercial interests to the government and to create new hierarchies of interest and dependency that would substitute for the absence of virtue and the apparently weak republican adhesives existing in America. "What other chain," asked Federalist congressman Christopher Gore, would be "so binding as that involving the interests of the men of property in the prosperity of the Government"?[12] In local areas Hamilton and the Federalist leaders built up followings among Revolutionary War veterans and members of the Society of the Cincinnati. They appointed important and respectable local figures to the federal judiciary and other federal offices. They exploited the patronage of the Treasury Department and its 800 or more customs officials, revenue agents, and postmasters with particular effectiveness. The Federalists carefully managed the Bank of the United States and the national debt to connect interested individuals to the government. By 1793 or so the Federalists had formed groups of "friends of government" in most of the states. Their hierarchies of patronage and dependency ran from the federal executive through Congress down to the various localities. In the eyes of their Jeffersonian Republican opponents the Federalists seemed to be taking Americans back to the monarchy that had been repudiated in 1776.

---

[10]The emergence of England's "fiscal-military" state, in John Brewer's apt term, was the miracle of the century. England mobilized wealth and waged war as no state in history ever had; with a population only a fraction the size of France's it had built the greatest empire since the fall of Rome. Hamilton saw that the secret of England's achievement was its system of funded debt together with its banking structure and market in public securities; he aimed to build the same kind of state for the United States. John Brewer, *The Sinews of Power: War, Money and the English State, 1688–1783* (New York, 1989).

[11]Hamilton, Speeches in the New York Ratifying Convention, 28, 27 June 1788, Syrett et al., eds., *Papers of Hamilton*, V, 118, 96.

[12]Helen R. Pickney, *Christopher More: Federalist of Massachusetts, 1758–1827* (Waltham, Mass., 1969), 37.

THE BILL OF RIGHTS

Articles in addition to, and Amendment of the Constitution of the United States of America, proposed by Congress, and ratified by the Legislatures of the several States, pursuant to the fifth Article of the original Constitution.

[The first ten amendments went into effect November 3, 1791.]

Art. I

Congress shall make no law respecting an establishment of religion, or prohibiting the free exercise thereof; or abridging the freedom of speech, or of the press; or the right of the people peaceably to assemble, and to petition the government for a redress of grievances.

Art. II

A well regulated Militia, being necessary to the security of a free State, the right of the people to keep and bear Arms, shall not be infringed.

Art. III

No Soldier shall, in time of peace be quartered in any house, without the consent of the Owner, nor in time of war, but in a manner to be prescribed by law.

Art. IV

The right of the people to be secure in their persons, houses, papers, and effects, against unreasonable searches and seizures, shall not be violated, and no Warrants shall issue, but upon probable cause, supported by Oath or affirmation, and particularly describing the place to be searched, and the persons or things to be seized.

Art. V

No person shall be held to answer for a capital, or otherwise infamous crime, unless on a presentment or indictment of a Grand Jury, except in cases arising in the land or naval forces, or in the Militia, when in actual service in time of War or public danger; nor shall any person be subject for the same offence to be twice put in jeopardy of life or limb; nor shall be compelled in any criminal case to be a witness against himself, nor be deprived of life, liberty, or property, without due process of law; nor shall private property be taken for public use, without just compensation.

Art. VI

In all criminal prosecutions, the accused shall enjoy the right to a speedy and public trial, by an impartial jury of the State and district wherein the crime shall have been committed, which district shall have been previously ascertained by law, and to be informed of the nature and cause of the accusation; to be confronted with the witnesses against him; to have compulsory process for obtaining witnesses in his favor, and to have the Assistance of Counsel for his defence.

Art. VII

In Suits at common law, where the value in controversy shall exceed twenty dollars, the right of trial by jury shall be preserved, and no fact tried by a jury, shall be otherwise re-examined in any Court of the United States, than according to the rules of the common law.

Art. VIII

Excessive bail shall not be required, nor excessive fines imposed, nor cruel and unusual punishments inflicted.

Art. IX

The enumeration in the Constitution, of certain rights, shall not be construed to deny or disparage others retained by the people.

Art. X

The powers not delegated to the United States by the Constitution, nor prohibited by it to the States, are reserved to the States respectively, or to the people.

2

Property and Commerce

Connections between economic prosperity and political power are ancient. In the *Republic,* Plato includes a discussion of plutocratic government, which is denoted as "oligarchic," in his criticism of "imperfect" species of the *polis.*[1] Aristotle continues this line of thought as he illustrates the formative impetus of wealth in the development of "oligarchies," which he considers to be among the forms of "perverse" or "deviated" constitutions.[2] Cicero provides a scathing indictment against plutocratic or oligarchic governance, inveighing against the rule by wealth and for the wealthy as "characterized by shamelessness and insufferable arrogance."[3] For Cicero, "There is indeed no uglier kind of state than one in which the richest men are thought to be the best."[4] Modern thinkers continued to examine the relationship between material affluence, political power, and successful government, arriving at numerous conclusions regarding the nature of these connections. James Harrington perceived important links between economic station and political influence, arguing for a restructuring of society that would militate against the concentration of wealth and thus ensure the achievement of a balanced system based upon the modest ownership of property and shared political power.[5] Significantly, John Locke, often considered to be the first great "liberal" theorist, placed property at the center of his justification for the social contract, explicitly stating in his *Second Treatise* that "The great and chief end" of government is the "preservation of property."[6] Ideally, Locke argued for a modest ownership of property with the right of property based upon one's labor and the limits of property drawn by appropriate use; however, with the introduction of money and commerce, Locke

[1]Cornford, F. M., trans. *The Republic of Plato* (New York: Oxford University Press, 1978), pp. 272–280.

[2]Aristotle, *The Politics,* H. Rackham, trans. (Cambridge: Harvard University Press/Loeb Classics, 1977), Books III and IV, *passim.*

[3]Cicero, *On the Commonwealth,* trans, by Sabine and Smith (Indianapolis: Bobbs-Merrill, 1976), p. 138.

[4]*Ibid.*

[5]J. G. A. Pocock, ed; *The Political Works of James Harrington* (Cambridge: Cambridge University Press, 1977), pp. 161–167, 169–171, 180–182, 200–201.

[6]John Locke, *Two Treatises of Government* (New York: New American Library, 1965), p. 395.

concludes that a limited degree of economic inequality cannot and perhaps should not be prevented.[7] Hume extends this notion even further, as he sees the production of luxury as beneficial to society, even morally edifying under the proper conditions.[8] Hume's republic would be a commercial one, modern in its economic orientation but still rooted in the social and political customs of the ancients. In France, the Physiocrats were more wary of the idea of commerce for its own sake and adhered instead to the notion that a nation's wealth and prosperity depend upon land and therefore are a function of a society based upon agrarian principles.[9]

Much of the debate revolving around the question of property and its relationship to power during the ratification controversy was already framed by the ideas of Harrington, Locke, Hume, and the Physiocrats. Consensus orbited around the assumption that private ownership of property was an inalienable right; even more "radical" thinkers such as Thomas Paine agreed on this point, and as an inalienable right, the opportunity to engage in acquisition was advanced as a shared condition for all. However, consensus yielded to controversy as the citizens of the young republic directed their attentions to the specific kind of economic system that was to be developed. At the center of these differences one finds the tension between arcadia and metropolis, or, that is to say, between the agrarian ideal and the movement toward new forms of enterprise through sophisticated, urban commerce and incipient industrialism. The former model was embraced with great ardor by Thomas Jefferson; the latter was vigorously advanced by Alexander Hamilton, and it is around the ideas of these two legendary minds that the debate over the economic, and ultimately the political and social, destiny of the republic would revolve.

Many of the opponents to the newly proposed Constitution concurred with the Jeffersonian vision of society—a society based both economically and politically upon the yeoman farmer. For Jefferson, an arcadian republic represented more than simply a sound economic arrangement; it was the fundamental condition for the creation of a virtuous body of citizens willing and able to participate in government and equipped with the moral attributes requisite to successful democratic rule. In Jefferson's view, property ownership not only guaranteed suffrage but also engendered the ethic of self-reliance and responsibility that is necessary to the character of a self-governing individual, and hence a self-governing citizenry. Several of the Antifederalists held the same view, as can be observed in the writings of such thinkers and activists as Melancton Smith, who praised the "middling class" of "respectable yeomen," claiming that it is through the interests of this class that the public good is most honestly pursued and the principles of liberty most firmly secured. However, as Professors William Allen and Gordon Lloyd remind us, the Antifederalists were concerned with both the cultivation of free enterprise and the cultivation of the earth, and much of the Antifederalist literature is strongly *laissez-faire*, favoring the development of an unfettered and ambitious merchant class. This is contrasted with the ideas and policies of Hamilton and his supporters, who favored a republic established upon the

---

[7]*Ibid.*, pp. 327–344.

[8]David Hume, *Essays Moral, Political, Literary* (Indianapolis: Liberty Classics, 1987), pp. 253–267.

[9]Lee McDonald, *Western Political Theory*, Part Two (New York: Harcourt, Brace, Jovanovich, 1968), pp. 346–348.

economic base of international commerce and manufacturing, emphasizing the gradual move toward the Metropole (while still sustaining a certain degree of agricultural independence) and propelled by dual efforts of business and government through an alliance that would lead to the emergence of state-assisted, and in some instances, state-directed capitalism. The very idea of this close relationship between the public and the private sector was oppressive to many of the Antifederalists. For them this was an unholy alliance that would further stimulate the acceleration of two unacceptable and perhaps irrevocable tendencies—the increasing encroachment of intrusive government upon private life and the accumulation of political power at the center. However, it must also be noted that, although these libertarian concerns obtain throughout most of the arguments within the Antifederalist dissent, concerns over property rights were often associated with the pernicious institution of slavery. Particularly in the Southern dissent, objections over the federal government's power to regulate commerce were raised in the full knowledge that the perpetuation of racial advantage might be more likely under the aegis of strong local and state governments capable of deflecting interference from the center. A review of subsequent history sheds further light on the issue.

Additionally, objections were raised over growing disparities between the wealthy class (both commercial and landed) and the majority of the citizenry. Madison observed that the unequal distribution of property was "the most common and durable source of faction" and approached economic inequality as an unfortunate but necessary aspect of the extended republic that he so adamantly embraced, an extended republic stabilized and strengthened by difference, including the difference between economic station. Arguments such as these, however subtle, did not escape those who believed that the new Constitution was the product of a plutocratic cabal. Surely the accomplishments of the Revolution would be lost once such an instrument, produced by and for the moneyed elite, was forced upon the political body. Republican government would be strangled in its cradle by the interest of mammon, to be replaced by the tyrannous changeling of a new class society.

In the articles below, several of these issues are addressed by those involved in the ratification controversy as well as more contemporary observers. Few American authors, past or present, would venture alternatives to capitalism; however, a tradition of radical thought in the United States that is often neglected is here represented in the essays by Greenberg and Slater. Plattner and Allen approach the connections between liberalism and capitalism in a more celebratory manner, informed by principles that assert the necessary connection between democratic success and commercial prosperity. In the excerpts from Charles Beard and Professor Brown, the role of wealth in the framing is provocatively assessed and debated. The essence of the debates over the relationship between property and democracy throughout all of these selections and excerpts seems to be reduced to a continuing concern over the tension between the ideal of political equality and social justice, which is a primary dimension of participatory democracy, and the realities of economic inequality, which is the inevitable and often disturbing result of capitalism. Representative institutions have been kind to wealth, but often at the expense of a broader participation from the whole body of citizens that we, perhaps too casually, refer to as "the people." We cannot help but continue to address this issue today as we continue to witness an expanding chasm between the empowered, privileged rich and the impotent, alienated poor throughout an American polity that contains a multitude of sins against the democratic creed.

THE CONSTITUTION (EXCERPTS)

ART. I

Sec. 1. Direct Taxes shall be apportioned among the several States which may be included within this Union, according to their respective Numbers, which shall be determined by adding to the whole Number of free Persons, including those bound to Service for a Term of Years, and excluding Indians not taxed, three fifths of all other Persons. . . .

Sec. 8. The Congress shall have Power

To lay and collect Taxes, Duties, Imposts and Excises, to pay the Debts and provide, for the common Defence and general Welfare of the United States; but all Duties, Imposts and Excises shall be uniform throughout the United States;

To borrow Money on the credit of the United States;

To regulate Commerce with foreign Nations, and among the several States, and with the Indian Tribes;

To establish an uniform Rule of Naturalization, and uniform Laws on the subject of Bankruptcies throughout the United States;

To coin Money, regulate the Value thereof, and of foreign Coin, and fix the Standard of Weights and Measures;

To provide for the Punishment of counterfeiting the Securities and current Coin of the United States;

To establish Post Offices and post Roads;

To promote the Progress of Science and useful Arts, by securing for limited Times to Authors and Inventors the exclusive Right to their respective Writings and Discoveries; . . .

Sec. 9. The Migration or Importation of such Persons as any of the States now existing shall think proper to admit, shall not be prohibited by the Congress prior to the Year one thousand eight hundred and eight, but a Tax or duty may be imposed on such Importation, not exceeding ten dollars for each Person.

No Capitation, or other direct, Tax shall be laid, unless in Proportion to the Census or Enumeration herein before directed to be taken.

No Tax or Duty shall be laid on Articles exported from any State.

No Preference shall be given by any Regulation of Commerce or Revenue to the Ports of one State over those of another: nor shall Vessels bound to, or from, one State, be obliged to enter, clear, or pay Duties in another.

No Money shall be drawn from the Treasury, but in Consequence of Appropriations made by Law; and a regular Statement and Account of the Receipts and Expenditures of all public Money shall be published from time to time.

ART. V

No person shall be . . . deprived of life, liberty, or property, without due process of law; nor shall private property be taken for public use, without just compensation.

ART. VI

All Debts contracted and Engagements entered into, before the Adoption of this Constitution, shall be as valid against the United States under this Constitution, as under the Confederation. . . .

Amendments

Art. XIV

July 28, 1868

Nor shall any State deprive any person of life, liberty, or property without due process of law; . . .

Art. XVI

February 25, 1913

The Congress shall have power to lay and collect taxes on incomes, from whatever source derived, without apportionment among the several States and without regard to any census or enumeration.

Art. XVIII

January 29, 1919

After one year from the ratification of this article, the manufacture, sale, or transportation of intoxicating liquors within, the importation thereof into, or the exportation thereof from the United States and all territory subject to the jurisdiction thereof for beverage purposes is hereby prohibited. . . .

Art. XXI

December 5, 1933

Sec. 1. The eighteenth article of amendment to the Constitution of the United States is hereby repealed. . . .

Article XXIV

January 24, 1964

Sec. 1. The right of citizens of the United States to vote in any primary or other election for President or Vice-President, for electors for President or Vice-President, or for Senator or Representative in Congress, shall not be denied or abridged by the United States or any state by reason of failure to pay any poll tax or other tax.

Sec. 2. The Congress shall have power to enforce this article by appropriate legislation.

THE JEFFERSONIAN VISION

Thomas Jefferson
Letter to John Jay

DISCUSSION QUESTIONS

1. What are the most essential elements of a democratic society in Jefferson's estimation? What implications are contained within the Jeffersonian model for modern democracy?
2. Discuss the elements of Jefferson's criticism of industrial society as he knew it in its incipient stage. Based upon these passages, how does Jefferson view human beings, and how does this help form his political vision?

Paris Aug. 23, 1785.

Dear Sir,

I shall sometimes ask your permission to write you letters, not official but private. The present is of this kind, and is occasioned by the question proposed in yours of June 14 "Whether it would be useful to us to carry all our own productions, or none?" Were we perfectly free to decide this question, I should reason as follows. We have now lands enough to employ an infinite number of people in their cultivation. Cultivators of the earth are the most valuable citizens. They are the most vigorous, the most independant, the most virtuous, and they are tied to their country and wedded to it's liberty and interests by the most lasting bands. As long therefore as they can find emploiment in this line, I would not convert them into mariners, artisans, or any thing else. But our citizens will find emploiment in this line till their numbers, and of course their productions, become too great for the demand both internal and foreign. This is not the case as yet, and probably will not be for a considerable time. As soon as it is, the surplus of hands must be turned to something else. I should then perhaps wish to turn them to the sea in preference to manufactures, because comparing the characters of the two classes I find the former the most valuable citizens. I consider the class of artificers as the panders of vice and the instruments by which the liberties of a country are generally overturned.

Thomas Jefferson
Letter to James Madison

DISCUSSION QUESTIONS

1. What are the implications, if any, in Jefferson's views regarding the connection between virtue and economic activity?
2. How does this relate to the political realm?

Fontainebleau Oct. 28. 1785.

Dear Sir,

Seven o'clock, and retired to my fireside, I have determined to enter into conversation with you; this is a village of about 5,000 inhabitants when the court is not here and 20,000 when they are, occupying a valley thro' which runs a brook, and on each side of it a ridge of small mountains most of which are naked rock. The king comes here in the fall always, to hunt. His court attend him, as do also the foreign diplomatic corps. But as this is not indispensably required, and my finances do not admit the expence of a continued residence here, I propose to come occasionally to attend the king's levees, returning again to Paris, distant 40 miles. This being the first trip, I set out yesterday morning to take a view of the place. For this purpose I shaped my course towards the highest of the mountains in sight, to the top of which was about a league. As soon as I had got clear of the town I fell in with a poor woman walking at the same rate with myself and going the same course.

Wishing to know the condition of the labouring poor I entered into conversation with her, which I began by enquiries for the path which would lead me into the mountain: and thence proceeded to enquiries into her vocation, condition and circumstances. She told me she was a day labourer, at 8. sous or 4 d. sterling the day; that she had two children to maintain, and to pay a rent of 30 livres for her house (which would consume the hire of 75 days), that often she could get no emploiment, and of course was without bread. As we had walked together near a mile and she had so far served me as a guide, I gave her, on parting 24 sous. She burst into tears of a gratitude which I could perceive was unfeigned, because she was unable to utter a word. She had probably never before received so great an aid. This little attendrissement, with the solitude of my walk led me into a train of reflections on that unequal division of property which occasions the numberless instances of wretchedness which I had observed in this country and is to be observed all over Europe. The property of this country is absolutely concentered in a very few hands, having revenues of from half a million of guineas a year downwards. These employ the flower of the country as servants, some of them having as many as 200 domestics, not labouring. They employ also a great number of manufacturers, and tradesmen, and lastly the class of labouring husbandmen. But after all these comes the most numerous of all the classes, that is, the poor who cannot find work. I asked myself what could be the reason that so many should be permitted to beg who are willing to work, in a country where there is a very considerable proportion of uncultivated lands? These lands are kept idle mostly for the sake of game. It should seem then that it must be because of the enormous wealth of the proprietors which places them above attention to the increase of their revenues by permitting these lands to be laboured. I am conscious that an equal division of property is impracticable. But the consequences of this enormous inequality producing so much misery to the bulk of mankind, legislators cannot invent too many devices for subdividing property, only taking care to let their subdivisions go hand in hand with the natural affections of the human mind. The descent of property of every kind therefore to all the children, or to all the brothers and sisters, or other relations in equal degree is a politic measure, and a practicable one. Another means of silently lessening the inequality of property is to exempt all from taxation below a certain point, and to tax the higher portions of property in geometrical progression as they rise. Whenever there is in any country, uncultivated lands and unemployed poor, it is clear that the laws of property have been so far extended as to violate natural right. The earth is given as a common stock for man to labour and live on. If, for the encouragement of industry we allow it to be appropriated, we must take care that other employment be furnished to those excluded from the appropriation. If we do not the fundamental right to labour the earth returns to the unemployed. It is too soon yet in our country to say that every man who cannot find employment but who can find uncultivated land, shall be at liberty to cultivate it, paying a moderate rent. But it is not too soon to provide by every possible means that as few as possible shall be without a little portion of land. The small landholders are the most precious part of a state.

ANTIFEDERALIST ARGUMENTS

"Centinel"
(Probably Samuel Bryan)
Essay, October 1787
(Excerpt)

DISCUSSION QUESTIONS

1. What might the author mean by the assertion that "commerce is the hand-maid of liberty"? Would Hamilton agree? In what way might Bryan and Hamilton disagree?
2. After reading Bryan's views on the extent of the "merchant's view," discuss the relationship between private gain and public concern.

The merchant, immersed in schemes of wealth, seldom extends his views beyond the immediate object of gain; he blindly pursues his seeming interest, and sees not the latent mischief; therefore it is, that he is the last to take the alarm when public liberty is threatened. This may account for the infatuation of some of our merchants, who, elated with the imaginary prospect of an improved commerce under the new government, overlook all danger: they do not consider that commerce is the hand-maid of liberty, a plant of free growth that withers under the hand of despotism, that every concern of individuals will be sacrificed to the gratification of the men in power, who will institute injurious monopolies and shackle commerce with every device of avarice; and that property of every species will be held at the will and pleasure of rulers.

If the nature of the case did not give birth to these well-founded apprehensions, the principles and characters of the authors and advocates of the measure ought. View the monopolising spirit of the principal of them. See him converting a bank, instituted for common benefit, to his own and creatures ['] emolument, and by the aid thereof, controuling the credit of the state, and dictating the measures of government. View the vassalage of our merchants, the thraldom of the city of Philadelphia, and the extinction of that spirit of independency in most of its citizens so essential to freedom. View this Collosus attempting to grasp the commerce of America and meeting with a sudden repulse, in the midst of his immense career, receiving a shock that threatens his very existence. View the desperate fortunes of many of his co-adjutors and dependants, particularly the bankrupt situation of the principal instrument under the *great man* in promoting the new government, whose superlative arrogance, ambition and rapacity, would need the spoils of thousands to gratify; view his towering aspect, he would have no bowels of compassion for the oppressed, he would *overlook* all their sufferings. Recollect the strenuous and unremitted exertions of these men, for years past, to destroy our admirable constitution, whose object is to secure equal liberty and advantages to all, and the great obstacle in the way of their ambitious schemes, and then answer, whether these apprehensions are chimerical, whether such characters will be less ambitious, less avaritious, more moderate, when the privileges, property, and every concern of the people of the United States shall lie at their mercy, when they shall be in possession of absolute sway?

CENTINEL

"John DeWitt" (Unknown) Essay IV (Excerpt)

DISCUSSION QUESTION

After reading this short excerpt from "John DeWitt," review the Constitution and identify the elements of the Constitution that might have led to his conclusions.

To the Free Citizens of the Commonwealth of Massachusetts.

Place the Frame of Government proposed, in the most favorable point of view, magnify the priviledges held forth to the people to their fullest extent, and enlarge as much as you please, upon the great checks therein provided, notwithstanding all which, there cannot remain a doubt in the mind of any reflecting man, that it is a System purely Aristocratical, calculated to find employment for men of ambition, and to furnish means of sporting with the sacred principles of human nature. The great object throughout, is the acquisition of property and power, and every possible opportunity has been embraced to make ample provision for supplying a redundancy of the one, to exercise the other in its fullest extent. They have engrossed to themselves the riches of America, and are carefully silent what use they intend to put them to. Powers are there granted, that shall give to persons, greater strangers, and perhaps greater enemies to you than the people of Great-Britain, the right of entry into your habitations without your consent, not a lisp being mentioned as to the mode or time when such powers shall be exercised. They have taken to themselves the Purse and Sword of your country.

Melancton Smith Speech June 21, 1788 (Excerpt)

DISCUSSION QUESTIONS

1. What are the participatory principles implicit in Smith's analysis of the relationship between economic class and representation?

2. How does Smith link democratic politics to a broader view of interest?
3. This speech is concluded in Chapter 5. Read the entire speech, and discuss Smith's views on the role of the "yeoman class" in a democratic society. Do you agree or disagree with his assumptions?

The idea that naturally suggests itself to our minds, when we speak of representatives is, that they resemble those they represent; they should be a true picture of the people; possess the knowledge of their circumstances and their wants; sympathize in all their distresses, and be disposed to seek their true interests. The knowledge necessary for the representatives of a free people, not only comprehends extensive political and commercial information, such as is acquired by men of refined education, who have leisure to attain to high degrees of improvement, but it should also comprehend that kind of acquaintance with the common concerns and occupations of the people, which men of the middling class of life are in general much better competent to, than those of a superior class. To understand the true commercial interests of a country, not only requires just ideas of the general commerce of the world, but also, and principally, a knowledge of the productions of your own country and their value, what your soil is capable of producing[,] the nature of your manufactures, and the capacity of the country to increase both. To exercise the power of laying taxes, duties and excises with discretion, requires something more than an acquaintance with the abstruse parts of the system of finance. It calls for a knowledge of the circumstances and ability of the people in general, a discernment how the burdens imposed will bear upon the different classes.

From these observations results this conclusion that the number of representatives should be so large, as that while it embraces men of the first class, it should admit those of the middling class of life. I am convinced that this Government is so constituted, that the representatives will generally be composed of the first class in the community, which I shall distinguish by the name of the natural aristocracy of the country. I do not mean to give offence by using this term. I am sensible this idea is treated by many gentlemen as chimerical. I shall be asked what is meant by the natural aristocracy—and told that no such distinction of classes of men exists among us. It is true it is our singular felicity that we have no legal or hereditary distinctions of this kind; but still there are real differences: Every society naturally divides itself into classes. The author of nature has bestowed on some greater capacities than on others—birth, education, talents and wealth, create distinctions among men as visible and of as much influence as titles, stars and garters. In every society, men of this class will command a superior degree of respect—and if the government is so constituted as to admit but few to exercise the powers of it, it will, according to the natural course of things, be in their hands. Men in the middling class, who are qualified as representatives, will not be so anxious to be chosen as those of the first. When the number is so small the office will be highly elevated and distinguished—the stile in which the members live will probably be high—circumstances of this kind, will render the place of a representative not a desirable one to sensible, substantial men, who have been used to walk in the plain and frugal paths of life.

"A Farmer and Planter"
(Unknown)
Essay, March 27, 1788
(Excerpts)

DISCUSSION QUESTIONS

1. Consider the concerns outlined in the essay by "A Farmer and Planter." What concerns still remain valid today? Has the essay's forecast of impending plutocracy materialized? Explain.
2. Why does the author of this essay argue that the wealthy can live well under any kind of government? What kind of government is necessary to provide the general welfare of the general citizenry? How should this be accomplished?

To the Farmers and Planters of Maryland

Fellow-Citizens,

The time is nearly at hand, when you are called upon to render up that glorious liberty you obtained, by resisting the tyranny and oppression of George the Third, King of England, and his ministers.— . . .

Let me entreat you, my fellows, to consider well what you are about—Read the said Constitution, and consider it well before you act—I have done so, and can find that we are to receive but little good, and a great deal of evil—Aristocracy, or government in the hands of a very few nobles, or RICH MEN, is therein concealed in the most artful wrote plan that ever was formed to entrap a free people. The contrivers of it have so completely entrapped you, and laid their plan so sure and secretly, that they have only left you to do one of two things; that is either to receive or refuse it. And in order to bring you into their snare, you may daily read new pieces published in the News-Papers, in favour of this new government; and should a writer dare to publish any piece against it, he is immediately abused and vilified.

Look around you and observe well the RICH MEN, who are to be your only rulers, lords and masters in future! Are they not all for it? Yes! Ought not this to put you on your guard? Does not riches beget power, and power, oppression and tyranny? . . . If you choose these men, or others like them, they certainly will do every thing in their power to adopt the new government—Should they succeed, your liberty is gone for ever; and you will then be nothing better than a strong ass crouching down between two burthens—The new form of government gives Congress liberty at any time, by their laws, to alter the state laws, and the time, places and manner of holding elections for representatives; by this clause they may command, by their laws, the people of Maryland to go to Georgia, and the people of Georgia to go to Boston, to choose their representatives—Congress, or our future lords and masters, are to have power to lay and collect taxes, duties, imposts, and excises—Excise is a new thing in America, and few country farmers and planters know the meaning of it; but it is not so in Old England, where I have seen the effects of it, and felt the smart. It is there a duty, or tax, laid upon almost every necessary of life and convenience, and a great number of other articles. . . .

. . . —View your danger, and find out good men to represent you in convention—men of your own profession and station in life—men who will not adopt this destructive and diabolical form of a federal government:—There are many among you that will not be led by the nose by rich men, and would scorn a bribe.—Rich men can live easy under any government, be it ever so tyrannical—they come in for a great share of the tyranny, because they are the ministers of tyrants, and always engross the places of honour and profit, whilst the greater part of the common people are led by the nose, and played about by these very men, for the destruction of themselves and their class.—Be wise, be virtuous, and catch the precious moment as it passes, to refuse this new-fangled federal government, and extricate yourselves and posterity from tyranny, oppression, aristocratical or monarchical government. . . .

. . . Some of you may say the rich men were virtuous in the last war; yes, my countrymen, they had reason then to be so! our liberty then was in dispute with a mighty and powerful tyrant, and it was for their interest to promote and carry on the opposition, as long as they could stay at home and send the common people into the field to fight their battles—After the war began, they could not with decency recede, for the sword and enemy were at the very entrance of their gates. The case is greatly altered now; *you* conquered the enemy, and the rich men now think to subdue you by their wiles and arts, or make you, or persuade you, to do it yourselves. Their aim, I perceive, is now to destroy that liberty which you set up as a reward for the blood and treasure you expended in the pursuit of and establishment of it. They well know that open force will not succeed at this time, and have chosen a safer method, by offering you a plan of a new Federal Government, contrived with great art, and shaded with obscurity, and recommended to you to adopt; which if you do, their scheme is compleated, the yoke is fixed on your necks, and you will be undone, perhaps for ever, and your boasted liberty is but a sound. Farewell!—be wise, be watchful, guard yourselves against the dangers that are concealed in this plan of a new Federal Government.

A Farmer and Planter

"A Farmer" (Probably John Francis Mercer) Essay VII (Excerpt)

DISCUSSION QUESTIONS

1. What are the primary philosophical and political principles that serve as the foundation for the author's essay? Do the author's ideas fit representative or participatory forms of democracy?

2. Consider the following phrase: "Laws are cobwebs, catching only flies and letting the wasps escape." Can you think of specific examples that might support the spirit of this assertion? What is the relationship between law, wealth, and power? What is the relationship between these element and representative government? Participatory government?

To examine and elucidate the great and leading principles of government, we must penetrate to the source of human action, and explore the heart and constitution of man;—a consciousness of the equal rights of nature, is a component part of that aetherial spirit, which we dignify with the appellation of soul; the ardent desire and unceasing pursuit of equality, can therefore be no more destroyed by human power, than the soul itself; the chains of terrestrial despotism may confine, afflict and bow down to the earth, this mould of flesh; but the soul more free than air, quits this mortal frame, surrounded by ills no longer supportable, and after witnessing the final overthrow of all its hopes in this world, retires with indignation, into a world unknown.

Let any people be personally and fairly consulted on the form of that government, which is to rule them and their children, and they will establish the *law of equality* as its basis;—the unequal division of property silently and gradually undermines this foundation, almost as soon as society is formed; or before a new compact is confirmed, this equality is materially injured if not destroyed. Montesquieu justly observes that men, in the advanced stages of government, quit the equality of nature, from the moment of their birth, never to re-enter it but by the force of equal law,—the law then that is equally enforced on all ranks of society, to which the *great* and the *humble*, are compelled to submit, is the next state of equality, to which this ever active principle of the mind aspires; with this it would be content, as the most perfect state of liberty, which exists only, in a just medium between two extremes; but in the attainment and preservation of this, the efforts of the human understanding never keep pace with the will.

Quicquid delirant reges, plectuntur achivi.

It is the poor people who suffer for the misrule of the great.

Laws are cobwebs, catching only the flies and letting the wasps escape. The great and powerful can easily bring to justice, the *poor and humble offender*; but who is to lead to punishment the *great*? These lords of the earth, who have extensive and powerful connexions, who aim at no trifling larcenies; but who plunder a people of their liberties and put public revenues into their private purses, under the sanction of laws made by themselves:—These are the men who deprive their fellow mortals of their fondest hopes, and compel them to resort to the supreme aim of a monarch—to the authority of a single person—who exalted far above all may reduce them all, once more to that common level of equal law, of which mankind never lose sight:—*Come we will choose one man to rule over us*! is the cry of a people who are tired of the rule of the *elders*—the meaning of the word senate, is an assembly of elders; but this the last and most fatal step, is never retrieved, until government returns through blood into that original chaos—from the discordant elements of which, new and equal forms of society arise, created upon first principles.

FEDERALIST ARGUMENTS

James Madison
Federalist *Paper 10*
(Excerpts)

DISCUSSION QUESTIONS

1. *Federalist* Paper 10 is considered by many to be Madison's masterpiece. A further excerpt from the essay is provided below in Chapter 4. Read the entire essay, and discuss the philosophical principles that are the formative elements of Madisonian political theory.
2. Why does property figure so prominently in Madison's work? What is the relationship between Madison's scheme of governing and his views on property, faction, and equality?
3. Why does Madison claim that property is "the most common and durable source of faction"? What are the implications of this assertion? How does this view affect his support of the Constitution? What does this mean to Madison?

The diversity in the faculties of men, from which the rights of property originate, is not less an insuperable obstacle to a uniformity of interests. The protection of these faculties is the first object of government. From the protection of different and unequal faculties of acquiring property, the possession of different degrees and kinds of property immediately results; and from the influence of these on the sentiments and views of the respective proprietors ensues a division of the society into different interests and parties.

The latent causes of faction are thus sown in the nature of man; and we see them everywhere brought into different degrees of activity, according to the different circumstances of civil society. . . . But the most common and durable source of factions has been the various and unequal distribution of property. Those who hold and those who are without property have ever formed distinct interests in society. Those who are creditors, and those who are debtors, fall under a like discrimination. A landed interest, a manufacturing interest, a mercantile interest, a moneyed interest, with many lesser interests, grow up of necessity in civilized nations, and divide them into different classes, actuated by different sentiments and views. The regulation of these various and interfering interests forms the principal task of modern legislation and involves the spirit of party and faction in the necessary and ordinary operations of government.

No man is allowed to be a judge in his own cause, because his interest would certainly bias his judgment, and, not improbably, corrupt his integrity. With equal, nay with greater reason, a body of men are unfit to be both judges and parties at the same time; yet what are many of the most important acts of legislation but so many judicial determinations, not indeed concerning the rights of single persons, but concerning the rights of large bodies of citizens? And what are the different classes of legislators but advocates and parties to the causes which they determine?

Is a law proposed concerning private debts? It is a question to which the creditors are parties on one side and the debtors on the other. Justice ought to hold the balance between them. Yet the parties are, and must be, themselves the judges; and the most numerous party, or in other words, the most powerful faction must be expected to prevail. Shall domestic manufacturers be encouraged, and in what degree, by restrictions on foreign manufacturers? are questions which would be differently decided by the landed and the manufacturing classes, and probably by neither with a sole regard to justice and the public good. The apportionment of taxes on the various descriptions of property is an act which seems to require the most exact impartiality; yet there is, perhaps, no legislative act in which greater opportunity and temptation are given to a predominant party to trample on the rules of justice. Every shilling with which they overburden the inferior number is a shilling saved to their own pockets.

Alexander Hamilton
Federalist *Paper 12*
(Excerpts)

DISCUSSION QUESTIONS

1. What is the difference between direct and indirect taxation? Why does Hamilton favor one over the other? How does Hamilton connect his views on taxation to his attitudes toward commerce? Why does Hamilton focus on the problem of government revenue in conjunction with his considerations of the link between economic processes and the political realm? How is this different from Jefferson's focus?
2. Compare the principles underlying Hamilton's arguments with those of Jefferson provided above. What are the essential differences between the two great minds? What do their arguments say about the importance of the connections between economics and politics? Which vision, the Jeffersonian or Hamiltonian, is more conducive to participatory democracy? Why?

To the People of the State of New York:

The prosperity of commerce is now perceived and acknowledged by all enlightened statesmen to be the most useful as well as the most productive source of national wealth, and has accordingly become a primary object of their political cares. By multiplying the means of gratification, by promoting the introduction and circulation of the precious metals, those darling objects of human avarice and enterprise, it serves to vivify and invigorate the channels of industry, and to make them flow with greater activity and copiousness. The assiduous merchant, the laborious husbandman, the active mechanic, and the industrious manufacturer,—all orders of men, look forward with eager expectation and growing alacrity to this pleasing reward of their toils. The often-agitated question between agriculture and commerce has, from indubitable experience, received a decision which has silenced the rivalship that once subsisted between them, and has proved, to the satisfaction of their friends, that their interests are intimately blended and interwoven. It has been found in various countries that, in proportion as commerce has flourished, land has risen in value. And how could it have happened otherwise? Could that which procures a freer vent for the products of the earth, which furnishes new incitements to the cultivation of land, which is the most powerful instrument in increasing the quantity of money in a state—could that, in fine, which is the faithful handmaid of labor and industry, in every shape, fail to augment that article, which is the prolific parent of far the greatest part of the objects upon which they are exerted? It is astonishing that so simple a truth should ever have had an adversary; and it is one, among a multitude of proofs, how apt a spirit of ill-informed jealousy, or of too great abstraction and refinement, is to lead men astray from the plainest truths of reason and conviction.

The ability of a country to pay taxes must always be proportioned, in a great degree, to the quantity of money in circulation, and to the celerity with which it circulates. Commerce, contributing to both these objects, must of necessity render the payment of taxes easier, and facilitate the requisite supplies to the treasury. The hereditary dominions of the Emperor of Germany contain a great extent of fertile, cultivated, and populous territory, a large proportion of which is situated in mild and luxuriant climates. In some parts of this territory are to be found the best gold and silver mines in Europe. And yet, from the want of the fostering influence of commerce, that monarch can boast but slender revenues. He has several times been compelled to owe obligations to the pecuniary succors of other nations for the preservation of his essential interests, and is unable, upon the strength of his own resources, to sustain a long or continued war.

But it is not in this aspect of the subject alone that Union will be seen to conduce to the purpose of revenue. There are other points of view, in which its influence will appear more immediate and decisive. It is evident from the state of the country, from the habits of the people, from the experience we have had on the point itself, that it is impracticable to raise any very considerable sums by direct taxation. Tax laws have in vain been multiplied; new methods to enforce the collection have in vain been tried; the public expectation has been uniformly disappointed, and the treasuries of the States have remained empty. The popular system of administration inherent in the nature of popular government, coinciding with the real scarcity of money incident to a languid and mutilated state of trade, has hitherto defeated every experiment for extensive collections, and has at length taught the different legislatures the folly of attempting them.

No person acquainted with what happens in other countries will be surprised at this circumstance. In so opulent a nation as that of Britain, where direct taxes from superior wealth must be much more tolerable, and, from the vigor of the government, much more practicable, than in America, far the greatest part of the national revenue is derived from taxes of the indirect kind, from imposts, and from excises. Duties on imported articles form a large branch of this latter description.

In America, it is evident that we must a long time depend for the means of revenue chiefly on such duties. In most parts of it, excises must be confined within a narrow compass. The genius of the people will ill brook the inquisitive and peremptory spirit of excise laws. The pockets of the farmers, on the other hand, will reluctantly yield but scanty supplies, in the unwelcome shape of impositions on their houses and lands; and personal property is too precarious and invisible a fund to be laid hold of in any other way than by the imperceptible agency of taxes on consumption.

If these remarks have any foundation, that state of things which will best enable us to improve and extend so valuable a resource must be best adapted to our political welfare. And it cannot admit of a serious doubt, that this state of things must rest on the basis of a general Union. As far as this would be conducive to the interests of commerce, so far it must tend to the extension of the revenue to be drawn from that source. As far as it would contribute to rendering regulations for the collection of the duties more simple and efficacious, so far it must serve to answer the purposes of making the same rate of duties more productive, and of putting it into the power of the government to increase the rate without prejudice to trade. . . .

. . . A nation cannot long exist without revenues. Destitute of this essential support, it must resign its independence, and sink into the degraded condition of a province. This is an extremity to which no government will of choice accede. Revenue, therefore, must be had at all events. In this country, if the principal part be not drawn from commerce, it must fall with oppressive weight upon land. It has been already intimated that excises, in their true signification, are too little in unison with the feelings of the people, to admit of great use being made of that mode of taxation; nor, indeed, in the States where almost the sole employment is agriculture, are the objects proper for excise sufficiently numerous to permit very ample collections in that way. Personal estate (as has been before remarked), from the difficulty in tracing it, cannot be subjected to large contributions, by any other means than by taxes on consumption. In populous cities, it may be enough the subject of conjecture, to occasion the oppression of individuals, without much aggregate benefit to the State; but beyond these circles, it must, in a great measure, escape the eye and the hand of the tax-gatherer. As the necessities of the State, nevertheless, must be satisfied in some mode or other, the defect of other resources must throw the principal weight of public burdens on the possessors of land. And as, on the other hand, the wants of the government can never obtain an adequate supply, unless all the sources of revenue are open to its demands, the finances of the community, under such embarrassments, cannot be put into a situation consistent with its respectability or its security. Thus we shall not even have the consolations of a full treasury, to atone for the oppression of that valuable class of the citizens who are employed in the cultivation of the soil. But public and private distress will keep pace with each other in gloomy concert; and unite in deploring the infatuation of those counsels which led to disunion.

PUBLIUS

Alexander Hamilton
Federalist *Paper 60*
(Excerpts)

DISCUSSION QUESTIONS

1. After reading the excerpts in this section (*Federalist* Papers 10, 12, and 60), and in comparison with the Antifederalist principles, both explicit and implicit in the Antifederalist excerpts, discuss the relationship between private property and political power. How do the supporters of the Constitution treat this issue? What is the response from the Antifederalist dissent?
2. Based upon the kinds of economic proposals that seem to underlie Hamilton's arguments, what kind of nation did Hamilton conceive? What questions does Madison raise that might be relevant to Hamilton's vision? Do you think that Hamilton and Madison are in accord in every instance? Explain.

To the People of the State of New York:

We have seen, that an uncontrollable power over the elections to the federal government could not, without hazard, be committed to the State legislatures. Let us now see, what would be the danger on the other side; that is, from confiding the ultimate right of regulating its own elections to the Union itself. It is not pretended, that this right would ever be used for the exclusion of any State from its share in the representation. The interest of all would, in this respect at least, be the security of all. But it is alleged, that it might be employed in such a manner as to promote the election of some favorite class of men in exclusion of others, by confining the places of election to particular districts, and rendering it impracticable to the citizens at large to partake in the choice. Of all chimerical suppositions, this seems to be the most chimerical. On the one hand, no rational calculation of probabilities would lead us to imagine that the disposition which a conduct so violent and extraordinary would imply, could ever find its way into the national councils; and on the other, it may be concluded with certainty, that if so improper a spirit should ever gain admittance into them, it would display itself in a form altogether different and far more decisive.

The improbability of the attempt may be satisfactorily inferred from this single reflection, that it could never be made without causing an immediate revolt of the great body of the people, headed and directed by the State governments. It is not difficult to conceive that this characteristic right of freedom may, in certain turbulent and factious seasons, be violated, in respect to a particular class of citizens, by a victorious and overbearing majority; but that so fundamental a privilege, in a country so situated and enlightened, should be invaded to the prejudice of the great mass of the people, by the deliberate policy of the government, without occasioning a popular revolution, is altogether inconceivable and incredible. . . .

What is to be the object of this capricious partiality in the national councils? Is it to be exercised in a discrimination between the different departments of industry, or between the different kinds of property, or between the different degrees of property? Will it lean in favor of the landed interest, or the moneyed interest, or the mercantile interest, or the manufacturing interest? Or, to speak in the fashionable language of the adversaries to the Constitution, will it court the elevation of "the wealthy and the well-born," to the exclusion and debasement of all the rest of the society?

If this partiality is to be exerted in favor of those who are concerned in any particular description of industry or property, I presume it will readily be admitted, that the competition for it will lie between landed men and merchants. And I scruple not to affirm, that it is infinitely less likely that either of them should gain an ascendant in the national councils, than that the one or the other of them should predominate in all the local councils. The inference will be, that a conduct tending to give an undue preference to either is much less to be dreaded from the former than from the latter.

The several States are in various degrees addicted to agriculture and commerce. In most, if not all of them, agriculture is predominant. In a few of them, however, commerce nearly divides its empire, and in most of them has a considerable share of influence. In proportion as either prevails, it will be conveyed into the national representation; and for the very reason, that this will be an emanation from a greater variety of interests, and in much more various proportions, than are to be found in any single State, it will be much less apt to espouse either of them with a decided partiality, than the representation of any single State.

In a country consisting chiefly of the cultivators of land, where the rules of an equal representation obtain, the landed interest must, upon the whole, preponderate in the government. As long as this interest prevails in most of the State legislatures, so long it must maintain a correspondent superiority in the national Senate, which will generally be a faithful copy of the majorities of those assemblies. It cannot therefore be presumed, that a sacrifice of the landed to the mercantile class will ever be a favorite object of this branch of the federal legislature. In applying thus particularly to the Senate a general observation suggested by the situation of the country, I am governed by the consideration, that the credulous votaries of State power cannot, upon their own principles, suspect, that the State legislatures would be warped from their duty by any external influence. But in reality the same situation must have the same effect, in the primitive composition at least of the federal House of Representatives: an improper bias towards the mercantile class is as little to be expected from this quarter as from the other.

In order, perhaps, to give countenance to the objection at any rate, it may be asked, is there not danger of an opposite bias in the national government, which may dispose it to endeavor to secure a monopoly of the federal administration to the landed class? As there is little likelihood that the supposition of such a bias will have any terrors for those who would be immediately injured by it, a labored answer to this question will be dispensed with. It will be sufficient to remark, first, that for the reasons elsewhere assigned, it is less likely that any decided partiality should prevail in the councils of the Union than in those of any of its members. Secondly, that there would be no temptation to violate the Constitution in favor of the landed class, because that class would, in the natural course of things, enjoy as great a preponderancy as itself could desire. And thirdly, that men accustomed to investigate the sources of public prosperity upon a large scale, must be too well convinced of the utility of commerce, to be inclined to inflict upon it so deep a wound as would result from the entire exclusion of those who would best understand its interest from a share in the management of them. The importance of commerce, in the view of revenue alone, must effectually guard it against the enmity of a body which would be continually importuned in its favor, by the urgent calls of public necessity.

I rather consult brevity in discussing the probability of a preference founded upon a discrimination between the different kinds of industry and property, because, as far as I understand the meaning of the objectors, they contemplate a discrimination of another kind. They appear to have in view, as the objects of the preference with which they endeavor to alarm us, those whom they designate by the description of "the wealthy and the well-born." These, it seems, are to be exalted to an odious preëminence over the rest of their fellow-citizens. At one time, however, their elevation is to be a necessary consequence of the smallness of the representative body; at another time it is to be effected by depriving the people at large of the opportunity of exercising their right of suffrage in the choice of that body.

But upon what principle is the discrimination of the places of election to be made, in order to answer the purpose of the meditated preference? Are "the wealthy and the well-born," as they are called, confined to particular spots in the several States? Have they, by some miraculous instinct or foresight, set apart in each of them a common place of residence? Are they only to be met with in the towns or cities? Or are they, on the contrary, scattered over the face of the country as avarice or chance may have happened to cast their own lot or that of their predecessors? If the latter is the case, (as every intelligent man knows it to be,*) is it not evident that the policy of confining the places of election to particular districts would be as subversive of its own aim as it would be exceptionable on every other account? The truth is, that there is no method of securing to the rich the preference apprehended, but by prescribing qualifications of property either for those who may elect or be elected. But this forms no part of the power to be conferred upon the national government. Its authority would be expressly restricted to the regulation of the *times*, the *places*, the *manner* of elections. The qualifications of the persons who may choose or be chosen, as has been remarked upon other occasions, are defined and fixed in the Constitution, and are unalterable by the legislature.

---

*Particularly in the Southern States and in this State.—PUBLIUS.

CONTEMPORARY INFLUENCES

W. B. Allen and G. Lloyd
"In Support of Capitalism and Democracy"
(Excerpt)

DISCUSSION QUESTIONS

1. According to the authors, what are the essential economic principles embraced by the Antifederalists?
2. Compare the authors' depiction of Antifederalist political economy with the Hamiltonian approach. Are either of these approaches compatible with democracy? If so, which one is more democratic? If not, why not?
3. In the issues mentioned by Allen and Lloyd, what clues are offered to help us understand the attitudes of the opponents of the Consitution? Are there kindred spirits today? What is different in today's society that might distance those who harbor these concerns from those who advance similar ideas in current politics? Explain.

The Antifederalists were deeply suspicious of economic and political privilege. They viewed the majority of the citizenry to be composed of people of moderate wealth who secured their position by means of honesty and diligence. The danger of faction did not originate with the majority so constituted. Rather, the danger came from the ambition of the few who would use political offices to advance their own interests. They believed that the purpose of republican government was to protect all the interests of the citizenry. With respect to trade, the Antifederalists believed that would be best accomplished by leaving commerce free to pursue natural courses, a policy which would benefit all since none could enjoy the advantage of government support. They warned that the unlimited power over trade bestowed on Congress by the new Constitution would lead to the establishment of monopolies which, in turn, would give undue influence in government to the ambitious few. The Antifederalists considered the effect of monopolies on trade analogous to the effect of aristocracy on government. They felt that faction resulted from rewarding ambition with public place amid inadequate constitutional precautions, rather than from the viciousness of mankind or the necessity of historical development as argued in *The Federalist.* Minority faction encouraged and protected by government constituted the danger to be avoided.

The kind of capitalism favored by the Antifederalists was the kind articulated by Adam Smith in *The Wealth of Nations.* They asserted that the prosperity of the nation was best served when a large number of buyers and sellers pursued their self-interest in a market place free from the regulation and intrusion of a central government. In addition to warning about the creation of monopolies, the An-

---

William B. Allen and Gordon Lloyd, eds., *The Essential Antifederalist* (Lanham, MD: University Press of America, 1985), pp. 225–226. Reprinted by kind permission of Professor Gordon Lloyd, University of Redlands.

tifederalists cautioned that the new plan gave Congress unlimited power over internal taxation. Such power not only distorted allocation decisions and enervated the enterprizing spirit, it also provided government with revenue for pursuing the aristocratic goals of international respect and grandeur. The Antifederalists saw a symbiotic relationship between monopoly capitalism and unlimited government. The solution to these twin dangers was free trade and restricted government.

The Antifederalists believed that substantial social equality prevailed in America and they wanted to preserve this equality. They admitted that in the nature of things certain inequalities were unavoidable. However, necessary inequalities were acceptable if they were compensated for by the elimination of unnecessary social inequality spilling over into the political realm which would, in turn, become the foundation for legitimizing both political and social inequality as natural. They accused the leading proponents of the Constitution with having a secret plan for the demise of social democracy and free commerce and the erection of a permanent political and economic aristocracy. Those governments which favor commerce seemed better suited to ameliorate the human condition, while those which *most* favor commerce seemed *best* of all.

Charles Beard *"An Economic Interpretation of the Constitution"* *(Excerpts)*

DISCUSSION QUESTIONS

1. How did Charles Beard interpret Madison's political theory? In what manner can it be said that Madison anticipated the development of modern political and economic ideas based upon Beard's interpretation?
2. How does Beard proceed in his attempt to prove the connection between economic interest and political founding? How does Beard challenge the common perception of the American framers? What conclusions can be drawn from Beard's approach?

Before taking up the economic implications of the structure of the federal government, it is important to ascertain what, in the opinion of *The Federalist*, is the basis of all government. The most philosophical examination of the foundations of political science is made by Madison in the tenth number. Here he lays down, in no uncertain language, the principle that the first and elemental concern of every government is economic.

1. "The first object of government," he declares, is the protection of "the diversity in the faculties of men, from which the rights of property originate." The

---

L. Levy, ed., *Essays on the Making of the Constitution.* (New York: Oxford University Press, 1969), pp. 8–10, 11–13. Reprinted by permission of the publisher.

chief business of government, from which, perforce, its essential nature must be derived, consists in the control and adjustment of conflicting economic interests. After enumerating the various forms of propertied interests which spring up inevitably in modern society, he adds: "The regulation of these various and interfering interests forms the principal task of modern legislation, and involves the spirit of party and faction in the ordinary operations of the government."

2. What are the chief causes of these conflicting political forces with which the government must concern itself? Madison answers. Of course fanciful and frivolous distinctions have sometimes been the cause of violent conflicts; "but the most common and durable source of factions has been the various and unequal distribution of property. Those who hold and those who are without property have ever formed distinct interests in society. Those who are creditors, and those who are debtors, fall under a like discrimination. A landed interest, a manufacturing interest, a mercantile interest, a moneyed interest, with many lesser interests grow up of necessity in civilized nations, and divide them into different classes actuated by different sentiments and views."

3. The theories of government which men entertain are emotional reactions to their property interests. "From the protection of different and unequal faculties of acquiring property, the possession of different degrees and kinds of property immediately results; *and from the influence of these on the sentiments and views of the respective proprietors, ensues a division of society into different interests and parties.*" Legislatures reflect these interests. "What," he asks, "are the different classes of legislators but advocates and parties to the causes which they determine." There is no help for it. "The causes of faction cannot be removed," and "we well know that neither moral nor religious motives can be relied on as an adequate control."

4. Unequal distribution of property is inevitable, and from it contending factions will rise in the state. The government will reflect them, for they will have their separate principles and "sentiments"; but the supreme danger will arise from the fusion of certain interests into an overbearing majority, which Madison, in another place, prophesied would be the landless proletariat,—an overbearing majority which will make its "rights" paramount, and sacrifice the "rights" of the minority. "To secure the public good," he declares, "and private rights against the danger of such a faction and at the same time preserve the spirit and the form of popular government is then the great object to which our inquiries are directed."

. . . Nevertheless, it may be asked why, if the protection of property rights lay at the basis of the new system, there is in the Constitution no provision for property qualifications for voters or for elected officials and representatives. This is, indeed, peculiar when it is recalled that the constitutional history of England is in a large part a record of conflict over the weight in the government to be enjoyed by definite economic groups, and over the removal of the property qualifications early imposed on members of the House of Commons and on the voters at large. But the explanation of the absence of property qualifications from the Constitution is not difficult.

The members of the Convention were, in general, not opposed to property qualifications as such, either for officers or voters. "Several propositions," says Mr. S. H. Miller, "were made in the federal Convention in regard to property qualifications. A motion was carried instructing the committee to fix upon such qualifications for members of Congress. The committee could not agree upon the amount and reported in favor of leaving the matter to the legislature. Charley Pinckney objected to this plan as giving too much power to the first legislature. . . . Ellsworth objected to a property qualification on account of the difficulty of fixing the amount. If it was made high enough for the South, it would not be applicable to the Eastern States. Franklin was the only speaker who opposed the proposition to require property on principle, saying that "some of the greatest rogues he was ever acquainted with were the richest rogues." A resolution was also carried to require a property qualification for the Presidency. Hence it was evident that the lack of all property requirements for office in the United States Constitution was not owing to any opposition of the convention to such qualifications per se."

Propositions to establish property restrictions were defeated, not because they were believed to be inherently opposed to the genius of American government, but for economic reasons—strange as it may seem. These economic reasons were clearly set forth by Madison in the debate over landed qualifications for legislators in July, when he showed, first, that slight property qualifications would not keep out the small farmers whose paper money schemes had been so disastrous to personalty; and, secondly, that landed property qualifications would exclude from Congress the representatives of "those classes of citizens who were not landholders," *i.e.* the personalty interests. This was true, he thought, because the mercantile and manufacturing classes would hardly be willing to turn their personalty into sufficient quantities of landed property to make them eligible for a seat in Congress.

The other members also knew that they had most to fear from the very electors who would be enfranchised under a slight freehold restriction, for the paper money party was everywhere bottomed on the small farming class. As Gorham remarked, the elections at Philadelphia, New York, and Boston, "where the merchants and mechanics vote, are at least as good as those made by freeholders only." The fact emerges, therefore, that the personalty interests reflected in the Convention could, in truth, see no safeguard at all in a freehold qualification against the assaults on vested personalty rights which had been made by the agrarians in every state. And it was obviously impossible to establish a personalty test, had they so desired, for there would have been no chance of securing a ratification of the Constitution at the hands of legislatures chosen by freeholders, or at the hands of conventions selected by them. . . .

Indeed, there was little risk to personalty in thus allowing the Constitution to go to the states for approval without any property qualifications on voters other than those which the state might see fit to impose. Only one branch of new government, the House of Representatives, was required to be elected by popular vote; and, in case popular choice of presidential electors might be established, a safeguard was secured by the indirect process. Two controlling bodies, the Senate and Supreme Court, were removed altogether from the possibility of popular election except by constitutional amendment. Finally, the conservative members of the Convention were doubly fortified in the fact that nearly all of the state constitutions then in force provided real or personal property qualifications for voters anyway, and radical democratic changes did not seem perilously near. . . .

The movement for the Constitution of the United States was originated and carried through principally by four groups of personalty interests which had been adversely affected under the Articles of Confederation: money, public securities, manufactures, and trade and shipping.

The first firm steps toward the formation of the Constitution were taken by a small and active group of men immediately interested through their personal possessions in the outcome of their labors.

No popular vote was taken directly or indirectly on the proposition to call the Convention which drafted the Constitution.

A large propertyless mass was, under the prevailing suffrage qualifications, excluded at the outset from participation (through representatives) in the work of framing the Constitution.

The members of the Philadelphia Convention which drafted the Constitution were, with a few exceptions, immediately, directly, and personally interested in, and derived economic advantages from, the establishment of the new system.

The Constitution was essentially an economic document based upon the concept that the fundamental private rights of property are anterior to government and morally beyond the reach of popular majorities.

Robert E. Brown
Charles Beard and the Constitution
(Excerpts)

DISCUSSION QUESTIONS

1. What does Brown conclude about Beard's emphasis on "personalty"?
2. Does Brown argue that property and economic interests are not significant?
3. How do economic and occupational interests affect political institutions?

The Constitution as an Economic Document

Having proved to his own satisfaction that the delegates to the Convention were the representatives of personalty, Beard then went on to show that the Constitution was fundamentally an economic rather than a political document, designed above all else to protect personalty from the leveling attacks of democracy. The true nature of the Constitution is not apparent on the surface, he said, for it contains no property qualifications for voting and does not outwardly recognize economic groups or confer special class privileges. . . .

The first question to be answered then is whether *The Federalist* presents

---

Robert E. Brown, *Charles Beard and the Constitution* (Westport, CT: Greenwood Press, 1956), pp. 92–111.

merely an "economic interpretation of politics." Can Jay's arguments on the need for a stronger union as protection from foreign enemies, presented in Nos. 2 to 5, be considered strictly economic? Was the danger of civil war between the states, as expounded by Hamilton, all due to economic causes? Is an appeal for the preservation of liberty and justice simply an appeal to man's economic instincts? Were all the criticisms of the Confederation and all the attempts to allay fears about the form and powers of the new government or freedom of the press purely economic? . . .

Even if we granted that *The Federalist* appealed only to the economic man, which, of course, we do not, this still would not support the Beard thesis that *personal* property was responsible for the Constitution. If he had said that Hamilton, Madison, and Jay based their appeal on the protection of *property in general*, Beard would have been correct as far as he went. There are appeals to economic interests, *all kinds* of economic interests—merchants, farmers, moneylenders, land speculators, artisans, everybody. Hamilton, Madison, and Jay were astute politicians. They knew then, just as politicians know now, that a winning combination under popular government must appeal to many groups and many interests. They were too astute to think that the Constitution could be adopted by an appeal to only 3.7 per cent of the country's property, even if the appeal had been all economic. But as I have said before, why would farmers not be interested in expanded markets for their products, or in a government that could open western lands for settlement and the Mississippi as an outlet for western products? And why would artisans and mechanics not vote for a government that would protect them from foreign competition? But all this is not to say that *The Federalist* appealed only to economic instincts, and especially that it appealed only to personalty interests.

Numerous other statements made in the Convention emphasize the absurdity of attributing the absence of property qualifications in the Constitution to personalty influences. George Mason proposed a landed qualification for members of Congress and exclusion from Congress of anyone having unsettled accounts with the United States. Gouverneur Morris called this a scheme of the landed against the moneyed interest, and maybe it was. But we must remember that Morris was one of the most vocal advocates of the freehold qualification for voters, which could also be a scheme of the landed against the moneyed interest. John Dickinson, another proponent of the freehold qualification, sided with Morris against Mason. On the other hand Gerry, one of the few real representatives of personalty, was ready not only to support Mason's motion requiring land as a qualification, but to go much further than Mason.[1] The delegates simply were not consistent, for if Morris and Dickinson favored personalty, as Beard claimed, they should have championed a personalty instead of a freehold qualification for voting, and security holder Gerry should never have backed Mason.

If the omission of property qualifications from the Constitution was not due to the delegates' fear of freeholders and their inability to get the kind of qualifications they wanted, what is the explanation? . . .

As a matter of fact, the two reasons for the exclusion of property qualifica-

---

[1]Max Farrand, ed., *The Records of the Federal Convention of 1787*, vol. II. (New Haven: Yale University Press 1937), p. 201.

tions from the Constitution were political, not economic, and they were not difficult to find in the *Records*.

One reason was that there were different qualifications in effect in different states and the delegates simply could not agree on a uniform qualification that would be satisfactory to all. Some wanted a freehold, others wanted to include any property, and a few would eliminate practically all qualifications. There was no great opposition to property qualifications for voting either in the Convention or in the country at large, for as Dickinson and Morris said, nine-tenths of the people were freeholders and would be pleased if voting were restricted to freeholders. But while most of the delegates favored a voting qualification, they could not agree on what that qualification should be. . . .

The second reason for omitting property qualifications from the Constitution was also political—the delegates were simply afraid that any innovations on this point might result in the rejection of the Constitution. Wilson wanted to avoid "unnecessary innovations," while Ellsworth thought the prevailing state qualifications were sufficient, and that "the people [would] not readily subscribe to the Natl. Constitution, if it should subject them to be disfranchised."[2] Men who wished for innovations on this point certainly were ignoring force of habit, declared Mason, for what would "the people say, if they should be disfranchised."[3] Franklin did not want to displease the common people by disfranchising them, for they had contributed much during the late war. Sons of substantial farmers would not be pleased at being disfranchised, he said, and if the common people were "denied the right of suffrage it would debase their spirit and detach them from the interest of the country."[4] Defending the habitual right of merchants and mechanics to vote, Gorham declared: "We must consult their rooted prejudices if we expect their concurrence in our propositions."[5] Rutledge explained why the committee had omitted the qualifications by saying its members could not agree among themselves for fear of displeasing the people if they made the qualifications high or having the qualifications be worthless if they were low.[6]

Since there were no personalty qualifications for voting in the Constitution, and since, as Beard said, the landed interests would control ratification either by state legislatures or by special conventions, the big question is this: Why was the Constitution ratified by the landed interests if it was designed to protect personalty? Beard never answered this question. . . .

There were a multitude of conflicting interests in the Convention, some economic and some not, and there simply had to be a great deal of compromising of interests for anything to be achieved. As one delegate said, he did not trust the other gentleman, and they all did everything possible to insure that their interests and principles got a hearing and that others' were checked as much as possible. Nobody could have his own way completely.

---

[2] *Ibid.*, p. 201.

[3] *Ibid.*, pp. 201–02.

[4] *Ibid.*, pp. 205, 210.

[5] *Ibid.*, p. 216.

[6] *Ibid.*, p. 249.

That the Constitution did not confer on Congress the power to make direct attacks on property is not to be wondered at. Given the America of 1787, in which most men owned property, the reverse would have been the more astonishing. A constitution which permitted an attack on property would not have received a hearing in a country that had fought a revolution for the preservation of life, liberty, and property. One of the colonists' chief complaints against Britain had been that the British, on whom the colonists had no check, were endangering the property rights of colonists. The opponents of the Constitution were not opposed to the protection of property rights. After all, were not the Antifederalists responsible for the adoption of the first ten amendments, and did not Articles IV, V, and VII provide for additional protection of property which these Antifederalists did not think the Constitution provided? . . .

So to prove that the Constitution was "an economic document drawn with superb skill by men whose property interests were immediately at stake," Beard had to violate the concepts of the historical method in many ways. These ran the gamut from omission to outright misrepresentation of evidence, and included the drawing of conclusions from evidence that not only did not warrant the conclusions but actually refuted them. To say that the Constitution was designed in part to protect property is true; to say that it was designed only to protect property is false; and to say that it was designed only to protect *personalty* is preposterous.

Mark F. Plattner
"American Democracy and the Acquisitive Spirit" (Excerpts)

DISCUSSION QUESTIONS

1. How do the liberal principles of American political thought relate to the economic principles of capitalism?
2. Does a democratic society depend upon a certain degree of affluence? If so, what kind and to what degree? If not, why not?
3. Why does the author dispute redistribution policies while supporting the essential principles behind the welfare state? How would Hamilton react? What would some of the Antifederalists argue in response to these issues?

More and more critics nowadays contend that there is a fundamental tension—or even contradiction—between America's capitalist economic order and its democratic political order. The late Arthur Okun opened his influential *Equality and Efficiency* with a discussion of the "double standard of capitalist democracy, professing and pursuing an egalitarian political and social system and simultaneously generat-

Robert Goldwin and William Schambra, eds., *How Capitalistic Is the Constitution?* (Washington, DC: American Enterprise Institute For Public Policy Research, 1982), pp. 1–21. Reprinted by permission.

ing gaping disparities in economic well-being."[1] In a similar vein, Kenneth Keniston, in his foreword to Richard de Lone's *Small Futures*, writes of "the inherent conflict between the inegalitarian consequences of a liberal economy and the egalitarian ideal of a liberal political democracy." De Lone spells out this view at greater length in the book:

> There is . . . a deep tension in liberal thought between the political and economic traditions. The political tradition emphasizes the equal *rights* of all individuals, rights conferred by the natural law from which human reason draws its strength. The economic tradition emphasizes not so much the rights as the *prerogatives* of individuals in the pursuit of self-interest, e.g., the accumulation of property and wealth. Rights and prerogatives often clash. The political tradition of rights embraces equality while the economic tradition of prerogatives leads to inequality.[2]

These critics are quite willing to affirm the democratic character of America's liberal political tradition and its commitment to guaranteeing equal political rights and liberties to all. They do not dispute the fact that the liberal tradition has historically been associated with support for a capitalist economy. What they do seem to deny is that there is any intrinsic connection between the political system whose protection of equal rights and liberties they applaud and the economic system whose inegalitarian outcomes they deplore. Accordingly, their prescription for the reform of American society consists chiefly of a call for a redistribution of incomes aimed at undoing the inequalities generated by a capitalist economy. They see no danger that such a policy might threaten the liberal political fabric that guarantees our liberties.

I believe that this view derives from a shallow and incorrect understanding of the bases of the American regime, one that overlooks certain critical connections between liberal democracy and capitalism. It is my contention that where the contemporary critics see only an adventitious and ill-matched association, the founders both of liberal political theory and of the government of the United States saw an intimate and indispensable link. In short, I believe that the regime instituted by the Constitution was understood by the framers to be essentially capitalistic. By the equivocal term "capitalistic" I do not mean, in this context, a "free market" economy devoid of any government interference or regulation. Rather, I refer more broadly to an economic system that allows all citizens freely to acquire, possess, and dispose of private property and encourages them to devote themselves to the pursuit and enjoyment of wealth.

The Rights of Property

Providing security for the rights of property is an absolutely central concern of the authors of *The Federalist.* Indeed, Madison, in a letter to Jefferson, suggests that the encroachments of unjust state laws on citizens' rights of private property were the principal factor that led both to the Constitutional Convention and to public readi-

---

[1]Arthur Okun, *Equality and Efficiency* (Washington, D.C.: The Brookings Institution, 1975), p. 1.

[2]Richard de Lone, *Small Futures*, a report of the Carnegie Council on Children (New York: Harcourt Brace Jovanovich, 1979), pp. xi, 28.

ness to accept " a general reform."[3] *The Federalist* itself is filled with condemnatory references to these problems, specifically attacking state laws that violated private contracts and paper-money measures and more generally deploring the mutability of state laws.[4] It is in these contexts, moreover, that Publius most frequently and emphatically invokes the language of justice and morality: "such atrocious breaches of moral obligation and social justice"; "an accumulation of guilt, which can be expiated no otherwise than by a voluntary sacrifice on the altar of justice of the power which has been the instrument of it"; "practices . . . which have . . . occasioned an almost universal prostration of morals"; "a rage for paper money, for an abolition of debts, for an equal division of property, or for any other improper or wicked project."[5]

The introductory paragraph of *Federalist* Paper 10 alludes to the instability and injustice of state governments, which Publius holds responsible for "that prevailing and increasing distrust of public engagements and alarm for private rights which are echoed from one end of the continent to the other." In the systematic analysis of the problem of faction that follows, he leaves no doubt that it is the violence and injustice prompted by economic motives that are his chief source of concern:

> The most common and durable source of factions has been the various and unequal distribution of property. Those who hold and those who are without property have ever formed distinct interests in society. Those who are creditors, and those who are debtors, fall under a like discrimination. A landed interest, a manufacturing interest, a mercantile interest, a moneyed interest, with many lesser interests, grow up of necessity in civilized nations, and divide them into different classes, actuated by different sentiments and views. The regulation of these various and interfering interests forms the principal task of modern legislation and involves the spirit of party and faction in the necessary and ordinary operations of government.[6]

Because in a republican government political power naturally comes to reside in majority factions, and because the rich are always in a minority, holds Publius, the greatest danger to property rights is that the poorer members of society may unite to defraud or despoil the wealthy. . . .

Publius's principal solution to the problem of faction is to enlarge the territory of a republic to encompass "a greater variety of parties and interests" (by which he appears primarily to mean economic interests). The purpose of this solution is to make the "various" distribution of property more politically salient than its "unequal" distribution. If both the poor and the rich earn their livelihood in a great variety of ways, there will be divergent and competing interests within each group, as well as certain common interests cutting across economic strata. Thus, Publius suggests, poor mechanics will be inclined to vote for the rich merchant as "their natural

---

[3]Madison to Jefferson, in Hunt, *Madison*, 5:27.

[4]In addition to the passages cited in notes 35 and 36 below, see *Federalist*, no. 37, p. 227; no. 44, pp. 282–83.

[5]*Ibid.*, no. 7, p. 65; no. 44, pp. 281–82; no. 85, pp. 521–22; no. 10, p. 84.

[6]*Ibid.*, no. 10, pp. 77–78, 79.

patron and friend," and a unity of political interest will exist between the "wealthiest landlord" and "the poorest tenant." Furthermore, the extended republic, with its large election districts, would be more likely to choose for its representatives men of "the most diffusive and established characters"—that is, presumably, men of greater wealth.[7] In sum, the large republic is meant to be structured so as to minimize the likelihood that a poor majority will coalesce to violate the property rights of the more prosperous.

The inviolability of the rights of property appears to have been accepted by the full range of American political thinkers of the constitutional era—anti-Federalists as well as supporters of the Constitution, agrarians as well as proponents of commerce and manufacturing.[8] Even Jefferson, despite the notably egalitarian character of some of his views, remained firmly committed to a concept of property rights which promoted and justified unequal material rewards. In his second inaugural address as president of the United States, he affirmed his wish that "equality of rights [be] maintained, and that state of property, equal or unequal, which results to every man from his own industry, or that of his fathers."[9] In a letter to Joseph Milligan, he stated:

> To take from one, because it is thought his own industry and that of his fathers has acquired too much, in order to spare to others, who, or whose fathers have not exercised equal industry and skill, is to violate arbitrarily the first principle of association, "the guarantee to everyone of a free exercise of his industry and the fruits acquired by it."[10]

This is not to deny that Jefferson, along with others of the founding generation, believed that a wide distribution of property, without vastly disproportionate wealth or acute poverty, best comported with republican government.[11] In a letter to the Reverend James Madison (a cousin of his more famous namesake), Jefferson suggests as one "means of silently lessening the inequality of property" the use of progressive taxation, a policy that had been approved by both Montesquieu and Adam Smith.[12] But the principal instrument advocated by Jefferson (and others) for preventing inequality of fortune sufficient to threaten republicanism was laws

---

[7] *Ibid.*, no. 35, pp. 214–15; no. 10, pp. 82–83.

[8] See Cecelia Kenyon, ed., *The Antifederalists* (Indianapolis: Bobbs Merrill, 1966), p. xxvii, and E. A. J. Johnson, *The Foundations of American Economic Freedom* (Minneapolis: University of Minnesota Press, 1973), pp. 191–92.

[9] Thomas Jefferson, "Second Inaugural Address," in Koch and Peden, *Jefferson*, p. 344.

[10] Thomas Jefferson to Joseph Milligan, 6 April 1816, in Albert Bergh, ed., *The Writings of Thomas Jefferson*, 20 vols. (Washington, D.C., 1907), 14:466.

[11] See Johnson, *American Economic Freedom*, pp. 310–11. James Madison (in Hunt, *Madison*, 6:86) asserts that republicanism is strengthened "by the *silent* operation of laws, which, *without violating the rights of property*, reduce extreme wealth towards a state of mediocrity, and raise extreme indigence toward a state of comfort" (italics added). The Founders' desire to reduce economic equality is always mitigated by their concern to preserve the legitimate rights of property. Hence they never advocate direct redistributive measures, but seek indirect and unobtrusive—that is, "silent"—means to this end.

[12] Thomas Jefferson to Rev. James Madison, 28 October 1785, in Koch and Peden, *Jefferson*, p. 390. Progressive taxation is endorsed by Montesquieu in *Spirit of the Laws*, 13:7, and by Adam Smith in *Wealth of Nations*, V, ii, Part II, Article 1.

encouraging the equal partition of inheritances. Shortly after the Declaration of Independence was adopted, Jefferson returned to the Virginia Legislature, where he led a successful fight to abolish the laws of primogeniture and entail (which required that landed estates be passed intact to the eldest son). In his autobiography he explains the purpose behind these reforms as follows:

> To annul this privilege, and instead of an aristocracy of wealth, of more harm and danger, than benefit, to society, to make an opening for the aristocracy of virtue and talent, which nature has wisely provided for the direction of the interests of society, and scattered with equal hand through all its conditions, was deemed essential to a well-ordered republic. To effect it, no violence was necessary, no deprivation of natural right, but rather an enlargement of it by repeal of the law [of entail]. For this would authorize the present holder to divide the property among his children equally, as his affections were divided; and would place them, by natural generation, on the level of their fellow citizens.[13]

If Tocqueville's account can be believed, the reformed law of inheritance fully achieved the democratizing effect Jefferson had intended. During the Revolutionary War, almost all the states had abolished the old aristocratic English laws of inheritance; sixty years later, "the law of partition [had] reduced all to one level." By this assertion Tocqueville means that the permanent concentration of vast wealth in certain great families had been eliminated:

> I do not mean that there is any lack of wealthy individuals in the United States; I know of no country, indeed, where the love of money has taken stronger hold on the affections of men and where a profounder contempt is expressed for the theory of the permanent equality of property. But wealth circulates with incredible rapidity, and experience shows that it is rare to find two succeeding generations in the full enjoyment of it.[14]

Results of the Framers' Work

The economic aspects of the framers' political theory may be summarized, then, in the following four points: (1) Industry and the pursuit of gain should be encouraged. (2) Superior industry and skill justly merit the greater material rewards they naturally tend to reap. (3) The rights of private property must be secured, both on grounds of justice and as a necessary condition for promoting industry. (4) The laws should favor the free and rapid circulation of property, so that all may have a chance to become rich and so that distinct and permanent classes of either the very rich or the very poor are unlikely to form.

The political ends these economic principles were meant to serve are the now traditional liberal goals of liberty and prosperity. National prosperity is the product of individual industry, supported by the security afforded to private property. Liberty is made possible because, given the proper political institutions (representative

---

[13]Thomas Jefferson, *Autobiography*, in Koch and Peden, *Jefferson*, pp. 38–39.

[14]Tocqueville, *Democracy in America*, vol. 1, ch. 3, pp. 49–50.

government, separation of powers, and a large territory), men devoted to industrious pursuits can largely be left to go their own way. The extended republic based on economic self-interest protects the private sphere and gives it unprecedented room to expand. In comparison with the classical republican ideal, the Madisonian version can be said to foster a far-reaching depoliticization of human society. Government no longer need closely supervise the morals, religion, and opinions of the people, for extraordinary public-spiritedness is neither demanded nor needed. The calculating pursuit of economic advantage and the habits of industry provide a check on people's most dangerous and politically destructive passions, and citizens readily give their allegiance to a government that guarantees their liberty and supplies the political conditions they need for prosperity.

I believe it is safe to say that Publius's vision of the large republic animated by economic self-interest has been remarkably successful in bringing the United States almost two hundred years of freedom and material well-being. I believe it is also fair to say that the economic views of the framers, at least as embodied in the principles summarized here, continue to prevail in this country today. To be sure, there have been enormous changes over the past two centuries in technology, in economic organization, and above all in the role played by the federal government in the economy. The modern welfare state certainly goes well beyond anything the framers of the Constitution might have envisioned. And it cannot be denied that the expanded scope of government activity has created difficulties for our political system that have not yet been fully resolved. But whatever the practical problems caused by the proliferation of government programs in the areas of regulation, social insurance, equal opportunity, and aid to the needy, I believe that on the level of principle, the welfare state remains compatible with the liberal capitalist society established by the Constitution—a society that guarantees the security of private property and generally allows material rewards to be allocated according to the "industry and skill" of individuals.

I would argue, however, that proposals for making it an explicit aim of government policy to combat economic inequality directly are a very different matter. In the first place, by focusing on the political competition among income classes (as opposed to that among interest groups formed along other lines), frankly redistributionist policies would intensify the very conflict between the rich and poor that the framers sought to minimize. Moreover, a direct governmental assault on economic inequality would seem to me even more fundamentally incompatible with the basic economic theory underlying the Constitution. It is no accident that the more sophisticated arguments for income redistribution are accompanied by an explicit denial that superior skill or industry conveys a just title to the greater material rewards it normally brings. (This denial is found in Okun's *Equality and Efficiency*, and it is a crucial premise of the most influential work in political theory of the past decade—John Rawls's *A Theory of Justice.*)[15] Having government determine

[15]Arthur Okun, *Equality and Efficiency*, pp. 42–50; John Rawls, *A Theory of Justice* (Cambridge: Harvard University Press, 1971), pp. 15, 74.

the level of people's income by redistribution can be morally justified only if those who originally earn income have no legitimate right to it.

By making the political process rather than the "honest industry" of private individuals the arbiter of each person's income, redistribution undermines the notion of genuinely private property. For the implicit assumption of such a policy is not that a society's wealth is the sum of the wealth of its individual citizens, but that individuals' wealth is merely the share of the society's wealth that government decides to allot them. By making everyone's income directly dependent on governmental largesse, a policy of explicit redistribution must necessarily politicize society. In effect, each citizen would become the equivalent of a government grantee or a welfare recipient, and it is hard to see how anyone could hope to avoid the government's solicitude about how he or she was spending the public's money. In addition, with everyone entitled to a goodly share of the society's total output, there would be inevitable pressure to regulate the contributions people make to the production of that output. Decisions about whether, where, and when individuals ought to work would tend to become subject to political determination. It seems unlikely, therefore, that a redistributionist society could maintain the protection of the private sphere necessary for personal liberty to flourish.[16]

One way of describing the error into which I believe the advocates of redistribution have fallen is that they seek to impose on the large republic an economic egalitarianism more appropriate to the small republic. Indeed, I think a very large portion of contemporary hostility to capitalism comes down to a longing for certain attractive features of the small republic—not only economic equality, but intense political participation, a strong sense of community, and selfless devotion to the public good. Few of the contemporary critics of capitalism, however, are willing to sacrifice the blessings of the large, modern, capitalistic republic—unprecedented wealth and personal liberty. Thus they often seem to wind up calling for a utopian combination of contradictory elements—diversity and unity, individualism and community, a high standard of living without resort to the pursuit of private gain. The danger, of course, is that trying to achieve this hybrid in practice will cause us to lose the advantages of the large republic without gaining the advantages of the small republic. In fact, modern totalitarianism can be viewed in some respects as the unfortunate result of just such a misguided attempt.

Lest I be misunderstood, let me hasten to make clear some things I do *not* mean to imply: that the large republic demands an unqualified reliance on self-interest and unbounded libertarianism, that it can or should *totally* dispense with every characteristic of the small republic, or that a capitalist economy is a sufficient condition for political liberty. Indeed, I think the gravest weakness of *The Federalist's* case for the large republic is its taking for granted the moral and customary props that are essential to the maintenance of self-government in any society. In this respect, an excellent supplement (or corrective) to *The Federalist* is provided by Tocqueville, with his emphasis on the importance of such factors as religion, local

[16]For a more extended critique of the redistributionist view, see Marc F. Plattner, "The Welfare State vs. the Redistributive State," in *The Public Interest*, no. 55 (Spring 1979), pp. 28–48.

government, civil association, and domestic morals to the health of American democracy. Tocqueville constantly stresses, however, the need to adapt these supports to the worldly and commercial spirit of a liberal capitalist society. For he perceived that self-interest—"rightly understood"—was the only reliable basis for political freedom in the modern world.

Certainly the historical record does not reveal any noncapitalist society that has given its citizens a high degree of personal liberty, or any large noncapitalist society that has long maintained a republican government. One hesitates, however, to rely too heavily on the evidence of the past in matters like these, remembering Publius's plea in behalf of "the experiment of an extended republic": "Hearken not to the voice which petulantly tells you that the form of government recommended for your adoption is a novelty in the political world; that it has never yet had a place in the theories of the wildest projectors; that it rashly attempts what it is impossible to accomplish."[17] Perhaps a country as large and diverse as the United States could continue to enjoy republican government and personal liberty even if it ceased to have a capitalist economy. This possibility will have to be taken seriously when it comes to be defended with the theoretical insight and persuasive power displayed in *The Federalist.*

Edward S. Greenberg
"Class Rule Under the Constitution"
(Excerpts)

DISCUSSION QUESTIONS

1. Are democratic principles impaired or advanced by modern capitalism?
2. Are the ideals of liberty and equality, central to the American creed, served or undermined by the combination of American constitutionalism and corporate capitalism?
3. What are the implications of "corporate-dominated planning" with regard to participatory government? Is the connection between economic control and political power important for a free society? Explain.

How capitalistic is the U.S. Constitution? To what extent does it support and encourage social and economic relations that may be described as capitalistic and discourage those that are anticapitalistic or noncapitalistic? I believe the Constitution is fundamentally and inescapably capitalistic; precisely how and to what degree, however, is historically contingent and seldom has been closely examined.

By the Constitution I mean more than simply the written document. Al-

---

[17]*Federalist*, no. 14, p. 104.

Robert Goldwin and William Schambra, eds., *How Capitalistic Is the Constitution?* (Washington, DC: American Enterprise Institute for Public Policy Research, 1982), pp. 22–48. Reprinted by permission.

though the express provisions of the document form the bedrock of any definition of it, a real understanding of the Constitution also must include the authoritative interpretations added over the years by Congress, the president, and the Supreme Court. To this I would add longstanding institutional practices and widely shared political traditions in the United States. By this broad (though hardly unusual) definition, the Constitution is clearly capitalistic. Except in times of instability and revolutionary upheaval, the dominant institutions in any society tend to be congruous and mutually supportive. The social arrangements, distributions of power, and prevailing ideas that characterize the political, economic, and cultural domains generally reinforce one another. Indeed, one of the key indicators of emerging tensions and potential disruptions to normal processes in any polity is the appearance of serious divergence among these domains. To claim that the U.S. Constitution is basically capitalistic, then, when it is the constitutive document of the world's leading capitalist nation, is no radical statement. What would be far more surprising—and would require far more justification—would be to claim that the constitutional-legal order and the prevailing economic arrangements in the United States are different, unrelated, or hostile to each other. Such a situation would make for a strange society indeed, and, as far as I am concerned, an untenable one.

By assuming the Constitution to be capitalistic, I do not mean to suggest that it is constant and fixed. On the contrary, the flexibility and adaptability of the U.S. Constitution have been cited so often that they have become one of the enduring clichés of American life. What is remarkable about the Constitution is that it manages to be both fixed and flexible at the same time. The document's constancy is its commitment to support, encourage, and nurture an economy based on private property. Its adaptability and flexibility grow out of its need to meet this fixed commitment in radically contrasting environments—environments created largely by the transformative qualities of a dynamic capitalism. It is this combination of constancy and adaptability in the American constitutional tradition that lies at the heart of its relationship to a capitalist economy. . . .

Capitalist and Constitutional Transformation

To argue that the Constitution is firm in its support of capitalism, as I have mentioned, is not necessarily to argue that it is unbending and inflexible. On the contrary, it is precisely the Constitution's ability to permit timely innovation in the face of dramatic transformations in economic society that best accounts for its historic staying power. While remaining capitalistic at its core, the Constitution has usually (though not invariably) allowed room for creative maneuver as different fractions of capital have vied for economic supremacy and for the opportunity to place their stamp on public policy. Thus, although capitalism is enshrined in the Constitution, no one particular form of capitalism is enshrined. . . .

In the late eighteenth century, the Constitution represented a tenuous accommodation between landed capitalism based on slavery (yet commercially oriented) and an emerging and dynamic capitalism based primarily but not solely on trade and small manufacturing. Those in both camps seem to have agreed that union and order were preferable to anarchy and the threat of impassioned antiproperty majorities. The debates surrounding the writing of the Constitution and its ratification were never between capitalist and noncapitalist interests, between capitalism and feudalism, or between capitalism and socialism. Neither feudalism nor socialism were on the agenda in Philadelphia because the American colonies were generally capitalistic in mood and organization from the beginning, being tied by culture, by arms, and by economics to an emerging capitalist world power in England.[1] Furthermore, the colonies were populated by eager entrepreneurs and situated far away from any viable competing systems of social organization. Although a panoply of debate surrounded particular provisions of the Constitution, its essential capitalist character was axiomatic. On this the main fractions of the property-owning class were in full agreement.

The precarious compromise among those fractions was exploded by the dramatic transformations in economic life and organization that took place in the first half of the nineteenth century. In the late eighteenth century, most American business activity was accounted for by trade, investments in land, and the sale and use of slaves. By 1807, overseas trade had expanded rapidly, fueled by the orders of the warring European powers. By 1830, the great trading houses that had arisen during the boom began shifting investments from external to internal ventures, particularly in transportation, banking, and manufacturing. By about 1850, financed directly by merchant capital or indirectly by it through the increasingly important investment banks, industrial capitalism had emerged in vigorous, though infant, form. In that year, the "value added" by manufacturing had already exceeded 50 percent of all agricultural production; the railroad, the sewing machine, and the reaper were in widespread use; large factories had appeared; and a sizable industrial proletariat had entered upon the historical stage. In short, capitalism in the Northern states had reached the take-off point for its subsequent leap into full-scale industrial capitalism.

Capitalism in the Southern states, on the other hand, remained mired in stagnation. Based as it was on slavery, vast landholdings, and aristocratic economic, cultural, and political hegemony, it was never able to discard its precapitalist, premodern economic impediments.[2] Plagued by the absence of a home market, low labor productivity, technological backwardness, and depleted soil, the slave-holding South was rapidly eclipsed economically by the dynamic capitalism of the Northern states. With its way of life under siege, economically threatened yet led by a relatively cohesive and politically astute ruling class, the South pursued strategies of expansion into the West and opposition to federal measures designed to further the interests of Northern capitalism (particularly the tariff). The clash between the two capitalisms, one forward-looking and dynamic, the

---

[1]By 1780, the enclosures were completed in England, agriculture was dominated by market-oriented farmers utilizing hired labor, and the great textile mills of the midlands were in full blossom, their looms manned by a vast population of depressed "free" labor.

[2]As Barrington Moore, Jr., has put it, "The South had a capitalist civilization . . . but hardly a bourgeois one." *The Social Origins of Dictatorship and Democracy* (Boston: Beacon Press, 1966), p. 121. The same point is elaborated by Eugene Genovese in *The Political Economy of Slavery* (New York: Pantheon Books, 1965).

other backward-looking and stagnant, was perhaps inevitable, and the ultimate results predictable.

For the only time in American constitutional history, capitalist factions were unable to settle their differences peacefully. Perhaps this was because their differences were irreconcilable; perhaps it was because the exploited class that might have forced their alliance by opposing them was too immature to represent a tangible threat; perhaps it was because competing ways of life were at issue.[3] The Civil War was the outcome of their failure, the ultimate and terrible conclusion to their struggle, and the only case when the Constitution proved inadequate to its mandate. Out of that intracapitalist struggle, merchant-industrial capitalism emerged supreme. Out of the shambles of the Civil War arose an economic society characterized by free enterprise, industrialization, the market mechanism, and commodicized ("free") labor, with the economic and political power of landed and slave capital erased forever from the United States. . . .

The late nineteenth century to World War II. With the dominance of industrial capitalism firmly established by the last third of the nineteenth century, the prevailing forms of the class struggle changed. The cause was the rapid advance of production, the appearance of large factories and urban concentrations, and the rise of the modern corporation, all brought about by the industrial and organizational revolutions. The most obvious result was the first serious, sustained, and organized struggles in the United States between wage labor and capital. That story is a familiar one. The other struggle, less familiar but more central to this discussion, took place within the capitalist class, between small and medium-sized regional businesses on the one hand and the giant national corporations on the other. That struggle was twofold, fought in the economic sphere for shares in the marketplace and in the political sphere for the form the capitalist state would take. Again, the outcome seems almost preordained: The corporate sector would win economic dominance by World War I, though it would not succeed in shaping the state in its image until World War II. . . .

The drive of business since the beginning of market society has been to dampen competition, mainly through cooperative efforts to limit production and set prices. Before the industrial revolution, the economy of the United States comprised a complex mixture of local and regional markets. Within these markets, leading enterprises customarily attempted to make arrangements to ease competition—most often, price and marketing agreements designed to provide the major firms within each region and industry with a relatively stable guaranteed rate of return. The combined impact of the industrial revolution, massive population increases, the appearance of the railroad and the telegraph line, and the rapid development of markets in the West destroyed these localized markets and local anticompetitive agreements. . . .

The final step in the process of dampening competition was for competing companies to merge, which was made possible by the states of New Jersey and Delaware in the 1890s. Each introduced liberal incorporation laws under which a

---

[3]The point cogently made by Genovese, *ibid.*

corporation could buy stock of a competing enterprise and merge with it into a single legal and economic entity. So momentous were these combined economic, legal, and organizational developments that in the relatively short time between the end of the Civil War and the beginning of World War I, the economy of the United States changed from one of farms and small businesses to one dominated by a handful of industrial and financial corporations.

The incorporated form of business thus culminated decades of efforts by large businesses to form cooperative arrangements aimed at limiting production, apportioning markets, and setting prices. Ultimately, however, these tactics proved inadequate to protect the major firms in each industry from intense competition, falling prices, and declining profits. Some of the most far-sighted business leaders in the corporate sector came to realize that what would help build the most formidable and lasting cartel-like intercorporate understandings would be the sponsorship of the federal government. Government support would legitimate intercorporate cooperation as being in the public interest; it would put new competitors at a disadvantage; and it would protect corporate prerogatives from the hostile inroads of state legislatures.

In the opening years of the twentieth century, then, with the encouragement of some of the leaders of the nation's largest corporations and financial institutions, a new corporate movement began. Its proponents lauded the economic and social benefits of concentrated corporate size and business cooperation—efficiency, economies of scale, technological advance, peaceful industrial relations, and the like—and urged that the federal government support and nurture this new "cooperative capitalism." Out of this movement, in a history too complex to review here, came such legal and political landmarks as the Federal Trade Commission Act, the Federal Reserve System, the War Industries Board of World War I, the trade association movement of the 1920s, the National Industrial Recovery Act and Wagner Labor Relations Act of Roosevelt's New Deal, and a host of other regulatory and subsidy programs, whose overall effect was to "quasi-cartelize" the American economy under federal government sponsorship.

From the early years of the twentieth century, then, the leaders of the largest corporations realized that a stable, ordered economy was possible only with the cooperative intervention of government. This was a view that was not initially shared by all leaders of large enterprises, though it gradually won over those who counted in the corporate sector. What eventually evolved was a protective umbrella of public policy under which the dominant corporations could legally cooperate with each other, stabilize and regularize their relationships in trade associations, standardize practices and products within industries, and receive assistance and subsidies from the government when the situation required. This structure has been the core of the American political economy ever since.

. . . By the end of the Second World War, the transformation of public policy was virtually complete, and the modern capitalist state was a reality. As yet, not all the machinery of regulation, subsidization, business-cycle management, militarization of the economy, welfare control of the underclass, collective bargaining, and protection of overseas business operations was in finished form. Still, the capitalist state as an institution committed to the support, protection, and sustenance of the major corporate enterprises was widely accepted by business, political, and academic leaders. Formally transforming the Constitution so as to change the definition of the state from an institution supportive of laissez-faire capitalism to one more attuned to concentrated corporate capitalism would naturally be a longer and more tortuous process than altering public policy, but the end would be the same.

Before 1900, when the corporations had not yet emerged as the dominant capitalist fraction, the Supreme Court functioned primarily as an instrument of the dominant class in general and not as an instrument of intraclass division. In the second half of the nineteenth century, the Supreme Court became the virtual handmaiden of private property. During that period, the Court rendered a series of decisions that reaffirmed the status of corporations as persons and holders of rights, and therefore as entities to be left free from interference in their operations. The Court interpreted the due process clause of the Fourteenth Amendment, originally intended to protect newly enfranchised black citizens, as a prohibition against state regulation of business enterprises and against efforts by working people to form unions. The Court also interpreted the Sherman Antitrust Act, originally directed at the problem of business monopoly, as prohibiting the unionization of workers.

For most of its history, in fact, from the era of John Marshall through the 1920s, the Court substantially agreed with the interests and needs of the leading national economic institutions. In the last decades of this era, in particular, the Court actively protected corporations from the dual threat of regulation by state governments and a unionized work force. This happy relationship was torn asunder by the events that surrounded the collapse of American capitalism in 1929. The crisis of capitalism was reflected in a crisis of the Court. In response to the Great Depression, the most advanced sectors of the business community and national political leadership moved in directions sharply at odds with prevailing notions on the Court. While members of the Court remained tied to fairly strict laissez-faire notions, corporate and political leaders were becoming sensitive to the necessity of constructing a form of cooperative corporate capitalism in which the national government would be actively involved in the protection, coordination, and stabilization of the entire economy. When the Roosevelt administration moved actively to implement this idea with legislation, the Court responded by rejecting many of the landmark programs of the New Deal, the most important ones being minimum-wage legislation, the National Industrial Recovery Act, and the Agricultural Adjustment Act.

Nevertheless, the constitutional crisis was short-lived. For reasons that are unclear, and without any change in personnel, the Court began to find New Deal legislation perfectly acceptable after 1937, including the new conception of governmental activism. Whether this transformation was influenced most centrally by the power of public opinion as reflected in FDR's smashing 1936 electoral victory, by the fear elicited among the justices by Roosevelt's ill-fated plan to pack the Court with friendly jurists, or by pressures from corporate and financial leaders, is largely immaterial. What mattered was that after 1937, the Court returned to the fold. From then until the present, the Court has allowed the federal government virtually a free hand in regulating and coordinating corporate capitalism.

. . . It is still too early to know which of the competing tendencies (assuming there remain only two general ones) will win out in the end, which one will eventually impose its vision on the form, operations, and purposes of the state. My guess, as I have suggested, is that corporate-oriented planning is the likely future of American capitalism. Still, the powerful appeal of laissez-faire may yet upset my expectations. We have no way of predicting, moreover, whether either conception of the capitalist state is capable of successfully taming the emerging crises in the system. In my view, neither seems up to the task, the one having proved already that it was not equal to the problems generated by a far simpler capitalist economy and the other being in some respects merely a further development of public policies that have contributed significantly to our present difficulties. I may be underestimating their flexibility, innovative potential, and staying power, however. Finally, because it is too early to know which policy will prevail, it is impossible to say what the future capitalist state and its supporting constitutional system will look like. My preliminary guess, based on some of the theoretical work already coming from the corporate-planning fraction[4] and on technical developments in information gathering, storing, and analysis, is that it will prove to be a more authoritarian system.[5]

One final observation about this new period is in order. The debate between the two main policy positions has been evident primarily within the capitalist class; it has not yet moved onto the terrain of public discourse. Indeed, debate in the political arena at present seems strangely divorced from that within the capitalist class, being confined mainly to the relative virtues of limited government and the free market versus New Deal–style liberalism. Yet it seems to me likely that planning is the probably capitalist future. If that is so, then the present shape of public discourse in the United States is diversionary and beside the point. If we as a people are not to drift unconsciously into corporate-dominated planning, we must begin to raise questions about the kind of planning system most appropriate to a democratic system. If we fail to do so, the issues will be settled for us.

---

[4]See especially Michael Crozier et al., eds., *The Crisis of Democracy* (New York: New York University Press, 1975).

[5]For a chilling discussion of these tendencies see Bertram Gross, *Friendly Fascism* (New York: Evans, 1980).

Philip Slater
A Dream Deferred
(Excerpt)

DISCUSSION QUESTIONS

1. Discuss the issue of economic empowerment and personal fulfillment.
2. Do the institutions and dynamics of American society inspire the "pursuit of happiness" or "promote the general welfare"?
3. What would Jefferson say about the observations shared in the last two paragraphs of Slater's article?
4. What does Slater mean when he states that the "vote is little more than a fingerhold on democracy"? Analyze this statement, and consider what might be necessary to ensure greater participation throughout the American citizenry.

Back to the Salt Mines

However poorly it may perform, bureaucracy is still the dominant species in the American economy. Most Americans work in settings that are resolutely authoritarian. This is particularly true of the working class, for whom democracy is more of a slogan than a fact of everyday life. What is the effect of this constant, grinding authoritarianism on the psyche of the average American worker? Can we expect democratic attitudes and responses from citizens who so rarely experience it in their daily lives? How can the reality of the workplace be reconciled with the democratic visions of our heritage?

We spend almost a third of our lives in the workplace, most of us in settings that are structurally antiquated, unfulfilling, uncreative, and antidemocratic. (Recent polls have suggested that more and more people are putting personal fulfillment ahead of money when considering a job, but other polls suggest that only a minority are finding it.) Perry Pascarella has shown that some of the most successful corporations are those that make work humanly fulfilling—that *empower* those who work in them—but these are still a small minority. We can never call ourselves a true democracy until the values of our heritage are reflected in the reality of our daily lives.

Rich and Poor

Democracy cannot survive inequality. If power and wealth are concentrated in the hands of a few, the fact that poor people can vote means very little. Only the wealthy can mount expensive advertising campaigns, lobby effectively, bribe legislators, conduct protracted legal battles, and so on. It takes money to run for office. Poor people do not hobnob with judges, diplomats, or U.S. senators. Given these circumstances the vote is little more than a fingerhold on democracy.

The last decade has witnessed an increase in the gap between rich and poor in America—enlarging the power, wealth, and immunity of the former and disen-

---

Philip Slater, *A Dream Deferred* (Boston: Beacon Press, 1991), pp. 68–70. Reprinted by permission.

franchising the latter. Even by the rosy-hued statistics of the Reagan administration, we have more poor people (in what was once the world's wealthiest nation) than most industrialized countries. Income figures show a consistent increase in the number of extremely wealthy individuals and in the very poor, while the middle class—once considered the bulwark of a healthy democracy—has been severely eroded. Instead of helping Latin America realize our democratic and equalitarian ideals, recent administrations seem to be trying to turn the United States into a replica of Guatemala or El Salvador.

During the last decade millions of people have slipped into the ranks of the destitute. Exactly how many we cannot determine, since so many of these people never get counted in the census and do not appear on voter registration rolls or any other official statistic. These people have literally been dumped out of our society. This is one of the great inventions of the Reagan era—the statistical forgetting of disaffected portions of the population. Unemployment figures remain low because those whose unemployment benefits run out are no longer classified as unemployed. People who have lost their homes and are living on the street often go uncounted and cannot vote to express their dissatisfaction because they have no addresses and are not registered.

And because the people who suffer under this regime are unlikely to mingle with the perpetrators of it, the latter are able to pretend they don't exist. Although for years millions of Americans have been eating in soup kitchens and out of garbage cans, officials proclaim that the "economy" is basically healthy. What is this "economy," that it can thrive on so much misery? What does it mean that the "economy" is basically healthy when there is more poverty in the United States than at any time since the Great Depression? This "economy" seems to consist of the exchange of goods and services merely among the well-to-do. Fewer and fewer Americans can afford to own a home, but the "economy" is basically healthy. Fewer and fewer Americans can afford a college education, but the "economy" is basically healthy. The infrastructure of our nation has deteriorated, our states, cities, and towns no longer can afford to provide any but the most rudimentary services, our schools have been starved into mere custodial institutions, and only the wealthy or heavily insured can afford medical care, but our "economy" is basically healthy.

This "economy" has very little to do with ordinary people. In theory it is supposed to benefit everyone, through the mysterious workings of the infamous "trickle-down theory"—the supply-side version of "the check is in the mail"—but since few supply-side economists ever bother to inspect a poor person's mailbox (and in the post-Reagan era the poor may not *have* a mailbox), they never discover that nothing is trickling down. How much, after all, is likely to slip through the fingers of people whose religion is greed?

The justification for all this is the archaic notion that giving more money to the rich will "encourage investment," which is supposed to "stimulate the economy" in ways that will "benefit everyone." Since "everyone" is very narrowly defined by those who advance this idea ("everyone who is anyone" would be a close translation) it isn't too surprising that the gap between rich and poor invariably widens when this view prevails. From a societal viewpoint the rich are poor investors—most likely to put their surplus dollars into corporate takeovers and other get-rich-quick schemes that will yield still more dollars for them and have a fundamentally destructive impact on the society as a whole; least likely to invest in anything of long-range benefit to the nation. We don't need to encourage them to find ways of making more money for themselves—they are addicted to it. To offer inducements—such as a lower capital gains tax—is like passing a law to encourage alcoholics to drink more.

The alarming increase in the gap between rich and poor is one of the most severe threats to American democracy today. Recent studies have shown, for example, that having affluent parents automatically adds an average of about twelve points to the IQ of a growing child. One result of supply-side economics, then, is to reduce the intelligence of future millions. Those who advocate policies that have this result can have no other goal but to reinstate the authoritarianism of centuries past.

3

Federalism

A federal system of government, in which substantial power is granted to both the nation and the states, is provided in the United States Constitution. The Preamble indicates the aim of forming "a more perfect union." Article I, Sections 8 through 10, set out the powers of Congress (the national government), the powers denied Congress, and the powers denied the states. The second paragraph of Article VI, the supremacy clause, establishes the national Constitution, laws, and treaties to be the "supreme law of the land." Amendment 10 is the familiar division of delegated powers to the national government and reserved powers to the states or to the people.

This federal relationship of nation to states was vigorously debated during the Constitutional ratification process in the states. The readings presented here represent some of the crucial arguments of opponents (Antifederalists) and advocates (Federalists) of the new constitution.

Patrick Henry in two fiery speeches contends that liberty is the first end of government and that personal freedoms and the protection rendered by one's state will be seriously threatened by the national government in the Constitution as drafted. He considers the national government under the Articles of Confederation to be sufficiently strong to protect the people. The people, he says, are not in fear of other nations.

Alexander Hamilton (Publius) discusses the shortcomings of the Articles of Confederation as they apply to the relations among the nation and the states and between states. Particular concerns revolve around the nation's raising money and men from the states, when needed, and some states being unfairly treated. John Jay, in *Federalist* Papers 3 and 4, suggests that safety of citizens is the primary role of government and that the national government under the Constitution can best provide safety against both "just" and "pretended" causes of war. Also, the strong national government will attract the best leaders to promote citizen safety. Alexander Hamilton, in a stirring *Federalist* Paper 6, argues that the danger of dissension exists among the states and from their leaders unless the Constitution is adopted.

The states have from time to time refused to comply with demands by the national government. Various names have been given to this noncompliance, such as "nullification," "interposition," and "states' rights." An example is the South Carolina Ordinance of Nullification of 1832, declaring null and void Congress' tariff of 1832. Excerpts from President Andrew Jackson's Proclamation to the People of South Carolina provides an answer to the "strange position that any one State may not only declare an act of Congress void, but prohibit its execution. . . . " He maintains that state action such as taken by South Carolina is dangerous to the Union.

The relationship between the nation and the states has evolved through various stages. Although known by a variety of names, these stages are often presented as in the Harrigan reading, as Dual, Cooperative, Creative, and New Federalism. Seldom is the federal relationship static from one Presidential administration to the next; by perceptive analysis the student may determine the current relationship of the nation to its states.

The inaugural addresses of Presidents Reagan and Clinton indicate their views on the role of government. President Reagan argues for less national government power whereas President Clinton advocates action and experimentation, presumably by government, as well as enhanced participation by citizens of the United States.

The readings in this chapter provide the beginnings and the echoes of Antifederalist and Federalist thought on the federal system. The Antifederalists' influence upon participatory democracy may be seen in demands for a smaller national government. The reason for this attitude is the belief that citizens cannot participate fully in large, overpowering governments.

THE CONSTITUTION (EXCERPTS)

THE PREAMBLE

We the People of the United States, in Order to form a more perfect Union, establish Justice, insure domestic Tranquility, provide for the common defence, promote the general Welfare, and secure the Blessings of Liberty to ourselves and our Posterity, do ordain and establish this Constitution for the United States of America.

ARTICLE I—THE LEGISLATIVE ARTICLE

Powers of Congress

Section 8 The Congress shall have Power To lay and collect Taxes, Duties, Imposts and Excises, to pay the Debts and provide for the common Defence and general Welfare of the United States; but all Duties, Imposts and Excises shall be uniform throughout the United States;

To borrow Money on the Credit of the United States;

To regulate Commerce with foreign Nations, and among the several States, and with the Indian Tribes;

To establish an uniform Rule of Naturalization, and uniform Laws on the subject of Bankruptcies throughout the United States;

To coin Money, regulate the Value thereof, and of foreign Coin, and fix the Standard of Weights and Measures;

To provide for the Punishment of counterfeiting the Securities and current Coin of the United States;

To establish Post Offices and post Roads;

To promote the Progress of Science and useful Arts, by securing for limited Times to Authors and Inventors the exclusive Right to their respective Writings and Discoveries,

To constitute Tribunals inferior to the supreme Court,

To define and punish Piracies and Felonies committed on the high Seas, and Offences against the Law of Nations;

To declare War, grant Letters of Marque and Reprisal, and make Rules concerning Captures on Land and Water;

To raise and support Armies, but no Appropriation of Money to that Use shall be for a longer Term than two Years;

To provide and maintain a Navy;

To make Rules for the Government and Regulation of the land and naval Forces;

To provide for calling for the Militia to execute the Laws of the Union, suppress Insurrections and repel Invasions;

To provide for organizing, arming, and disciplining, the Militia, and for governing such Part of them as may be employed in the Service of the United States, reserving to the States respectively, the Appointment of the Officers, and the Authority of training the Militia according to the discipline prescribed by Congress;

To exercise exclusive Legislation in all Cases whatsoever, over such District (not exceeding ten Miles square) as may, by Cession of particular States, and the Acceptance of Congress, become the Seat of the Government of the United States, and to exercise like Authority over all Places purchased by the Consent of the Legislature of the State in which the Same shall be, for the Erection of Forts, Magazines, Arsenals, dock-Yards, and other needful Buildings;—And

To make all Laws which shall be necessary and proper for carrying into Execution the foregoing Powers, and all other Powers vested by this Constitution in the Government of the United States, or in any Department or Officer thereof.

Powers Denied to Congress

Section 9 The Migration or Importation of such Persons as any of the States now existing shall think proper to admit, shall not be prohibited by the Congress prior to the Year one thousand eight hundred and eight, but a Tax or Duty may be imposed on such Importation, not exceeding ten dollars for each Person.

The privilege of the Writ of Habeas Corpus shall not be suspended, unless when in Cases of Rebellion or Invasion the public Safety may require it.

No Bill of Attainder or ex post facto Laws shall be passed.

No Capitation, or other direct, Tax shall be laid, unless in Proportion to the Census or Enumeration herein before directed to be taken.

No Tax or Duty shall be laid on Articles exported from any State.

No Preference shall be given by any Regulation of Commerce or Revenue to the Ports of one State over those of another; nor shall Vessels bound to, or from, one State, be obliged to enter, clear, or pay Duties in another.

No Money shall be drawn from the Treasury, but in Consequence of Appropriations made by Law; and a regular Statement and Account of the Receipts and Expenditures of all public Money shall be published from time to time.

No Title of Nobility shall be granted by the United States; And no Person holding any Office of Profit or Trust under them, shall, without the Consent of the Congress, accept of any present, Emolument, Office, or Title, of any kind whatever, from any King, Prince, or foreign State.

Powers Denied to the States

Section 10 No State shall enter into any Treaty, Alliance, or Confederation; grant Letters of Marque and Reprisal; coin Money; emit Bills of Credit; make any Thing but gold and silver Coin a Tender in Payment of Debts; pass any Bill of Attainder, ex post facto Law, or Law impairing the Obligation of Contracts, or grant any Title of Nobility.

No State shall, without the Consent of the Congress, lay any Imposts or Duties on Imports or Exports, except what may be absolutely necessary for executing it's inspection Laws: and the net Produce of all Duties and Imposts, laid by any State on Imports or Exports, shall be for the Use of the Treasury of the United States; and all such Laws shall be subject to the Revision and Controul of the Congress.

No State shall, without the Consent of Congress, lay any Duty of Tonnage, keep Troops, or Ships of War in time of Peace, enter into any Agreement or Compact with another State, or with a foreign Power, or engage in War, unless actually invaded, or in such imminent Danger as will not admit of Delay.

Article VI—The Supremacy Act

This Constitution, and the Laws of the United States which shall be made in Pursuance thereof; and all Treaties made, or which shall be made, under the Authority of the United States, shall be the supreme Law of the Land; and the Judges in every State shall be bound thereby, any Thing in the Constitution or Laws of any State to the Contrary notwithstanding.

Amendment 10—
Reserved Powers of the States

The powers not delegated to the United States by the Constitution, nor prohibited by it to the States, are reserved to the States respectively, or to the people.

ANTIFEDERALIST ARGUMENTS

Patrick Henry
Speech
June 5, 1788
(Excerpts)

DISCUSSION QUESTIONS

1. How does Patrick Henry rank liberty, trade, and power as proper ends of government?
2. What does Henry have to say about the strength of the Confederation in protecting the nation?
3. Does Henry believe the nation to be in danger? Explain.
4. What does Henry relate as matters of concern for the common man and the constitution?

Mr. Chairman—I am much obliged to the very worthy Gentleman [Henry Lee] for his encomium. I wish I was possessed of talents, or possessed of any thing, that might enable me to elucidate this great subject. I am not free from suspicion: I am apt to entertain doubts: I rose yesterday to ask a question, which arose in my own mind. When I asked the question, I thought the meaning of my interrogation was obvious: The fate of this question and America may depend on this: Have they said, we the States? Have they made a proposal of a compact between States? If they had, this would be a confederation: It is otherwise most clearly a consolidated government. The question turns, Sir, on that poor little thing—the expression, *We, the people*, instead of the States of America. I need not take much pains to show, that the principles of this system, are extremely pernicious, impolitic, and dangerous. Is this a Monarchy, like England—a compact between Prince and people; with checks on the former, to secure the liberty of the latter? Is this a Confederacy, like Holland—an association of a number of independent States, each of which retain its individual sovereignty? It is not a democracy, wherein the people retain all their rights securely. Had these principles been adhered to, we should not have been brought to this alarming transition, from a Confederacy to a consolidated Government. We have no detail of those great considerations which, in my opinion, ought to have abounded before we should recur to a government of this kind. Here is a revolution as radical as that which separated us from Great Britain. It is as radical, if in this transition our rights and privileges are endangered, and the sovereignty of the States be relinquished: And cannot we plainly see, that this is actually the case? The rights of conscience, trial by jury, liberty of the press, all your immunities and franchises, all pretensions to human rights and privileges, are rendered insecure, if not lost, by this change so loudly talked of by some, and inconsiderately by others. Is this same relinquishment of rights worthy of freemen? Is it worthy of that manly fortitude that ought to characterize republicans: It is said eight States have adopted this plan. I declare that if twelve States and an half had adopted it, I would with manly firmness, and in spite of an erring world, reject it. You are not to inquire how your trade may be increased, nor how you are to become a great and powerful people, but how your liberties can be secured; for liberty ought to be the direct end of your Government. Having premised these things, I shall, with the aid of my judgment and information, which I confess are not extensive, go into the discussion of this system more minutely. Is it necessary for your liberty, that you should abandon those great rights by the adoption of this system? Is the relinquishment of the trial by jury, and the liberty of the press, necessary for your liberty? Will the abandonment of your most sacred rights tend to the security of your liberty? Liberty the greatest of all earthly blessings—give us that precious jewel, and you may take every thing else: But I am fearful I have lived long enough to become an old fashioned fellow: Perhaps an invincible attachment to the dearest rights of man, may, in these refined enlightened days, be deemed *old fashioned:* If so, I am contended to be so: I say, the time has been, when every pore of my heart beat for American liberty, and which, I believe, had a counterpart in the breast of every true American:

. . . Guard with jealous attention the public liberty. Suspect every one who approaches that jewel. Unfortunately, nothing will preserve it, but downright force: Whenever you give up that force, you are inevitably ruined. I am answered by Gentlemen, that though I might speak of terrors, yet the fact was, that we were surrounded by none of the dangers I apprehended. I conceive this new Government to be one of those dangers: It has produced those horrors, which distress many of our best citizens. We are come hither to preserve the poor Commonwealth of Virginia, if it can be possibly done: Something must be done to preserve your liberty and mine: The Confederation; this same despised Government, merits, in my opinion, the highest encomium: It carried us through a long and dangerous war: It rendered us victorious in that bloody conflict with a powerful nation: It has secured us a territory greater than any European Monarch possesses: And shall a Government which has been thus strong and vigorous, be accused of imbecility and abandoned for want of energy? Consider what you are about to do before you part with this Government. Take longer time in reckoning things: Revolutions like this have happened in almost every country in Europe: Similar examples are to be found in ancient Greece and ancient Rome: Instances of the people loosing their liberty by their own carelessness and the ambition of a few. We are cautioned by the Honorable Gentleman who presides, against faction and turbulence: I acknowledge that licentiousness is dangerous, and that it ought to be provided against: I acknowledge also the new form of Government may effectually prevent it: Yet, there is another thing it will as effectually do: it will oppress and ruin the people. There are sufficient guards placed against sedition and licentiousness:

. . . And those nations who have gone in search of grandeur, power and splendor, have also fallen a sacrifice, and been the victims of their own folly: While they acquired those visionary blessings, they lost their freedom. My great objection to this Government is, that it does not leave us the means of defending our rights; or, of waging war against tyrants: It is urged by some Gentlemen, that this new plan will bring us an acquisition of strength, an army, and the militia of the States: This is an idea extremely ridiculous: Gentlemen cannot be in earnest. This acquisition will trample on your fallen liberty: Let my beloved Americans guard against that fatal lethargy that has pervaded the universe: Have we the means of resisting disciplined armies, when our only defence, the militia is put into the hands of Congress? The Honorable Gentleman said, that great danger would ensue if the Convention rose without adopting this system: I ask, where is that danger? I see none: Other Gentlemen have told us within these walls, that the Union is gone—or, that the Union will be gone: Is not this trifling with the judgment of their fellow-citizens? Till they tell us the ground of their fears, I will consider them as imaginary: I rose to make enquiry where those dangers were; they could make no answer: I believe I never shall have that answer: Is there a disposition in the people of this country to revolt against the dominion of laws? Has there been a single tumult in Virginia? Have not the people of Virginia, when labouring under the severest pressure of accumulated distresses, manifested the most cordial acquiescence in the execution of the laws? What could be more awful than their unamious acquiescence under general distresses? Is there any revolution in Virginia? Whither is the spirit of America gone? Whither is the genius of America fled? It was but yesterday, when our enemies marched in triumph through our country: Yet the people of this country could not be appalled by their pompous armaments: They stopped their career, and victoriously captured them: Where is the peril now compared to that? Some minds are agitated by foreign alarms: Happily for us, there is no real danger from Europe: that country is engaged in more arduous business; from that quarter there is no cause of fear: You may sleep in safety forever for them. Where is the danger? If, Sir, there was any, I would recur to the American spirit to defend us;—that spirit which has enabled us to surmount the greatest difficulties: To that illustrious spirit I address my most fervent prayer, to prevent our adopting a system destructive to liberty. Let not Gentlemen be told, that it is not safe to reject this Government. Wherefore is it not safe? We are told there are dangers; but those dangers are ideal; they cannot be demonstrated:

. . . When the American spirit was in its youth, the language of America was different: Liberty, Sir, was then the primary object. We are descended from a people whose Government was founded on liberty: Our glorious forefathers of Great Britain, made liberty the foundation of every thing. That country is become a great, mighty, and splendid nation; not because their Government is strong and energetic; but, Sir, because liberty is its direct end and foundation: We drew the spirit of liberty from our British ancestors; by that spirit we have triumphed over every difficulty: But now, Sir, the American spirit, assisted by the ropes and chains of consolidation, is about to convert this country to a powerful and mighty empire: If you make the citizens of this country agree to become the subjects of one great consolidated empire of America, your Government will not have sufficent energy to keep them together: Such a Government is incompatible with the genius of republicanism: There will be no checks, no real balances, in this Government: What can avail your specious imaginary balances, your rope-dancing, chain-rattling, ridiculous ideal checks and contrivances? But, Sir, we are not feared by foreigners: we do not make nations tremble: Would this, Sir, constitute happiness, or secure liberty? I trust, Sir, our political hemisphere will ever direct their operations to the security of those objects. Consider our situation, Sir: Go to the poor man, ask him what he does; he will inform you, that he enjoys the fruits of his labour, under his own fig-tree, with his wife and children around him, in peace and security. Go to every other member of the society, you will find the same tranquil ease and content; you will find no alarms or disturbances: Why then tell us of dangers to terrify us into an adoption of this new Government? and yet who knows the dangers that this new system may produce; they are out of the sight of the common people: They cannot foresee latent consequences: I dread the operation of it on the middling and lower class of people: It is for them I fear the adoption of this system. I fear I tire the patience of the Committee, but I beg to be indulged with a few more observations: When I thus profess myself an advocate for the liberty of the people, I shall be told, I am a designing man, that I am to be a great man, that I am to be a demagogue; and many similar illiberal insinuations will be thrown out; but, Sir, conscious rectitude, out-weighs these things with me: I see great jeopardy in this new Government. I see none from our present one: I hope some Gentleman or other will bring forth, in full array, those dangers, if there be any, that we may see and touch them.

Patrick Henry
Speech
June 7, 1788
(Excerpts)

DISCUSSION QUESTIONS

1. Why does Patrick Henry believe the claims and fears of advocates of the new Constitution to be groundless?
2. What threats to his state (Virginia) does Henry anticipate under the new Constitution?

I have thought, and still think, that a full investigation of the actual situation of America, ought to precede any decision on this great and important question. That Government is no more than a choice among evils, is acknowledged by the most intelligent among mankind, and has been a standing maxim for ages. If it be demonstrated that the adoption of the new plan is a little or a trifling evil, then, Sir, I acknowledge that adoption ought to follow: But, Sir, if this be a truth that its adoption may entail misery on the free people of this country, I then insist, that rejection ought to follow. Gentlemen strongly urge its adoption will be a mighty benefit to us: But, Sir, I am made of such incredulous materials that assertions and declarations, do not satisfy me. I must be convinced, Sir. I shall retain my infidelity on that subject, till I see our liberties secured in a manner perfectly satisfactory to my understanding. . . .

You are told [by Governor Randolph] there is no peace, although you fondly flatter yourselves that all is peace—No peace—a general cry and alarm in the country—Commerce, riches, and wealth vanished—Citizens going to seek comforts in other parts of the world—Laws insulted—Many instances of tyrannical legislation. These things, Sir, are new to me. He has made the discovery—As to the administration of justice, I believe that failures in commerce, &c. cannot be attributed to it. My age enables me to recollect its progress under the old Government. I can justify it by saying, that it continues in the same manner in this State, as it did under former Government. As to other parts of the Continent, I refer that to other Gentlemen. As to the ability of those who administer it, I believe they would not suffer by a comparison with those who administered it under the royal authority. Where is the cause of complaint if the wealthy go away? Is this added to the other circumstances, of such enormity, and does it bring such danger over this Commonwealth as to warrant so important, and so awful a change in so precipitate a manner? As to insults offered to the laws, I know of none. In this respect I believe this Commonwealth would not suffer by a comparison with the former Government. The laws are as well executed, and as patiently acquiesced in, as they were under the royal administration. Compare the situation of the country—Compare that of our citizens to what they were then, and decide whether persons and property are not as safe and secure as they were at that time. Is there a man in this Commonwealth, whose person can be insulted with impunity? Cannot redress be had here for personal insults or injuries, as well as in any part of the world—as well as in those countries where Aristocrats and Monarchs triumph and reign? Is not the protection of property in full operation here? The contrary cannot with truth be charged on this Commonwealth. Those severe charges which are exhibited against it, appear to me totally groundless. On a fair investigation, we shall be found to be surrounded by no real dangers. We have the animating fortitude and persevering alacrity of republican men, to carry us through misfortunes and calamities. 'Tis the fortune of a republic to be able to withstand the stormy ocean of human vicissitudes. I know of no danger awaiting us. Public and private security are to be found here in the highest degree. Sir, it is the fortune of a free people, not to be intimidated by imaginary dangers. Fear is the passion of slaves. Our political and natural hemisphere are now equally tranquil. Let us recollect the awful magnitude of the subject of our deliberation. Let us consider the latent consequences of an erroneous decision—and let not our minds be led away by unfair misrepresentations and uncandid suggestions. There have been many instances of uncommon lenity and temperance used in the exercise of power in this Commonwealth. I could call your recollection to many that happened during the war and since—But every Gentleman here must be apprized of them.

The Honorable member has given you an elaborate account of what he judges tyrannical legislation, and an *ex post facto law* (in the case of Josiah Philips.) He has misrepresented the facts. That man was not executed by a tyrannical stroke of power. He was a fugitive murderer and an out-law—a man who commanded an infamous banditti, at a time when the war was at the most perilous stage. He committed the most cruel and shocking barbarities. He was an enemy to the human name.—Those who declare war against the human race, may be struck out of existence as soon as they are apprehended. He was not executed according to those beautiful legal ceremonies which are pointed out by the laws, in criminal cases. The enormity of his crimes did not entitle him to it. I am truly a friend to legal forms and methods; but, Sir, the occasion warranted the measure. A pirate, an outlaw, or a common enemy to all mankind, may be put to death at any time. It is justified by the laws of nature and nations. The Honorable member tells us then, that there are burnings and discontents in the hearts of our citizens in general, and that they are dissatisfied with their Government. I have no doubt the Honorable member believes this to be the case, because he says so. But I have the comfortable assurance, that it is a certain fact, *that it is not so.* The middle and lower ranks of people have not those illumined ideas, which the well-born are so happily possessed of—They cannot so readily perceive latent objects. The microscopic eyes of modern States-men can see abundance of defects in old systems; and their illumined imaginations discover the necessity of change.

. . . I have said that I thought this a Consolidated Government: I will now prove it. Will the great rights of the people be secured by this Government? Suppose it should prove oppressive, how can it be altered? Our Bill of Rights declares,

"That a majority of the community hath an *undubitable, unalienable,* and *indefeasible right* to reform, alter, or abolish it, in such manner as shall be judged most conducive to the public weal." I have just proved that one tenth, or less, of the people of America, a most despicable minority may prevent this reform or alteration. Suppose the people of Virginia should wish to alter their Government, can a majority of them do it? No, because they are connected with other men; or, in other words, consolidated with other States: When the people of Virginia at a future day shall wish to alter their Government, though they should be unanimous in this desire, yet they may be prevented therefrom by a despicable minority at the extremity of the United States: The founders of your own Constitution made your Government changeable: But the power of changing it is gone from you! Whither is it gone? It is placed in the same hands that hold the rights of twelve other States; and those who hold those rights, have right and power to keep them: It is not the particular Government of Virginia: One of the leading features of that Government is, that a majority can alter it, when necessary for the public good. This Government is not a Virginian but an American Government. Is it not therefore a Consolidated Government? The sixth clause of your Bill of Rights tells you, "That elections of members to serve as Representatives of the people in Assembly, ought to be free, and that all men having sufficient evidence of permanent common interest with, and attachment to the community, have the right of suffrage, and *cannot* be *taxed* or *deprived* of *their property* for public uses, without their own consent, or that of their Representatives so elected, nor bound by any law to which they have not in like manner assented for the public good." But what does this Constitution say? The clause under consideration gives an unlimited and unbounded power of taxation: Suppose every delegate from Virginia opposes a law laying a tax, what will it avail? They are opposed by a majority: Eleven members can destroy their efforts: Those feeble ten cannot prevent the passing the most oppressive tax law. So that in direct opposition to the spirit and express language of your Declaration of Rights, you are taxed not by your own consent, but by people who have no connection with you. The next clause of the Bill of Rights tells you, "That all power of suspending law, or the execution of laws, by any authority without the consent of the Representatives of the people, is injurious to their rights, and ought not to be exercised." This tells us that there can be no suspension of Government, or laws without our own consent: Yet this Constitution can counteract and suspend any of our laws, that contravene its oppressive operation; for they have the power of direct taxation; which suspends our Bill of Rights; and it is expressly provided, that they can make all laws necessary for carrying their powers into execution; and it is declared paramount to the laws and constitutions of the States. Consider how the only remaining defence we have left is destroyed in this manner: Besides the expences of maintaining the Senate and other House in as much splendor as they please, there is to be a great and mighty President, with very extensive powers; the powers of a King: He is to be supported in extravagant magnificence: So that the whole of our property may be taken by this American Government, by laying what taxes they please, giving themselves what salaries they please, and suspending our laws at their pleasure: I might be thought too inquisitive, but I believe I should take up but very little of your time in enumerating the little power that is left to the Government of Virginia; for this power is reduced to little or nothing: Their garrisons, magazines, arsenals, and forts, which will be situated in the strongest places within the States: Their ten miles square, with all the fine ornaments of human life, added to their powers, and taken from the States, will reduce the power of the latter to nothing. The voice of tradition, I trust, will inform posterity of our struggles for freedom: If our descendants be worthy the name of Americans, they will preserve and hand down to their latest posterity, the transactions of the present times; and though, I confess, my exclamations are not worthy the hearing, they will see that I have done my utmost to preserve their liberty: For I never will give up the power of direct taxation, but for a scourge: I am willing to give it conditionally; that is, after non-compliance with requisitions: I will do more, Sir, and what I hope will convince the most sceptical man, that I am a lover of the American Union, that in case Virginia shall not make punctual payment, the controul of our custom houses, and the whole regulation of trade, shall be given to Congress, and that Virginia shall depend on Congress even for passports, till Virginia shall have paid the last farthing; and furnished the last soldier: Nay, Sir, there is another alternative to which I would consent: Even that they should strike us out of the Union, and take away from us all federal privileges till we comply with federal requisitions; but let it depend upon our own pleasure to pay our money in the most easy manner for our people. Were all the States, more terrible than the mother country, to join against us, I hope Virginia could defend herself; but, Sir, the dissolution of the Union is most abhorent to my mind: The first thing I have at heart is American *liberty*; the second thing is American Union; and I hope the people of Virginia will endeavor to preserve that Union: The increasing population of the southern States, is far greater than that of New-England: Consequently, in a short time, they will be far more numerous than the people of that country: Consider this, and you will find this State more particularly interested to support American liberty, and not bind our posterity by an improvident relinquishment of our rights. I would give the best security for a punctual compliance with requisitions; but I beseech Gentlemen, at all hazards, not to give up this unlimited power of taxation: The Honorable Gentleman has told us these powers given to Congress, are accompanied by a Judiciary which will connect all: On examination you will find this very Judiciary oppressively constructed; your jury trial destroyed, and the Judges dependent on Congress. In this scheme of energetic Government, the people will find two sets of tax-gatherers—the State and the Federal Sheriffs. This it seems to me will produce such dreadful oppression, as the people cannot possibly bear: The Federal Sheriff may commit what oppression, make what distresses he pleases, and ruin you with impunity: For how are you to tie his hands?

FEDERALIST ARGUMENTS

Alexander Hamilton
Federalist *Paper 15*
(Excerpt)

DISCUSSION QUESTIONS

1. What are the drawbacks of a confederacy?
2. Who are the "proper objects" of government?
3. What means are available to require the obedience to the laws?
4. What problems exist in the exercise of power by a confederacy?

The great and radical vice in the construction of the existing Confederation, is in the principle of *legislation* for *States* or *Governments*, in their *corporate* or *collective capacities*, and as contradistinguished from the *individuals* of whom they consist. Though this principle does not run through all the powers delegated to the Union: yet it pervades and governs those on which the efficacy of the rest depends. Except as to the rule of apportionment, the United States have an infinite discretion to make requisitions for men and money; but they have no authority to raise either, by regulations extending to the individual citizens of America. The consequence of this is, that though in theory, their resolutions concerning those objects, are laws, constitutionally binding on the members of the Union, yet, in practice, they are mere recommendations, which the States observe or disregard at their option.

It is a singular instance of the capriciousness of the human mind, that, after all the admonitions we have had from experience on this head, there should still be found men, who object to the new Constitution, for deviating from a principle which has been found the bane of the old; and which is, in itself, evidently incompatible with the idea of a *government*; a principle in short, which, if it is to be executed at all, must substitute the violent and sanguinary agency of the sword, to the mild influence of the magistracy.

There is nothing absurd or impracticable, in the idea of a league or alliance between independent nations, for certain defined purposes precisely stated in a treaty; regulating all the details of time, place, circumstance, and quantity; leaving nothing to future discretion; and depending for its execution on the good faith of the parties. Compacts of this kind exist among all civilized nations, subject to the usual vicissitudes of peace and war; of observance and non-observance, as the interests or passions of the contracting Powers dictate. In the early part of the present century, there was an epidemical rage in Europe for this species of compacts; from which the politicians of the times fondly hoped for benefits which were never realized. With a view to establishing the equilibrium of power, and the peace of that part of the world, all the resources of negotiation were exhausted, and triple and quadruple alliances were formed; but they were scarcely formed before they were broken, giving an instructive, but afflicting lesson to mankind, how little dependence is to be placed on treaties which have no other sanction than the obligations of good faith; and which oppose general considerations of peace and justice, to the impulse of any immediate interest or passion.

If the particular States in this country are disposed to stand in a similar relation to each other, and to drop the project of a general *discretionary superintendence,* the scheme would indeed be pernicious, and would entail upon us all the mischiefs which have been enumerated under the first head; but it would have the merit of being at least consistent and practicable. Abandoning all views towards a Confederate Government, this would bring us to a simple alliance, offensive and defensive; and would place us in a situation to be alternately friends and enemies of each other, as our mutual jealousies and rivalships, nourished by the intrigues of foreign nations, should prescribe to us.

But if we are unwilling to be placed in this perilous situation; if we still adhere to the design of a National Government, or, which is the same thing, of a superintending power, under the direction of a common council, we must resolve to incorporate into our plan those ingredients, which may be considered as forming the characteristic difference between a league and a government; we must extend the authority of the Union to the persons of the citizens—the only proper objects of government.

Government implies the power of making laws.—It is essential to the idea of a law, that it be attended with a sanction; or, in other words, a penalty or punishment for disobedience. If there be no penalty annexed to disobedience, the resolutions or commands which pretend to be laws, will in fact amount to nothing more than advice or recommendation.—This penalty, whatever it may be, can only be inflicted in two ways; by the agency of the courts and ministers of justice, or by military force; by the *coercion* of the magistracy, or by the *coercion* of arms. The first kind can evidently apply only to men; the last kind must of necessity be employed against bodies politic, or communities or States. It is evident, that there is no process of a court by which their observance of the laws can, in the last resort, be enforced. Sentences may be denounced against them for violations of their duty; but these sentences can only be carried into execution by the sword. In an association, where the general authority is confined to the collective bodies of the communities that compose it, every breach of the laws must involve a state of war, and military execution must become the only instrument of civil obedience. Such a state of things can certainly not deserve the name of Government, nor would any prudent man choose to commit his happiness to it.

There was a time when we were told that breaches by the States, of the regulations of the Federal authority, were not to be expected, that a sense of common interest would preside over the conduct of the respective members, and would beget a full compliance with all the constitutional requisitions of the Union. This language, at the present day, would appear as wild as a great part of what we now hear from the same quarter will be thought, when we shall have received further lessons from that best oracle of wisdom, experience. It at all times betrayed an ignorance of the true springs by which human conduct is actuated, and belied the original inducements to the establishment of civil power. Why has government been instituted at all? Because the passions of men will not conform to the dictates of reason and justice, without constraint. Has it been found that bodies of men act with more rectitude or greater disinterestedness than individuals? The contrary of this has been inferred by all accurate observers of the conduct of mankind; and the inference is founded on obvious reasons. Regard to reputation has a less active influence, when the infamy of a bad action is to be divided among a number, than when it is to fall singly upon one. A spirit of faction, which is apt to mingle its poison in the deliberations of all bodies of men, will often hurry the persons, of whom they are composed, into improprieties and excesses, for which they would blush in a private capacity.

In addition to all this, there is, in the nature of sovereign power, an impatience of control, which disposes those who are invested with the exercise of it, to look with an evil eye upon all external attempts to restrain or direct its operations. From this spirit it happens, that in every political association which is formed upon the principle of uniting in a common interest a number of lesser sovereignties, there will be found a kind of eccentric tendency in the subordinate or inferior orbs, by the operation of which, there will be a perpetual effort in each, to fly off from the common centre. This tendency is not difficult to be accounted for. It has its origin in the love of power. Power, controlled or abridged, is almost always the rival and enemy of that power by which it is controlled or abridged. This simple proposition will teach us how little reason there is to expect, that the persons entrusted with the administration of the affairs of the particular members of a Confederacy, will at all times be ready, with perfect good-humor, and an unbiased regard to the public weal, to execute the resolutions or decrees of the general authority. The reverse of this results from the constitution of man.

If therefore the measures of the Confederacy cannot be executed, without the intervention of the particular administrations, there will be little prospect of their being executed at all. The rulers of the respective members, whether they have a constitutional right to do it or not, will undertake to judge of the propriety of the measures themselves. They will consider the conformity of the thing proposed or required to their immediate interests or aims; the momentary conveniences or inconveniences that would attend its adoption. All this will be done; and in a spirit of interested and suspicious scrutiny, without that knowledge of national circumstances and reasons of state, which is essential to a right judgment, and with that strong predilection in favor of local objects, which can hardly fail to mislead the decision. The same process must be repeated in every member of which the body is constituted; and the execution of the plans, framed by the councils of the whole, will always fluctuate on the discretion of the ill informed and prejudiced opinion of every part. Those who have been conversant in the proceedings of popular assemblies; who have seen how difficult it often is, when there is no exterior pressure of circumstances to bring them to harmonious resolutions on important points, will readily conceive how impossible it must be to induce a number of such assemblies, deliberating at a distance from each other, at different times, and under different impressions, long to co-operate in the same views and pursuits.

In our case, the concurrence of thirteen distinct sovereign wills is requisite under the Confederation, to the complete execution of every important measure, that proceeds from the Union. It has happened, as was to have been foreseen. The measures of the Union have not been executed; the delinquencies of the States have, step by step, matured themselves to an extreme, which has at length arrested all the wheels of the National Government, and brought them to an awful stand. Congress at this time scarcely possess the means of keeping up the forms of administration till, the States can have time to agree upon a more substantial substitute for the present shadow of a Federal Government. Things did not come to this desperate extremity at once. The causes which have been specified, produced at first only unequal and disproportionate degrees of compliance with the requisitions of the Union. The greater deficiencies of some States furnished the pretext of example, and the temptation of interest to the complying, or at least delinquent States. Why should we do more in proportion than those who are embarked with us in the same political voyage? Why should we consent to bear more than our proper share of the common burden? These were suggestions which human selfishness could not withstand, and which even speculative men, who looked forward to remote consequences, could not without hesitation combat. Each State, yielding to the persuasive voice of immediate interest or convenience, has successively withdrawn its support, till the frail and tottering edifice seems ready to fall upon our heads, and to crush us beneath its ruins.

PUBLIUS

John Jay
Federalist *Paper 3*
(Excerpt)

DISCUSSION QUESTIONS

1. How is the safety of the people promoted under the new Constitution?
2. What are the "just causes of war"?
3. Why will the "best men in the country" be available for positions in the national government?

It is not a new observation, that the people of any country (if, like the Americans, intelligent and well informed), seldom adopt and steadily persevere for many years, in any erroneous opinion respecting their interests. That consideration naturally tends to create great respect for the high opinion which the people of America have so long and uniformly entertained of the importance of their continuing firmly united under one Federal Government, vested with sufficient powers for all general and national purposes.

The more attentively I consider and investigate the reasons which appear to have given birth to this opinion, the more I become convinced that they are cogent and conclusive.

Among the many objects to which a wise and free people find it necessary to direct their attention, that of providing for their *safety* seems to be the first. The *safety* of the people doubtless has relation to a great variety of circumstances and considerations, and consequently affords great latitude to those who wish to define it precisely and comprehensively.

At present I mean only to consider it as it respects security for the preservation of peace and tranquillity, as well against dangers from *foreign arms and influence*, as against dangers arising from domestic causes. As the former of these comes first in order, it is proper it should be first discussed. Let us therefore proceed to examine whether the people are not right in their opinion, that a cordial union under an efficient National Government, affords them the best security that can be devised against *hostilities* from abroad.

The number of wars which have happened, or may happen in the world, will always be found to be in proportion to the number and weight of the causes, whether *real* or *pretended*, which *provoke* or *invite* them. If this remark be just, it becomes useful to inquire, whether so many just causes of war are likely to be given by *united* America, as by *disunited* America; for if it should turn out that united America will probably give the fewest, then it will follow, that in this respect, the Union tends most to preserve the people in a state of peace with other nations.

The *just* causes of war, for the most part, arise either from violations of treaties, or from direct violence. America has already formed treaties with no less than six foreign nations, and all of them, except Prussia, are maritime, and therefore able to annoy and injure us: she has also extensive commerce with Portugal, Spain, and Britain; and with respect to the two latter, has the additional circumstance of neighborhood to attend to.

It is of high importance to the peace of America, that she observe the law of nations towards all these Powers; and to me it appears evident, that this will be more perfectly and punctually done by one National Government, than it could be either by thirteen separate States, or by three or four distinct confederacies. For this opinion various reasons may be assigned.

When once an efficient National Government is established, the best men in the country will not only consent to serve, but will also generally be appointed to manage it; for although town, or country, or other contracted influence, may place men in State Assemblies, or Senates, or Courts of Justice, or Executive Departments; yet more general and extensive reputation for talents and other qualifications, will be necessary to recommend men to offices under the National Government, especially as it will have the widest field for choice, and never experience that want of proper persons, which is not uncommon in some of the States. Hence it will result, that the administration, the political councils, and the judicial decisions of the National Government will be more wise, systematical, and judicious, than those of individual States, and consequently more satisfactory with respect to the other nations, as well as more *safe* with respect to ourselves.

Under the National Government, treaties and articles of treaties, as well as the law of nations, will always be expounded in one sense, and executed in the same manner: whereas adjudications on the same points and questions, in thirteen States, or in three or four confederacies, will not always accord, or be consistent;

and that as well from the variety of independent courts and judges, appointed by different and independent Governments, as from the different local laws and interests which may affect and influence them. The wisdom of the Convention in committing such questions to the jurisdiction and judgment of courts appointed by, and responsible only to one National Government, cannot be too much commended.

The prospect of present loss or advantage, may often tempt the governing party in one or two States to swerve from good faith and justice; but those temptations not reaching the other States, and consequently having little or no influence on the National Government, the temptations will be fruitless, and good faith and justice be preserved. The case of the Treaty of Peace with Britain, adds great weight to this reasoning.

If even the governing party in a State should be disposed to resist such temptations, yet as such temptations may, and commonly do, result from circumstances peculiar to the States, and may affect a great number of the inhabitants, the governing party may not always be able, if willing, to prevent the injustice meditated, or to punish the aggressors. But the National Government, not being affected by those local circumstances, will neither be induced to commit the wrong themselves, nor want power or inclination to prevent, or punish its commission by others.

John Jay
Federalist *Paper 4*
(Excerpt)

DISCUSSION QUESTIONS

1. What are the "pretended causes of war"?
2. What examples does Hamilton give of potential "jealousies" among nations?
3. What advantages does "one good Government" have over separate governments?

My last paper assigned several reasons why the safety of the people would be best secured by union against the danger it may be exposed to by *just* causes of war given to other nations; and those reasons show that such causes would not only be more rarely given, but would also be more easily accommodated by a National Government, than either by the State Governments, or the proposed Confederacies.

But the safety of the people of America against dangers from foreign force, depends not only on their forbearing to give just causes of war to other nations, but also on their placing and continuing themselves in such a situation as not to invite hostility or insult: for it need not be observed, that there are pretended as well as just causes of war.

It is too true, however disgraceful it may be to human nature, that nations in general will make war whenever they have a prospect of getting anything by it: nay, that absolute monarchs will often make war when their nations are to get nothing by it; but for purposes and objects merely personal, such as a thirst for military glory, revenge for personal affronts, ambition, or private compacts to aggrandize or support their particular families, or partisans. These, and a variety of motives, which affect only the mind of the sovereign, often lead him to engage in wars not sanctioned by justice, or the voice and interests of his people. But, independent of these inducements to war, which are most prevalent in absolute monarchies, but which well deserve our attention, there are others which affect nations, as often as kings; and some of them will, on examination, be found to grow out of our relative situation and circumstances.

With France and with Britain we are rivals in the fisheries, and can supply their markets cheaper than they can themselves, notwithstanding any efforts to prevent it by bounties on their own, or duties on foreign fish.

With them, and with most other European nations, we are rivals in navigation, and the carrying trade: and we shall deceive ourselves if we suppose that any of them will rejoice to see these flourish in our hands; for as our carrying trade cannot increase, without in some degree diminishing theirs, it is more their interest, and will be more their policy, to restrain than to promote it.

In the trade to China and India, we interfere with more than one nation, inasmuch as it enables us to partake in advantages which they had in a manner monopolized, and as we thereby supply ourselves with commodities which we used to purchase from them.

The extension of our own commerce in our own vessels, cannot give pleasure to any nations who possess territories on or near this continent, because the cheapness and excellence of our productions, added to the circumstance of vicinity, and the enterprise and address of our merchants and navigators, will give us a greater share in the advantages which those territories afford, than consists with the wishes or policy of their respective sovereigns.

Spain thinks it convenient to shut the Mississippi against us on the one side, and Britain excludes us from the St. Lawrence on the other; nor will either of them permit the other waters, which are between them and us, to become the means of mutual intercourse and traffic.

From these, and like considerations, which might, if consistent with prudence, be more amplified and detailed, it is easy to see that jealousies and uneasinesses may gradually slide into the minds and cabinets of other nations; and that we are not to expect they should regard our advancement in union, in power and consequence, by land and by sea, with an eye of indifference and composure.

The people of America are aware that inducements to war may arise out of these circumstances, as well as from others not so obvious at present; and that whenever such inducements may find fit time and opportunity for operation, pretences to color and justify them will not be wanting. Wisely therefore do they consider union and a good National Government, as necessary to put and keep them in such a situation, as, instead of inviting war, will tend to repress and discourage it. That situation consists in the best possible state of defence, and necessarily depends on the Government, the arms, and the resources of the country.

As the safety of the whole is the interest of the whole, and cannot be provided for without Government, either one or more, or many, let us inquire whether one good Government is not, relative to the object in question, more competent than any other given number whatever.

One Government can collect and avail itself of the talents and experience of the ablest men, in whatever part of the Union they may be found. It can move on uniform principles of policy. It can harmonize, assimilate, and protect the several parts and members, and extend the benefit of its foresight and precautions to each. In the formation of treaties it will regard the interest of the whole, and the particular interest of the parts as connected with that of the whole. It can apply the resources and power of the whole to the defence of any particular part, and that more easily and expeditiously than State Governments, or separate Confederacies, can possibly do, for want of concert and unity of system. It can place the militia under one plan of discipline, and by putting their officers in a proper line of subordination to the Chief Magistrate, will in a manner consolidate them into one corps, and thereby render them more efficient than if divided into thirteen, or into three or four distinct independent bodies.

Alexander Hamilton
Federalist *Paper 6*
(Excerpts)

DISCUSSION QUESTIONS

1. What are the causes of hostility among nations that might be applied to the states?
2. What examples does Hamilton give of actions by men endangering the people?
3. How does Hamilton answer the argument that commerce among nations and states tends to reduce the danger of war?

The three last numbers of this work have been dedicated to an enumeration of the dangers to which we should be exposed, in a state of disunion, from the arms and arts of foreign nations. I shall now proceed to delineate dangers of a different, and, perhaps, still more alarming kind; those which will in all probability flow from dissensions between the States themselves, and from domestic factions and convulsions. These have been already in some instances slightly anticipated; but they deserve a more particular and more full investigation.

If these States should either be wholly disunited, or only united in partial confederacies, a man must be far gone in Utopian speculations, who can seriously doubt, that the subdivisions into which they might be thrown, would have frequent and violent contests with each other. To presume a want of motives for such contests, as an argument against their existence, would be to forget that men are ambitious, vindictive, and rapacious. To look for a continuation of harmony between a number of independent unconnected sovereignties, situated in the same neighborhood, would be to disregard the uniform course of human events, and to set at defiance the accumulated experience of ages.

The causes of hostility among nations are innumerable. There are some which have a general and almost constant operation upon the collective bodies of society. Of this description are the love of power, or the desire of pre-eminence and dominion—the jealousy of power, or the desire of equality and safety. There are others which have a more circumscribed, though an equally operative influence, within their spheres; such as the rivalships and competitions of commerce between commercial nations. And there are others, not less numerous than either of the former, which take their origin entirely in private passions; in the attachments, enmities, interests, hopes, and fears, of leading individuals in the communities of which they are members. Men of this class, whether the favorites of a king or of a people, have in too many instances abused the confidence they possessed; and assuming the pretext of some public motive, have not scrupled to sacrifice the national tranquillity to personal advantage, or personal gratification.

The celebrated Pericles, in compliance with the resentments of a prostitute,[1] at the expense of much of the blood and treasure of his countrymen, attacked, vanquished, and destroyed the city of the *Samnians*. The same man, stimulated by private pique against the *Magarensians*, another nation of Greece, or to avoid a prosecution with which he was threatened as an accomplice in a supposed theft of the statuary *Phidias*, or to get rid of the accusations prepared to be brought against him for dissipatings the funds of the state in the purchase of popularity, or from a combination of all these causes, was the primitive author of that famous and fatal war, distinguished in the Grecian annals by the name of the Peloponnesian War; which, after various vicissitudes, intermissions, and renewals, terminated in the ruin of the Athenian Common wealth.

The ambitious Cardinal, who was Prime Minister to Henry VIII., permitting his vanity to aspire to the triple-crown, entertained hopes of succeeding in the acquisition of that splendid prize by the influence of the Emperor Charles V. To secure the favor and interest of this enterprising and powerful monarch, he precipitated England into a war with France, contrary to the plainest dictates of policy, and at the hazard of the safety and independence, as well of the kingdom over which he presided by his counsels, as of Europe in general. For if there ever was a sovereign who bid fair to realize the project of universal monarchy, it was the Emperor Charles V., of whose intrigues Wolsey was at once the instrument and the dupe. . . .

. . . To multiply examples of the agency of personal considerations in the production of great national events, either foreign or domestic, according to their direction, would be an unnecessary waste of time. Those who have but a superficial acquaintance with the sources from which they are to be drawn, will themselves recollect a variety of instances; and those who have a tolerable knowledge of human nature, will not stand in need of such lights, to form their opinion either of the reality or extent of that agency. Perhaps, however, a reference, tending to illustrate the general principle, may with propriety be made to a case which has lately happened among ourselves. If SHAYS had not been a *desperate debtor*, it is much to be doubted whether Massachusetts would have been plunged into a civil war.

But, notwithstanding the concurring testimony of experience in this particu-

[1]Aspasia, *vide* Plutarch's *Life of Pericles*.

lar, there are still to be found visionary or designing men, who stand ready to advocate the paradox of perpetual peace between the States, though dismembered and alienated from each other. The genius of republics, say they, is pacific; the spirit of commerce has a tendency to soften the manners of men, and to extinguish those inflammable humors which have so often kindled into wars. Commercial republics, like ours, will never be disposed to waste themselves in ruinous contentions with each other. They will be governed by mutual interest, and will cultivate a spirit of mutual amity and concord.

We may ask these projectors in politics, whether it is not the true interest of all nations to cultivate the same benevolent and philosophic spirit? If this be their true interest, have they in fact pursued it? Has it not, on the contrary, invariably been found, that momentary passions, and immediate interests, have a more active and imperious control over human conduct, than general or remote considerations of policy, utility, or justice? Have republics in practice been less addicted to war than monarchies? Are not the former administered by men as well as the latter? Are there not aversions, predilections, rivalships, and desires of unjust acquisitions, that affect nations as well as kings? Are not popular assemblies frequently subject to the impulses of rage, resentment, jealousy, avarice, and of other irregular and violent propensities? Is it not well known, that their determinations are often governed by a few individuals in whom they place confidence, and that they are of course liable to be tinctured by the passions and views of those individuals? Has commerce hitherto done anything more than change the objects of war? Is not the love of wealth as domineering and enterprising a passion as that of power or glory? Have there not been as many wars founded upon commercial motives, since that has become the prevailing system of nations, as were before occasioned by the cupidity of territory or dominion? Has not the spirit of commerce, in many instances, administered new incentives to the appetite both for the one and for the other? Let experience, the least fallible guide of human opinions, be appealed to for an answer to these inquiries.

Sparta, Athens, Rome, and Carthage, were all republics; two of them, Athens and Carthage, of the commercial kind. Yet were they as often engaged in wars, offensive and defensive, as the neighboring monarchies of the same times. Sparta was little better than a well regulated camp; and Rome was never sated of carnage and conquest.

Carthage, though a commercial republic, was the aggressor in the very war that ended in her destruction. Hannibal had carried her arms into the heart of Italy, and even to the gates of Rome, before Scipio, in turn, gave him an overthrow in the territories of Carthage, and made a conquest of the Commonwealth.

Venice, in latter times, figured more than once in wars of ambition; till becoming an object of terror to the other Italian States, Pope Julius the Second found means to accomplish that formidable league,[2] which gave a deadly blow to the power and pride of that haughty republic.

---

[2]The league of CAMBRAY, comprehending the Emperor, the King of France, the King of Arragon, and most of the Italian Princes and States.

The provinces of Holland, till they were overwhelmed in debts and taxes, took a leading and conspicuous part in the wars of Europe. They had furious contests with England for the dominion of the sea; and were among the most persevering and most implacable opponents of Louis XIV.

In the Government of Britain the representatives of the people compose one branch of the National Legislature. Commerce has been for ages the predominant pursuit of that country. Yet few nations have been more frequently engaged in war; and the wars in which that kingdom has been engaged, have, in numerous instances, proceeded from the people. There have been, if I may so express it, almost as many popular, as royal wars. The cries of the nation and the importunities of their representatives, have, upon various occasions, dragged their monarchs into war, or continued them in it contrary to their inclinations, and sometimes contrary to the real interests of the State. In that memorable struggle for superiority between the rival houses of Austria and Bourbon, which so long kept Europe in a flame, it is well known that the antipathies of the English against the French, seconding the ambition, or rather the avarice of a favorite leader,[3] protracted the war beyond the limits marked out by sound policy, and for a considerable time in opposition to the views of the Court.

The wars of these two last mentioned nations have in a great measure grown out of commercial considerations. The desire of supplanting, and the fear of being supplanted, either in particular branches of traffic, or in the general advantages of trade and navigation; and sometimes even the more culpable desire of sharing in the commerce of other nations, without their consent.

The last war but two between Britain and Spain, sprang from the attempts of the English merchants, to prosecute an illicit trade with the Spanish Main. These unjustifiable practices on their part, produced severities on the part of the Spaniards, towards the subjects of Great Britain, which were not more justifiable; because they exceeded the bounds of a just retaliation, and were chargeable with inhumanity and cruelty. Many of the English who were taken on the Spanish coast, were sent to dig in the mines of Potosi; and by the usual progress of a spirit of resentment, the innocent were after a while confounded with the guilty in indiscriminate punishment. The complaints of the merchants kindled a violent flame throughout the nation, which soon after broke out in the House of Commons, and was communicated from that body to the Ministry. Letters of reprisal were granted and a war ensued; which in its consequences, overthrew all the alliances that but twenty years before had been formed, with sanguine expectations of the most beneficial fruits.

From this summary of what has taken place in other countries, whose situations have borne the nearest resemblance to our own, what reason can we have to confide in those reveries, which would seduce us into the expectation of peace and cordiality between the members of the present Confederacy, in a state of separation? Have we not already seen enough of the fallacy and extravagance of those idle theories which have amused us with promises of an exemption from the imperfections, the weaknesses, and the evils incident to society in every shape? Is it

[3]The Duke of Marlborough.

not time to awake from the deceitful dream of a golden age, and to adopt as a practical maxim for the direction of our political conduct, that we, as well as the other inhabitants of the globe, are yet remote from the happy empire of perfect wisdom and perfect virtue?

Let the point of extreme depression to which our national dignity and credit have sunk; let the inconveniences felt everywhere from a lax and ill administration of Government; let the revolt of a part of the State of North Carolina; the late menacing disturbances in Pennsylvania, and the actual insurrections and rebellions in Massachusetts, declare!

So far is the general sense of mankind from corresponding with the tenets of those who endeavor to lull asleep our apprehensions of discord and hostility between the States, in the event of disunion, that it has, from long observation of the progress of society, become a sort of axiom in politics, that vicinity or nearness of situation, constitutes nations natural enemies. An intelligent writer expresses himself on this subject to this effect: "NEIGHBORING NATIONS (says he), are naturally ENEMIES of each other, unless their common weakness forces them to league in a CONFEDERATE REPUBLIC, and their constitution prevents the differences that neighborhood occasions, extinguishing that secret jealousy, which disposes all States to aggrandize themselves at the expense of their neighbors."[4] This passage, at the same time, points out the EVIL and suggests the REMEDY.

PUBLIUS

South Carolina Ordinance of Nullification November 24, 1832 (Excerpts)

DISCUSSION QUESTIONS

1. Was Congress acting properly under its assigned powers when it passed the tariff? Explain.
2. What will be South Carolina's response to any use of force by the United States Government?

An Ordinance to Nullify certain acts of the Congress of the United States, purporting to be laws laying duties and imposts on the importation of foreign commodities.

Whereas the Congress of the United States, by various acts, purporting to be acts laying duties and imposts on foreign imports, but in reality intended for the protection of domestic manufactures, and the giving of bounties to classes and individuals engaged in particular employments, at the expense and to the injury and oppression of other classes and individuals, and by wholly exempting from taxation certain foreign commodities, such as are not produced or manufactured in

[4] *Vide Principles des Negotiations par l'Abbe de Mably.*

the United States, to afford a pretext for imposing higher and excessive duties on articles similar to those intended to be protected, hath exceeded its just powers under the Constitution, which confers on it no authority to afford such protection, and hath violated the true meaning and intent of the Constitution, which provides for equality in imposing the burthens of taxation upon the several States and portions of the Confederacy: *And whereas* the said Congress, exceeding its just power to impose taxes and collect revenue for the purpose of effecting and accomplishing the specific objects and purposes which the Constitution of the United States authorizes it to effect and accomplish, hath raised and collected unnecessary revenue for objects unauthorized by the Constitution:—

We, therefore, the people of the State of South Carolina in Convention assembled, do declare and ordain, . . . That the several acts and parts of acts of the Congress of the United States, purporting to be laws for the imposing of duties and imposts on the importation of foreign commodities, . . . and, more, especially, . . . [the tariff acts of 1828 and 1832] . . . , are unauthorized by the Constitution of the United States, and violate the true meaning and intent thereof, and are null, void, and no law, nor binding upon this State, its officers or citizens; and all promises, contracts, and obligations, made or entered into, or to be made or entered into, with purpose to secure the duties imposed by the said acts, and all judicial proceedings which shall be hereafter had in affirmance thereof, are and shall be held utterly null and void . . . .

And we, the People of South Carolina, to the end that it may be fully understood by the Government of the United States, and the people of the co-States, that we are determined to maintain this, our Ordinance and Declaration, at every hazard, *Do further Declare* that we will not submit to the application of force, on the part of the Federal Government, to reduce this State to obedience; but that we will consider the passage, by Congress, of any act . . . to coerce the State, shut up her ports, destroy or harass her commerce, or to enforce the acts hereby declared to be null and void, otherwise than through the civil tribunals of the country, as inconsistent with the longer continuance of South Carolina in the Union: and that the people of this State will thenceforth hold themselves absolved from all further obligation to maintain or preserve their political connexion with the people of the other States, and will forthwith proceed to organize a separate Government, and do all other acts and things which sovereign and independent States may of right to do.

President Andrew Jackson "Proclamation to the People of South Carolina" December 10, 1832 (Excerpts)

DISCUSSION QUESTIONS

1. Is the South Carolina ordinance based upon resistance to unconditional or oppressive acts by the United States government? Explain.

2. What problems arise from a state's declaring unconstitutional any national law that the state believes to be harmful?
3. How does the provision "to form a more perfect union" in the Preamble to the Constitution relate to South Carolina's ordinance of nullification?

Whereas a convention assembled in the State of South Carolina have passed an ordinance by which they declare "that the several acts and parts of acts of the Congress of the United States purporting to be laws for the imposing of duties and imposts on the importation of foreign commodities, . . . are unauthorized by the Constitution of the United States, and violate the true meaning and intent thereof, and are null and void and no law," nor binding on the citizens of that State or its officers; . . . .

Whereas the said ordinance prescribes to the people of South Carolina a course of conduct in direct violation of their duty as citizens of the United States, contrary to the laws of their country, subversive of its Constitution, and having for its object the destruction of the Union—

To preserve this bond of our political existence from destruction, to maintain inviolate this state of national honor and prosperity, and to justify the confidence my fellow-citizens have reposed in me, I, Andrew Jackson, President of the United States, have thought proper to issue this my proclamation, stating my views of the Constitution and laws applicable to the measures adopted by the convention of South Carolina and to the reasons they have put forth to sustain them, declaring the course which duty will require me to pursue, and, appealing to the understanding and patriotism of the people, warn them of the consequences that must inevitably result from an observance of the dictates of the convention. . . .

The ordinance is founded, not on the indefeasible right of resisting acts which are plainly unconstitutional and too oppressive to be endured, but on the strange position that any one State may not only declare an act of Congress void, but prohibit its execution; that they may do this consistently with the Constitution; that the true construction of that instrument permits a State to retain its place in the Union and yet be bound by no other of its laws than those it may choose to consider as constitutional. It is true, they add, that to justify this abrogation of a law it must be palpably contrary to the Constitution; but it is evident that to give the right of resisting laws of that description, coupled with the uncontrolled right to decide what laws deserve that character, is to give the power of resisting all laws; for as by the theory there is no appeal, the reasons alleged by the State, good or bad, must prevail. If it should be said that public opinion is a sufficient check against the abuse of this power, it may be asked why it is not deemed a sufficient guard against the passage of an unconstitutional act by Congress? There is, however, a restraint in this last case which makes the assumed power of a State more indefensible, and which does not exist in the other. There are two appeals from an unconstitutional act passed by Congress—one to the judiciary, the other to the people and the States. There is no appeal from the State decision in theory, and the practical illustration shows that the courts are closed against an application to review it, both judges and jurors being sworn to decide in its favor. But reasoning on this subject is superfluous when our social compact, in express terms, declares that the laws of the United States, its Constitution, and treaties made under it are the supreme law of the land, and, for greater caution, adds "that the judges in every State shall be bound thereby, anything in the constitution or laws of any State to the contrary notwithstanding." And it may be asserted without fear of refutation that no federative government could exist without a similar provision. Look for a moment to the consequence. If South Carolina considers the revenue laws unconstitutional and has a right to prevent their execution in the port of Charleston, there would be a clear constitutional objection to their collection in every other port; and no revenue could be collected anywhere, for all imposts must be equal. It is no answer to repeat that an unconstitutional law is no law so long as the question of its legality is to be decided by the State itself, for every law operating injuriously upon any local interest will be perhaps thought, and certainly represented, as unconstitutional, and, as has been shown, there is no appeal.

If this doctrine had been established at an earlier day, the Union would have been dissolved in its infancy. The excise law in Pennsylvania, the embargo and nonintercourse law in the Eastern States, the carriage tax in Virginia, were all deemed unconstitutional, and were more unequal in their operation than any of the laws now complained of; but, fortunately, none of those States discovered that they had the right now claimed by South Carolina. The war into which we were forced to support the dignity of the nation and the rights of our citizens might have ended in defeat and disgrace, instead of victory and honor, if the States who supposed it a ruinous and unconstitutional measure had thought they possessed the right of nullifying the act by which it was declared and denying supplies for its prosecution. Hardly and unequally as those measures bore upon several members of the Union, to the legislatures of none did this efficient and peaceable remedy, as it is called, suggest itself. The discovery of this important feature in our Constitution was reserved to the present day. To the statesmen of South Carolina belongs the invention, and upon the citizens of that State will unfortunately fall the evils of reducing it to practice.

If the doctrine of a State veto upon the laws of the Union carries with it internal evidence of its impracticable absurdity, our constitutional history will also afford abundant proof that it would have been repudiated with indignation had it been proposed to form a feature in our Government.

Our present Constitution was formed . . . in vain if this fatal doctrine prevails. It was formed for important objects that are announced in the preamble, made in the name and by the authority of the people of the United States, whose delegates framed and whose conventions approved it. The most important among these objects—that which is placed first in rank, on which all the others rest—is "*to form a more perfect union.*" Now, is it possible that even if there were no express provision giving supremacy to the Constitution and laws of the United States over those of the States, can it be conceived that an instrument made for the purpose of "*forming a more perfect union*" than that of the Confederation could be so constructed by the assembled wisdom of our country as to substitute for that Confederation a form of government dependent for its existence on the local interest, the party spirit, of a State, or of a prevailing faction in a State? Every man of plain, unsophisticated understanding who hears the question will give such an answer as will preserve the Union. Metaphysical subtlety, in pursuit of an impracticable theory, could alone have devised one that is calculated to destroy it.

I consider, then, the power to annul a law of the United States, assumed by one State, *incompatible with the existence of the Union, contradicted expressly by the letter of the Constitution, unauthorized by its spirit, inconsistent with every principle on which it was founded, and destructive of the great object for which it was formed.*

CONTEMPORARY INFLUENCES

John J. Harrigan
"The Evolution of Federalism"

DISCUSSION QUESTIONS

1. Describe the evolution from dual federalism to new federalism.
2. Which form of Federalism do you believe is most prevalent today? Why?

Federalism today is very different from federalism in 1787, when the Constitution was written. Federalism has evolved through different stages,[1] which has led us from a dual-federalism concept of state-national relations to cooperative federalism.

Dual federalism: pre-1937. Before 1937, dual federalism was the prevailing view of the relations between the state and national governments. Each level of government was viewed as having its own separate source of authority and areas of responsibility.[2] The states were not supposed to interfere in foreign affairs, for example, and the federal government was not supposed to intervene in areas of state responsibility.

The entire history of dual federalism was marked by intense conflicts for dominance between the federal government and the states. The Civil War (1861–1865) established the ultimate dominance of the national government by determining that states could not secede from the union. After the Civil War, the main conflicts centered on federal government attempts to regulate business and stimulate the economy. National dominance in this sphere was affirmed by the Supreme Court in 1937, when it legitimized the federal government's right to regulate major aspects of the national economy.[3]

---

[1]See Deil S. Wright, "Intergovernmental Relations: An Analytical Overview," *Annals of the American Academy of Political and Social Science* 416 (November 1974): 5.

[2]See Daniel J. Elazar, *The American Partnership* (Chicago: University of Chicago Press, 1962), p. 20.

[3]*National Labor Relations Board* v. *Jones and Laughlin Steel Corp.*, 300 U.S. 1 (1937).

John J. Harrigan, *Politics and Policy in States and Communities* 5th ed. Copyright © 1994 by Harper-Collins College Publishers, pp. 36–46.

Cooperative federalism: 1933–1961. The dual federalism concept concentrates on constitutional divisions of authority. In the actual operation of governments, however, the division of powers is not so tidy as it appears in the Constitution. The very achievement of federal dominance by the 1930s brought basic changes in the federal system. The federal government began working directly with local governments, thus introducing a three-level relationship. By the end of the 1930s, the three levels had become deeply intertwined. . . .

. . . the levels of government are no longer separate, like the layers of a layer cake. Rather, as Morton Grodzins has said, the functions of government overlap so much among all three levels of government that they have the appearance of a "rainbow or marble cake, characterized by an inseparable mingling of differently colored ingredients, the colors appearing in vertical and diagonal strains and unexpected whirls. As colors are mixed in the marble cake, so functions are mixed in the American federal system."[4] This feature of federalism is labeled cooperative federalism,[5] because the federal government is seeking to cooperate with state and local governments to provide financial support for their traditional services. It is also sometimes called marble cake federalism, in contrast to layer cake federalism, or dual federalism.

An inevitable byproduct of the shift toward cooperative or marble cake federalism was a growing centralization of the power to control governmental expenditures. At the beginning of the twentieth century, local governments spent about three-fifths of all the money spent by all governments in America, and the federal government spent barely one-third. By 1987, the federal government's share had grown to almost two-thirds and local government's share dropped to about one-fourth.[6]

Creative federalism: 1961–1969. During the administrations of Presidents Kennedy and Johnson (1961–1969), intergovernmental politics moved into a third phase. The national government increasingly relied on the grant-in-aid system (see next section) to impose the federal government's priorities on the states. The number of federal grant programs increased dramatically from about one hundred at the start of the decade to about five hundred at the decade's end—from about $7 billion to about $24 billion. President Johnson labeled his administration the Great Society. He persuaded Congress to pass a variety of imaginative programs with catchy names such as the War on Poverty, Model Cities, Headstart, legal services for the poor, and compensatory education.

This phase of intergovernmental relations was called *creative federalism*, because the policy initiatives were often created at the national level and then imposed on the states. As such, it also entailed a massive shift of power over domestic policies from the state-local levels to the federal level. With its superior ability to

[4]Morton Grodzins, "The Federal System," *Goals for Americans: The Report of the President's Commission on National Goals* (Englewood Cliffs, N.J.: Prentice-Hall, 1960), pp. 365–366. In this article, Grodzins provided the example of the sanitarian on which the example of the child-protection worker is modeled.

[5]Elazar, *The American Partnership*, p. 20.

[6]Bureau of the Census, *Statistical Abstract of the United States: 1990* (Washington D.C.: U.S. Government Printing Office, 1991), p. 273.

raise revenues and the willingness of federal courts to impose desegregation, affirmative action, and other guidelines throughout the nation, the federal government by 1969 had in fact become supreme over the states. In reaction to this, Republican Presidents Nixon (1969–1974) and Reagan (1981–1989) pushed for a *New Federalism* that would reverse the flow of power to Washington. . . .

The New Federalism

Each presidential administration has reacted differently to these complaints about cooperative federalism. During the Eisenhower years (1953–1961), grants-in-aid came under attack by conservatives as undermining state autonomy. President Eisenhower formed a national committee to find grant-in-aid programs that could be turned over to the states, but not a single program was shifted to the states.

As we saw, the Kennedy-Johnson years (1961–1969) brought a dramatic increase in the number of grant programs, from 100 to about 500. These were the Great Society years, in which categorical grants were used to entice the states to participate in a number of federally initiated social welfare programs: Model Cities, Medicaid, Food Stamps, legal services for the poor, compensatory education, and the War on Poverty, among others.

During the 1970s, the number of categorical grant programs ceased growing as the Nixon administration (1969–1974) sponsored general revenue sharing and the first extensive block grants. Although the number of grant programs stayed stable in the 1970s, the money involved grew rapidly to $94 billion in 1981, supplying about a fourth of all state and local government revenue.

In the early 1980s the Reagan administration proposed a New Federalism in which, the new president proclaimed: "It is my intention to curb the size and influence of the federal establishment."[7] The key to this curbing of the federal government was "devolution," or spinning off the federal government's responsibilities to state and local governments and to the private sector. Devolution has four components: the budget, regulation, the private sector, and courts.

Budgetary devolution. Reagan sought to spin off substantial federal budgetary responsibilities to state and local governments by consolidating seventy-seven categorical grants into nine new block grants, which would be administered by the states with minimal federal strings attached, and by making severe budget cutbacks in social service programs in an effort to shift more of the burden for these services onto the states. He also sought from Congress, but failed to get, a *Great Swap*, under which the federal government would assume all responsibility for Medicaid, a very expensive and rapidly growing program of health care for the indigent, the elderly, and people on welfare. In exchange, the states would take over responsibility for Food Stamps, Aid to Families with Dependent Children (AFDC), and 43 other categorical programs.

The important point about these complicated proposals is that they were the most significant attempts to date to reverse federal dominance of the federal-fiscal partnership that has existed since the 1930s. The original intent of the Reagan ad-

---

[7]President Ronald Reagan, "Inaugural Address," January 20, 1981.

ministration was to cut the total amount of federal grants almost in half, which would have consequently cut much of the federal government's ability to set budget priorities for the states.

While Reagan scored stunning successes on his block grant and social services cutback proposals, Congress rejected his Great Swap proposal. Local officials resisted taking over these new responsibilities from the federal government. Many of them viewed poverty and welfare as national problems, and for years they had urged the federal government to assume full financial responsibility for the major welfare programs. Reagan's Great Swap proposal to devolve Food Stamps and AFDC onto the states directly contradicted this goal. Against opposition from the states, Reagan succeeded in cutting federal grants-in-aid back to $86 billion in 1982. Despite this reduction, federal aid continued to grow and by 1991 had reached $152 billion.

Regulatory devolution. A second aspect of Reagan's New Federalism was regulatory devolution. Between 1965 and 1980, there was a virtual explosion of federal laws, administrative agency rules, and court orders that put the sharpest regulation in American history on several aspects of the economy, ranging from environmental protection to antidiscrimination and occupational health and safety. Because these new regulations added to the cost of doing business, American business leaders bitterly resented many of them. Thus the Carter administration took some early steps toward deregulation by phasing out federal controls over the price of petroleum and natural gas and deregulating the airline industry. President Reagan made further reductions of federal regulatory activities and sought legislation that would shift major regulatory responsibilities to the states, especially in environmental protection. Under Reagan, the Environmental Protection Agency cut back sharply the number of regulations it issued. . . . Reagan threw his support behind attempts to rewrite the Clean Air Act in ways that would put greater responsibility on the states for reducing air pollution.

Devolution to the private sector. When the Reagan administration cut funds for social programs in the early 1980s, it called on the private sector to take up the slack. In cutting social expenditures, for example, Reagan argued that some federally funded programs providing food and shelter for the destitute could be replaced by volunteers from churches and nonprofit organizations. The heart of his proposals for tackling urban problems was to create so-called *urban enterprise zones.* These would be city neighborhoods in which taxes and regulatory restrictions (such as occupational safety and minimum wages) would be relaxed for companies that moved facilities into those neighborhoods and created jobs there. This reliance on the private sector to accomplish public goals did not, of course, initiate with Reagan. But he pushed for this objective more strongly than any other recent president.

Curbing federal courts. Finally, the 1980s saw concerted efforts to pressure the federal courts into a conservative posture on highly volatile issues such as abortion, desegregation, and voting rights, in which the federal courts have ordered states to comply with federal laws and with the Supreme Court's interpretation of the Constitution. By consistently appointing conservative judges and Supreme Court Justices,[8] Presidents Reagan and Bush effectively reduced the role of the federal courts in pursuit of a liberal agenda in social policy.

Assessing the new federalism. Did Reagan's New Federalism achieve his goal of returning more power and authority to the states and communities? On the surface it may seem that the goal was not achieved, since the president lost most of the major battles involved and eventually seemed to lose interest in the issue itself.

Reagan may, however, have won the war. He capped the growth rate of most domestic social programs, reduced the number of federal grant-in-aid programs, got nine new block grants passed, terminated General Revenue Sharing, and provoked an ongoing debate over the sorting out of federal from state and local responsibilities. As a result of all this, the federal role in domestic policy has shrunk. Furthermore, because of the huge budget deficits built up during the Reagan-Bush years, there is little room for reversing the shrinkage of the federal government's domestic policy role. This shrinkage has given cities and states greater independence to run domestic programs with less interference from Washington than they have had since the 1960s. And toward the end of his presidency, Reagan pointed to this as one of his major achievements. . . .

The states and cities have, however, paid a very high price for their renewed independence from Washington.[9] A survey of municipal finance officers in 1989 found that 86 percent of them received fewer federal dollars than they had at the beginning of the decade. More than a third of them reported eliminating some city services or laying off city employees as a result of the cuts in federal aid. And generally they found themselves turning to regressive revenue sources such as user fees and sales taxes to make up for the losses in aid. . . .[10] Other surveys of cities have found similar results.[11] In summary, the New Federalism not only brought about a significant revenue shift from the federal level to the state and local levels, but it also helped shift the revenue burden from upper-middle income taxpayers to less affluent taxpayers who fare less well under most state and local tax systems than they do under the federal tax system.

Finally, despite the New Federalism's rhetoric about returning power to states and communities, neither Reagan nor his successor George Bush stemmed the growing number of federal mandates on states and communities. Mandates are program requirements that a higher level government imposes on a lower level government. During the 1980s and early 1990s, state or local governments were required by federal law, among other things, to raise the minimum drinking age from 18 to 21, remove asbestos from public schools, implement stricter water pol-

---

[8]Sheldon Goldman, "Reagan's Second Term Judicial Appointments: The Battle at Midway," *Judicature* 70, no. 6 (April–May 1987): 324–339.

[9]Richard L. Cole, Delbert A. Taebel, and Rodney V. Hissong, "America's Cities and the 1980s: The Legacy of the Reagan Years," *Journal of Urban Affairs* 12, no. 4 (1990): 345–360.

[10]Ibid.

[11]Vincent L. Marando, "General Revenue Sharing: Termination and City Response," *State and Local Government Review* 22, no. 3 (Fall 1990): 98–106.

lution regulations, establish programs to protect workers against certain dangerous chemicals, and make reports on measures to protect more than 150 new endangered species.[12] In the year 1990 alone, 20 new mandates were passed into law.[13] Due to its own budget problems, moreover, Washington is seldom able to provide sufficient funds to implement these mandated programs. As the costs for these mandated expenditures go up, the ability of state and local governments to set their own policy priorities among other programs goes down.[14]

In sum, the New Federalism of the Reagan and Bush administrations did not dismantle the federal government's domestic policy machine, but it did reduce the machine's abilities to advance the liberal agenda which had dominated federal policy makers during the 1960s. Ironically, despite the attempt of the New Federalism to impose conservative social policies on the nation, many states have liberalized their own social service expenditures to make up for the federal budget cutbacks. One study examined the responses of 14 states to federal cuts in social services. Of the 14, 13 either increased their own expenditures to make up for the federal cuts or adopted stronger policymaking roles than they previously had.[15] The net result of the New Federalism has probably been less spending on social services and welfare, but it clearly did not bring about the extensive reduction in the overall size and scope of government in welfare and domestic policy that had originally been envisioned by Reagan and Bush.

President Ronald Reagan Inauguration Address January 20, 1981 (Excerpt)

DISCUSSION QUESTIONS

1. Why did President Reagan believe that the role of government should be curbed?
2. What is the relation of the states to the national government?

So, as we begin, let us take inventory. We are a nation that has a government—not the other way around. And this makes us special among the nations of the Earth. Our government has no power except that granted it by the people. It is time to check and reverse the growth of government which shows signs of having grown beyond the consent of the governed.

[12] *The New York Times*, May 21, 1990, p. A11.

[13] *The New York Times*, March 24, 1992, p. 1

[14] Martha A. Fabricius, "The 102nd's Multiplying Mandates," *State Legislatures* 18, no. 1 (January 1992): 17–18 and "More Dictates from the Feds," *State Legislatures* 17, no. 2 (February 1991): 28–30.

[15] Richard P. Nathan and Fred C. Doolittle, "The Untold Story of Reagan's 'New Federalism,'" *Public Interest* no. 77 (Fall 1984): 96–105.

It is my intention to curb the size and influence of the Federal establishment and to demand recognition of the distinction between the powers granted to the Federal Government and those reserved to the States or to the people. All of us need to be reminded that the Federal government did not create the states; the states created the Federal Government.

Now, so there will be no misunderstanding, it's not my intention to do away with government. It is rather to make it work—work with us, not over us; to stand by our side, not ride on our back. Government can and must provide opportunity, not smother it; foster productivity, not stifle it.

If we look to the answer as to why for so many years we achieved so much, prospered as no other people on Earth, it was because here in this land we unleashed the energy and individual genius of man to a greater extent than had ever been done before. Freedom and the dignity of the individual have been more available and assured here than in any other place on Earth. The price for this freedom at times has been high. But we have never been unwilling to pay that price.

It is no coincidence that our present troubles parallel and are proportionate to the intervention and intrusion in our lives that result from unnecessary and excessive growth of government. It is time for us to realize that we are too great a nation to limit ourselves to small dreams. We're not, as some would have us believe, doomed to an inevitable decline. I do not believe in a fate that will fall on us no matter what we do. I do believe in a fate that will fall on us if we do nothing. So, with all the creative energy at our command, let us begin an era of national renewal. Let us renew our determination, our courage, and our strength. And let us renew our faith and our hope.

President William Clinton
Inauguration Address
January 20, 1993
(Excerpt)

DISCUSSION QUESTIONS

1. What evidence of a desire for change and for action do you see in President Clinton's words?
2. How do you interpret government's role in Franklin Roosevelt's "bold, persistent experimentation"?
3. How do the ideas of Presidents Reagan and Clinton relate to Antifederalist and Federalist thoughts?

Profound and powerful forces are shaking and remaking our world, and the urgent question of our time is whether we can make change our friend and not our enemy.

This new world has already enriched the lives of millions of Americans who are able to compete and win in it. But when most people are working harder for less; when others cannot work at all; when the cost of health care devastates families and threatens to bankrupt many of our enterprises, great and small; when fear of crime robs law-abiding citizens of their freedom; and when millions of poor children cannot even imagine the lives we are calling them to lead—we have not made change our friend.

We know we have to face hard truths and take strong steps. But we have not done so. Instead, we have drifted, and that drifting has eroded our resources, fractured our economy and shaken our confidence.

Though our challenges are fearsome, so are our strengths. And Americans have ever been a restless, questing, hopeful people. We must bring to our task today the vision and will of those who came before us.

From our revolution to the Civil War, to the Great Depression to the civil rights movement, our people have always mustered the determination to construct from these crises the pillars of our history.

Thomas Jefferson believed that to preserve the very foundations of our nation, we would need dramatic change from time to time. Well, my fellow citizens, this is our time. Let us embrace it.

Our democracy must be not only the envy of the world but the engine of our own renewal. There is nothing wrong with American that cannot be cured by what is right with America.

And so today, we pledge an end to the era of deadlock and drift—a new season of American renewal has begun.

To renew America, we must be bold.

We must do what no generation has had to do before. We must invest more in our own people, in their jobs, in their future, and at the same time cut our massive debt. And we must do so in a world in which we must compete for every opportunity.

It will not be easy; it will require sacrifice. But it can be done, and done fairly, not choosing sacrifice for its own sake, but for our own sake. We must provide for our nation the way a family provides for its children.

Our Founders saw themselves in the light of posterity. We can do no less. Anyone who has ever watched a child's eyes wander into sleep knows what posterity is. Posterity is the world to come—the world for whom we hold our ideals, from whom we have borrowed our planet, and to whom we bear sacred responsibility.

We must do what America does best: offer more opportunity to all and demand responsibility from all.

It is time to break the bad habit of expecting something for nothing, from our government or from each other. Let us all take more responsibility, not only for ourselves and our families but for our communities and our country.

To renew America, we must revitalize our democracy.

This beautiful capital, like every capital since the dawn of civilization, is often a place of intrigue and calculation. Powerful people maneuver for position and worry endlessly about who is in and who is out, who is up and who is down, forgetting those people whose toil and sweat sends us here and pays our way.

Americans deserve better, and in this city today, there are people who want to do better. And so I say to all of us here, let us resolve to reform our politics, so that power and privilege no longer shout down the voice of the people. Let us put aside personal advantage so that we can feel the pain and see the promise of America.

Let us resolve to make our government a place for what Franklin Roosevelt called "bold, persistent experimentation," a government for our tomorrows, not our yesterdays.

Let us give this capital back to the people to whom it belongs.

To renew America, we must meet challenges abroad as well as at home. There is no longer division between what is foreign and what is domestic—the world economy, the world environment, the world AIDS crisis, the world arms race—they affect us all.

4

Political Parties and Interest Groups

The Federalists and Antifederalists both had concerns about factions becoming too powerful. The factions that existed at the time of the adoption of the Constitution are described in both satiric and serious fashion in three Antifederalist writings. In the first, a satire by "John Humble," the extremes between the "low-born" and the "well-born" are compared. In a second, serious essay, the Federal Farmer comments on the unprincipled parties who existed on the fringes of the majority of the population. The same writer believed that the views of representatives to the state conventions would reflect the will of the people to a greater extent than did the Philadelphia delegates.

Finally, "A Farmer," while describing the three classes of persons in America, advances two major themes with regard to the effects of the new Constitution. First, it is impossible to have two governments control the same individual, and, second, freedom depends upon the existence of parties; conversely, "public liberty" will be harmed by the existence of a single party.

In an answer to the Antifederalists' fears of a dominant faction, James Madison (Publius) in *Federalist* Paper 10 argues that having a majority included in a faction permits citizens to protect their liberties. He contends that the Antifederalists' preference for societies of smaller groups of citizens is no guarantee of liberty or "cure for the mischiefs of faction."

In "Interest Groups Liberalism," Theodore J. Lowi harks back to both the Antifederalists and the Federalists, especially Madison's *Federalist* Paper 10, by showing the extensive powers of interest groups in modern times. Perhaps our current interest-group–dominated political system can be viewed as Madisonianism out of control. The price of interest-group liberalism is high and includes the destruction of political responsibility. With the rise in interest-group influence came the decline of political parties as described by James MacGregor Burns in "How to Dismember a Party."

This decline in party leadership is more the pity when considered in light of Burns' contention that parties are fusion "devices that counteract the divisive tendencies of interest groups." Lloyd Cutler likewise argues for strong political parties in "Political Parties and a Workable Government." He sees the party as a force that can moderate the pressures of single-interest groups.

Eksterowicz and Cline bring the Antifederalist-Federalist arguments to the present day by showing the efforts of "modern Antifederalists" to reform the system of electing our representatives by admitting more citizen participation. For instance, the recommendations of the Committee on the Constitutional System emphasize ways of ending the deadlock that occurs when the executive and legislative branches are controlled by different parties.

The article by Eksterowicz and Cline advances the theme of Antifederalist participatory democracy through the incorporation of "citizen assemblies" into the political party system. These assemblies would permit the rank-and-file party members to have a voice in party decision making.

ANTIFEDERALIST ARGUMENTS

"John Humble"
(Unknown)
"Address to the Low-Born of America"

DISSUSSION QUESTIONS

1. Since "John Humble" is speaking satirically, what is he really saying about the new Constitution?
2. What does "John Humble" argue about the national government's collecting taxes?

The humble address of the *low- born* of the United States of America, to their fellow slaves scattered throughout the world—greeting:

Whereas it hath been represented unto us that a most dreadful disease hath for these five years last past infected, preyed upon and almost ruined the government and people of this our country; and of this malady we ourselves have had perfect demonstration, not mentally, but bodily, through every one of the five senses. For although our sensations in regard to the mind be not just so nice as those of the *well born*, yet our feeling, through the medium of the plow, the hoe and the grubbing ax, is as acute as any nobleman's in the world. And, whereas, a number of skillful physicians having met together at Philadelphia last summer, for the purpose of exploring, and, if possible, removing the cause of this direful disease, have, through the assistance of John Adams, Esq., in the profundity of their great political knowledge, found out and discovered that nothing but a new government, consisting of three different branches, namely, king, lords, and commons—or, in the American language, President, Senate and Representatives—can save this, our country, from inevitable destruction. And, whereas, it has been reported that several of our *low-born* brethren have had the horrid audacity to think for themselves in regard to this new system of government, and, dreadful thought! have wickedly begun to doubt concerning the perfection of this evangelical constitution, which our political doctors have declared to be a panacea, which (by inspiration) they

---

The Philadelphia *Independent Gazetteer*, October 29, 1787

know will infallibly heal every distemper in the confederation, and finally terminate in the salvation of America.

Now we the *low born*, that is, all the people of the United States, except 600 thereabouts, *well born*, do by this our humble address, declare and most solemnly engage, that we will allow and admit the said 600 *well born*, immediately to establish and confirm this most noble, most excellent and truly divine constitution. And we further declare that without any equivocation or mental reservation whatever we will support and maintain the same according to the best of our power, and after the manner and custom of all other slaves in foreign countries, namely by the sweat and toil of our body. Nor will we at any future period of time ever attempt to complain of this our royal government, let the consequences be what they may.

And although it appears to us that a standing army, composed of the purgings of the jails of Great Britain, Ireland and Germany, shall be employed in collecting the revenues of this our king and government, yet, we again in the most solemn manner declare, that we will abide by our present determination of non- resistance and passive obedience—so that we shall not dare to molest or disturb those military gentlemen in the service of our royal government. And (which is not improbable) should any one of those soldiers when employed on duty in collecting the taxes, strike off the arm (with his sword) of one of our fellow slaves, we will conceive our case remarkably fortunate if he leaves the other arm on. And moreover, because we are aware that many of our fellow slaves shall be unable to pay their taxes, and this incapacity of theirs is a just cause of impeachment of treason; wherefore in such cases we will use our utmost endeavors, in conjunction with the standing army, to bring such atrocious offenders before our federal judges, who shall have power, without jury or trial, to order the said miscreants for immediate execution; nor will we think their sentence severe unless after being hanged they are also to be both beheaded and quartered. And finally we shall henceforth and forever leave all power, authority and dominion over our persons and properties in the hands of the *well born*, who were designed by Providence to govern. And in regard to the liberty of the press, we renounce all claim to it forever more, Amen; and we shall in future be perfectly contented if our tongues be left us to lick the feet of our *well born* masters.

Done on behalf of three millions of low- born American slaves.

JOHN HUMBLE, Secretary

"The Federal Farmer" (Richard Henry Lee) Essay (Excerpt)

DISCUSSION QUESTIONS

1. Describe the two parties that exist in the United States.
2. What is the relationship of these parties to the new Constitution?
3. How will the state conventions differ from the federal Constitutional convention?

And I see the danger in either case will arise principally from the conduct and views of two very unprincipled parties in the United States—two fires, between which the honest and substantial people have long found themselves situated. One party is composed of little insurgents, men in debt, who want no law, and who want a share of the property of others; these are called levellers, Shayites, etc. The other party is composed of a few, but more dangerous men, with their servile dependents; these avariciously grasp at all power and property; you may discover in all the actions of these men, an evident dislike to free and equal government, and they will go systematically to work to change, essentially, the forms of government in this country; these are called aristocrats, monarchists, etc. Between these two parties is the weight of the community; the men of middling property, men not in debt on the one hand, and men, on the other, content with republican governments, and not aiming at immense fortunes, offices, and power. In 1786, the little insurgents, the levellers, came forth, invaded the rights of others, and attempted to establish governments according to their wills. Their movements evidently gave encouragement to the other party, which, in 1787, has taken the political field, and with its fashionable dependents, and the tongue and the pen, is endeavoring to establish in a great haste, a politer kind of government. These two parties, which will probably be opposed or united as it may suit their interests and views, are really insignificant, compared with the solid, free, and independent part of the community. It is not my intention to suggest, that either of these parties, and the real friends of the proposed constitution, are the same men. The fact is, these aristocrats support and hasten the adoption of the proposed constitution, merely because they think it is a stepping stone to their favorite object. I think I am well founded in this idea. I think the general politics of these men support it, as well as the common observation among them: That the proffered plan is the best that can be got at present, it will do for a few years, and lead to something better. The sensible and judicious part of the community will carefully weigh all these circumstances; they will view the late convention as a respectable body of men—America probably never will see an assembly of men, of a like number, more respectable. But the members of the convention met without knowing the sentiments of one man in ten thousand in these states respecting the new ground taken. Their doings are but the first attempts in the most important scene ever opened. Though each individual in the state conventions will not, probably, be so respectable as each individual in the federal convention, yet as the state conventions will probably consist of fifteen hundred or two thousand men of abilities, and versed in the science of government, collected from all parts of the community and from all orders of men, it must be acknowledged that the weight of respectability will be in them. In them will be collected the solid sense and the real political character of the country. Being revisers of the subject, they will possess peculiar advantages. To say that these conventions ought not to attempt, coolly and deliberately, the revision of the system, or that they cannot amend it, is very foolish or very assuming. . . .

THE FEDERAL FARMER

"A Farmer" (Probably John Francis Mercer) Essay, March 18, 1788 (Excerpt)

DISCUSSION QUESTIONS

1. Describe the three classes of persons in the United States.
2. Why should parties be preserved?
3. Why should the parties be balanced?

As our citizens are now apprized of the progress of parties or political opinions on the continent, it is fit they should also be informed of the present state, force and designs of each, in order that they may form their decisions with safety to the public and themselves—this shall be given with all the precision and impartiality the author is capable of.

America is at present divided into three classes or descriptions of men, and in a few years there will be but two.

[*First*]. The first class comprehends all those men of fortune and reputation who stepped forward in the late revolution, from opposition to the administration, rather than the government of Great Britain. All those aristocrats whose pride disdains equal law. Many men of very large fortune, who entertain real or imaginary fears for the security of property. Those young men, who have sacrificed their time and their talents to public service, without any prospect of an adequate pecuniary or honorary reward. All your people of fashion and pleasure who are corrupted by the dissipation of the French, English and American armies; and a love of European manners and luxury. The public creditors of the continent, whose interest has been heretofore sacrificed by their friends, in order to retain their services on this occasion. A large majority of the mercantile people, which is at present a very unformed and consequently dangerous interest. Our old native merchants have been almost universally ruined by the receipt of their debts in paper during the war, and the payment in hard money of what they owed their British correspondents since peace. Those who are not bankrupts, have generally retired and given place to a set of young men, who conducting themselves as rashly as ignorantly, have embarrassed their affairs and lay the blame on the government, and who are really unacquainted with the true mercantile interest of the country—which is perplexed from circumstances rather temporary than permanent. The foreign merchants are generally not to be trusted with influence in our government—they are most of them birds of passage. Some, perhaps British emissaries increasing and rejoicing in our political mistakes, and even those who have settled among us with an intention to fix themselves and their posterity in our soil, have brought with them more foreign prejudices than wealth. Time must

The *Maryland Gazette and Baltimore Advisor*, March 18, 1788 elapse before the mercantile interest will be so organized as to govern themselves, much less others, with propriety. And lastly, to this class I suppose we may ultimately add the *tory interest,* with the exception of very many respectable characters, who reflect with a gratification mixed with disdain, that those principles are now become fashionable for which they have been persecuted and hunted down—which, although by no means so formidable as is generally imagined, is still considerable. They are at present wavering. They are generally, though with very many exceptions, openly for the proposed, but secretly against any American government. *A burnt child dreads the fire.* But should they see any fair prospect of confusion arise, these gentry will be off at any moment for these five and twenty years to come. Ultimately, should the administration promise stability to the new government, they may be counted on as the Janizaries of power, ready to efface all suspicion by the violence of their zeal.

In general, all these various people would prefer a government, as nearly copied after that of Great Britain, as our circumstances will permit. Some would strain these circumstances. Others still retain a deep rooted jealousy of the executive branch and strong republican prejudices as they are called. Finally, this class contains more aggregate wisdom and moral virtue than both the other two together. It commands nearly two thirds of the property and almost one half the numbers of America, and has at present, become almost irresistible from the name of the truly great and amiable man who it has been said, is disposed to patronize it, and from the influence which it has over the second class. This [first] class is nearly at the height of their power; they must decline or moderate, or another revolution will ensue, for the opinion of America is becoming daily more unfavorable to those radical changes which high- toned government requires. A conflict would terminate in the destruction of this class, or the liberties of their country. May the Guardian Angel of America prevent both!

[*Second*]. The second class is composed of those descriptions of men who are certainly more numerous with us than in any other part of the globe. *First,* those men who are so wise as to discover that their ancestors and indeed all the rest of mankind were and are fools. We have a vast overproportion of these great men, who, when you tell them that from the earliest period at which mankind devoted their attention to social happiness, it has been their uniform judgment, that a government over governments cannot exist—*that is two governments* operating on the same individual—assume the smile of confidence, and tell you of two people travelling the same road—of a perfect and precise division of the duties of the individual. Still, however, the political apothegm is as old as the proverb—*That no man can serve two masters*—and whoever will run their noddles against old proverbs will be sure to break them, however hard they may be. And if they broke only their own, all would be right; but it is very horrible to reflect that all our numskulls must be cracked in concert. *Second.* The *trimmers,* who from sympathetic indecision are always united with, and when not regularly employed, always fight under the banners of these great men. These people are forever at market, and when parties are nearly equally divided, they get very well paid for their services. *Thirdly.* The *indolent,* that is almost every second man of independent fortune you meet with in America—*these are quite easy, and can live under any government.* If men can be said to live, who scarcely breathe; and if breathing was attended with any bodily exertion, would give up their small portion of life in despair. These men do not swim with the stream as the trimmers do, but are dragged like mud at the bottom. As they have no other weight than their fat flesh, they are hardly worth mentioning when we speak of the sentiments and opinions of America. As this second class never can include any of the yeomanry of the union, who never affect superior wisdom, and can have no interests but the public good, it can be only said to exist at the birth of government, and as soon as the first and third classes become more decided in their views, this will divide with each and dissipate like a mist, or sink down into what are called moderate men, and become the tools and instruments of others. These people are prevented by a cloud from having *any* view; and if they are not virtuous, they at least preserve the appearance, which in this world amounts to the same thing.

[*Third*]. At the head of the third class appear the old rigid republicans, who although few in number, are still formidable. Reverence will follow these men in spite of detraction, as long as wisdom and virtue are esteemed among mankind. They are joined by the true *democrats*, who are in general fanatics and enthusiasts, and some few sensible, charming madmen. A decided majority of the *yeomanry* of America will, for a length of years, be ready to support these two descriptions of men. But as this last class is forced to act as a residuary legatee, and receive all the trash and filth, it is in some measure disgraced and its influence weakened. 3dly. The free- booters and plunderers, who infest all countries and ours perhaps as little as any other whatever. These men have that natural antipathy to any kind or sort of government, that a rogue has to a halter. In number they are few indeed—such characters are the offspring of dissipation and want, and there is not that country in the world where so much real property is shared so equally among so few citizens, for where property is as easily acquired by fair means, very few indeed will resort to foul. Lastly, by the *poor mob, infoelix pecus!* The property of whoever will feed them and take care of them—let them be spared. Let the burden of taxation sit lightly on their shoulders. But alas! This is not their fate. It is here that government forever falls with all its weight. It is here that the proposed government will press where it should scarcely be felt. . . .

In this [third] class may be counted men of the greatest mental powers and of as sublime virtue as any in America. They at present command nearly one- third of the property and above half the numbers of the United States, and in either event they must continue to increase in influence by great desertions from both the other classes. . . . If the [proposed] government is not adopted, theirs will be the prevalent opinion. The object of this class either is or will be purely federal—an union of independent States, not a government of individuals. And should the proposed federal plan fail, from the obstinacy of those who will listen to no *conditional* amendments, although such as they cannot disapprove; or should it ultimately in its execution upon a fair trial, disappoint the wishes and expectations of our country—[then] an union purely federal is what the reasonable and dispassionate patriots of America must bend their views to.

My countrymen, preserve your jealousy—reject suspicion, it is the fiend that destroys public and private happiness. I know some weak, but very few if any wicked men in public confidence. And *learn* this most difficult and necessary lesson: That on the preservation of parties, public liberty depends. Whenever men are unanimous on great public questions, whenever there is but one party, freedom ceases and despotism commences. The object of a free and wise people should be so to balance parties, that *from the weakness of all you may be governed by the moderation of the combined judgments of the whole, not tyrannized over by the blind passions of a few individuals.*

A FARMER

FEDERALIST ARGUMENTS

James Madison
Federalist *Paper 10*
(Excerpts)

DISCUSSION QUESTIONS

1. How does Madison define "faction"?
2. How may the "mischiefs of faction" be cured?
3. Why is it important to have a majority of people in a faction?
4. What are the differences between a democracy and a republic?
5. What are the effects of these differences?

Among the numerous advantages promised by a well constructed Union, none deserves to be more accurately developed, than its tendency to break and control the violence of faction. The friend of popular governments, never finds himself so much alarmed for their character and fate, as when he contemplates their propensity to this dangerous vice. He will not fail, therefore, to set a due value on any plan which, without violating the principles to which he is attached, provides a proper cure for it. The instability, injustice, and confusion introduced into the public councils, have, in truth, been the mortal diseases under which popular governments have everywhere perished; as they continue to be the favorite and fruitful topics from which the adversaries to liberty derive their most precious declamations. The valuable improvements made by the American Constitutions on the popular models, both ancient and modern, cannot certainly be too much admired; but it would be an unwarrantable partiality, to contend that they have as effectually obviated the danger on this side, as was wished and expected. Complaints are everywhere heard from our most considerate and virtuous citizens, equally the friends of public and private faith, and of public and personal liberty, that our governments are too unstable; that the public good is disregarded in the conflicts of rival parties; and that measures are too often decided, not according to the rules of justice, and the rights of the minor party, but by the superior force of an interested and overbearing majority. However anxiously we may wish that these complaints had no foundation, the evidence of known facts will not permit us to deny that they are in some degree true. It will be found, indeed, on a candid review of our situation, that some of the distresses under which we labor, have been erroneously charged on the operations of our governments: but it will be found, at the same time, that other causes will not alone account for many of our heaviest misfortunes; and, particularly, for that prevailing and increasing distrust of public engagements, and alarm for private rights, which were echoed from one end of the continent to the other. These must be chiefly, if not wholly, effects of the unsteadiness and injustice, with which a factious spirit has tainted our public administration;

By a faction, I understand a number of citizens, whether amounting to a majority or minority of the whole, who are united and actuated by some common impulse of passion, or of interest, adverse to the rights of other citizens, or to the permanent and aggregate interests of the community.

There are two methods of curing the mischiefs of faction: The one by removing its causes; the other by controlling its effects.

There are again two methods of removing the causes of faction: The one by destroying the liberty which is essential to its existence; the other, by giving to every citizen the same opinions, the same passions, and the same interests.

It could never be more truly said, than of the first remedy, that it is worse than the disease. Liberty is to faction, what air is to fire, an aliment, without which it instantly expires. But it could not be a less folly to abolish liberty, which is essential to political life, because it nourishes faction, than it would be to wish the annihilation of air, which is essential to animal life, because it imparts to fire its destructive agency.

The second expedient is as impracticable, as the first would be unwise. As long as the reason of man continues fallible, and he is at liberty to exercise it, different opinions will be formed. As long as the connection subsists between his reason and his self- love, his opinions and his passions will have a reciprocal influence on each other; and the former will be the objects to which the latter will attach themselves.

. . . It is in vain to say, that enlightened statesmen will be able to adjust these clashing interests, and render them all subservient to the public good. Enlightened statesmen will not always be at the helm: nor, in many cases, can such an adjustment be made at all, without taking into view indirect and remote considerations, which will rarely prevail over the immediate interest which one party may find in disregarding the rights of another, or the good of the whole.

The inference to which we are brought is, that the *causes* of faction cannot be removed; and that relief is only to be sought in the means of controlling its *effects*.

If a faction consists of less than a majority, relief is supplied by the republican principle, which enables the majority to defeat its sinister views, by regular vote. It may clog the administration, it may convulse the society; but it will be unable to execute and mask its violence under the forms of the Constitution. When a majority is included in a faction, the form of popular government, on the other hand, enables it to sacrifice to its ruling passion or interest, both the public good and the rights of other citizens. To secure the public good and private rights against the danger of such a faction, and at the same time to preserve the spirit and the form of popular government, is then the great object to which our inquiries are directed. Let me add, that it is the great desideratum, by which alone this form of government can be rescued from the opprobrium under which it has so long labored, and be recommended to the esteem and adoption of mankind.

By what means is this object attainable? Evidently by one of two only. Either the existence of the same passion or interest in a majority, at the same time, must be prevented; or the majority, having such co-existent passion or interest, must be rendered, by their number and local situation, unable to concert and carry into effect schemes of oppression. If the impulse and the opportunity be suffered to coincide, we well know, that neither moral nor religious motives can be relied on as an adequate control. They are not found to be such on the injustice and violence of individuals, and lose their efficacy in proportion to the number combined together; that is, in proportion as their efficacy becomes needful.

From this view of the subject, it may be concluded that a pure democracy, by which I mean a society consisting of a small number of citizens, who assemble and administer the government in person, can admit of no cure for the mischiefs of faction. A common passion or interest will, in almost every case, be felt by a majority of the whole; a communication and concert, results from the form of government itself; and there is nothing to check the inducements to sacrifice the weaker party, or an obnoxious individual. Hence it is, that such democracies have ever been spectacles of turbulence and contention; have ever been found incompatible with personal security, or the rights of property; and have, in general, been as short in their lives, as they have been violent in their deaths. Theoretic politicians, who have patronized this species of government, have erroneously supposed, that by reducing mankind to a perfect equality in their political rights, they would, at the same time, be perfectly equalized and assimilated in their possessions, their opinions, and their passions.

A republic, by which I mean a government in which the scheme of representation takes place, opens a different prospect, and promises the cure for which we are seeking. Let us examine the points in which it varies from pure democracy, and we shall comprehend both the nature of the cure, and the efficacy which it must derive from the union.

The two great points of difference, between a democracy and a republic, are, first, the delegation of the government, in the latter, to a small number of citizens elected by the rest; secondly, the greater number of citizens, and greater sphere of country, over which the latter may be extended.

The effect of the first difference is, on the one hand, to refine and enlarge the public views, by passing them through the medium of a chosen body of citizens, whose wisdom may best discern the true interest of their country, and whose patriotism and love of justice will be least likely to sacrifice it to temporary or partial considerations. Under such a regulation, it may well happen, that the public voice, pronounced by the representatives of the people, will be more consonant to the public good, than if pronounced by the people themselves, convened for the purpose. On the other hand, the effect may be inverted. Men of factious tempers, of local prejudices, or of sinister designs, may by intrigue, by corruption, or by other means, first obtain the suffrages, and then betray the interest of the people. The question resulting is whether small or extensive republics are most favorable to the election of proper guardians of the public weal; and it is clearly decided in favor of the latter by two obvious considerations.

In the first place, it is to be remarked, that however small the republic may be, the representatives must be raised to a certain number, in order to guard against the cabals of a few; and that however large it may be, they must be limited to a certain number, in order to guard against the confusion of a multitude. Hence the number of representatives in the two cases not being in proportion to that of the constituents, and being proportionably greatest in the small republic, it follows, that if the proportion of fit characters be not less in the large than in the small republic, the former will present a greater option, and consequently a greater probability of a fit choice.

In the next place, as each representative will be chosen by a greater number of citizens in the large than in the small republic, it will be more difficult for unworthy candidates to practice with success the vicious arts, by which elections are too often carried; and the suffrages of the people being more free, will be more likely to centre in men who possess the most attractive merit, and the most diffusive and established characters.

It must be confessed, that in this, as in most other cases, there is a mean, on both sides of which inconveniences will be found to lie. By enlarging too much the number of electors, you render the representative too little acquainted with all their local circumstances and lesser interests; as by reducing it too much, you render him unduly attached to these, and too little fit to comprehend and pursue great and national objects. The Federal Constitution forms, in this respect, a happy combination; the great and aggregate interest being referred to the National—the local and particular, to the State Legislatures.

The other point of difference is, the greater number of citizens and extent of territory, which may be brought within the compass of republican, than of democratic government; and it is this circumstance principally which renders factious combinations less to be dreaded in the former, than in the latter. The smaller the society, the fewer probably will be the distinct parties and interests composing it; the fewer the distinct parties and interests, the more frequently will a majority be found of the same party; and the smaller the number of individuals composing a majority, and the smaller the compass within which they are placed, the more easily will they concert and execute their plans of oppression. Extend the sphere, and you take in a greater variety of parties and interest; you make it less probable that a majority of the whole will have a common motive to invade the rights of other citizens; or if such a common motive exists, it will be more difficult for all who feel it to discover their own strength, and to act in unison with each other. Besides other impediments, it may be remarked, that where there is a consciousness of unjust or dishonorable purpose, communication is always checked by distrust, in proportion to the number whose concurrence is necessary.

Hence it clearly appears, that the same advantage, which a republic has over a democracy, in controlling the effects of faction, is enjoyed by a large over a small republic—is enjoyed by the Union over the States composing it. Does this advantage consist in the substitution of representatives, whose enlightened views and virtuous sentiments render them superior to local prejudices, and to schemes of injustice? It will not be denied, that the representation of the Union will be most likely to possess these requisite endowments. Does it consist in the greater security afforded by a greater variety of parties, against the event of any one party being able to outnumber and oppress the rest? In an equal degree does the increased variety of parties, comprised within the Union, increase this security. Does it, in fine, consist in the greater obstacles opposed to the concert and accomplishment of the secret wishes of an unjust and interested majority? Here, again, the extent of the Union gives it the most palpable advantage.

The influence of factious leaders may kindle a flame within their particular States, but will be unable to spread a general conflagration through the other States. A religious sect may degenerate into a political faction in a part of the Confederacy; but the variety of sects dispersed over the entire face of it must secure the national councils against any danger from that source. A rage for paper money, for an abolition of debts, for an equal division of property, or for any other improper or wicked project, will be less apt to pervade the whole body of the Union, than a particular member of it; in the same proportion as such a malady is more likely to taint a particular county or district, than an entire State.

In the extent and proper structure of the Union, therefore, we behold a republican remedy for the diseases most incident to a republican government. And according to the degree of pleasure and pride we feel in being republicans, ought to be our zeal in cherishing the spirit, and supporting the character, of Federalists.

PUBLIUS

CONTEMPORARY INFLUENCES

Theodore J. Lowi
"The End of Liberalism"
(Excerpts)

DISCUSSION QUESTIONS

1. What are the assumptions of the interest-group liberal model?
2. Describe the three major consequences, or costs, of interest-group liberalism.
3. Can you detect Antifederalist and Federalist thoughts running through Lowi's arguments?

The most clinically accurate term to describe the American variant is *interest-group liberalism.* It may be called liberalism because it expects to use government in a positive and expansive role, it is motivated by the highest sentiments, and it possesses strong faith that what is good for government is good for the society. It is "interest-group liberalism" because it sees as both necessary and good that the policy agenda and the public interest be defined in terms of the organized interests in society. In brief sketch, the working model of the interest group liberal is a vulgarized version of the pluralist model of modern political science. It assumes: (1) Organized interests are homogeneous and easy to define, sometimes monolithic. Any "duly elected" spokesman for any interest is taken as speaking in close approximation for each and every member.[1] (2) Organized interests pretty much fill up and adequately represent most of the sectors of our lives, so that one organized group can be found effectively answering and checking some other organized group as it seeks to prosecute its claims against society.[2] And (3) the role of government is one of ensuring access particularly to the most effectively organized, and of ratifying the agreements and adjustments worked out among the competing leaders and their claims. This last assumption is supposed to be a statement of how our democracy works and how it ought to work.

These assumptions are the basis of the new public philosophy. The policy behavior of old-school liberals and conservatives, of Republicans and Democrats, so inconsistent with liberalism-conservatism criteria, are fully consistent with the criteria drawn from interest-group liberalism: *The most important difference between liberals and conservatives, Republicans and Democrats*—however they define themselves—*is to be found in the interest groups they identify with. Congressmen are guided in their votes, Presidents in their programs, and administrators in their discretion by whatever organized interests they have taken for themselves as the most legitimate; and that is the measure of the legitimacy of demands. . . .*

. . . For all the political advantages interest-group liberals have in their ideology, there are high costs involved. Unfortunately, these costs are not strongly apparent at the time of the creation of a group-based program. As Wallace Sayre has observed, the gains of a change tend to be immediate, the costs tend to be cumulative. However, it takes no long-run patience or the spinning of fine webs to capture and assess the consequences of group-based policy solutions. Three major consequences are suggested and assessed here: (1) the atrophy of institutions of popular control; (2) the maintenance of old and creation of new structures of privilege; and (3) conservatism, in several senses of the world. These consequences will guide later analysis.

(1) In *The Public Philosophy*, Walter Lippmann was rightfully concerned over the "derangement of power" whereby modern democracies tend first toward unchecked elective leadership and then toward drainage of public authority from elective leaders down into their constituencies. However, Lippmann erred if he thought of constituencies only as voting constituencies. Drainage has tended toward "support group constituencies," and with special consequence. Parceling out policy-making power to the most interested parties destroys political responsibility. A program split off with a special imperium to govern itself is not merely an ad-

---

[1]For an excellent inquiry into this assumption and into the realities of the internal life of the interests, see McConnell, *op. cit.*; see also Clark Kerr, *Unions and Union Leaders of Their Own Choosing* (Santa Barbara: Fund for the Republic, 1957); S. M Lipset et al., *Union Democracy* (New York: Anchor, 1962); and Arthur S. Miller, *Private Governments and the Constitution* (Santa Barbara: Fund for the Republic, 1959).

[2]It is assumed that "countervailing power" usually crops up somehow. Where it does not, government ought to help create it. See John Kenneth Galbraith, *American Capitalism* (Boston: Houghton Mifflin, 1952).

ministrative unit. It is a structure of power with impressive capacities to resist central political control.

Besides making conflict-of-interest a principle of government rather than a criminal act, participatory programs shut out the public. To be more precise, programs of this sort tend to cut out all that part of the mass that is not specifically organized around values strongly salient to the goals of the program. They shut out the public, first, at the most creative phase of policy-making—the phase where the problem is first defined. Once problems are defined, alliances form accordingly and the outcome is both a policy and a reflection of superior power. If the definition is laid out by groups along lines of established group organization, there is always great difficulty for an amorphous public to be organized in any other terms.

The public is shut out, secondly, at the phase of accountability. In programs in which group self-administration is legitimate, the administrators are accountable primarily to the groups, only secondarily to the President or Congress as institutions. In brief, to the extent that organized interests legitimately control a program there is functional rather than substantive accountability. This means questions of equity, balance, and equilibrium to the exclusion of questions of overall social policy and questions of whether or not the program should be maintained or discontinued. It also means accountability to experts first and amateurs last; and an expert is a man trained and skilled in the mysteries and technologies of the program. This is the final victory of functional over substantive considerations. . . .

Finally, there is a conspiracy to shut out the public. One of the assumptions underlying direct group representation is that on the boards and in the staff and among the recognized outside consultants there will be regular countervailing, checks, and balances. In Schattschneider's terms, this would be expected to expand the "scope of conflict." But there is nothing inevitable about that, and the safer assumption might well be the converse. . . .

(2) Programs following the principles of interest-group liberalism create privilege, and it is a type of privilege particularly hard to bear or combat because it is touched with the symbolism of the state. The large national interest groups that walk the terrains of national politics are already fairly tight structures of power. We need no more research to support Michels' iron tendency toward oligarchy in these "private governments." Pluralists ease our problem of abiding the existence of organized interests by characterizing oligarchy as simply a negative name for organization: In combat people want and need to be organized and led. Another, somewhat less assuaging, assertion of pluralism is that the member approves the goals of the group or is free to leave it for another, or can turn his attention to one of his "overlapping memberships" in other groups. But however true this may be in pluralistic *politics*, everything changes when some of the groups are co-opted by the state in pluralistic government. . . .

The more clear and legitimized the representation of a group or its leaders in policy formation, the less voluntary is membership in that group and the more necessary is loyalty to its leadership for people who share the interests in question. And, the more clear the official practice of recognizing only organized interests, the more hierarchy is introduced into the society. It is a well-recognized and widely appreciated function of formal groups in modern societies to provide much of the necessary everyday social control. However, when the very thought processes behind public policy are geared toward those groups they are bound to take on much of the involuntary character of *public* control. . . .

Even when the purpose of the program is the uplifting of the underprivileged, the administrative arrangement favored by interest-group liberalism tends toward creation of new privilege instead. Urban redevelopment programs based upon federal support of private plans do not necessarily, but do all too easily, become means by which the building industry regularizes itself. . . .

(3) Government by and through interest groups is in its impact conservative in almost every sense of that term. Part of its conservatism can be seen in another look at the two foregoing objections: Weakening of popular government and support of privilege are, in other words, two aspects of conservatism. It is beside the point to argue that these consequences are not intended. A third dimension of conservatism, stressed here separately, is the simple conservatism of resistance to change.

James MacGregor Burns
"How to Dismember a Party"
(Excerpt)

DISCUSSION QUESTIONS

1. What triggered the political transformation of 1896?
2. What devices did reformers introduce to combat corruption in political parties?
3. What have been the effects of the decline in party leadership?

What triggers a massive political transformation? The upsetting of the party balance in 1896 probably had its roots in the economic and social disarray of Cleveland's second term—panic on Wall Street, spreading financial fear, industrial failures, soaring unemployment, widening strikes and violence. Farmers had been suffering for years from falling prices, tightening credit, high interest rates, and exploitation by shippers and wholesalers; now the economic crises brought long-simmering feelings to a boil. The political result was a crisis within the Democratic Party as the conservative Cleveland, who once had denied federal funds to send seed corn to Texas after a drought, refused now to take strong action in face of economic want, except of course on behalf of capital. The aroused populist and labor leadership in the Democracy struck back against Cleveland in 1896 with the nomination of William Jennings Bryan.

The candidacy of the Great Commoner precipitated the first ideological confrontation in American presidential politics for decades. Never mind that Bryan was a social conservative, anti-urban, anti-cosmopolitan, anti-immigrant. To the men who controlled the Republican Party Bryan was anathema—a threat to credit,

---

capital, and Constitution. Bryan "would steal from the creditors of the nation half of what they saved," Theodore Roosevelt ranted. Republican newspapers labeled him an anarchist, assassin, revolutionary. At the same time the Republican nominee for president, William McKinley, showed a fine talent for coalition building as he united eastern and northern capital and agriculture and labor, Civil War veterans and Negroes, Republican liberals and conservatives, against the populist threat from West and South.

The outcome was a vast imbalancing of the national two-party balance, as McKinley swept the North and East. The Republicans carried even the urban counties of New England and won every northern state east of the Mississippi. It was the lopsided state results that were crucial, for this was the most sectional of elections. Eighteen ninety-six brought not merely a shift of the pendulum, one that would swing the opposite direction in the next election. The pendulum would not shift for a long time. McKinley won again in 1900—the only man who could stop him was not a Democratic candidate but an anarchist with a gun—and Republicans Roosevelt and William Howard Taft came along to win the next two elections.

Thus the decade of the 1890s witnessed, in Paul Kleppner's summary, "an abrupt, massive, and durable shift in the competitive balance between the nation's major parties, ending two decades of partisan stalemate in which neither major party regularly commanded the allegiance of a majority of the nation's voters." This was not only more than a pendulum swing. It was more, even, than a realigning election, or realigning era, in which the long-term strategic relationships of parties are changed. The 1890s brought a *structural* or *institutional* change that profoundly affected the future of political parties and American politics in general. The 1890s elections were so sectional that the one-partyism in northern and southern states, which had long existed to some degree beneath the surface of national two-party politics, intensified and reacted back on national politics. State legislatures dramatically reflected the imbalance. For decades after '96 hardly more than a few Democrats made their way into the upper or lower houses of Vermont or Pennsylvania or Michigan; for decades only handfuls of Republicans could gain seats in the Alabama or South Carolina or other southern legislatures. And by the same token, northern delegations to Congress were heavily Republican, southern delegations even more heavily Democratic.

This was one-partyism with a vengeance, and meant that many states lacked a healthy, competitive party balance. And it had massive and enduring consequences. The health of the party system—its vitality and stability and justification—had lain in that party balance. Now, in state after state, one party could always expect to win, unless it nominated Caligula, and the other party could expect to lose, even if it nominated Cinderella. The pressure on party leaders to perform—to offer good candidates and programs, to govern wisely and compassionately—fell off. If you always would win, why make the effort? Or if you always would lose, why make the effort?

Party leaders, whether local bosses or national chairmen, had long been attacked in press and pulpit as venal, arbitrary, and incompetent. Party leadership had been strong and competitive enough to withstand these assaults. Now, after the turn of the century, political moralists and purists renewed their campaign, and now they had a far better case. What had happened to the opposition party as watchdog? they could ask. They painted lurid pictures of party bosses meeting in smoke-filled rooms and handing out nominations to henchmen who were entirely unfit for the offices they sought, but who would win because of one-party control. Middle-class moralists, most of them white Protestants, had long detested the vulgar, lower-class types who ran the parties at the grass roots. Often they found themselves at the polls choosing between unsavory types from both parties. Now they seemed vindicated.

How to combat the heightened corruption, incompetence, and autocracy in party? Middle-class reformers had the solution: more democracy, participation, and representation within the parties. And they had the devices—the initiative, referendum and recall, and direct primary—that could purify and democratize the government. Civil Service reform was another means of striking at boss control.

The primary was by far the most powerful of these reforms, for it struck at the heart of party power, the nominating process. The essence of the role of party leader had been his influence over the choosing of party nominees. The unique role of party had always been its control of nominating; interest groups, reform organizations, mass movements, could affect the outcome of elections, but they did not have that precious and unique authority, safeguarded by state law, actually to put the names of nominees on ballots. In the early years of the new century, state after state, responding to the iniquities of boss-controlled conventions in particular and to the moral force of progressive, middle-class reformers and "muckrakers" in general, adopted party primaries, along with the initiative and referendum and recall. These reformers were protesting against the party "machine" that had allegedly monopolized politics just as they had turned against the corporate machines that had allegedly monopolized meat packing, utilities ("Trusts"), steel, and oil.

The revolt against party leadership—not just against the Democratic or Republican party leadership but against *party leadership as such*—manifested itself most dramatically in Congress. In the House of Representatives, Speaker Joseph G. Cannon had been acting virtually like a prime minister, controlling the order of business, committee and chairmanship appointments, procedure on the floor, until he was challenged by a young insurgent, George W. Norris, and stripped of much of his power. In the Senate, Robert La Follette of Wisconsin led the fight against "Aldrichism"—Old Guard control of the upper chamber by Senator Nelson Aldrich of Rhode Island and his cronies. La Follette was less successful than Norris, but reformers' and liberals' indignation over the conservative Senate oligarchy helped lead to passage of the 17th Amendment, shifting election of senators out of state legislatures and placing it directly in the hands of the voters. Perhaps it was fitting that the place where national parties were first established—in Congress—was the place where the start of their decline was first evident.

It was in state and congressional politics, though, that the disintegration of party leadership was most evident. There the direct primary fundamentally altered the relationship among party leaders, party nominees, and voters in ways that on balance continued to cripple parties not only in their nominating role but in other functions. Much has been made of the decline of local parties as service and welfare organizations—a result, it is said, of the rise of the New Deal welfare state. But that decline was probably as much a result of parties' earlier organizational erosion as a cause of it. Party "bosses" were able to extract services for their people (and boodle for themselves) out of government because they had held a central role in the "hiring and firing" of city officials. Once they lost their candidate-choosing power, much of their clout was gone.

The rise of "direct democracy" and the decline of party were not dramatic. These alterations in the political system, moreover, proceeded at an uneven pace from state to state. California, under Hiram Johnson and other progressives, took the lead in dismantling the state parties, not only by establishing primaries but also by making city and county elective posts nonpartisan, introducing cross-filing (through which candidates could run for more than one party's nomination), and discouraging straight-party voting. New York, on the other hand, retained significant party conventions and machinery, which for a time heavily influenced even primary outcomes. Hence it was not wholly surprising that New York continued to produce strong state party leaders—Democrats like Al Smith, Franklin D. Roosevelt, Senators Herbert Lehman and Robert Wagner, Republicans like Henry Stimson, Charles Evans Hughes, Thomas E. Dewey, and Nelson Rockefeller. Most of these men, whatever their individual strengths and failings, had a sense of the need for collective leadership, teamwork, and responsibility.

As the collective leadership of party declined, the individual leadership of candidates and officeholders flourished. As parties came to be less effective in furnishing votes and political money to their nominees, office seekers increasingly built their own personal organizations independent of party. A spiral of weakness developed as individual politicians grew increasingly dependent on their own political resources, with parties increasingly cut off from those resources. More and more politicians played King of the Rock as five or ten or more aspirants plunged into primaries, fought for money and publicity, and won or lost on their own, while the party leadership stood by passively, forced to be neutral.

All this had crucial implications for government; it meant that officeholders responded more to diverse and shifting constellations of money givers, organized interests, single-issue groups, and ideological movements than to party programs, interests, and memberships. Teamwork among officeholders, unity across branches of government, collective responsibility and accountability—all these suffered. As the force of the party constitution dwindled, the problems of the first Constitution intensified.

Lloyd N. Cutler
"Political Parties and a Workable Government"
(Excerpt)

DISCUSSION QUESTIONS

1. Describe the trend toward divided government in America.
2. What are the causes of the weakness in political parties?
3. What are the values of a strong national party system?
4. How may a strong national party system be achieved?

Many Americans are deeply concerned about the government's seeming inability to tackle critical problems, such as the need to make the decisions necessary to correct our continuing budget and trade deficits. That inability does not derive from a lack of consensus about the gravity of these problems. Indeed, there is virtual unanimity among our elected leaders that the twin deficits are spreading cancers that may soon become irreversible. Every one of them has a cure to propose, but they are unable to agree on what cure to adopt. Meanwhile, the cancers continue to grow.

Although we are now celebrating the 200th anniversary of the Constitution, few of us associate these massive failures of the political system with faults in our political structure. Most of us blame the individuals we elect to office. Like horse-players disappointed in our choices for the last race, we turn immediately to the entries in the next. But by and large, the 537 incumbents we elect today—435 members of Congress, 100 senators, the president, and the vice-president—are as able and decent as the incumbents of 1937 or 1887. If the national government has greater difficulties in meeting its responsibilities today than at earlier times, the reasons must lie elsewhere.

One glaring reason is the recent decline in the cohesion of the political parties. It is true, of course, that the Constitution makes no mention of political parties, and that James Madison warned against the "rise of faction" in *Federalist Paper No. 10.* But to the political theorists of the eighteenth century, there were three kinds of faction, based on allegiance to a person or family, on a desire for personal political power, or on a shared view of the national interest. There is strong circumstantial evidence that the framers were more concerned about the first two rather than the third. When the new government was formed, Madison and Thomas Jefferson, along with Alexander Hamilton and John Adams, quickly took the lead in establishing two broadly based political parties rooted in their differing views of the national interest. During their presidencies, Adams, Jefferson, Madison, and James Monroe were the de facto leaders of their parties' delegations in Congress. And until President Andrew Jackson, at odds with the congressional

---

Burke Marshall, ed., *A Workable Government? The Constitution After 200 Years.* (New York: W. W. Norton & Company), pp. 49–57.

wing of his party, invented the national political convention to achieve his renomination, the congressional caucus of each party played the dominant role in nominating the party's presidential candidate.

While the constitutional separation of the executive and legislative branches did exert its intended centrifugal effect, presidents and legislators of the same party worked remarkably well together to govern the young nation. John Adams and Jefferson never had to cast a single veto, Madison did so only seven times, and Monroe only once. During the seven consecutive terms of these four presidents, divided government (one party holding the White House and the other party a majority of one or both houses) never occurred. In fact, only three nineteenth-century presidents (Millard Fillmore, Rutherford B. Hayes, and Grover Cleveland in his first term) were elected without carrying majorities for their parties in both houses. In the twentieth century, this did not happen until 1956, when President Dwight D. Eisenhower, even while winning his own reelection by a huge margin, failed to carry a majority for his party in both houses. This phenomenon of divided government resulted in five of the eight presidential elections from 1956 to 1984—more often in these three decades than in the first 170 years of the Republic. In the presidential elections from 1968 to 1984, it occurred four times out of five.

Woodrow Wilson campaigned against divided government when he ran for president in 1912, a time when the Republicans held the presidency and a majority of the Senate, and the Democrats held a majority of the House. Wilson said:

> [Under divided government] you have an arrested government. You have a government that is not responding to the wishes of the people. You have a government that is not functioning, a government whose very energies are stayed and postponed. If you want to release the force of the American people, you have got to get possession of the Senate and the presidency as well as the House.

Wilson won the presidency and a solid majority for the Democrats in both houses. His first term carried out the party program by laying the legislative foundation of the New Freedom, generally regarded as the most productive period of American government between the abolition of slavery and the New Deal.

This recent trend toward divided government parallels the growing weakness of the political parties. That weakness has several causes.

First, voters have lost their earlier sense of party consciousness. In 1900, 4 percent of the nation's congressional districts cast a majority vote for one party's presidential candidate and for the other party's candidate for the House of Representatives. Ticket splitting increased to the point where this happened in 45 percent of all districts in 1984. Polls taken in 1987 showed that nearly one-third of all voters did not think of themselves as adhering to a party.

Second, party cohesion in Congress, and between the legislators and president of the same party, has been greatly weakened by twentieth-century reforms such as the civil service system, the primary elections, and the "democratization" of Congress, as well as by technological innovations such as radio and television. National, state, and local party leaders no longer select or provide most of the financing to the party's candidates for federal office; the candidates get themselves nominated and financed with little or no help from party leaders. Well-heeled single-interest groups have accelerated this process. They have learned they can exert greater influence on the single issues they care about by contributing directly to the candidate and by making additional "independent expenditures" on his or her behalf than by contributing indirectly through the party. For the past two decades, congressional candidates have become less and less dependent on the parties' leaders to get themselves elected and reelected, and they have little incentive to support these leaders while in office.

Two features of the Constitution itself have accelerated the weakening of political parties. One is the ban, which the Supreme Court has read into the First Amendment, on laws limiting campaign expenditures. Congress may set such limits only as a condition imposed on those candidates who accept public financing, which is currently available only to presidential nominees. This ban enhances the divisive power of single-interest blocs willing to spend any amount to achieve their goals. The other constitutional feature that has weakened political parties is the staggering of electoral terms and the brief two-year term of the House of Representatives—the shortest of any major democratic nation. Presidents are elected for a four-year term, but all representatives and one-third of the senators always face an election within two years. With the carefully balanced sharing of legislative and executive power that is designed into the Constitution, the shorter time horizon of most legislators becomes dominant and creates deadlock between the branches and between the president and the legislators of the president's party. It is a political truism that nothing can be done to reduce deficits in an election year, which now means nothing can be done every other year.

The results are apparent. The percentage of congressional votes in which a majority of one party is on one side and a majority of the other party is on the other side has fallen below 50 percent. Most controversial legislation is passed by cross-party coalitions whose makeup shifts from one issue to the next. With so little cohesion on either side of the aisle, the party holding the White House has great difficulty in legislating the program on which its candidates ran for office. This is especially true at times of divided government, when the administration's success rate on major bills is only about 66 percent (except in 1981, President Ronald Reagan did no better). Even at times when the administration party has majorities in both houses, its success rate is only 80 percent. These rates considerably overstate the actual degree of success, because they include many bills in which the administration has accepted major modifications it dislikes in order to get at least half of what it wants.

The sum of all these decisions is often inconsistent and self-defeating. Moreover, neither party nor any individual we elect can fairly be held accountable for the hodgepodge of unwanted outcomes such as the huge budget and trade deficits. Indeed, they mostly succeed in escaping accountability. About 90 percent of the incumbent legislators of *both* parties who run for reelection are reelected, even when their party loses the White House. And Presidents Eisenhower, Richard Nixon, and Reagan, who ran for reelection at times of divided government, were reelected by landslide margins.

Benjamin Franklin's 1776 maxim, "We must all hang together, or most assuredly we shall all hang separately," is a dead letter for either party's incumbents today. They adhere more closely to the motto of the Damon Runyon character who said, "It's every man for theirself."

The values of a strong national party system are threefold. First, a broadly based party, able to select and finance its own candidates and maintain cohesion among them in office, can serve as a moderating force between the financial and voting pressures of single-interest groups and the individual candidates we elect to conduct the government. Second, it can blend these conflicting pressures and a broader view of the national interest into a coherent program for governing. Third, if it wins the presidency and a working majority of both houses, it can legislate and execute that program, and stand clearly accountable at the next election for its good, bad, or indifferent results.

Nevertheless, some believe that weak parties and divided government are better than their opposites. They fear that stronger political parties and a greater degree of party government would lead to wild swings of the pendulum between extreme policies, such as the shifts between nationalization and privatization in Britain. But wild extremes did not happen under the stronger parties that took turns governing this nation for most of the first 150 years of our history. They have not happened in the Federal Republic of Germany or in our own state governments, many of which still function under strong and cohesive state party systems. The centrifugal forces in our constitutional structure and in our ocean-to-ocean continent of a nation are far too strong for such extreme swings to occur.

Some also believe that the primary reason for deadlock and incoherence is a lack of public consensus on major controversial issues, and that it is the duty of elected officials to reflect this lack until a true public consensus forms. But the framers never intended the national government to be run as a town meeting of the entire citizenry. The framers created *representative* government, and expected these elected representatives to govern by making decisions in the national interest as they saw it. They did not intend these representatives to vote in perfect reflection of the weekly public opinion polls.

Is it too late to strengthen the political parties to the point where they can resume their natural functions of intermediation and accountability? Some of us believe it is not too late. For the past several years, the Committee on the Constitutional System, composed of several hundred present and former senators and representatives, cabinet officials, White House staffers, academics, and grass-roots political, business, and labor leaders, has been studying this question. It has just published its analysis and recommendations.

The committee recognizes the many virtues in our 200-year-old constitutional structure and in the reforms of the political party system that have been made during this century. It sees no reason to reverse any of these reforms or to alter the basic constitutional framework, and accepts that in any event it is not feasible to do so. But a broad consensus of the committee agrees that a few modest improvements in our electoral arrangements would greatly improve the chances of strengthening the parties and enabling them to resume the role they filled so well until the 1950s. Some of these suggestions would require changes in party rules, some would require legislation, and some would require very moderate changes in the Constitution itself. The following are among the most important improvements.

Change party rules for presidential nominating conventions. Give the party's nominees for the House and Senate races plus the holdover senators 535 additional seats as uncommitted voting delegates. This would give them a major voice in close races for the presidential nomination, make them politically accountable for the convention's choice, and enhance the possibilities of party cohesion with the president after the election.

Provide funding for congressional election campaigns. Enact a statute to provide public funding for congressional election campaigns, as we now do for presidential elections. Nominees who accept public funding would be barred from raising or spending any other funds, as the presidential nominees are now barred, and as the Supreme Court approved in *Buckley v. Valeo* (1976). Half or more of the funds would be allocated to the nominees directly under a population-based formula. The balance would go to each party's congressional campaign committees, usually made up of party leaders in each house, to be allocated among the close races as the committees decide in order to maximize the party's chances of winning majority control. This would reduce the pressure of well-heeled single-interest groups on nominees and incumbents, and improve their cohesion with the party's legislative leaders after election.

Limit campaign expenditures. Amend the Constitution to permit Congress to set reasonable limits on all campaign expenditures in primaries and general elections, something the Supreme Court has held the Constitution presently forbids. In 1986 midterm election candidates raised and spent $350 million, most of which was contributed directly or spent on behalf of individual candidates by wealthy single-interest pressure groups. This was considerably above the amount spent four years earlier, and the trend is moving steadily up. These pressure groups weaken party cohesion and are largely responsible for the hodgepodge of inconsistent government actions we see today.

Change terms of office. Amend the Constitution to establish a four-year term for the House of Representatives, running simultaneously with the presidential term, and an eight-year term for the Senate, with two classes of senators rather than the present three. Every four years we would vote at the same time for president, vice-president, all members of the House, and one senator from each state. This would create a common political time horizon of at least four years for all elected officials. It would lengthen the "honeymoon" period in which major but controversial legislation can be enacted, such as deficit-reduction measures that may create unpopular pains within two years, but produce popular benefits within four. It would also cut the cost of campaigning in half and assure a much larger voter turnout for congressional elections than the 35 percent of eligible voters who turned out for the 1986 midterm election. It would enhance the party consciousness of voters and, since they all would be running in the same election and reelection, it would enhance cohesion among each party's elected officials while in office.

Anthony J. Eksterowicz and Paul C. Cline "Is Citizen Participation Consistent with Effective Political Parties?"

DISCUSSION QUESTIONS

1. Why have the progressive reforms "taken their toll" on political parties?
2. How do the proposals of the Committee on the Constitutional System reflect Antifederalist and Federalist thought?
3. Evaluate the proposal for citizen assemblies in light of Antifederalist and Federalist ideas.

In American Political Science literature, it has become axiomatic that political parties have declined in electoral influence. Gone are the days of the old city party machines of Bosses Plunkett, Daley and Rizzo along with their consequent party nomination deals in the proverbial smoke-filled back rooms.

Scholars and political commentators have noted the new movement toward direct participation of the people in the political candidate nomination process. Many have been critical of this movement for it seems to imply the decline of American political parties. Indeed, according to this analysis, political parties have suffered since the inception of the Progressive Reform Movement at the turn of this century. Progressive, "populist" devices such as the initiative, referendum and recall, and especially the direct primary have combined to weaken political parties and perhaps render them relics of a past age. A few scholars advocate a reduction in the use of these devices as a first step toward party regeneration. It should be noted that the type of political participation fostered by these Progressive reforms emphasizes citizen impact upon electoral politics in contrast to the type of strong citizen participation emphasizing enlightened and informed debate complete with education functions.

What seems implicit in contemporary party literature is the argument that we can have either strong citizen participation or strong parties but not both. This remains a rather curious belief since Thomas Jefferson, whom many cite as the founder of American political parties, fervently believed in the right of citizens to participate in the decisions that would affect them. This would be accomplished via regular meetings in the context of what he termed ward republics.[1]

In this essay, we will first examine the claims concerning Progressive citizen initiatives and their effect upon political parties. Second, we will discuss the origins of the mutual exclusivity argument between citizen participation and strong political parties. Finally, we will challenge this argument largely by proposing a method aimed at fusing citizen participation with strengthened parties.

[1]Richard K. Matthews, *The Radical Politics of Thomas Jefferson* (Lawrence: The University of Kansas Press, 1984), pp. 81–85. See also Jefferson's July 12, 1816 letter to Samuel Kercheval in Walter E. Volkmer, Ed., *The Liberal Tradition in American Thought* (New York: Capricorn Books, 1969), pp. 116–123.

National Civic Review. LXXIX, No. 6 (November-December, 1990), pp. 529–545.

Progressive Reforms

The list of reforms attributed to the turn-of-the-century Progressives is a long one. Some of the measures were economic, such as control of street railways by cities, new taxes and regulations in the states and support for tariffs nationally.

V. O. Key's list of progressive reforms relating to political parties is instructive. He indicated a variety of motivations behind the changes.

> That movement, whose temper is difficult to reconstruct, was a mixture of economic discontent, of middle-class protest against plutocratic influences, and of moral and religious fervor, as well as of more than a trace of sectionalism. It denounced special privilege and bossism, and fought popular rule.[2]

His list included the direct primary, the initiative and referendum, direct election of Senators and urban political reform.

Other students of the progressive era have added to the list numerous other demands for change in government and in political party activity. These demands include civil service instead of patronage, regulation of the operation of parties, registration of voters, women's suffrage, dropping partisan designations in local elections, and adoption of the office-block ballot.[3]

Heading nearly every observer's list of progressive action that has affected political parties is the direct primary as a replacement for the convention as a nominating device. The aim in adopting the direct primary was "to substitute the party electorate for the party organization as the nominator."[4]

The effect of the use of the direct primary has been otherwise. Austin Ranney suggests that the direct primary has removed not only boss control but also party control of the nomination process.[5] While the weakening of party control has depended upon both a state's formulation of the direct primary nominating system and the extent of the state party leadership's ability to act within that legal framework, the overall effect of the direct primary is to weaken the party "as an organization."

Frank Sorauf maintains that the advocates of the primary "succeeded in multiplying the party oligarchies rather than in democratizing them."[6] This is accomplished through shifting control to nonparty actors and individual candidates. Since the party must control the nominating process in order to be effective in its major task of electing persons to office, the role of the political party has been re-

---

[2]V. O. Key, Jr., *Politics, Parties, and Pressure Groups*, 4th Ed. (New York: Thomas Y. Crowell Company, 1958), pp. 194–95.

[3]See, for example, David E. Price, *Bringing Back the Parties* (Washington: CQ Press, 1984), p. 101; Frank J. Sorauf and Paul Allen Beck, *Party Politics in America*, 6th Ed. (Boston: Scott, Foresman and Company, 1988), pp. 217, 224, and 244–45.

[4]Sorauf, p. 267.

[5]Austin Ranney, *Curing the Mischiefs of Faction* (Berkeley: University of California Press, 1975), p. 129.

[6]Sorauf, p. 267.

duced by the advent of primaries. With the opening of the nomination role to persons who have little affiliation or loyalty to the party, the political party is little more than a sponsor rather than an actor in the process of candidate selection.

The perception of the party in the minds of citizens is not enhanced by the direct primary. Not only is the effectiveness of the party reduced, but its representativeness also suffers. Persons on the lower end of the socioeconomic scale tend to play a lesser role, permitting the higher status individuals to engage in what amounts to "stuffing the ballot box."[7] Voters and citizens contemplating voting find it difficult to identify with the political party that they cannot see acting in their behalf. Still worse, voters can barely see the party acting in any fashion during the nomination process in direct primary situations.

In order to render the parties more effective and active, a respected student of parties has recommended that they choose the nominating method, with the caucus and convention preferred. If the direct primary is retained, he suggests the closed rather than the open version with the pre-primary endorsement of party-favored candidates by a party convention.[8]

The initiative, referendum and recall have taken their toll on the importance of political parties. These devices were designed to permit a larger role for the individual citizens in deciding important issues. Various factors have reduced this democratizing effect, such as the often low turnout in referenda elections. Although these devices have not competed with political parties as extensively as has the direct primary, the use of statewide initiatives increased in the 1980s. With the growth of the initiative, an "initiative industry" has risen to perform the tasks necessary to place measures on the ballot. The professionals in this industry are experts in the use of direct mail, polling and media.[9]

With the growth of the initiative, the political party has been surpassed as a policy facilitator. Issues of party interest are often the very ones that are accomplished through the initiative; these include matters of health, welfare, housing, revenues and taxes. With the rising costs of the initiative process, the democratic nature of the activity is reduced for the use of the process is restricted to groups with significant financial resources, thus effectively eliminating the citizen of below-average means.

The Progressive reformers reduced the effectiveness of political parties from the selection process of a host of elective and appointive offices. Examples include changes brought about by the direct election of Senators, elimination of political party designations in local elections and the civil service movement.

Much has been written on each of these changes. An illustration of the problems created by these reforms is the mitigation of overt party activity at the local

---

[7]Nelson W. Polsby, *Consequences of Party Reform* (Oxford: Oxford University Press, 1983), p. 160.

[8]Larry J. Sabato, *The Party's Just Begun: Shaping Political Parties for America's Future* (Boston: Scott, Foresman and Company, 1988), pp. 205–6 and 210.

[9]David B. Magleby, "Taking the Initiative: Direct Legislation and Direct Democracy in the 1980s," *PS: Political Science and Politics*, Vol. 21 (Summer 1988), pp. 602–5.

government level. Many municipal elections are held without the inclusion of party labels on the ballot. The advent of the professional city manager reduced the role and party position of the elected mayor.

Because local government nonpartisanship occurs at the lowest level, the opportunity is removed for citizens to be involved in the initial level of the political party process, the level closest to the ordinary person. The educational value of joining the process, learning party skills, and being exposed to party procedures at this less sophisticated and less threatening stage is missing. Further, the opportunity to recruit party officeholders and allow them to run for local office before representing larger constituencies is less available.

The Progressive reformers have gone over, around and under political parties in their efforts to open the political process to more participants. In doing so, they have enhanced the quantity of persons who are admitted to the game; however, the composition of these participants has not fulfilled the expectations of the reformers. Further, the quality of participation has suffered with the decline in political party strength.

Mechanisms that have increased citizen input to either the political party candidate nomination and selection process or more broadly to government policy formulation are linked to the decline in the strength of political parties. This belief highlights the dilemma of mutual exclusivity between citizen participation and strong political parties. But are these two ideas really mutually exclusive? Where is the genesis of such thinking? Might it be possible to fuse these two seemingly contradictory ideas and if so, how? These are the questions to which we now turn.

The Origins of Mutual Exclusivity: Federalists and Antifederalists

The genesis of the mutual exclusivity argument can be traced to the Constitutional ratification debates. Much has been written about the republican nature of our Constitution and the elements of the elite consensus at Philadelphia. The Founders' antipathy to mass participation and direct democracy was noted by James Madison when he stated, " . . . Had every Athenian citizen been a Socrates, every Athenian assembly would still have been a mob."[10] Roger Sherman echoed this sentiment by remarking, " . . . The people should have as little to do as may be about the government. They want information and are constantly liabled to be mislead."[11] Hamilton's aristocratic views led to an even more strident view concerning widespread citizen participation. Indeed, the Founders constructed elaborate filtering devices between the people and their government: the electoral college, election of senators via state legislatures, a rather small House of Representatives which might, in the beginning, ensure rule by the privileged classes and the failure of the founders at the Constitutional Convention to deal with the restrictive property qualifications attached to the franchise by many of the states. Their purpose was the protection of private property from the type of revolt illustrated by Shay's Rebellion. With this, they believed, would come stability:

---

[10]Clinton Rossiter, Ed., *The Federalist Papers* (New York: Mentor Books, 1961), p. 342.

[11]Ferdinand Lundberg, *Cracks in the Constitution* (Secaucus, N.J.: Lyle Stuart, Inc., 1980), p. 157.

> Inherent in Hamilton's grand design is a set of political implications with profound importance. He created an intricate central government machine that encouraged and rewarded behavior appropriate to his vision of a national-commercial-financial-industrial economy—the entrepreneurial, productive, growth-oriented behavior that was to define our economic, political, and cultural life and identity for centuries. . . .
>
> Hamilton also insulated the machine against the possibility that popular majorities or political chicanery might alter the outcomes he deemed essential to the creation of a great nation. In the process, by building upon the dark side of the Constitution, the Framers' property protecting provisions and fear of democracy, Hamilton succeeded in almost completely removing the substance of public policy from popular hands. . . .[12]

Madison reflected Hamilton's thoughts concerning collective meetings of the people by remarking that, ". . . Ignorance will be the dupe of cunning and passion the slave of sophistry and declamation."[13] Thus, the Founders desired a strict republican form of government which would be ruled by the wisdom inherent in men associated with the privileged classes.

While the Constitution does not mention political parties, they quickly emerged not only as electoral institutions but as institutions for the transmission of popular will into government policy. It is possible to view these institutions as additional filtering devices between the people and their government so necessary to the Founders' republican ideas. As a result, political parties were more republican and representative in nature and not strictly participatory. Contemporary arguments aimed at reestablishing strong political parties stress the intermediary role of such institutions.[14] The argument for strong and hence elite republican institutions like political parties, among others, was entrenched in our national psyche during the Constitution ratification debates. These ideas, however, were not the only ones debated during the ratification period.

Antifederalist ideas concerning the nature of our republic were also extremely important. If we can generally characterize the Founders' ideas of government as elite and republican in nature, then we can surely characterize Antifederalist notions as more democratic. As Gordon Wood has observed:

> The Antifederalists thus came to oppose the new national government for the same reasons the Federalists favored it: because its very structure and detachment from the people would work to exclude any kind of actual and local interest representation and prevent those who were not rich, well born, or prominent from exercising political power. Both sides fully appreciated the central issue the Constitution posed and grappled with it throughout the debates: whether a professedly popular government should actually be in the hands of, rather than simply derived from, common ordinary people.[15]

---

[12]Kenneth M. Dolbeare and Linda Medcalf, "The Dark Side of the Constitution" in John F. Manley and Kenneth M. Dolbeare, Eds., *The Case Against the Constitution* (New York: M. E. Sharpe, Inc., 1987), p. 121.

[13]Rossiter, Ed., p. 360.

[14]See, for example, the argument of Lloyd N. Cutler, "Political Parties and a Workable Government" in Burke Marshall, Ed., *A Workable Government: The Constitution After 200 Years* (New York: W.W. Norton & Co., 1987), pp. 49–58.

[15]Gordon S. Wood, *The Creation of the American Republic 1776–1787* (Chapel Hill: University of North Carolina Press, 1969), p. 516.

There are a number of important elements comprising the Antifederalist argument:

- First, most Antifederalists resented the secrecy surrounding the Constitutional Convention. Some compared the pledges of secrecy to the chains of despotism. Thus, secrecy was seen by some as a calculated attempt to keep information from the people.[16]
- Second, Antifederalists objected to the idea that wisdom resides in the natural aristocracy instead of the people. The minority delegation to the Philadelphia Convention, for example, resented the influence of the representatives from the City of Philadelphia in the state legislature to the detriment of more rural areas. The rule agreed to by the Pennsylvania legislature that there was to be no compensation for the delegates to the Constitutional Convention worked against rural delegates living great distances from the city and conversely worked in favor of those more aristocratic delegates nearer the city.[17]
- Third, Antifederalists argued for more and frequent elections. The idea was to have the government close to the people and prevent isolation of the people from their governmental representatives. For this reason, the Antifederalists also favored the rotation of governmental offices.[18]
- Fourth, Antifederalists objected to the representation in the proposed House of Representatives. The membership in such a House was judged to be too small to ensure adequate representation. To the Antifederalist, adequate representation implied an equality of representation from all classes and professions. Balance was to be the key here and this, it was thought, would help to preclude representation by natural aristocracy. The formula of one representative for every 30,000 to 40,000 inhabitants derived at the Convention was judged inadequate by Antifederalist standards. As Richard Henry Lee argued, " . . . It is deceiving a people to tell them they are electors, and can chuse their legislators, if they cannot, in the nature of things, chuse men from among themselves, and genuinely like themselves."[19]

There were other Antifederalist objections to the Constitution such as the absence of a Bill of Rights. Since such a bill was included in amendment form to the Constitution, it is perhaps too commonly thought that this action detracts from the Antifederalist argument. However, the major Antifederalist claims concerning participatory democracy still stand. It is important to characterize the nature of these objections. Some Antifederalists were not objecting to republican institutions per se but to the type of republican institutions agreed to at the Convention. There were areas

---

[16]See, for example, "The Addresses and Reasons of Dissent of the Minority of the Convention of Pennsylvania to Their Constituents" in Manley and Dolbeare, Eds., p. 74.

[17]Manley and Dolbeare, Eds., p. 73.

[18]Samuel E. Morison and Henry S. Commager, *The Growth of the American Republic, volume I* (New York: Oxford University Press, 1962), p. 290.

[19]Richard Henry Lee, "Letter from the Federal Farmer," in Manley and Dolbeare, Eds., p. 94.

of agreement between the Federalists and Antifederalists. Both disagreed with rule by a monarch. Both agreed to some form of representation. Both saw the need for a government with some centralizing tendencies. The question was rather over what type of government and the extent of centralizing tendencies. Some Antifederalists would probably have accepted a representative governmental structure which ensured a greater equality of representation in the House. This would have implied a larger House with emphasis upon equality of representation by class and profession. It would have implied more frequent elections with rotation of office provisions. It would have probably also implied government with less secrecy and dispatch. This type of government could have occurred within a republican framework. All of this suggests that the two ideas of participatory and republican representative democracy need not necessarily be inimicable. There has been a tendency to view our choices here in an either/or framework, but reality is rarely that kind. Gray areas predominate reality simultaneously creating more options but complicating our choices.

The Contemporary Debate Revisited

In point of fact, the United States has been deeply affected by the ideas of participatory democracy. It is possible to view, "... United States political history ... as a process of democratizing a republican government structure."[20] From the efforts of Thomas Jefferson to the Age of Jackson through the Progressive Reform Movement, New Deal, Civil Rights, Vietnam Protest, Women's Movement, and Environmental periods, some form of participatory effort was stressed usually by Congressional mandate. Many of the Great Society programs required citizen participation. For example, the Equal Opportunity Act of 1964 mobilized the poor and involved them in policy-making decisions. Other acts, like the Coastal Zone Act and the Housing and Community Development Act required citizen participation either by legislation or regulation. Many federal legislative programs have also been amended to include citizen participation provisions.[21] As a result, citizens have been incorporated into many planning bodies across diverse fields like health, education, transportation and the environment.

Upon examination, one finds in the citizen participation literature a rich diversity concerning the goals of such participation. Some participatory advocates urge the utilization of (and building upon) participatory instrumentalities from the Progressive Reform Era.[22] Others have focused their efforts on instituting participatory mechanisms for industrial use.[23] Others seek to remove the restrictions associated with majority rule constructed by the Founders.[24] Still others seek to

---

[20]Mary G. Kweit and Robert W. Kweit, *Implementing Citizen Participation in a Bureaucratic Society* (New York: Praeger Publishers, 1981), p. 4.

[21]Stuart Langton, *Citizen Participation in America* (Mass.: D.C. Heath & Co., 1978), p. 3.

[22]Joseph F. Zimmerman, *Participatory Democracy: Populism Revived* (New York: Praeger, 1986).

[23]D. H. Cole, *Self Government in Industry* (London: G. Bell & Sons, 1919), passim, and Carole Pateman, *Participation and Democratic Theory* (Cambridge: Cambridge University Press, 1970), passim.

[24]Robert A. Dahl, "On Removing Certain Impediments to Democracy in the United States," *Political Science Quarterly*, Vol. 92, 1977, pp. 1–20.

utilize emerging communications technologies in participatory schemes that vary from establishing participatory institutions[25] to replacing these institutions or eclipsing them with direct democracy.[26] The debate therefore appears to be largely over whether to replace existing representation institutions or merely influence them.

The ideas expressed in this literature have much in common with Antifederalist arguments. Indeed, one scholar has referred to contemporary political reformers of the 1960s and 1970s as modern Antifederalists. Four themes seem to link the modern reformers with their Antifederalist counterparts. First, both expressed goals of democratizing our political structure. These reformers see participation as valid for its own sake and not a means towards some other end. Second, while both are portrayed as radical, they are perhaps best viewed as liberal reformers committed to systemic values such as the rule of law. Third, both were deeply suspicious of capitalism, but the emphasis of at least the contemporary activists has been on reforming the system, not eliminating it. Fourth, there is a hostility towards special interests which the Antifederalists would have termed privileged interests. As Brand notes:

> When the four principles that animated reform in the 1960s and 1970s were combined, they impelled reformers beyond narrowly conceived piecemeal reforms. Indeed, the conjunction of direct democracy, legal formalism, suspicion of capitalism, and suspicion of interest group politics posits a fundamentally different political system than established by the American Framers in 1789.[27]

Perhaps the present system can best be characterized as one emphasizing representative institutions tinged with democratic measures. The debate concerning the methods for strengthening our governmental structure and process illustrates this mixture.

During the Bicentennial year, the Committee on the Constitutional System was formed to examine the problems facing government and to propose solutions in the form of reforms. Generally, the Committee found the problem of divided government ending in policy deadlock to be the one overriding problem facing the United States in the near future. They proposed a number of reforms aimed at alleviating the problem. Many of these reforms were in the form of constitutional amendments but others were suggested federal statutes and party rule changes. Table 1 summarizes these proposals.[28]

These proposals touched off a debate with striking similarities to the one during the Constitutional ratification period. For example, critics of the committee ar-

---

[25]Robert A. Dahl, *Controlling Nuclear Weapons: Democracy Versus Guardianship* (New York: Syracuse University Press, 1985).

[26]Richard Hollander, *Video Democracy: The Vote from Home Revolution* (Mt. Airy: Lomand Publications, 1985).

[27]Donald R. Brand, "Reformers of the 1960's and 1970's: Modern Anti-Federalists?" in Richard A. Harris and Sidney M. Milkis, Eds., *Remaking American Politics* (Boulder: Westview Press, 1989), p. 39.

[28]For a discussion of these proposals see, Donald L. Robinson, Ed., *Reforming American Government* (Boulder: Westview Press, 1985), *passim.*

TABLE 4-1 Proposals of the Committee on the Constitutional System

I. Constitutional Amendments
  A. *To solve primarily the problem of divided government:*
    1. Coordinated terms of office for elected members of the executive and legislative branches would be established;
    2. Presidential and congressional candidates would run as a team on a political party slate;
    3. The party electing the President would receive bonus seats in the Senate and House;
    4. Members of the Senate and House would be eligible to fill offices in the executive branch;
    5. The President would have the power to appoint cabinet secretaries to the Senate and House;
    6. The two-term limit on the presidency (twenty-second amendment) would be repealed.
  B. *To solve primarily the problem of deadlock:*
    1. The President and Congress would have the power to issue a proclamation or resolution of no confidence which would result in special elections for President and all members of Congress;
    2. Provisions would be made for a national referendum;
    3. The one house override would be available to House and Senate;
    4. The President would be empowered with the item veto;
    5. Congress would be empowered with the legislative veto;
    6. Treaty ratification would occur by a reduced majority.

II. Federal Statutes to Reform the Electoral System
  1. Two phase federal elections would be established in which the President would be elected four weeks prior to Congress;
  2. Candidates for federal office would have the option to run on party slates;
  3. Public financing of campaign broadcasts would be provided.

III. Party Rules to Reform the Electoral System
  1. Restrictions would be placed on campaign expenditures;
  2. Bicameral nominating conventions would divide delegates to national conventions into a popular and a congressional chamber.

Source: Jeanne Hahn, "Neohamiltonianism; A Democratic Critique," in John F. Manley and Kenneth M. Dolbeare, Eds., *The Case Against the Constitution: From Antifederalist to the Present* (New York: M. E. Sharpe, Inc., 1987), pp. 147–48.

gued that the first three proposed constitutional amendments would have the effect of diminishing third party movements. Since there were no proposals concerning the single-member districts, the winner-take-all representation model, a competitive multi-party system would be discouraged. The same could be said of the federal statutes aimed at coupling federal candidates to party slates, encouraging public financing of campaign broadcasts which could be construed to restrict third party efforts, and changes in the congressional campaign finance laws that would distribute contributions only to the two established parties.[29] Generally, modern reformers favor widening the representative institutions for debate. As Jeanne Hahn argues concerning the committee's proposals:

---

[29]Jeanne H. Hahn, "Neohamiltonianism: A Democratic Critique" in Manley and Dolbeare, Eds., pp. 147–52.

> As for the Committee's professed twin goals of efficiency and accountability, the first would be achieved with a vengeance. Once in place, the package would work to purify parties, to make them more internally homogenous and like-minded, and to muffle the voice of those groups that had begun to be heard for the first time. . . .
>
> It would be a very efficient government indeed. But accountable to whom? Certainly not the people, from whom it would be largely insulated. The people are excluded from the proposed process except in their role as atomized voters — disciplined or required by constitutional directive to vote a party slate.[30]

The committee's proposals were viewed as Hamiltonian in nature by the critics. Given the nature of this contemporary debate, we now must ask if there might be a way to fuse the participatory ideals of Antifederalism with republican institutions like political parties.

Toward a Fusion: Strong BUT Participatory Political Parties

In *The Party's Just Begun,* Larry J. Sabato correctly notes that political parties are stronger than conventional wisdom would have us believe. He wishes to encourage this trend for as he notes, in a world without parties special interests, PACs, wealthy and celebrity candidates, incumbents, the news media, and political consultants would all gain in political prominence. In this type of world, Antifederalist ideals would surely suffer. Sabato provides an agenda for strong party renewal consisting of actions initiated by the parties and those initiated with the aid of government-assisted reforms.

Under these proposals, parties would engage more in education and policy formulation, and provide more tangible and material services to members. They would offer campaign services to party candidates. Sabato also advocates an expansion of party fund raising with greater efforts to recruit party volunteers and candidates. Government-assisted reforms aimed at strengthening political parties include: deregulation of parties, an emphasis upon conventions and caucuses with fewer primaries, provisions for public financing along with a party role in this financing, provisions for free radio and television time, changes in federal election laws, re-institution of a universal straight party lever, universal party registration, consolidation of elections and government structure to increase the coattail effect and strengthen governorships, an increase in patronage, and prohibitions on primary losers' launching election bids as incumbents.[31]

Modern reformers would, no doubt, raise concerns similar to those raised against the suggested proposals by the Committee on the Constitutional System. Under many of Sabato's proposals, for example, there would be a debilitating effect upon third party movements. Although one, perhaps, can argue that strengthened parties may attract previously nonparticipating citizens because party activity would become more worthwhile and relevant, active participation of the people in important party deliberations such as policy formulation seems to be negligible. Yet, Sabato's observations about a world without parties can be frightening. There

---

[30] Manley and Dolbeare, Eds., p. 163.

[31] Sabato, pp. 176–242.

may be a way to fuse the best Jeffersonian notions of citizen participation with Sabato's proposals concerning strong political parties. We should note that this attempt to fuse participatory functions with republican political party structures would not please all modern Antifederalists or dedicated republicans. Neither would it address the problem of third parties and single-member districts, but it could lead to a more open, decentralized and participatory two-party system, and this should do for a start.

The belief behind strong participatory politics stems from Jefferson. As James MacGregor Burns notes:

> . . . Jefferson believed that virtue must be nurtured at the bottom, among the "little republics" of states, where as he wrote later, 'every man is a sharer in the direction of his ward, republic, or of some of the higher ones, and feels that he is a participator in the government of affairs, not merely at an election one day in the year, but every day; where there shall not be a man in the state who will not be a member of some one of its councils, great or small, he will let the heart be torn out of his body sooner than his power wrested from him by a Caesar or Bonaparte.'[32]

With this spirit in mind Robert Dahl, in *Controlling Nuclear Weapons*, suggests one possible participatory institution that would possess educational and equality-of-representation functions. The goal is to develop a body of competent citizens able to make adequately enlightened judgments about public issues or the terms for delegation of authority. This institution, which we term a "citizen's assembly" would ensure a broad dissemination of information on the issues to all members of the Assembly. All citizens would be provided with opportunities to be heard on the issues. For these ends, the Assembly could utilize modern interactive communications technologies to aid in the questioning of government officials, expressing citizen preference, and debating the issues. Dahl has also advocated random selection of citizens to establish a greater equality of representation.[33] His focus was on a national Citizen's Assembly of about 1,000 people. A variation of this idea was put into practice by the Roosevelt Center for American Policy Studies during the Fall of 1988. The purpose was to convene citizen's assemblies across the nation and forge a citizen's agenda for the new President. The effort met with some success.[34] Arguments have been advanced for the establishment of citizen assemblies at the state level[35] and at other levels of local government.[36] While Dahl originally envi-

---

[32]James M. Burns, *The Vineyard of Liberty* (New York: Alfred A. Knopf, 1982), pp. 62–3.

[33]For a more complete discussion of these ideas see, Robert A. Dahl, *Controlling Nuclear Weapons . . . , passim.*

[34]*A Citizen's Agenda for the President*, Roosevelt Center for American Policy Studies, 316 Pennsylvania Avenue, Suite 500, Washington, D. C., November 1988.

[35]Anthony Eksterowicz, *The Citizen's Assembly: A Participatory Experiment for Social Science and the State*, paper delivered at the Annual Meeting of the Southwest Political Science Association, March 1988, Houston, Texas.

[36]Anthony J. Eksterowicz and Paul C. Cline, "Citizen Participation: Opportunities to Influence Public Policy," *University of Virginia Newsletter*, The Center for Public Service, Vol. 65, No. 1, September 1988.

sioned these efforts as an addition to republican institutions, other reformers would view these assemblies as replacements for current institutions. These assemblies could also be utilized within the framework of political parties to increase party representation and thus add to party strength.

One of the problems concerning modern political parties is the relationship of the rank-and-file membership with the party leadership. In both parties, there seems to be a gap between leadership and member ideology. This creates problems for the direction or public policy stands of the parties. The Republican Party leadership appears to be more conservative than its membership, and the Democrat Party leaders are more liberal than the rank-and-file members. Indeed, the problems regarding the Southern wing of the Democratic Party are becoming legendary.

A political party sponsored citizen's assembly could help alleviate this problem. Such an assembly could be initiated by the leadership of the party at any level—local, state or national. Participation in the assembly could be fixed either by random invitation of members from party lists, or simply by invitation alone. These efforts should be geared to establish the widest possible range of citizen participation in party matters. These assemblies could be construed to give a representative sample of members a role in party rules or party policy and issue formulation. They can be utilized to break party deadlocks over policy initiatives. Most importantly, they would give rank-and-file members an opportunity to educate themselves in party affairs. Membership in the assembly would have a fixed time period and members could not serve for a set period of time after their initial tenure. This would guarantee the rotation of membership that the original Antifederalists championed. Thus, the Jeffersonian goals of participation *and* enlightened education would be fulfilled. Furthermore, the party most adept at mobilizing not only its rank-and-file members but also attracting significant numbers of independents into the party fold could reap electoral rewards. Public opinion polling of party members could be utilized to determine the most salient issues or concerns of party members. The duration, structure, and work schedule of the assembly could be determined by the leadership of the party, perhaps in conjunction with a commission of randomly selected rank-and-file members. Finally, a portion of public finance money (if established) dedicated to such assemblies could hasten their initiation.

A party sponsored citizen's assembly would seem to possess a number of advantages. Since it would, by its constitution, be more representative than current party structures, it could provide a voice for old and new members that they would not otherwise have. This might lead to an increase of intra-party comity. While parties have established formal policy committees, councils and think tanks, a distinction between these groups and citizen assemblies is the broader representational base for the assemblies. Such assemblies could foster an enlightened and more educated party membership willing to devote time to party business and electoral tasks. This might lead to the establishment of continuous parties that do not disappear between elections. It could thus aid in candidate recruitment as party members rose within the ranks of the assembly or otherwise distinguished themselves. In addition, such an assembly could foster a new sense of volunteerism by members that might reach beyond the electoral cycles. It could provide an increase in party patronage power especially when coupled with the support services such an institution will require. It might ensure greater representation of the rank-and-file membership in party caucuses and conventions, and increase the pool of contributors and the level of their contributions. In addition, the importance of parties could be conveyed to the general public because of the inevitable media attention devoted to these assemblies. Finally, parties could compete more effectively with highly financed special interests ensuring a more open and competitive electoral system.

The existence of party sponsored citizen assemblies would take the harsh edge off of many proposals aimed at rejuvenating political parties. The task is to combine strength with greater representation and participation fusing republican and Antifederalist ideals. The result might be enhanced party prestige and status. Without such an effort, moves to strengthen political parties will inevitably suffer from charges of party elitism leading to a continuity of political party decline.

Conclusion

A variety of Progressive reforms have been instituted since the early 20th century. These reforms have included the direct primary; the initiative, referendum, and recall; and nonpartisan elections at the local level. The reforms were defended as devices which would increase citizen participation in political party activity. The effect of these reforms has been the weakening of political parties and the perpetuation of mutual exclusivity between citizen participation and party government.

The premise of this mutual exclusivity argument has its origin in the Constitutional ratification debates between the Federalists and Antifederalists. Recently, these debates have been revisited in the proposals for reform by the Committee on the Constitutional System and the reactions of critics to these proposals.

Nonetheless, a means exists for the fusing of participation with the political party in such a way as to strengthen the party. The device advocated for enhancing political party strength is a citizen assembly called to give continuing input into the positions to be taken by the party. Additional advantages to the party of a practical nature include assistance provided by the citizen assembly in the party's recruitment of members, leaders, and money.

While this proposal would certainly be opposed by some strong party advocates as chimerical, unrealistic, naive, unworkable and costly, some of these same adjectives can be utilized to describe reforms aimed at strengthening political parties, such as PAC reform, free radio and television time, and Congressional action to neutralize key Supreme Court decisions. Furthermore, movement towards these ends will be met with strong anti-party feeling that has always existed in this nation. Thus, without significant and meaningful involvement of the people, political parties will continue to decline in electoral influence.

On the other hand, there are those who would actively hope for such a decline and suggest that the proposal herein presented would bolster decaying institutions of bygone days. Some modern reformers would tear down our two-party system and rebuild it perhaps along the lines of a parliamentary form of government with a competitive multi-party system. Without an active movement toward the elimination of single-member districts and the institution of proportional representation, however, such developments are even less likely. Moreover, efforts toward those ends would be opposed by the current party system. These parties may be weak, but they can still wage a powerful defensive battle for their very existence.

5

Voting, Elections, and Representation

Article I, Section 4 of the Constitution serves as the catalyst for an Antifederalist-Federalist debate over state versus federal powers in regulating congressional elections, the type of representation these elections would ensure, and, in a more subtle way, which part of the populace would do the voting. In general, the Antifederalists, represented by the writings in this chapter, were wary of the federal control that might be exercised under Article I, Section 4. Brutus in Essay IV argues that national elections set by the federal government could subvert the people's elections in the states. This would result in government farther from the people. Brutus argues for a provision that would give the local level of government more power in regulating these elections. Cato echoes Brutus' arguments but, in addition, calls for annual elections in order to keep the government closer to the people. John DeWitt notes that the House of Representatives under the Constitutional scheme would be unlike the people. For DeWitt, frequent voting would keep the federal government from being populated by strangers. In a very subtle way, the Antifederalists may have been suggesting that voting procedures matter because these procedures may facilitate the election of representatives who could be divorced from the middle and poor classes. Therefore, the policies that these representatives might advocate could also differ from the interests of the poor and middle classes. In this sense, voting is linked more to possible substantive policies than to mere procedures for elections. This is essentially the argument of Melancton Smith. Smith also addresses the issue of slavery and apportionment for Congressional elections.

Alexander Hamilton, in a stinging response to the Antifederalists, argues that an election law could not be framed so as to include all states and probable changes in the nation. A discretionary power over elections must exist somewhere. He also notes that the federal government is to intervene only in extraordinary circumstances. If the power of elections rested solely with the states, it would leave the federal government at the mercy of the states. Under this circumstance the federal union would not last very long. Madison responds to the Antifederalist proposal for one-year House terms by arguing that federal officials have to acquire more knowledge than their state counterparts, who were generally serving one-year terms. Madison then answers the charges of Melancton Smith concerning slavery and apportionment for representation in the House of Representatives. In *Federalist* Paper 49 Madison argues against frequent change in the Constitution. He was responding to Jefferson, who advocated such change. The reading is included here to illustrate Madison's view of Constitutional government and his belief in preserving its equilibric qualities. It also illustrates his views concerning the general public. Madison refutes the Antifederalist desire for large assemblies of representatives, equating these not with reason but pure destructive passion.

By the time of Alexis de Tocqueville's visit in 1831, America was already well on her way toward a more democratic society. The franchise had been extended, and aristocratic influences in government were subsiding. As Thomas Cronin notes, this trend continued with populism and the reforms of the progressive movement like the referendum, recall, and citizen initiative. A split developed in the views concerning the utility of voting. As William Riker observes, the liberal interpretation of voting was heavily influenced by the ideas of Madison. The populistic, more participatory, interpretation of voting was influenced by the ideas of Rousseau. However, this interpretation may have found a ready audience in America, influenced by the ideas of Antifederalism. Robert Dahl's advocacy of a minipopulus—a type of representative citizen's assembly—may have something in common with the ideas of John DeWitt.

THE CONSTITUTION (EXCERPTS)

Article I—The Legislative Article

Congressional Elections: Times, Places, Manner

Section 4 The Times, Places and Manner of holding Elections for Senators and Representatives, shall be prescribed in each State by the Legislature thereof; but the Congress may at any time by Law make or alter such Regulations, except as to the Places of chusing Senators.

The Congress shall assemble at least once in every Year, *and such Meeting shall be on the first Monday in December, unless they shall by Law appoint a different Day.*

Article V—The Amending Power

The Congress, whenever two thirds of both Houses shall deem it necessary, shall propose Amendments to this Constitution, or, on the Application of the Legislatures of two thirds of several States, shall call a Convention for proposing Amendments, which, in either Case, shall be valid to all Intents and Purposes, as Part of this Constitution, when ratified by the Legislatures of three fourths of the several States, or by Conventions in three fourths thereof, as the one or the other Mode of Ratification may be proposed by the Congress; Provided that no Amendment which may be made prior to the Year One thousand eight hundred and eight shall in any Manner affect the first and fourth Clauses in the Ninth Section of the first Article; and that no State, without its Consent, shall be deprived of its equal Suffrage in the Senate.

ANTIFEDERALIST ARGUMENTS

"Brutus" *(Probably Robert Yates)* *Essay IV* *(Excerpt)*

DISCUSSION QUESTIONS

1. Under Article I, Section 4 of the Constitution, how could the federal legislature institute rules that would favor a certain class of men?
2. What is the nature of the division between less populous and more populous areas of a state in electing representatives to the Congress?
3. According to Brutus, what provisions *should have been made* if the national legislature was going to regulate state elections?
4. How does Brutus respond to the charge that normally the national legislature under the new Constitution would perform its role without prejudice?

By section 4, article I, the Congress are authorized, at any time, by law, to make, or alter, regulations respecting the time, place, and manner of holding elections for senators and representatives, except as to the places of choosing senators. By this clause the right of election itself, is, in a great measure, transferred from the people to their rulers.—One would think, that if any thing was necessary to be made a fundamental article of the original compact, it would be, that of fixing the branches of the legislature, so as to put it out of its power to alter itself by modifying the election of its own members at will and pleasure. When a people once resign the privilege of a fair election, they clearly have none left worth contending for.

It is clear that, under this article, the federal legislature may institute such rules respecting elections as to lead to the choice of one description of men. The weakness of the representation, tends but too certainly to confer on the rich and well-born, all honours; but the power granted in this article, may be so exercised, as to secure it almost beyond a possibility of control. The proposed Congress may make the whole state one district, and direct, that the capital (the city of New York, for instance) shall be the place for holding the election; the consequence would be, that none but men of the most elevated rank in society would attend, and they would as certainly choose men of their own class; as it is true what the Apostle Paul saith, that "no man ever yet hated his own flesh, but nourisheth and cherisheth it."—They may declare that those members who have the greatest number of votes, shall be considered as duly elected; the consequence would be that the people, who are dispersed in the interior parts of the state, would give their votes for a variety of candidates, while any order, or profession, residing in populous places, by uniting their interests, might procure whom they pleased to be chosen—and by this means the representatives of the states may be elected by one tenth part of the people who actually vote. This may be effected constitutionally, and by one of those silent operations which frequently takes place without being noticed, but which often produces such changes as entirely to alter a government, subvert a free constitution, and rivet the chains on a free people before they perceive they are forged. Had the power of regulating elections been left under the direction of the state legislature, where the people are not only nominally but substantially represented, it would have been secure; but if it was taken out of their hands, it surely ought to have been fixed on such a basis as to have put it out of the power of the federal legislature to deprive the people of it by law. Provision should have been made for marking out the states into districts, and for choosing, by a majority of votes, a person out of each of them of permanent property and residence in the district which he was to represent.

If the people of America will submit to a constitution that will vest in the hands of any body of men a right deprive them by law of the privilege of a fair election, they will submit to almost any thing. Reasoning with them will be in vain, they must be left until they are brought to reflection by feeling oppression—they will then have to wrest from their oppressors, by a strong hand, that which they now possess, and which they may retain if they will exercise but a moderate share of prudence and firmness.

I know it is said that the dangers apprehended from this clause are merely imaginary, that the proposed general legislature will be disposed to regulate elections upon proper principles, and to use their power with discretion, and to promote the public good. On this, I would observe, that constitutions are not so necessary to regulate the conduct of good rulers as to restrain that of bad ones.—Wise and good men will exercise power so as to promote the public happiness under any form of government. If we are to take it for granted, that those who administer the government under this system, will always pay proper attention to the rights and interests of the people, nothing more was necessary than to say who should be invested with the powers of government, and leave them to exercise it at will and pleasure. Men are apt to be deceived both with respect to their own dispositions and those of others. Though this truth is proved by almost every page of the history of nations, to wit, that power lodged in the hands of rulers to be used at discretion, is almost always exercised to the oppression of the people, and the aggrandizement of themselves; yet most men think if it was lodged in their hands they would not employ it in this manner.

"Cato"
(Unknown)
Essay VII
(Excerpt)

DISCUSSION QUESTIONS

1. According to Cato, how will the power of the national Congress under the Constitution impinge upon the state's ability to regulate elections?

2. What will these restrictions do to the linkages between the people and their government?

Among the many evils that are incorporated in this new system of government, is that of congress having the power of making or altering the regulations prescribed by the different legislatures, respecting the time, place, and manner of holding elections for representatives, and the time, and manner of choosing senators. If it is enquired, in what manner this regulation may be exercised to your injury—the answer is easy.

By the first article the house of representatives shall consist of members, chosen every second year by the people of the several states, who are qualified to vote for members of their several state assemblies; it can therefore readily be believed, that the different state legislatures, provided such can exist after the adoption of this government, will continue those easy and convenient modes for the election of representatives for the national legislature, that are in use, for the election of members of assembly for their own states; but the congress have, by the constitution, a power to make other regulations, or alter those in practice, prescribed by your own state legislature; hence, instead of having the places of elections in the precincts, and brought home almost to your own doors, Congress may establish a place, or places, at either the extremes, center, or outer parts of the states; at a time and season too, when it may be very inconvenient to attend; and by these means destroy the rights of election; but in opposition to this reasoning, it is asserted, that it is a necessary power because the states might omit making rules for the purpose, and thereby defeat the existence of that branch of the government; this is what logicians call *argumentum absurdum*, for the different states, if they will have any security at all in this government, will find it in the house of representatives, and they, therefore, would not be very ready to eradicate a principle in which it dwells, or involve their country in an instantaneous revolution. Besides, if this was the apprehension of the framers, and the ground of that provision, why did not they extend this controlling power to the other duties of the several state legislatures. To exemplify this the states are to appoint senators and electors for choosing of a president; but the time is to be under the direction of congress. Now, suppose they were to omit the appointment of senators and electors, though congress was to appoint the time, which might [as] well be apprehended as the omission of regulations for the election of members of the house of representatives, provided they had that power; or suppose they were not to meet at all: of course, the government cannot proceed in its exercise. And from this motive, or apprehension, congress ought to have taken these duties entirely in their own hands, and, by a decisive declaration, annihilated them, which they in fact have done by leaving them without the means of support, or at least resting on their bounty. To this, the advocates for this system oppose the common, empty declamation, that there is no danger that congress will abuse this power; but such language, as relative to so important a subject, is mere vapour, and sound without sense. Is it not in their power, however, to make such regulations as may be inconvenient to you? It must be admitted, because the words are unlimited in their sense. It is a good rule, in the construction of a contract, to support, that what may be done will be; therefore, in considering this subject, you are to suppose, that in the exercise of this government, a regulation of congress will be made, for holding an election for the whole state at Poughkeepsie, at New York, or, perhaps, at Fort Stanwix: who will then be the actual electors for the house of representatives? Very few more than those who may live in the vicinity of these places. Could any others afford the expense and time of attending? And would not the government by this means have it in their power to put whom they pleased in the house of representatives? You ought certainly to have as much or more distrust with respect to the exercise of these powers by congress, than congress ought to have with respect to the exercise of those duties which ought to be entrusted to the several states, because over them congress can have a legislative controlling power.

"Cato"
(Probably George Clinton)
Essay V
(Excerpts)

DISCUSSION QUESTIONS

1. According to Cato, frequent elections will lead to what development?
2. What is Cato's opinion of the frequency of Constitutional elections for the House and Senate?
3. What remark does Cato make against the size of the House of Representatives?

If annual elections were to exist in this government, and learning and information to become more prevalent, you never will want men to execute whatever you could design—Sidney observes "that a well governed state is as fruitful to all good purposes as the seven headed serpent is said to have been in evil; when one head is cut off, many rise up in the place of it." He remarks further, that "it was also thought, that free cities by frequent elections of magistrates became nurseries of great and able men, every man endeavoring to excel others, that he might be advanced to the honor he had no other title to, than what might arise from his merit, or reputation," but the framers of this *perfect government*, as it is called, have departed from this democratical principle, and established bi-ennial elections for the house of representatives, who are to be chosen by the people, and sextennial for the senate, who are to be chosen by the legislatures of the different states, and have given to the executive the unprecedented power of making temporary senators, in case of vacancies, by resignation or otherwise; and so far forth establishing a precedent for virtual representation (though in fact, their original appointment is virtual) thereby influencing the choice of the legislatures, or if they should not be so complaisant as to conform to his appointment—offence will be given to the executive and the temporary members will appear ridiculous by rejection; this temporary member, during his time of appointment, will of course act by a power derived from the executive, and for, and under his immediate influence.

. . . Another thing [that] may be suggested against the small number of representatives is, that but few of you will have the chance of sharing even in this branch of the legislature; and that the choice will be confined to a very few; the more complete it is, the better will your interests be preserved, and the greater the opportunity you will have to participate in government, one of the principal securities of a free people; but this subject has been so ably and fully treated by a writer under the signature of Brutus, that I shall content myself with referring you to him thereon, reserving further observations on the other objections I have mentioned, for my future numbers.

"John DeWitt"
(Unknown)
Essay III
(Excerpt)

DISCUSSION QUESTIONS

1. According to John DeWitt, does the House of Representatives contain the "sense of the people"? Why or why not?
2. What type of people will be elected to the legislative branch?
3. How does DeWitt propose to bring the legislative branch closer to the people?

But, my fellow-citizens, the important question here arises, who are this House of Representatives? "A representative Assembly, says the celebrated Mr. Adams, is the sense of the people, and the perfection of the portrait, consists in the likeness."—Can this Assembly be said to contain the sense of the people?—Do they resemble the people in any one single feature?—Do you represent your wants, your grievances, your wishes, in person? If that is impracticable, have you a right to send one of your townsmen for that purpose?—Have you a right to send one from your county? Have you a right to send more than one for every thirty thousand of you? Can he be presumed knowing to your different, peculiar situations—your abilities to pay public taxes, when they ought to be abated, and when increased? Or is there any possibility of giving him information? All these questions must be answered in the negative. But how are these men to be chosen? Is there any other way than by dividing the Senate into districts? May not you as well at once invest your annual Assemblies with the power of choosing them—where is the essential difference? The nature of the thing will admit of none. Nay, you give them the power to prescribe the mode. They may invest it in themselves.—If you choose them yourselves, you must take them upon credit, and elect those persons you know only by common fame. Even this privilege is denied you annually, through fear that you might withhold the shadow of control over them. In this view of the System, let me sincerely ask you, where is the people in this House of Representatives?—Where is the boasted popular part of this much admired System?—Are they not cousins-german in every sense to the Senate? May they not with propriety be termed an Assistant Aristocratical Branch, who will be infinitely more inclined to co-operate and compromise with each other, than to be the careful guardians of the rights of their constituents? Who is there among you would not start at being told, that instead of your present House of Representatives, consisting of members chosen from every town, your future Houses were to consist of but ten in number, and these to be chosen by districts?—What man among you would betray his country and approve of it? And yet how infinitely preferable to the plan proposed?—In the one case the elections would be annual, the persons elected would reside in the center of you, their interests would be yours, they would be subject to your immediate control, and nobody to consult in their deliberations—But in the other, they are chosen for double the time, during which, however well disposed, they become strangers to the very people choosing them, they reside at a distance from you, you have no control over them, you cannot observe their conduct, and they have to consult and finally be guided by twelve other States, whose interests are, in all material points, directly opposed to yours. Let me again ask you, What citizen is there in the Commonwealth of Massachusetts, that would deliberately consent laying aside the mode proposed, that the several Senates of the several States, should be the popular Branch, and together, form one National House of Representatives?—And yet one moment's attention will evince to you, that this blessed proposed Representation of the People, this apparent faithful Mirror, this striking Likeness, is to be still further refined, and more Aristocratical four times told—Where now is the exact balance which has been so diligently attended to? Where lies the security of the people? What assurances have they that either their taxes will not be exacted but in the greatest emergencies, and then sparingly, or that standing armies will be raised and supported for the very plausible purpose only of cantoning them upon their frontiers? There is but one answer to these questions—They have none.

Melancton Smith
Speech
June 20, 1788
(Excerpts)

DISCUSSION QUESTION

Explain Smith's ideas on the apportionment of representatives for the House and the issue of slavery.

He would now proceed to state his objections to the clause just read, (section 2 of article I, clause 3.) His objections were comprised under three heads: 1st the rule of appointment is unjust; 2d. there is no precise number fixed on below which the house shall not be reduced; 3d. it is inadequate. In the first place the rule of apportionment of the representatives is to be according to the whole number of the white inhabitants, with three fifths of all others; that is in plain English, each state is to send Representatives in proportion to the number of freemen, and three fifths of the slaves it contains. He could not see any rule by which slaves are to be included in the ratio of representation: The principle of a representation, being that every free agent should be concerned in governing himself, it was absurd to give that power to a man who could not exercise it—slaves have no will of their own: The very operation of it was to give certain privileges to those people who were so wicked as to keep slaves. He knew it would be admitted that this rule of apportionment was founded on unjust principles, but that it was the result of accommodation; which he supposed we should be under the necessity of admitting, if we meant to be in union with the Southern States, though utterly repugnant to his feelings. . . .

He who is controlled by another is a slave; and that government which is directed by the will of any one or a few, or any number less than is the will of the community, is a government for slaves.

Melancton Smith
Speech
June 21, 1788
(Excerpt)

DISCUSSION QUESTIONS

1. What does Smith have to say about elections for the House of Representatives and the middle class?
2. What about elections and the poor class?
3. Describe Smith's opinion of great men in the governing class. Who should control this "great" class of people?

Besides, the influence of the great will generally enable them to succeed in elections—it will be difficult to combine a district of country containing 30 or 40,000 inhabitants, frame your election laws as you please, in any one character; unless it be in one of conspicuous, military, popular, civil or legal talents. The great easily form associations; the poor and middling class form them with difficulty. If the elections be by plurality, as probably will be the case in this state, it is almost certain, none but the great will be chosen—for they easily unite their interest—The common people will divide, and their divisions will be promoted by the others. There will be scarcely a chance of their uniting, in any other but some great man, unless in some popular demagogue, who will probably be destitute of principle. A substantial yeoman of sense and discernment, will hardly ever be chosen. From these remarks it appears that the government will fall into the hands of the few and the great. This will be a government of oppression. I do not mean to declaim against the great, and charge them indiscriminately with want of principle and honesty.—The same passions and prejudices govern all men. The circumstances in which men are placed in a great measure give a cast to the human character. Those in middling circumstances, have less temptation—they are inclined by habit and the company with whom they associate, to set bounds to their passions and appetites—if this is not sufficient, the want of means to gratify them will be a restraint—they are obliged to employ their time in their respective callings—hence the substantial yeomanry of the country are more temperate, of better morals and less ambition than the great. The latter do not feel for the poor and middling class; the reasons are obvious—they are not obliged to use the pains and labour to procure property as the other—They feel not the inconveniences arising from the payment of small sums. The great consider themselves above the common people—entitled to more respect—do not associate with them—they fancy themselves to have a right of pre-eminence in every thing. In short, they possess the same feelings, and are under the influence of the same motives, as an hereditary nobility. I know the idea that such a distinction exists in this country is ridiculed by some—But I am not the less apprehensive of anger from their influence on this account—Such distinctions exist all the world over—have been taken notice of by all writers on free government—and are founded in the nature of things. It has been the principal care of free governments to guard against the encroachments of the great. Common observation and experience prove the existence of such distinctions. Will any one say, that there does not exist in this country the pride of family, of wealth, of talents; and that they do not command influence and respect among the common people? Congress, in their address to the habitants of the province of Quebec, in 1775, state this distinction in the following forcible words quoted from the Marquis Beccaria. "In every human society, there is an essay continually tending to confer on one part of the height of power and happiness, and to reduce the other to the extreme of weakness and misery. The intent of good laws is to oppose this effort, and to diffuse their influence universally and equally." We ought to guard against the government being placed in the hands of this class—They cannot have that sympathy with their constituents which is necessary to connect them closely to their interest: Being in the habit of profuse living, they will be profuse in the public expenses. They find no difficulty in paying their taxes, and therefore do not feel public burthens: Besides if they govern, they will enjoy the emoluments of the government. The middling class, from their frugal habits, and feeling themselves the public burdens, will be careful how they increase them.

But I may be asked, would you exclude the first class in the community, from any share in legislation? I answer by no means—they would be more dangerous out of power than in it—they would be factious—discontented and constantly disturbing the government—it would also be unjust—they have their liberties to protect as well as others—and the largest share of property. But my idea is, that the Constitution should be so framed as to admit this class, together with a sufficient number of the middling class to control them. You will then combine the abilities and honesty of the community—a proper degree of information, and a disposition to pursue the public good. A representative body, composed principally of respectable yeomanry is the best possible security to liberty—When the interest of this part of the community is pursued, the public good is pursued; because the body of every nation consists of this class. And because the interest of both the rich and the poor are involved in that of the middling class. No burden can be laid on the poor, but what will sensibly affect the middling class. Any law rendering property insecure, would be injurious to them—When therefore this class in society pursue their own interest, they promote that of the public, for it is involved in it.

FEDERALIST ARGUMENTS

Alexander Hamilton
Federalist *Paper 59*

DISCUSSION QUESTIONS

1. Hamilton presents a plain proposition as evidence of the propriety of Article I, Section 4 of the Constitution. What is this proposition?
2. According to Hamilton, what would have happened if the exclusive power for regulating government elections was in the hands of the state governments?
3. At which level of government does Hamilton believe abuses are more likely to occur? Why?
4. Brutus, in Essay IV, argued that certain provisions should have been made in the Constitution. Hamilton answers him in this essay. What is the gist of Hamilton's response? (Review Brutus IV before answering this question.)
5. What seems to be Hamilton's main concern about giving the states the power of regulating elections for the House of Representatives?

The natural order of the subject leads us to consider in this place that provision of the Constitution which authorizes the national legislature to regulate, in the last resort, the election of its own members.

It is in these words: "The times, places, and manner of holding elections for senators and representatives shall be prescribed in each State by the legislature thereof; but the Congress may, at any time, by law, make or alter such regulations, except as to the places of choosing senators."[1] This provision has not only been declaimed against by those who condemn the Constitution in the gross, but it has been censured by those who have objected with less latitude and greater moderation; and, in one instance, it has been thought exceptionable by a gentleman who has declared himself the advocate of every other part of the system.

I am greatly mistaken, notwithstanding, if there be any article in the whole plan more completely defensible than this. Its propriety rests upon the evidence of this plain proposition, that every government ought to contain in itself the means of its own preservation. Every just reasoner will, at first sight, approve an adherence to this rule, in the work of the Convention; and will disapprove every deviation from it which may not appear to have been dictated by the necessity of incorporating into the work some particular ingredient with which a rigid conformity to the rule was incompatible. Even in this case, though he may acquiesce in the necessity, yet he will not cease to regard and to regret a departure from so fundamental a principle as a portion of imperfection in the system which may prove the seed of future weakness and perhaps anarchy.

It will not be alleged that an election law could have been framed and inserted in the Constitution, which would have been always applicable to every prob-

---

[1]Clause I, section 4, of article I.

able change in the situation of the country; and it will, therefore, not be denied that a discretionary power over elections ought to exist somewhere. It will, I presume, be as readily conceded that there were only three ways in which this power could have been reasonably modified and disposed; that it must either have been lodged wholly in the national legislature or wholly in the State legislatures, or primarily in the latter and ultimately in the former. The last mode has, with reason, been preferred by the Convention. They have submitted the regulation of elections for the federal government, in the first instance, to the local administrations, which, in ordinary cases, and when no improper views prevail, may be both more convenient and more satisfactory; but they have reserved to the national authority a right to interpose, whenever extraordinary circumstances might render that interposition necessary to its safety.

Nothing can be more evident than that an exclusive power of regulating elections for the national government, in the hands of the State legislatures, would leave the existence of the Union entirely at their mercy. They could at any moment annihilate it by neglecting to provide for the choice of persons to administer its affairs. It is to little purpose to say that a neglect or omission of this kind would not be likely to take place. The constitutional possibility of the thing, without an equivalent for the risk, is an unanswerable objection. Nor has any satisfactory reason been yet assigned for incurring that risk. The extravagant surmises of a distempered jealousy can never be dignified with that character. If we are in a humor to presume abuses of power, it is as fair to presume them on the part of the State governments as on the part of the general government; and as it is more consonant to the rules of a just theory to intrust the Union with the care of its own existence than to transfer that care to any other hands, if abuses of power are to be hazarded on the one side or on the other, it is more rational to hazard them where the power would naturally be placed than where it would unnaturally be placed.

Suppose an article had been introduced into the Constitution empowering the United States to regulate the elections for the particular States, would any man have hesitated to condemn it, both as an unwarrantable transposition of power and as a premeditated engine for the destruction of the State governments? The violation of principle in this case would have required no comment; and, to an unbiassed observer, it will not be less apparent in the project of subjecting the existence of the national government, in a similar respect, to the pleasure of the State governments. An impartial view of the matter cannot fail to result in a conviction, that each, as far as possible, ought to depend on itself for its own preservation.

As an objection to this position, it may be remarked that the constitution of the national Senate would involve, in its full extent, the danger which it is suggested might flow from an exclusive power in the State legislatures to regulate the federal elections. It may be alleged, that by declining the appointment of senators, they might at any time give a fatal blow to the Union, and from this it may be inferred that as its existence would be thus rendered dependent upon them in so essential a point, there can be no objection to intrusting them with it in the particular case under consideration. The interest of each State, it may be added, to maintain its representation in the national councils, would be a complete security against an abuse of the trust.

This argument, though specious, will not, upon examination, be found solid. It is certainly true that the State legislatures, by forbearing the appointment of senators, may destroy the national government; but it will not follow that because they have the power to do this in one instance, they ought to have it in every other. There are cases in which the pernicious tendency of such a power may be far more decisive, without any motive equally cogent with that which must have regulated the conduct of the Convention in respect to the formation of the Senate, to recommend their admission into the system. So far as that construction may expose the Union to the possibility of injury from the State legislatures, it is an evil; but it is an evil which could not have been avoided without excluding the States, in their political capacities, wholly from a place in the organization of the national government. If this had been done, it would doubtless have been interpreted into an entire dereliction of the federal principle, and would certainly have deprived the State governments of that absolute safeguard which they will enjoy under this provision; but however wise it may have been, to have submitted in this instance to an inconvenience, for the attainment of a necessary advantage or a greater good, no inference can be drawn from thence to favor an accumulation of the evil, where no necessity urges nor any greater good invites.

It may be easily discerned, also, that the national government would run a much greater risk, from a power in the State legislatures over the elections of its House of Representatives, than from their power of appointing the members of its Senate. The senators are to be chosen for the period of six years; there is to be a rotation, by which the seats of a third part of them are to be vacated and replenished every two years; and no State is to be entitled to more than two senators. A quorum of the body is to consist of sixteen members. The joint result of these circumstances would be that a temporary combination of a few States, to intermit the appointment of senators, could neither annul the existence nor impair the activity of the body; and it is not from a general and permanent combination of the States that we can have anything to fear. The first might proceed from sinister designs in the leading members of a few of the State legislatures: the last would suppose a fixed and rooted disaffection in the great body of the people, which will either never exist at all or will in all probability proceed from an experience of the inaptitude of the general government to the advancement of their happiness; in which event no good citizen could desire its continuance.

But with regard to the federal House of Representatives, there is intended to be a general election of members once in two years. If the State legislatures were to be invested with an exclusive power of regulating these elections, every period of making them would be a delicate crisis in the national situation, which might issue in a dissolution of the Union if the leaders of a few of the most important States should have entered into a previous conspiracy to prevent an election.

I shall not deny that there is a degree of weight in the observation that the interest of each State, to be represented in the federal councils, will be a security against the abuse of a power over its elections in the hands of the State legislatures. But the security will not be considered as complete, by those who attend to the force of an obvious distinction between the interest of the people in the public felicity, and the interest of their local rulers in the power and consequence of their offices. The people of America may be warmly attached to the government of the Union, at times when the particular rulers of particular States, stimulated by the natural rivalship of power, and by the hopes of personal aggrandizement, and supported by a strong faction in each of those States, may be in a very opposite temper. This diversity of sentiment between a majority of the people and the individuals who have the greatest credit in their councils, is exemplified in some of the States at the present moment, on the present question. The scheme of separate confederacies, which will always multiply the chances of ambition, will be a never-failing bait to all such influential characters in the State administrations as are capable of preferring their own emolument and advancement to the public weal. With so effectual a weapon in their hands as the exclusive power of regulating elections for the national government, a combination of a few such men, in a few of the most considerable States, where the temptation will always be the strongest, might accomplish the destruction of the Union, by seizing the opportunity of some casual dissatisfaction among the people (and which, perhaps, they may themselves have excited), to discontinue the choice of members for the federal House of Representatives. It ought never to be forgotten that a firm Union of this country, under an efficient government, will probably be an increasing object of jealousy to more than one nation of Europe; and that enterprises to subvert it will sometimes originate in the intrigues of foreign powers, and will seldom fail to be patronized and abetted by some of them. Its preservation, therefore, ought, in no case that can be avoided, to be committed to the guardianship of any but those whose situation will uniformly beget an immediate interest in the faithful and vigilant performance of the trust.

PUBLIUS

James Madison
Federalist *Paper 53*
(Excerpts)

DISCUSSION QUESTION

What are the reasons for Madison's advocacy of two-year terms for the House?

No man can be a competent legislator who does not add to an upright intention and a sound judgment a certain degree of knowledge of the subjects on which he is to legislate. A part of this knowledge may be acquired by means of information which lie within the compass of men in private as well as public stations. Another part can only be attained, or at least thoroughly attained, by actual experience in the station which requires the use of it. The period of service ought, therefore, in all such cases to bear some proportion to the extent of practical knowledge requisite to the due performance of the service. The period of legislative service established in most of the States for the more numerous branch is, as we have seen, one year. The question, then, may be put into this simple form: Does the period of two years bear no greater proportion to the knowledge requisite for federal legislation than one year does to the knowledge requisite for State legislation? The very statement of the question in this form suggests the answer that ought to be given to it.

In a single State the requisite knowledge relates to the existing laws, which are uniform throughout the State, and with which all the citizens are more or less conversant, and to the general affairs of the State, which lie within a small compass, are not very diversified, and occupy much of the attention and conversation of every class of people. The great theatre of the United States presents a very different scene. The laws are so far from being uniform that they vary in every State; while the public affairs of the Union are spread throughout a very extensive region, and are extremely diversified by the local affairs connected with them, and can with difficulty be correctly learned in any other place than in the central councils, to which a knowledge of them will be brought by the representatives of every part of the empire. Yet some knowledge of the affairs, and even of the laws, of all the States ought to be possessed by the members from each of the States. How can foreign trade be properly regulated by uniform laws without some acquaintance with the commerce, the ports, the usages, and the regulations of the different States? How can the trade between the different States be duly regulated without some knowledge of their relative situations in these and other respects? . . .

A branch of knowledge which belongs to the acquirements of a federal representative, and which has not been mentioned, is that of foreign affairs. In regulating our own commerce he ought to be not only acquainted with the treaties between the United States and other nations, but also with the commercial policy and laws of other nations. He ought not to be altogether ignorant of the law of nations; for that, as far as it is a proper object of municipal legislation, is submitted to the federal government, and although the House of Representatives is not immediately to participate in foreign negotiations and arrangements, yet from the necessary connection between the several branches of public affairs those particular branches will frequently deserve attention in the ordinary course of legislation, and will sometimes demand particular legislative sanction and co-operation. Some portion of this knowledge may, no doubt, be acquired in a man's closet, but some of it also can only be derived from the public sources of information; and all of it will be acquired to best effect by a practical attention to the subject during the period of actual service in the legislature.

There are other considerations, of less importance, perhaps, but which are not unworthy of notice. The distance which many of the representatives will be obliged to travel, and the arrangements rendered necessary by that circumstance, might be much more serious objections with fit men to this service if limited to a single year than if extended to two years. No argument can be drawn on this subject from the case of the delegates to the existing Congress. They are elected annually, it is true; but their re-election is considered by the legislative assemblies almost as a matter of course. The election of the representatives by the people would not be governed by the same principle.

James Madison
Federalist *Paper 54*
(Excerpt)

DISCUSSION QUESTION

How does Madison answer the charge of Melancton Smith regarding the counting of slaves as part of the ratio of population for representation?

"We subscribe to the doctrine," might one of our Southern brethren observe, "that representation relates more immediately to persons, and taxation more immediately to property, and we join in the application of this distinction to the case of our slaves." But we must deny the fact that slaves are considered merely as property, and in no respect whatever as persons. The true state of the case is that they partake of both these qualities; being considered by our laws, in some respects as persons, and in other respects as property. In being compelled to labor, not for himself, but for a master; in being vendible by one master to another master; and in being subject at all times to be restrained in his liberty and chastised in his body, by the capricious will of another—the slave may appear to be degraded from the human rank, and classed with those irrational animals which fall under the legal denomination of property. In being protected, on the other hand, in his life and in his limbs, against the violence of all others, even the master of his labor and his liberty, and in being punishable himself for all violence committed against others—the slave is no less evidently regarded by the law as a member of the society, not as a part of the irrational creation; as a moral person, not as a mere article of property. The federal Constitution, therefore, decides with great propriety on the case of our slaves, when it views them in the mixed character of persons and of property. This is in fact their true character. It is the character bestowed on them by the laws under which they live; and it will not be denied that these are the proper criterion; because it is only under the pretext that the laws have transformed the negroes into subjects of property, that a place is disputed them in the computation of numbers; and it is admitted that if the laws were to restore the rights which have been taken away, the negroes could no longer be refused an equal share of representation with the other inhabitants.

James Madison
Federalist *Paper 49*
(Excerpt)

DISCUSSION QUESTIONS

1. What are Madison's reasons against the institution of frequent elections?
2. How would you describe Madison's view of individual man as opposed to aggregate men or people in groups?

3. Does Madison seem to trust people? Why or why not?
4. According to Madison, what is the greatest reason for opposing frequent change in the Constitution?
5. What are the similarities between Madison's argument against frequent changes in the Constitution and Hamilton's argument against allowing the states the power of regulating elections in the House of Representatives?
6. How do Madison's and Hamilton's ideas contrast with the ideas of the Antifederalists on the above issues?

In the next place, it may be considered, as an objection inherent in the principle, that as every appeal to the people would carry an implication of some defect in the government, frequent appeals would in a great measure deprive the government of that veneration which time bestows on everything, and without which perhaps the wisest and freest governments would not possess the requisite stability. If it be true that all governments rest on opinion, it is no less true that the strength of opinion in each individual, and its practical influence on his conduct, depend much on the number which he supposes to have entertained the same opinion. The reason of man, like man himself, is timid and cautious when left alone, and acquires firmness and confidence in proportion to the number with which it is associated. When the examples which fortify opinion are ancient as well as numerous, they are known to have a double effect. In a nation of philosophers, this consideration ought to be disregarded. A reverence for the laws would be sufficiently inculcated by the voice of an enlightened reason. But a nation of philosophers is as little to be expected as the philosophical race of kings wished for by Plato. And in every other nation the most rational government will not find it a superfluous advantage to have the prejudices of the community on its side.

The danger of disturbing the public tranquility by interesting too strongly the public passions is a still more serious objection against a frequent reference of constitutional questions to the decision of the whole society. Notwithstanding the success which has attended the revisions of our established forms of government, and which does so much honor to the virtue and intelligence of the people of America, it must be confessed that the experiments are of too ticklish a nature to be unnecessarily multiplied. We are to recollect that all the existing constitutions were formed in the midst of a danger which repressed the passions most unfriendly to order and concord; of an enthusiastic confidence of the people in their patriotic leaders, which stifled the ordinary diversity of opinions on great national questions; of a universal ardor for new and opposite forms, produced by a universal resentment and indignation against the ancient government; and while no spirit of party, connected with the changes to be made, or the abuses to be reformed, could mingle its leaven in the operation. The future situations in which we must expect to be usually placed do not present any equivalent security against the danger which is apprehended.

But the greatest objection of all is that the decisions which would probably result from such appeals would not answer the purpose of maintaining the constitutional equilibrium of the government.

James Madison
Federalist *Paper 55*
(Excerpts)

DISCUSSION QUESTIONS

1. Why does Madison warn against finding our political calculations in arithmetical principles?
2. What is Madison's opinion of large assemblies of people?
3. What is the relationship between reason and passion in large assemblies as opposed to small assemblies?

The number of which the House of Representatives is to consist forms another and a very interesting point of view under which this branch of the federal legislature may be contemplated. Scarce any article, indeed, in the whole Constitution seems to be rendered more worthy of attention by the weight of character and the apparent force of argument with which it has been assailed. The charges exhibited against it are: First, that so small a number of representatives will be an unsafe depositary of the public interests; secondly, that they will not possess a proper knowledge of the local circumstances of their numerous constituents; thirdly, that they will be taken from that class of citizens which will sympathize least with the feelings of the mass of the people and be most likely to aim at a permanent elevation of the few, on the depression of the many; fourthly, that defective as the number will be in the first instance, it will be more and more disproportionate, by the increase of the people, and the obstacles which will prevent a correspondent increase of the representatives. . . .

Another general remark to be made is that the ratio between the representatives and the people ought not to be the same where the latter are very numerous as where they are very few. Were the representatives in Virginia to be regulated by the standard in Rhode Island they would at this time amount to between 400 and 500; and twenty or thirty years hence, to 1,000. On the other hand, the ratio of Pennsylvania, if applied to the State of Delaware, would reduce the representative Assembly of the latter to seven or eight members. Nothing can be more fallacious than to found our political calculations on arithmetical principles. Sixty or seventy men may be more properly trusted with a given degree of power than six or seven. But it does not follow that 600 or 700 would be proportionably a better depositary. And if we carry on the supposition to 6,000 or 7,000, the whole reasoning ought to be reversed. The truth is that in all cases a certain number at least seems to be necessary to secure the benefits of free consultation and discussion, and to guard against too easy a combination for improper purposes; as, on the other hand, the number ought at most to be kept within a certain limit in order to avoid the confusion and intemperance of a multitude. In all very numerous assemblies, of whatever characters composed, passion never fails to wrest the sceptre from reason. Had every Athenian citizen been a Socrates, every Athenian assembly would still have been a mob.

Alexis de Tocqueville
Democracy in America
(Excerpt)

DISCUSSION QUESTION

After reading de Tocqueville's observations of America on his visit in 1831, what might we infer about the influences of Antifederalist ideas on the extension of the franchise and democracy?

The American Revolution broke out, and the doctrine of the sovereignty of the people came out of the townships and took possession of the state. Every class was enlisted in its cause; battles were fought and victories obtained for it; it became the law of laws.

A change almost as rapid was effected in the interior of society, where the law of inheritance completed the abolition of local influences.

As soon as this effect of the laws and of the Revolution became apparent to every eye, victory was irrevocably pronounced in favor of the democratic cause. All power was, in fact, in its hands, and resistance was no longer possible. The higher orders submitted without a murmur and without a struggle to an evil that was thenceforth inevitable. The ordinary fate of falling powers awaited them: each of their members followed his own interest; and as it was impossible to wring the power from the hands of a people whom they did not detest sufficiently to brave, their only aim was to secure its goodwill at any price. The most democratic laws were consequently voted by the very men whose interests they impaired: and thus, although the higher classes did not excite the passions of the people against their order, they themselves accelerated the triumph of the new state of things; so that, by a singular change, the democratic impulse was found to be most irresistible in the very states where the aristocracy had the firmest hold. The state of Maryland, which had been founded by men of rank, was the first to proclaim universal suffrage[1] and to introduce the most democratic forms into the whole of its government.

When a nation begins to modify the elective qualification, it may easily be foreseen that, sooner or later, that qualification will be entirely abolished. There is no more invariable rule in the history of society: the further electoral rights are extended, the greater is the need of extending them; for after each concession the strength of the democracy increases, and its demands increase with its strength. The ambition of those who are below the appointed rate is irritated in exact proportion to the great number of those who are above it. The exception at last becomes the rule, concession follows concession, and no stop can be made short of universal suffrage.

Alexis de Tocqueville, *Democracy in America* (New York: Vintage Books, 1945), pp. 58–60. Reprinted with the permission of Random House, Inc., and Alfred A. Knopf, Inc.

[1]Amendment made to the Constitution of Maryland in 1801 and 1809.

At the present day the principle of the sovereignty of the people has acquired in the United States all the practical development that the imagination can conceive. It is unencumbered by those fictions that are thrown over it in other countries, and it appears in every possible form, according to the exigency of the occasion. Sometimes the laws are made by the people in a body, as at Athens; and sometimes its representatives, chosen by universal suffrage, transact business in its name and under its immediate supervision.

In some countries a power exists which, though it is in a degree foreign to the social body, directs it, and forces it to pursue a certain track. In others the ruling force is divided, being partly within and partly without the ranks of the people. But nothing of the kind is to be seen in the United States; there society governs itself for itself. All power centers in its bosom, and scarcely an individual is to be met with who would venture to conceive or, still less, to express the idea of seeking it elsewhere. The nation participates in the making of its laws by the choice of its legislators, and in the execution of them by the choice of the agents of the executive government; it may almost be said to govern itself, so feeble and so restricted is the share left to the administration, so little do the authorities forget their popular origin and the power from which they emanate. The people reign in the American political world as the Deity does in the universe. They are the cause and the aim of all things; everything comes from them, and everything is absorbed in them.

CONTEMPORARY INFLUENCES

William H. Riker
Liberalism Against Populism
(Excerpt)

DISCUSSION QUESTIONS

1. What are the elements that comprise the liberal interpretation of voting?
2. Are there any omissions in this interpretation?
3. How would you define the populist interpretation of voting?
4. How may Federalist and Antifederalist ideas have affected the two interpretations of voting?

The Liberal Interpretation of Voting

Democrats of all persuasions would probably agree that participation built on the act of voting is the focus of democracy. But they certainly interpret voting in different ways. What does it accomplish? What does it mean? The sharp dispute on these questions can be summarized in two views—one of which I call *liberal* or Madisonian, the other *populist* or Rousseauistic.[1]

In the liberal view, the function of voting is to control officials, *and no more.* Madison, who is the original American spokesman for liberal democracy (or republicanism, as he called it) defined a republic as "a government that derives all its powers directly or indirectly from the great body of the people, and is administered by people holding their offices during pleasure, for a limited period, as during good behavior."[2] The first requirement, popularness, he called essential (that is, *necessary*); the second, election and limited tenure, he called *sufficient.* Thus his definition is *logically* complete, and there is nothing to add. Madison said nothing about the quality of popular decision, whether good or bad.

Since all democrats would accept the necessary condition, it is the sufficient condition that is distinctive and hence deserving of detailed explication. Why is election and limited tenure sufficient? Popularness, the necessary condition, ensures participation and equality. The sufficient condition is intended to ensure liberty. In Madison's view, the danger for liberty lies in government officials who might deprive citizens of liberty or fail as agents of citizens' participation. In either case, the liberal remedy is the next election. That is all that is needed to protect liberty; so election and limited tenure are sufficient.

To consider first the protection of citizens' liberty: The replacement of officials is, in the liberal view, the only available instrument. The liberal fear is that the force of government can easily be deployed against citizens to make them support unpopular policies that officials believe necessary. The liberal hope is that officials will be restrained from such behavior out of fear of the next election. It is true that Madison and other framers of the Constitution provided the separation of powers as auxiliary protection, but Madison regarded that protection as distinctly secondary to "a dependence on the people." And the contemporary liberal agrees with Madison that the defense of liberty lies in the discipline of elections.

In the twentieth century it has sometimes (but not lately) been fashionable for populists to dismiss the liberal fear of oppression as an anachronism. Populists believe that, by reason of popular participation, democratic governments embody the will of the people and cannot therefore oppress. Only in the eighteenth century, they say, when executives were officers of the Crown was this danger real; now that elected executives supposedly embody the popular will, they cannot oppress. In *Roosevelt and Hopkins,* Robert Sherwood, for example, disputed Lord Acton's assertion that power corrupts with his (that is, Sherwood's) own belief that power en-

---

[1]The words "Madisonian" and "populist" are used in Dahl, *A Preface to Democratic Theory*; my usage, however, is quite different.

[2]James Madison, *The Federalist,* No. 39. That "democracy" and "republic" meant about the same thing in Madison's day is indicated by Thomas Nugent's translation (1750) of Montesquieu's *Spirit of the Laws,* Bk. II, chap. 2: "When the body of the people in a republic are possessed of supreme power, this is called a democracy." Adrienne Koch, in her preface to *Madison's Notes of Debates in the Federal Convention of 1787* (New York: Norton, 1966), p. xix, argues that by "republic" Madison meant "representative democracy."

nobled Franklin Roosevelt.[3] But it was Sherwood's other subject, Harry Hopkins, who presumably uttered that epitome of corruption: "We will tax and tax, spend and spend, elect and elect." Lately, of course, even populists have been shaken by the imperial presidency of Johnson and Nixon, who, however popularly elected, persisted in a hated and oppressive war. In both cases the threat of the next election proved decisive for liberty because it made one not try for reelection and the other (ultimately) end the war. Even more impressive, the possibility of impeachment, a kind of negative election, made Nixon resign. Moreover, it was elections themselves, not just the threat of them, that as recently as 1977 disposed of two putatively tyrannical rulers in India and Sri Lanka.

The other part of Madison's concern was a fear of tyranny by the majority. This is a fear that officials acting for a majority created in the last election will persecute the minority of that election. Madison hoped that such oppression would be minimized by the fact of shifting majorities, so that a future majority might throw out of office the officials who oppressed in the name of the former majority. This is the reason he stressed diversity in the electorate. The way, he said, "to guard one part of society against the injustice of the other part" is to comprehend "in the society so many separate descriptions of citizens as will render an unjust combination of a majority of the whole very improbable, if not impracticable."[4]

Viewed statically, this sounds like just another version of the separation of powers.[5] Viewed dynamically, however, this is simply the claim that an unjust majority cannot last through several elections. Looking at the oppression of blacks, the most persistent issue in American politics and the clearest case of tyranny by the majority, it appears that the Madisonian hope has been justified. As long as blacks were excluded from the political system (from the beginning to 1867 and from the end of Reconstruction in 1877 to the emergence of a substantial number of black voters in the 1930s), they were persecuted. But including them in the system, especially as they became a marginal bloc between the political parties, led to political reform and even to reorientation of the judiciary, so that national political leaders (followed by the courts) have mitigated and are gradually eliminating that tyranny by the majority.

To consider the other danger to liberty (that officials be inefficient agents): The only possible remedy—and one recommended by both populists and liberals—is to elect new officials. So again the next election promotes liberty. Notice, however, that in the liberal view it is not assumed that the electorate is right. This assumption characterizes populism, as I will show. The liberal assumes not popular competence, but merely that the electorate can change officials if many people are dissatisfied or hope for better performance.

It may seem that in the liberal view officials, who are only negatively controlled by voting, cannot really act as agents of the electorate. By reason of regular

---

[3]Robert Sherwood, *Roosevelt and Hopkins* (New York: Harper and Row, 1948), p. 127; see also p. 102 for the controversy over Hopkins' remark, mentioned subsequently in the text.

[4]Madison, *The Federalist*, No. 51. See also No. 10.

[5]Dahl, in *A Preface to Democratic Theory*, so interprets it. In my terms, Dahl turns out to be a liberal and Madisonian; his "polyarchal" democracy is very similar to my interpretation of Madison.

elections, however, officials may be rejected. In their efforts to avoid rejection they usually act in some rough way as agents of the electorate, at least attempting to avoid giving offense to some future majority. Since this future majority cannot at any moment be clearly specified, officials seeking to placate it in advance must anticipate several kinds of potential majorities, the union of which is often most of the electorate. By reason of this anticipation of the next election, officials are, even in the liberal view, subject to electoral discipline as the agents of democratic self-control.

The Populist Interpretation of Voting

For the populist, liberty and hence self-control through participation are obtained by embodying the will of the people in the action of officials. The fundamental notion goes back at least to Rousseau. There is a social contract, which creates a "moral and collective body" that has "life" and "will," that is the famous "general will," the will of the incorporated people, the Sovereign. Individual liberty, for Rousseau and subsequent populists, is the participation of the citizen in this sovereignty. "Liberty," Rousseau says, "is obedience to a law we have prescribed for ourselves," understanding, of course, that the prescription is through the acts of the anthropomorphized Sovereign.[6] The way to discover the general will, which is the objectively correct common interest of the incorporated citizens, is to compute it by consulting the citizens. The computation will be accurate if each citizen, when giving an opinion or vote, considers and chooses only the common interest, not a personal or private interest. Thus, by summing the common interest regarding wills (votes) of real persons, one can arrive at the will of the great artificial person, the Sovereign.

In the Middle Ages it was sometimes (blasphemously) said that the voice of the people is the voice of God. Rosseau did not invest the people with quite such divine authority—indeed he believed they might be mistaken about the general will—but he did assert that the general will is always correct and embodies the objective good for society. Later populists have continued to attribute some special character to the voice of the people: What the sovereign people, when speaking for the public interest, want is justified because the sovereign people want it and because it is their liberty.

To summarize: According to the populist interpretation of voting, participation in rule-making is necessary for liberty. The rules thus made must be respected as right and proper because they embody that liberty. Were they not so respected, liberty itself might vanish.

---

[6]Jean Jacques Rousseau, *Social Contract*, Bk. I, chap. 8

Thomas E. Cronin
Direct Democracy
(Excerpt)

DISCUSSION QUESTIONS

1. List some of the historical results in the movement toward direct democracy.
2. Describe the paradox of our American style of democracy.
3. What are the pros and cons associated with direct democracy?
4. After reading the Antifederalist writings and Professor Cronin's ideas, is there a link between Antifederalist and populist ideas? If so, what is the nature of this link?

Americans of the Revolutionary era were profoundly ambivalent about democracy. About one-third would gladly have continued as loyal subjects of the king; another third did not want to be bothered by tedious debates about forms of government, representation, and election schemes: they wanted to be left alone and to leave what limited governing was necessary to those who were willing to do it. A positive embrace of democracy in any real sense came well after the writing of the Constitution.

When democracy, even in its limited forms, did evolve, it did so too quickly for many people. The very notion of direct and frequent popular participation in state or national decision making frightened many of those in privileged positions. Many worried about tyranny by the majority and held the protection of the minority to be of equal if not superior importance to majority rule. The purpose of elections, most people then believed, was to select leaders—not to get the public wholly involved in the affairs of government. Once basic rules of constitutionalism could be agreed on, political leaders would govern and the governed would obey. Even the desirability of a representative government with the suffrage limited to white males was debated well into the nineteenth century.

Yet the reasonable voice of the people has always been accorded a special significance in theories of American governance. And the impetus for the American Revolution surely emerged from the protests of the common people as much as, if not more than, from the well bred, well read, and well fed. In urging American unity in the war effort, Thomas Jefferson emphasized the fundamental right of a people to rebel and end the illegitimate rule of unreasonable and unresponsive leaders. Even Alexander Hamilton, whom one could hardly accuse of being a professional democrat, later wrote that the fabric of the new American republic ought to rest on the solid basis of the consent of the people. "The streams of national power ought to flow immediately from that pure original foundation of all legitimate authority."[1] James Madison emphasized it was essential for the new republic to derive its legitimacy from "the great body of the society, not from any inconsid-

[1]Alexander Hamilton, *The Federalist*, no. 22, in *The Federalist Papers*, ed. Jacob E. Cooke (New York: Meridian, 1961), p. 146. All subsequent citations of *The Federalist* are to this edition.

erable portion, or a favored class of it."[2] But although Madison and his peers conceded that government should be carried on with steady attention to the expectations and preferences of the American voter, they opposed widespread and continuous public participation in the conduct and operations of government decision making. Regular elections would be sufficient to render elected officials sensitive to the public's wishes.

A hundred years later, populists and progressives began to call for more direct participation in the democratic process. The cure for the ills of representative democracy, they argued, was more democracy, and three of the proposed cures were the initiative, referendum, and recall. Today we hear similar calls for more direct democracy, including the direct election of the American president, easier voter registration procedures at all levels, and even, occasionally, two-way interactive, electronic town meetings and teledemocracy technologies. Certain writers and reformers in American politics say it is time to consider bolder, more innovative forms of citizen education and citizen involvement if we want to become a robust, healthy, and strong democracy.[3]

If we have learned anything about democracy in the twentieth century, it is that the slogan "The cure for democracy is more democracy" is only a partial truth. A democracy requires more than popular majority rule and a system of democratic procedures to flatter the voters. A vital democracy puts faith not only in the people but also in their ability to select representatives who will provide a heightened sense of the best aspirations for the whole country and who can make sense of the key issues.

In practice, Americans are torn between wanting responsible leaders to make decisions and wanting the general public to be consulted (see Table 5–1). There exists in America both an uncertainty about the ability of the average voter to make policy and about the desirability of having elected officials make unilateral decisions.

Democracy American style is fraught with paradox. Most Americans believe that majority rule is both their right and "what democracy is all about." Although most Americans realize they do not have all the answers, they believe that on important issues the voting public can be trusted to do what is right just about as often as their elected public officials.

Most Americans are not inclined to exercise their political rights fully. But the right they exercise most often is the right to choose elected officials. They believe that representative assemblies are better suited than ordinary citizens to decide technical and legal policy matters. They believe, too, that legislative bodies provide an opportunity for the views and concerns of minorities to be expressed and balanced against the interests of majorities.

---

[2]James Madison, *The Federalist*, no. 39, p. 251. See also Charles S. Hyneman, "Republican Government in America," in *Founding Principles of American Government: Two Hundred Years of Democracy on Trial*, ed. George J. Graham, Jr., and Scarlett G. Graham (Bloomington: Indiana University Press, 1977), p. 18.

[3]See, for example, Barber, *Strong Democracy*; and Patrick B. McGuigan, *The Politics of Direct Democracy in the 1980s: Case Studies in Popular Decision Making* (Washington, D.C.: Institute for Government and Politics, 1985).

TABLE 5-1 Informed Leadership vs. Democratic Values (%) (N = 1026)

1. To be realistic about it, our elected officials:	
—know much more than the voters about issues, and should be allowed to make whatever decisions they think best	8
—would badly misuse their power if they weren't watched and guided by the voters	68
—Decline to choose	23
2. When making new laws, the government should pay most attention to:	
—the opinion of the people who really know something about the subject	53
—the opinions of average citizens, regardless of how little they know	22
—Decline to choose	25
3. Should people with more intelligence and character have greater influence over the country's decisions than other people?	
—Yes, because they have more to offer and can do more to benefit society.	39
—No, because every citizen must have an equal right to decide what's best for the country.	45
—Decline to choose	16

Source: Civil liberties national survey, 1978–79, reported in Herbert McClosky and John Zaller, *The American Ethos: Public Attitudes toward Capitalism and Democracy* (Cambridge, Mass.: Harvard University Press, 1984), p. 79.

Americans' ambivalence toward procedural democracy is explained in large measure by their general satisfaction with the capacity of elected officials to reconcile their objective needs with their expectations. Perhaps, though, Americans have for too long underestimated the potential of a citizenry that is well educated and informed. Such a citizenry would be motivated to participate more vigorously in the political process. Ironically, public leadership of a major kind would be needed to implement programs to heighten citizen interest in more fully exercising their democratic rights!

A populist impulse, incorporating notions of "power to the people" and skepticism about the system has always existed in America. Americans seldom abide quietly the failings and deficiencies of capitalism, the welfare state, or the political decision rules by which we live. We are, as historian Richard Hofstadter wrote, "forever restlessly pitting ourselves against them, demanding changes, improvements, remedies."[4] Demand for more democracy occurs when there is growing distrust of legislative bodies and when there is a growing suspicion that privileged interests exert far greater influences on the typical politician than does the common voter.

Direct democracy, especially as embodied in the referendum, initiative, and recall, is sometimes viewed as a typically American political response to perceived abuses of the public trust. Voters periodically become frustrated with taxes, regulations, inefficiency in government programs, the inequalities or injustices of the system, the arms race, environmental hazards, and countless other irritations. This frustration arises in part because more public policy decisions are now made in dis-

[4]Richard Hofstadter, *The Age of Reform* (New York: Vintage Books, 1955), p. 16.

tant capitals, by remote agencies or private yet unaccountable entities—such as regulatory bodies, the Federal Reserve Board, foreign governments, multinational alliances, or foreign trading combines—instead of at the local or county level as once was the case, or as perhaps we like to remember.

Champions of populist democracy claim many benefits will accrue from their reforms. Here are some:

> Citizen initiatives will promote government responsiveness and accountability. If officials ignore the voice of the people, the people will have an available means to make needed law.
>
> Initiatives are freer from special interest domination than the legislative branches of most states, and so provide a desirable safeguard that can be called into use when legislators are corrupt, irresponsible, or dominated by privileged special interests.
>
> The initiative and referendum will produce open, educational debate on critical issues that otherwise might be inadequately discussed.
>
> Referendum, initiative, and recall are nonviolent means of political participation that fulfill a citizen's right to petition the government for redress of grievances.
>
> Direct democracy increases voter interest and election-day turnout. Perhaps, too, giving the citizen more of a role in governmental processes might lessen alienation and apathy.
>
> Finally (although this hardly exhausts the claims), citizen initiatives are needed because legislators often evade the tough issues. Fearing to be ahead of their time, they frequently adopt a zero-risk mentality. Concern with staying in office often makes them timid and perhaps too wedded to the status quo. One result is that controversial social issues frequently have to be resolved in the judicial branch. But who elected the judges?

For every claim put forward on behalf of direct democracy, however, there is an almost equally compelling criticism. Many opponents believe the ordinary citizen usually is not well enough informed about complicated matters to arrive at sound public policy judgments. They also fear the influence of slick television advertisements or bumper sticker messages.

Some critics of direct democracy contend the best way to restore faith in representative institutions is to find better people to run for office. They prefer the deliberations and the collective judgment of elected representatives who have the time to study complicated public policy matters, matters that should be decided within the give-and-take process of politics. That process, they say, takes better account of civil liberties.

Critics also contend that in normal times initiative and referendum voter turnout is often a small proportion of the general population and so the results are unduly influenced by special interests: big money will win eight out of ten times.

A paradox runs throughout this debate. As the United States has aged, we have extended the suffrage in an impressive way. The older the country, the more we have preached the gospel of civic participation. Yet we also have experienced centralization of power in the national government and the development of the professional politician. The citizen-politician has become an endangered species.

Representative government is always in the process of development and decay. Its fortunes rise and fall depending upon various factors, not least the quality of people involved and the resources devoted to making it work effectively. When the slumps come, proposals that would reform and change the character of representative government soon follow. Direct democracy notions have never been entirely foreign to our country—countless proponents from Benjamin Franklin to Jesse Jackson, Jack Kemp, and Richard Gephardt have urged us to listen more to the common citizen. . . .

Robert Dahl
Controlling Nuclear Weapons
(Excerpt)

DISCUSSION QUESTIONS

1. Describe Dahl's concept of a minipopulus.
2. Can we link this idea to the ideas embodied in Antifederalism, populism, and other direct democracy ideas or reforms?
3. Are there any similarities in the ideas of John DeWitt and Robert Dahl on representation and representative assemblies?

Representing Public Opinion

Finally, how can we possibly achieve the third objective, which on the face of it looks self-contradictory: to provide a highly informed body of public opinion that *except for being highly informed* is *representative* of the entire citizen body?

Certainly the solutions described thus far could substantially raise the average level of civic understanding of complex issues, increase the size and representativeness of attentive elites, improve the quality of public discussion and debate, and help to make political elites, both elective and bureaucratic, responsive to a more informed body of citizens. Yet even if everything I have suggested were in place and working satisfactorily, the problem that has emerged in these essays as a central and formidable obstacle to the democratic process—the interdependence of moral and technical judgments—would not necessarily be satisfactorily solved. The organizations and processes sketched out here would hardly provide for a systematic exploration, in depth, of the interdependent moral and technical questions involved in complex issues.

Because of the limitations of elections mentioned in the first chapter, and despite the numerous ways in which public opinion helps to influence the agenda of political decisions as well as the decisions themselves, it is often crucial to the democratic process for both citizens and officials to know what alternative would be favored by, or at least acceptable to, a majority of citizens. Advocates of plebiscitary democracy would of course make government policy highly dependent on referenda. Yet even if public opinion were to reflect considerably greater competence on public matters than is now the case, referenda and other techniques of direct

---

democracy would tend to suffer, like opinion surveys, from many of the defects we are trying to remedy. One view of participatory democracy assumes by implication that *all* citizens, or most of them at any rate, would somehow come to possess a high degree of political competence on *all* major issues—something approximating the competence, let us say, of a well informed member of Congress. But this looks to be flatly impossible. Arguably it is not even a particularly worthy ideal. After all, political life is not the whole of life, and all of us ought not to be obliged to devote all of our daily lives to becoming extraordinarily well-informed and active citizens.

A more attainable and perhaps even more desirable alternative might be adopted. Imagine that a representative group of citizens were to acquire a high degree of political competence and were to "stand for," and in this sense of the term to "represent," the rest. But in order to "stand for" the citizen body as a whole, so far as humanly possible they ought not to develop additional interests stemming from the very role of representation itself, such as a primary interest in re-election. To avoid this possibility, and to insure that their interests were essentially no other than the interests they possess as ordinary citizens, citizens would need to be chosen randomly, and for a limited period. Election by lot is an ancient democratic idea that preceded elected representation by several thousand years. So to insure that our representative bodies of citizens were truly representative, its members would be chosen by a random process, rather like respondents are chosen in scientifically designed opinion surveys.

We might call such a body a *minipopulus.* As to the size of a minipopulus, suppose we say about a thousand: a compromise between the lower limits set by the risk of excessive sampling error and upper limits set by opportunities to participate in discussion. In my experience, a thousand is large for a town meeting, but manageable. One minipopulus might decide on the agenda of issues, while several others might each concern itself with one of the major issues. A minipopulus could exist at any level of government: national, state or local. Citizens selected for membership in a minipopulus would be paid. They would serve for a year—and no more than once in a lifetime.

Members of a minipopulus would not need to assemble in one place, for they could easily meet instead by means of telecommunications. Indeed, it would be advantageous for them to remain in their own communities, with their own friends and acquaintances. They could meet for a year, let us say, during which they would be expected to work through a single important issue. Each minipopulus could be attended—again by telecommunications—by an advisory committee of scholars chosen along the lines suggested earlier, and by an administrative staff monitored by the advisory committee. A minipopulus could hold hearings, commission research, and engage in debate and discussion.

By the end of its year, a minipopulus could indicate the preference ordering of its members among the most relevant alternatives in the policy area assigned to it. Its "decision" however, would have no binding effect—on the relevant legislature or executive, for example. For a minipopulus would not be a law making or rule making body. Rather it would "stand for" the public: it would represent what the public would itself prefer if members of the public were as well informed as the members of the minipopulation had become. A minipopulus would reflect public opinion at a higher level of competence.

A vital task of a minipopulus would be to assess *risks, uncertainties, and trade offs.* . . . On these crucial presuppositions of policy decisions, specialists can make no special claim to expertise. On many important issues, to arrive at judgments requires assumptions about the world and its tendencies, the relative worth of lives, present and future, under alternative circumstances and conditions that may be highly uncertain and radically different from one another, and how much risk and uncertainty it is prudent to accept in the hope of achieving the best possible outcome. Decisions about nuclear weapons strategies are of course jam-packed with such crucial presuppositions. So too are many other complex issues. Who could justifiably claim to possess a more reasonable judgment on these matters than a minipopulus that had grappled with the issue for a year?

The relevant decision makers, whether congress and president, a state governor and legislature, or mayor and council, could and at times probably would disagree with the majority views expressed by the minipopulus, particularly if no overwhelming consensus had emerged. In disagreeing, however, decision makers would need to explain their reasons for doing so, and in this way their disagreement would itself contribute still further to the continuing process of civic teaching and learning.

6

The Public's Opinion

Wide differences appear to exist in the positions of Antifederalists and Federalists concerning the public's opinion. Generally, Antifederalist literature displays a greater trust in the capacity of the public to know and understand the Constitutional issues affecting them. Federalist literature tends to display a skepticism concerning the public's capacity to make informed and intelligent decisions concerning these Constitutional issues. However, one must be cautious because a continuum along the preceding lines of thought exists. Some Antifederalists were more trusting than others, and some Federalists were less skeptical than others. With this cautionary note in mind, we can gain some insight about these differences by examining excerpts from the various essays in both camps.

John DeWitt, in his essay of October 22, 1787, encourages the public to examine the Constitution in a "candid and strict" way. He sees this as a duty of every citizen. Antifederalists were concerned with a number of issues affecting the Constitution, and they sought the public's opinion on these issues. Brutus, in his essay of October 18, 1787, argues against extending the republic to a large geographical area because this would diminish the people's ability to meet and deliberate on the issues affecting them. Antifederalists were also worried about the potential for aristocratic government. On November 5, 1787, John DeWitt warned that the Constitution in theory was different from the Constitution in practice. In theory it favors the people, but in practice it would favor the aristocracy. These thoughts are echoed by Brutus Junior, who notes the aristocratic nature of the founding fathers. He believes that the aristocratic founders had nothing but contempt for the people. Melancton Smith admits that there are problems with the public's competence to judge public issues. He also admits that there is a chance for corruption concerning the Constitutional selection of senators. But his cure for such corruption is a greater dose of democracy for the purposes of bringing government representatives closer to the people via shorter terms and rotation of offices. Thus, although he shares a skeptical view of the public with the Federalists, he simultaneously desires to provide the public with frequent opportunity for representational voting. In two essays, one on March 20 and the other on April, 10, 1788, Brutus remains uncomfortable with the plan for the judicial branch under the Constitution. This branch is the farthest from the people. Brutus advocates greater control of the judicial branch by the people. Thomas Jefferson, although not an Antifederalist opponent of the Constitution, champions the notion of a natural aristocracy based not upon wealth and heredity but on education and civic involvement. It was his answer to those who believed the public too ignorant and incompetent to be involved in public affairs. Jefferson desired to create an enlightened public to counter the aristocratic tendencies of our young nation.

Federalist writers are skeptical of the public and its opinions. James Madison in *Federalist* Paper 49 warns that, ". . . it is reason, alone, of the public, that ought to control and regulate the governed. The passions ought to be controlled and regulated by the government." In a stirring and uncompromising essay of October 17, 1787, Alexander Hamilton states clearly his opinion of the public. As he indicates, he was ". . . not much attached to the majesty of the multitude." We must offer a note of caution concerning this letter in that a controversy exists over Hamilton's authorship of it. Whereas traditional historians have long attributed this letter to Hamilton, Professor Jacob E. Cooke argues that Hamilton did not write this letter and that it was probably authored by some other New York Federalist.[1] Nevertheless, this essay illustrates that Federalist fears were many and real. Madison, in *Federalist* Paper 51, argues that the rights of people will be protected better in an extended republic than in a small one. This is a direct response to the arguments of Brutus. In *Federalist* Paper 48, Madison argues against direct democracy because the people are ill suited for regular deliberation. He is concerned with the passions of the people. His republic combines reason in order to temper passion. In *Federalist* Paper 51 he indicates that one of the methods for achieving this result is to temper ambition with ambition. The different interests in the republic will counteract the majority and protect minority rights. Hamilton, in *Federalist* Paper 59, fears giving people in the states the power over national elections, for this could lead to the dissolution of the Union. In *Federalist* Paper 34, Hamilton notes that the zeal for the rights of the people masks tyranny. In *Federalist* Paper 71, Hamilton argues that people may have good intentions but may not achieve good results. Representative guardians are thus necessary for the realization of the public good. In *Federalist* Paper 45, Madison notes that state sovereignty may have to be sacrificed for the happiness of all the people.

The arguments of Antifederalists and Federalists over the public's opinion have survived the ages. One of the foremost public opinion pollsters of our era, Daniel Yankelovich, documents the views of the media, public policy experts, political scientists, and the polling professionals concerning public opinion. He notes their skepticism concerning the public's ability to arrive at informed opinions. It seems that modern experts have much in common with Federalist beliefs. In a rather poignant excerpt, Yankelovich shares his thoughts about the expert view of public opinion. He then presents a vision for the future which, at first blush, appears to draw upon Antifederalist confidence in the public and Jeffersonian ideals of civic education.

---

[1]Jacob E. Cooke, "Alexander Hamilton's Authorship of the 'Caesar' Letters," *The William and Mary Quarterly*, Vol. 17, 1960: 78–85.

ANTIFEDERALIST ARGUMENTS

"John DeWitt"
(Unknown)
"To the Free Citizens of the Commonwealth of Massachusetts"
(Excerpt)

DISCUSSION QUESTIONS

1. According to DeWitt, why should citizens carefully examine the new Constitution?
2. Why should citizens question the motives of the members of the constitutional convention?
3. What does John DeWitt say about the need for a strong union?

Are we to adopt this Government, without an examination?—Some there are, who, literally speaking, are for pressing it upon us at all events. The name of the man who but lisps a sentiment in objection to it, is to be handed to the printer, by the printer to the publick, and by the publick he is to be led to execution. They are themselves stabbing its reputation. For my part, I am a stranger to the necessity for all this haste! Is it not a subject of some small importance? Certainly it is.—Are not your lives, your liberties and properties intimately involved in it?—Certainly they are. Is it a government for a moment, a day, or a year? By no means—but for ages—Altered it may possibly be, but it is easier to correct before it is adopted.—Is it for a family, a state, or a small number of people? It is for a number no less respectable than three millions. Are the enemy at our gates, and have we not time to consider it? Certainly we have. Is it so simple in its form as to be comprehended instantly?—Every letter, if I may be allowed the expression, is an idea. Does it consist of but few additions to our present confederation, and those which have been from time to time described among us, and known to be necessary?—Far otherwise. It is a compleat system of government, and armed with every power, that a people in any circumstances ought to bestow. It is a path newly struck out, and a new set of ideas are introduced that have neither occurred or been digested.—A government for national purposes, preserving our constitution entire, hath been the only plan hitherto agitated. I do not pretend to say, but it is in theory the most unexceptionable, and in practice will be the most conductive to our happiness of any possible to be adopted:—But it ought to undergo a candid and strict examination. It is the duty of every one in the Commonwealth to communicate his sentiments to his neighbour, divested of passion, and equally so of prejudices. If they are honest and he is a real friend to his country, he will do it and embrace every opportunity to do it. If thoroughly looked into before it is adopted, the people will be more apt to approve of it in practice, and every man is a TRAITOR to himself and his posterity, who shall ratify it with his signature, without first endeavouring to understand it.—We are but yet in infancy; and we had better proceed slow than too fast.—It is much easier to dispense powers, than recall them.—The present generation will not be drawn into any system; they are too enlightened; they have not forfeited their right to a share in government, and they ought to enjoy it.

Some are heard to say, "When we consider the men who made it, we ought to take it for sterling, and without hesitation—that they were the collected wisdom of the States, and had no object but the general good." —I do not doubt all this, but facts ought not to be winked out of sight:—They were delegated from different States, and nearly equally represented, though vastly disproportionate both in wealth and numbers. They had local prejudices to combat, and in many instances, totally opposite interests to consult. Their situations, their habits, their extent, and their particular interest, varied each from the other. The gentlemen themselves acknowledge that they have been less rigid upon some points, in consequence of those difficulties than they otherwise should have been.—Others again tell you that the Convention is or will be dissolved; that we must take their proceedings in whole or reject them.—But this surely cannot be a reason for their speedy adoption; it rather works the other way. If evils are acknowledged in the composition, we ought, at least, to see whose shoulders are to bear the most; to compare ours with those of other States, and take care that we are not saddled with more than our proportion: That the citizens of Philadelphia are running mad after it, can be no argument for us to do the like:—Their situation is almost contrasted with ours; they suppose themselves a central State; they expect the perpetual residence of Congress, which of itself alone will ensure their aggrandizement: We, on the contrary, are sure to be near one of the extremes; neither the loaves or fishes will be so plenty with us, or shall we be so handy to procure them.

We are told by some people, that upon the adopting this New Government, we are to become every thing in a moment:—Our foreign and domestic debts will be as a feather; our ports will be crowded with the ships of all the world, soliciting our commerce and our produce: Our manufactures will increase and multiply; and, in short, if we STAND still, our country, notwithstanding, will be like the blessed Canaan, a land flowing with milk and honey. Let us not deceive ourselves; the only excellency of any government is in exact proportion to the administration of it:—Idleness and luxury will be as much a bane as ever; our passions will be equally at war with us then as now; and if we have men among us trying with all their ability to undermine our present Constitution, these very persons will direct their force to sap the vitals of the new one.—

Upon the whole, my fellow countrymen, I am as much a federal man as any person: In a federal union lies our political salvation—To preserve that union, and make it respectable to foreign opticks, the National Government ought to be armed with all necessary powers; but the subject I conceive of infinite delicacy, and requires both ability and reflection. In discussing points of such moment, America has nothing to do with passions or hard words; every citizen has an undoubted right to examine for himself, neither ought he to be ill treated and abused, because he does not think at the same moment exactly as we do. It is true, that many of us have but our liberties to lose, but they are dearly bought, and are not the least precious in estimation:—In the mean time, is it not of infinite consequence, that we pursue inflexibly that path, which I feel persuaded we are now approaching, wherein we shall discourage all foreign importations; shall see the necessity of greater oeconomy and industry; shall smile upon the husbandman, and reward the industrious mechanick; shall promote the growth of our own country, and wear the produce of our own farms; and, finally, shall support measures in proportion to their honesty and wisdom, without any respect to men. Nothing more is wanted to make us happy at home, and respectable abroad.

JOHN DEWITT

"Brutus" (Probably Robert Yates) Essay I (Excerpt)

DISCUSSION QUESTIONS

1. According to Brutus, what are the dangers associated with large republics?
2. What is the relationship of public opinion and government?
3. What is Brutus advocating in this essay?

History furnishes no example of a free republic, any thing like the extent of the United States. The Grecian republics were of small extent; so also was that of the Romans. Both of these, it is true, in process of time, extended their conquests over large territories of country; and the consequence was, that their governments were changed from that of free governments to those of the most tyrannical that ever existed in the world.

Not only the opinion of the greatest men, and the experience of mankind, are against the idea of an extensive republic, but a variety of reasons may be drawn from the reason and nature of things, against it. In every government, the will of the sovereign is the law. In despotic governments, the supreme authority being lodged in one, his will is law, and can be as easily expressed to a large extensive territory as to a small one. In a pure democracy the people are the sovereign, and their will is declared by themselves; for this purpose they must all come together to deliberate, and decide. This kind of government cannot be exercised, therefore, over a country of any considerable extent; it must be confined to a single city, or at least limited to such bounds as that the people can conveniently assemble, be able to debate, understand the subject submitted to them, and declare their opinion concerning it.

In a free republic, although all laws are derived from the consent of the people, yet the people do not declare their consent by themselves in person, but by representatives, chosen by them, who are supposed to know the minds of their constituents, and to be possessed of integrity to declare this mind.

In every free government, the people must give their assent to the laws by which they are governed. This is the true criterion between a free government and an arbitrary one. The former are ruled by the will of the whole, expressed in any manner they may agree upon; the latter by the will of one, or a few. If the people are to give their assent to the laws, by persons chosen and appointed by them, the manner of the choice and the number chosen, must be such, as to possess, be disposed, and consequently qualified to declare the sentiments of the people; for if they do not know, or are not disposed to speak the sentiments of the people, the people do not govern, but the sovereignty is in a few. Now, in a large extended country, it is impossible to have a representation, possessing the sentiments, and of integrity, to declare the minds of the people, without having it so numerous and unwieldly, as to be subject in great measure to the inconveniency of a democratic government.

"Brutus Junior"
(Unknown)
Essay, November 8, 1787
(Excerpts)

DISCUSSION QUESTIONS

1. What is the point that Brutus Junior is attempting to make concerning the aristocratic tendencies of the founders?
2. What can we note about the framers and their confidence in the people?
3. According to Brutus Junior, what is the relationship of the framers with the common people?

I have read with a degree of attention several publications which have lately appeared in favor of the new Constitution; and as far as I am able to discern, the arguments (if they can be so termed) of most weight, which are urged in its favor, may be reduced to the two following:

1st. That the men who formed it, were wise and experienced; that they were an illustrious band of patriots, and had the happiness of their country at heart; that they were four months deliberating on the subject, and therefore, it must be a perfect system. . . .

It is readily admitted that many individuals who composed this body were men of the first talents and integrity in the union. It is at the same time, well known to every man, who is but moderately acquainted with the characters of the members, that many of them are possessed of high aristocratic ideas, and the most sovereign contempt of the common people; that not a few were strongly disposed in favor of monarchy; that there were some of no small talents and of great influence, of consummate cunning and masters of intrigue, whom the war found poor or in embarrassed circumstances, and left with princely fortunes acquired in public employment. . . . that there were others who were young, ardent, and ambitious, who wished for a government corresponding with their feelings, while they were destitute of experience . . . in political researches; that there were not a few who were gaping for posts of honor and emolument—these we find exulting in the idea of a change which will divert places of honor, influence and emolument, into a different channel, where the confidence of the people will not be necessary to their acquirement. It is not to be wondered at, that an assembly thus composed should produce a system liable to well founded objections, and which will require very essential alterations. We are told by one of themselves (Mr. [James] Wilson of Philadelphia) the plan was [a] matter of accommodation, and it is not unreasonable to suppose, that in this accommodation, principles might be introduced which would render the liberties of the people very insecure.

"John DeWitt"
(Unknown)
Essay, November 5, 1787
(Excerpt)

DISCUSSION QUESTIONS

1. Why and how does DeWitt make a distinction between the Constitution in theory and practice?
2. Will the government under the Constitution listen to public opinion? Why or why not?

All contracts are to be construed according to the meaning of the parties at the time of making them. By which is meant, that mutual communications shall take place, and each shall explain to the other their ideas of the contract before them.—If any unfair practices are made use of, if its real tendency is concealed by either party, or any advantage taken in the execution of it, it is in itself fraudulent and may be avoided. There is no difference in the constitution of government—Consent it is allowed is the spring—The form is the mode in which the people choose to direct their affairs, and the magistrates are but trustees to put that mode in force.—It will not be denied, that this people, of any under Heaven, have a right of living under a government of their own choosing.—That government, originally consented to, which is in practice, what it purports to be in theory, is a government of choice; on the contrary, that which is essentially different in practice, from its appearance in theory, however it may be in letter a government of choice, it never can be so in spirit. Of this latter kind appear to me to be the proceedings of the Federal Convention—They are presented as a Frame of Government purely Republican, and perfectly consistent with the individual governments in the Union. It is declared to be constructed for national purposes only, and not calculated to interfere with domestic concerns. You are told, that the rights of the people are very amply secured, and when the wheels of it are put in motion, it will wear a milder aspect than its present one. Whereas the very contrary of all this doctrine appears to be true. Upon an attentive examination you can pronounce it nothing less, than a government which in a few years, will degenerate to a complete Aristocracy, armed with powers unnecessary in any case to bestow, and which in its vortex swallows up every other Government upon the Continent. In short, my fellow-citizens, it can be said to be nothing less than a hasty stride to Universal Empire in this Western World, flattering, very flattering to young ambitious minds, but fatal to the liberties of the people. The cord is strained to the very utmost.—There is every spice of the SIC. JUBEO possible in the composition. Your consent is requested, because it is essential to the introduction of it; after having received-confirmation, your complaints may increase the whistling of the wind, and they will be equally regarded.

Melancton Smith
Essay
June 25, 1788
(Excerpts)

DISCUSSION QUESTIONS

1. Describe Smith's view of the public.
2. How does Smith propose to reduce governmental corruption?
3. What might this imply about his opinion of the public?

The amendment embraces two objects: First, that the senators shall be eligible for only six years in any term of twelve years: Second, that they shall be subject to the recall of the legislatures of their several states. . . .

Against this part of the amendment a great deal of argument has been used, and with considerable plausibility. It is said if the amendment takes place, the senators will hold their office only during the pleasure of the state legislatures, and consequently will not possess the necessary firmness and stability. I conceive, Sir, there is a fallacy in this argument, founded upon the suspicion that the legislature of a state will possess the qualities of a mob, and be incapable of any regular conduct. I know that the impulses of the multitude are inconsistent with systematic government. The people are frequently incompetent to deliberate discussion, and subject to errors and imprudencies. Is this the complexion of the state legislatures? I presume it is not. I presume that they are never actuated by blind impulses—that they rarely do things hastily and without consideration. The state legislatures were select bodies of men, chosen for their superior wisdom, and so organized as to be capable of calm and regular conduct. My apprehension is, that the power of recall would not be exercised as often as it ought. It is highly improbable that a man, in whom the state has confided, and who has an established influence, will be recalled, unless his conduct has been notoriously wicked—The arguments of the gentleman therefore, do not apply in this case. It is further observed, that it would be improper to give the legislatures this power, because the local interests and prejudices of the states ought not to be admitted into the general government; and that if the senator is rendered too independent of his constituents, he will sacrifice the interests of the Union to the policy of his state. Sir, the senate has been generally held up by all parties as a safe guard to the rights of the several states. In this view, the closest connection between them has been considered as necessary. But now it seems we speak a different language—We now look upon the least attachment to their state as dangerous—We are now for separating them, and rendering them entirely independent, that we may root out the last vestige of state sovereignty. . . .

More than one of the gentlemen have ridiculed my apprehensions of corruption. How, say they, are the people to be corrupted? By their own money? Sir, in many countries, the people pay money to corrupt themselves: why should it not happen in this? Certainly, the congress will be as liable to corruption as other bodies of men. Have they not the same frailties, and the same temptations? With respect to the corruption arising from the disposal of offices, the gentlemen have treated the argument as insignificant. But let any one make a calculation, and see whether there will not be good offices enough, to dispose of to every man who goes there, who will then freely resign his seat: for, can any one suppose, that a member of congress would not go out and relinquish his four dollars a day, for two or three thousand pounds a year? It is here objected that no man can hold an office created during the time he is in Congress—But it will be easy for a man of influence, who has in his eye a favorite office previously created and already filled, to say to his friend, who holds it—Here—I will procure you another place of more emolument, provided you will relinquish yours in favor of me. The constitution appears to be a restraint, when in fact it is none at all. I presume, sir, there is not a government in the world in which there is greater scope for influence and corruption in the disposal of offices. Sir, I will not declaim, and say all men are dishonest; but I think that, in forming a constitution, if we presume this, we shall be on the safest side. The extreme is certainly less dangerous than the other. It is wise to multiply checks to a greater degree than the present state of things requires. It is said that corruption has never taken place under the old government—I believe, gentlemen hazard this assertion without proofs. That it has taken place in some degree is very probable. Many millions of money have been put into the hands of government, which have never yet, been accounted for: The accounts are not yet settled, and Heaven only knows when they will be.

I have frequently observed a restraint upon the state governments, which Congress never can be under, construct that body as you please. It is a truth, capable of demonstration, that the nearer the representative is to his constituent, the more attached and dependent he will be—In the states, the elections are frequent, and the representatives numerous: They transact business in the midst of their constituents, and every man may be called upon to account for his conduct. In this state the council of appointment are elected for one year.—The proposed constitution establishes a council of appointment who will be perpetual—Is there any comparison between the two governments in point of security? It is said that the governor of this state is limited in his powers—Indeed his authority is small and insignificant, compared to that of the senate of the United States.

"Brutus" (Probably Robert Yates) Essay, March 20, 1788 (Excerpt)

DISCUSSION QUESTIONS

1. According to Brutus, under the Constitution, which government institution would be responsible for explaining the Constitution?
2. Why is Brutus wary of such an arrangement?
3. What would he prefer?
4. What does this imply about his beliefs concerning public opinion?

Perhaps nothing could have been better conceived to facilitate the abolition of the state governments than the constitution of the judicial. They will be able to extend the limits of the general government gradually, and by insensible degrees, and to accommodate themselves to the temper of the people. Their decisions on the meaning of the constitution will commonly take place in cases which arise between individuals, with which the public will not be generally acquainted; one adjudication will form a precedent to the next, and this to a following one. These cases will immediately affect individuals only; so that a series of determinations will probably take place before even the people will be informed of them. In the mean time all the art and address of those who wish for the change will be employed to make converts to their opinion. The people will be told, that their state officers, and state legislatures are a burden and expence without affording any solid advantage, for that all the laws passed by them, might be equally well made by the general legislature. If to those who will be interested in the change, be added, those who will be under their influence, and such who will submit to almost any change of government, which they can be persuaded to believe will ease them of taxes, it is easy to see, the party who will favor the abolition of the state governments would be far from being inconsiderable.—In this situation, the general legislature, might pass one law after another, extending the general and abridging the state jurisdictions, and to sanction their proceedings would have a course of decisions of the judicial to whom the constitution has committed the power of explaining the constitution.—If the states remonstrated, the constitutional mode of deciding upon the validity of the law, is with the supreme court, and neither people, nor state legislatures, not the general legislature can remove them or reverse their decrees.

Had the construction of the constitution been left with the legislature, they would have explained it at their peril; if they exceed their powers, or sought to find, in the spirit of the constitution, more than was expressed in the letter, the people from whom they derived their power could remove them, and do themselves right; and indeed I can see no other remedy that the people can have against their rulers for encroachments of this nature. A constitution is a compact of a people with their rulers; if the rulers break the compact, the people have a right and ought to remove them and do themselves justice; but in order to enable them to do this with the greater facility, those whom the people choose at stated periods, should have the power in the last resort to determine the sense of the compact; if they determine contrary to the understanding of the people, an appeal will lie to the people at the period when the rulers are to be elected, and they will have it in their power to remedy the evil; but when this power is lodged in the hands of men independent of the people, and of their representatives, and who are not, constitutionally, accountable for their opinions, no way is left to control them but *with a high hand and an outstretched arm.*

"Brutus"
(Probably Robert Yates)
Essay, April 10, 1788
(Excerpt)

DISCUSSION QUESTIONS

1. According to Brutus, who is the superior power in republican governments?
2. Describe his arguments concerning the judicial branch.

When great and extraordinary powers are vested in any man, or body of men, which in their exercise, may operate to the oppression of the people, it is of high importance that powerful checks should be formed to prevent the abuse of it.

Perhaps no restraints are more forcible, than such as arise from responsibility to some superior power.—Hence it is that the true policy of a republican government is, to frame it in such manner, that all persons who are concerned in the government, are made accountable to some superior for their conduct in office.—This responsibility should ultimately rest with the People. To have a government well administered in all its parts, it is requisite the different departments of it should be separated and lodged as much as may be in different hands. The legislative power should be in one body, the executive in another, and the judicial in one different from either—But still each of these bodies should be accountable for their conduct. Hence it is impracticable, perhaps, to maintain a perfect distinction between these several departments—For it is difficult, if not impossible, to call to account the several officers in government, without in some degree mixing the legislative and judicial. The legislature in a free republic are chosen by the people at stated periods, and their responsibility consists, in their being amenable to the people. When the term, for which they are chosen, shall expire, who will then have opportunity to displace them if they disapprove of their conduct—but it would be improper that the judicial should be elective, because their business requires that they should possess a degree of law knowledge, which is acquired only by a regular education, and besides it is fit that they should be placed, in a certain degree in an independent situation, that they may maintain firmness and steadiness in their decisions. As the people therefore ought not to elect the judges, they cannot be amenable to them immediately, some other mode of amenability must therefore be devised for these, as well as for all other officers which do not spring from the immediate choice of the people: this is to be effected by making one court subordinate to another, and by giving them cognizance of the behaviour of all officers; but on this plan we at last arrive at some supreme, over whom there is no power to control but the people themselves. This supreme controlling power should be in the choice of the people, or else you establish an authority independent, and not amenable at all, which is repugnant to the principles of a free government. Agreeable to these principles I suppose the supreme judicial ought to be liable to be called to account, for any misconduct, by some body of men, who depend upon the people for their places; and so also should all other great officers in the State, who are not made amenable to some superior officers.

Thomas Jefferson
Letter to John Adams
October 28, 1813
(Excerpt)

DISCUSSION QUESTIONS

1. What types of aristocracies does Jefferson describe?
2. What is the role of education?
3. Does Jefferson seem more Federalist or Antifederalist in his thinking concerning public opinion? Why?

Dear Sir,—According to the reservation between us, of taking up one of the subjects of our correspondence at a time, I turn to your letters of August the 16th and September the 2d. . . .

. . . I agree with you that there is a natural aristocracy among men. The grounds of this are virtue and talents. Formerly, bodily powers gave place among the *aristoi.* But since the invention of gunpowder has armed the weak as well as the strong with missile death, bodily strength, like beauty, good humor, politeness and other accomplishments, has become but an auxiliary ground for distinction. There is also an artificial aristocracy, founded on wealth and birth, without either virtue or talents; for with these it would belong to the first class. The natural aristocracy I consider as the most precious gift of nature, for the instruction, the trusts, and government of society. And indeed, it would have been inconsistent in creation to have formed man for the social state, and not to have provided virtue and wisdom enough to manage the concerns of the society. May we not even say, that that form of government is the best, which provides the most effectually for a pure selection of these natural *aristoi* into the offices of government? The artificial aristocracy is a mischievous ingredient in government, and provision should be made to prevent its ascendancy. On the question, what is the best provision, you and I differ; but we differ as rational friends, using the free exercise of our own reason, and mutually indulging its errors. You think it best to put the *pseudo-aristoi* into a separate chamber of legislation, where they may be hindered from doing mischief by their co-ordinate branches, and where, also, they may be a protection to wealth against the Agrarian and plundering enterprises of the majority of the people. I think that to give them power in order to prevent them from doing mischief, is arming them for it, and increasing instead of remedying the evil. For if the co-ordinate branches can arrest their action, so may they that of the co-ordinates. Mischief may be done negatively as well as positively. Of this, a cabal in the Senate of the United States has furnished many proofs. Nor do I believe them necessary to protect the wealthy; because enough of these will find their way into every branch of the legislation, to protect themselves. From fifteen to twenty legislatures of our own, in action for thirty years past, have proved that no fears of an equalization of property are to be apprehended from them. I think the best remedy is exactly that provided by all our constitutions, to leave to the citizens the free election and separation of the *aristoi* from the *pseudo-aristoi*, of the wheat from the chaff. In general they will elect the really good and wise. In some instances, wealth may corrupt, and birth blind them; but not in sufficient degree to endanger the society.

It is probable that our difference of opinion may, in some measure, be produced by a difference of character in those among whom we live. From what I have seen of Massachusetts and Connecticut myself, and still more from what I have heard, and the character given of the former by yourself, who know them so much better, there seems to be in those two states a traditionary reverence for certain families, which has rendered the offices of the government nearly hereditary in those families. I presume that from an early period of your history, members of those families happening to possess virtue and talents, have honestly exercised them for the good of the people, and by their services have endeared their names to them. In coupling Connecticut with you, I mean it politically only, not morally. For having made the Bible the common law of their land, they seemed to have modeled their morality on the story of Jacob and Laban. But although this hereditary succession to office with you, may, in some degree, be founded in real family merit, yet in a much higher degree, it has proceeded from your strict alliance of Church and State. These families are canonised in the eyes of the people on common principles, "you tickle me, and I will tickle you." In Virginia we have nothing of this. Our clergy, before the revolution, having been secured against rivalship by fixed salaries, did not give themselves the trouble of acquiring influence over the people. Of wealth, there were great accumulations in particular families, handed down from generation to generation, under the English law of entails. But the only object of ambition for the wealthy was a seat in the King's Council. All their court then was paid to the crown and its creatures; and they Philipised in all collisions between the King and the people. Hence they were unpopular; and that unpopularity continues attached to their names. A Randolph, a Carter, or a Burwell must have great personal superiority over a common competitor to be elected by the people even at this day. At the first session of our legislature after the Declaration of Independence, we passed a law abolishing entails. And this was followed by one abolishing the privilege of primogeniture, and dividing the lands of intestates equally among all their children, or other representatives. These laws, drawn by myself, laid the ax to the foot of pseudo-aristocracy. And had another which I prepared been adopted by the legislature, our work would have been complete. It was a bill for the more general diffusion of learning. This proposed to divide every county into wards of five or six miles square, like your townships; to establish in each ward a free school for reading, writing and common arithmetic; to provide for the annual selection of the best subjects from these schools, who might receive, at the public expense, a higher degree of education at a district school; and from these district schools to select a certain number of the most promising subjects, to be completed at an University, where all the useful sciences should be taught. Worth and genius would thus have been sought out from every condition of life, and completely prepared by education for defeating the competition of wealth and birth for public trusts. My proposition had, for a further object, to impart to these wards those portions of self-government for which they are best qualified, by confiding to them the care of their poor, their roads, police, elections, the nomination of jurors, administration of justice in small cases, elementary exercises of militia; in short, to have made them little republics, with a warden at the head of each, for all those concerns which, being under their eye, they would better manage than the larger republics of the county or State. A general call of ward meetings by their wardens on the same day through the State, would at any time produce the genuine sense of the people on any required point, and would enable the State to act in mass, as your people have so often done, and with so much effect by their town meetings.

FEDERALIST ARGUMENTS

Alexander Hamilton
Essay
October 17, 1787
(Excerpt)

DISCUSSION QUESTIONS

1. Why does Hamilton distrust the qualifications of people to choose a form of government?
2. How are citizens to determine what form of government is in their best interest?
3. Of what types of persons and arguments should citizens beware?

I know there are Citizens, who, to gain their own private ends, enflame the minds of the well-meaning, tho' less intelligent parts of the community, by sating their

The Daily Advertiser, October 17, 1787.

vanity with that cordial and unfailing specific, that *all power is seated in the people.* For my part, I am not much attached to the *majesty of the multitude,* and therefore waive all pretensions (founded on such conduct), to their countenance. I consider them in general as very ill qualified to judge for themselves what government will best suit their peculiar situations; nor is this to be wondered at. The science of government is not easily understood. Cato will admit, I presume, that men of good education and deep reflection, only, are judges of the *form* of a government; whether it is constituted on such principles as will restrain arbitrary power, on the one hand and equal to the exclusion of corruption and the destruction of licentiousness on the other; whether the New Constitution, if adopted, will prove adequate to such desirable ends, time, the mother of events, will show. For my own part, I sincerely esteem it a system, which, without the finger of *God,* never could have been suggested and agreed upon by such a diversity of interests. I will not presume to say that a more perfect system might not have been fabricated; but who expects perfection at once? And it may be asked, *who are judges of it?* Few, I believe, who have leisure to study the nature of Government scientifically, but will frequently disagree about the quantum of power to be delegated to Rulers, and the different modifications of it. Ingenious men will give every plausible, and it may be pretty substantial reasons, for the adoption of two plans of Government, which shall be fundamentally different in their construction, and not less so in their operation; yet both, if honestly administered, might operate with safety and advantage. When a new form of government is fabricated, it lies with the people at large to receive or reject it—that is their *inherent right.* Now, I would ask (without intending to triumph over the weaknesses or follies of any men), how are the people to profit by this inherent right? By what conduct do they discover that they are sensible of their own interests in this situation? Is it by the exercise of a well-disciplined reason, and a correspondent education? I believe not. How then? As I humbly conceive, by a tractable and docile disposition, and by honest men endeavoring to keep their minds easy, while others, of the same disposition, with the advantages of genius and learning, are constructing the bark that may, by the blessing of Heaven, carry them to the port of rest and happiness if they will embark without diffidence and proceed without mutiny I know this is blunt and ungracious reasoning; it is the best, however, which I am prepared to offer on this momentous business and since my own heart does not reproach me, I shall not be very solicitous about its reception. If truth, then, is permitted to speak, the mass of the people of America (any more than the mass of other countries) cannot judge with any degree of precision concerning the fitness of this New Constitution to the peculiar situation of America; they have, however, done wisely in delegating the power of framing a government to those every way worthy and well-qualified; and, if this Government is snatched untasted, from them, it may not be amiss to inquire into the causes which will probably occasion their disappointment. Out of several, which present to my mind, I shall venture to select *one,* baneful enough, in my opinion, to work this dreadful evil. There are always men in society of some talents, but more ambition, in quest of *that* which it would be impossible for them to obtain in any other way than by working on the passions and prejudices of the less discerning classes of citizens and yeomanry. It is the plan of men of this stamp to frighten the people with ideal bugbears, in order to mould them to their own purposes. The unceasing cry of these designing croakers is, My friends, your liberty is invaded! Have you thrown off the yoke of one tyrant to invest yourselves with that of another? Have you fought, bled and conquered for *such a change*? If you have—go—retire into silent obscurity, and kiss the rod that scourges you.

To be serious: These state empiries leave no species of deceit untried to convince the unthinking people that they have power to do—what? Why truly to do much mischief, and to occasion anarchy and wild uproar. And for what reason do these political jugglers incite the peaceably disposed to such extravagant commotions? Because until the people really discover that they have *power*, by some outrageous act, they never can become of any importance. The misguided people never reflect during this frenzy, that the moment they become riotous, they renounce, from that moment, their independence, and commence vassals to their ambitious leaders, who instantly, and with a high hand, rob them of their consequence, and apply it to their own present or future aggrandisement; nor will these tyrants over the people stick at sacrificing *their* good, if an advantageous compromise can be effected for *themselves*.

James Madison
Federalist *Paper 51*
(Excerpts)

DISCUSSION QUESTIONS

1. What is Madison's view of the people and their opinions as a check on or control of government?
2. How does Madison plan to guard society against itself?
3. What are the advantages of extended republics?
4. What are the disadvantages of small republics?
5. Where does one find more stability and justice?
6. Which type of republic is more respectful of public opinion?

Ambition must be made to counteract ambition. The interest of the man must be connected with the constitutional rights of the place. It may be a reflection on human nature that such devices should be necessary to control the abuses of government. But what is government itself but the greatest of all reflections on human nature? If men were angels, no government would be necessary. If angels were to govern men, neither external nor internal controls on government would be necessary. In framing a government which is to be administered by men over men, the great difficulty lies in this: you must first enable the government to control the governed; and in the next place oblige it to control itself. A dependence on the people is, no doubt, the primary control on the government; but experience has taught mankind the necessity of auxiliary precautions. . . .

Second. It is of great importance in a republic not only to guard the society against the oppression of its rulers, but to guard one part of the society against the injustice of the other part. Different interests necessarily exist in different classes of citizens. If a majority be united by a common interest, the rights of the minority will be insecure. There are but two methods of providing against this evil: the one by creating a will in the community independent of the majority—that is, of the society itself; the other, by comprehending in the society so many separate descriptions of citizens as will render an unjust combination of a majority of the whole very improbable, if not impracticable. The first method prevails in all governments possessing an hereditary or self-appointed authority. This, at best, is but a precarious security; because a power independent of the society may as well espouse the unjust views of the major as the rightful interests of the minor party, and may possibly be turned against both parties. The second method will be exemplified in the federal republic of the United States. Whilst all authority in it will be derived from and dependent on the society, the society itself will be broken into so many parts, interests and classes of citizens, that the rights of individuals, or of the minority, will be in little danger from interested combinations of the majority. In a free government the security for civil rights must be the same as that for religious rights. It consists in the one case in the multiplicity of interests, and in the other in the multiplicity of sects. The degree of security in both cases will depend on the number of interests and sects; and this may be presumed to depend on the extent of country and number of people comprehended under the same government. This view of the subject must particularly recommend a proper federal system to all the sincere and considerate friends of republican government, since it shows that in exact proportion as the territory of the Union may be formed into more circumscribed Confederacies, or States, oppressive combinations of a majority will be facilitated; the best security, under the republican forms, for the rights of every class of citizen, will be diminished; and consequently the stability and independence of some member of the government, the only other security, must be proportionally increased. Justice is the end of government. It is the end of civil society. It ever has been and ever will be pursued until it be obtained, or until liberty be lost in the pursuit. In a society under the forms of which the stronger faction can readily unite and oppress the weaker, anarchy may as truly be said to reign as in a state of nature, where the weaker individual is not secured against the violence of the stronger; and as, in the latter state, even the stronger individuals are prompted, by the uncertainty of their condition, to submit to a government which may protect the weak as well as themselves; so, in the former state, will the more powerful factions or parties be gradually induced, by a like motive, to wish for a government which will protect all parties, the weaker as well as the more powerful. It can be little doubted that if the State of Rhode Island was separated from the Confederacy and left to itself, the insecurity of rights under the popular form of government within such narrow limits would be displayed by such reiterated oppressions of factious majorities that some power altogether independent of the people would soon be called for by the voice of the very factions whose misrule had proved the necessity of it. In the extended republic of the United States, and among the great variety of interests, parties, and sects which it embraces, a coalition of a majority of the whole society could seldom take place on any other principles than those of justice and the general good; whilst there being thus less danger to a minor from the will of a major party, there must be less pretext, also, to provide for the security of the former, by introducing into the government a will not dependent on the latter, or, in other words, a will independent of the society itself. It is no less certain than it is important, notwithstanding the contrary opinions which have been entertained, that the larger the society, provided it lie within a practicable sphere, the more duly capable it will be of self-government. And happily for the *republican cause*, the practicable sphere may be carried to a very great extent by a judicious modification and mixture of the *federal principle.*

James Madison
Federalist *Paper 48*
(Excerpt)

DISCUSSION QUESTIONS

1. Describe Madison's feeling about a hereditary monarchy, a democracy, and a representative republic.
2. What does this tell us about his belief in public opinion? (*Hint*: passion and reason)

In a government where numerous and extensive prerogatives are placed in the hands of an hereditary monarch, the executive department is very justly regarded as the source of danger, and watched with all the jealousy which a zeal for liberty ought to inspire. In a democracy, where a multitude of people exercise in person the legislative functions and are continually exposed, by their incapacity for regular deliberation and concerted measures, to the ambitious intrigues of their executive magistrates, tyranny may well be apprehended, on some favorable emergency, to start up in the same quarter. But in a representative republic where the executive magistracy is carefully limited, both in the extent and the duration of its power; and where the legislative power is exercised by an assembly, which is inspired by a supposed influence over the people with an intrepid confidence in its own strength; which is sufficiently numerous to feel all the passions which actuate a multitude, yet not so numerous as to be incapable of pursuing the objects of its passions by means which reason prescribes; it is against the enterprising ambition of this department that the people ought to indulge all their jealousy and exhaust all their precautions.

Alexander Hamilton
Federalist *Paper 59*
(Excerpt)

DISCUSSION QUESTIONS

1. What would be the result of giving state governments greater control in setting the procedures for federal elections?
2. Could this be a reason for Hamilton's skepticism of the public's opinion?

I shall not deny that there is a degree of weight in the observation that the interests of each State, to be represented in the federal councils, will be a security against the abuse of a power over its elections in the hands of the State legislatures. But the security will not be considered as complete by those who attend to the force of an obvious distinction between the interest of the people in the public felicity and the interest of their local rulers in the power and consequence of their offices. The people of America may be warmly attached to the government of the Union, at times when the particular rulers of particular States, stimulated by the natural rivalship of power, and by the hopes of personal aggrandizement, and supported by a strong faction in each of those States, may be in a very opposite temper. This diversity of sentiment between a majority of the people and the individuals who have the greatest credit in their councils is exemplified in some of the States at the present moment, on the present question. The scheme of separate confederacies, which will always multiply the chances of ambition, will be a never-failing bait to all such influential characters in the State administrations as are capable of preferring their own emolument and advancement to the public weal. With so effectual a weapon in their hands as the exclusive power of regulating elections for the national government, a combination of a few such men, in a few of the most considerable States, where the temptation will always be the strongest, might accomplish the destruction of the Union by seizing the opportunity of some casual dissatisfaction among the people (and which perhaps they may themselves have excited) to discontinue the choice of members for the federal House of Representatives. It ought never to be forgotten that a firm union of this country, under an efficient government, will probably be an increasing object of jealousy to more than one nation of Europe; and that enterprises to subvert it will sometimes originate in the intrigues of foreign powers and will seldom fail to be patronized and abetted by some of them. Its preservation, therefore, ought in no case that can be avoided to be committed to the guardianship of any but those whose situation will uniformly beget an immediate interest in the faithful and vigilant performance of the trust.

Alexander Hamilton
Federalist *Paper 34*
(Excerpt)

DISCUSSION QUESTIONS

1. What does Hamilton argue about the rights of the people, the head, and the heart?
2. What is essential to the security of liberty?
3. What does Hamilton say about the zeal for efficiency and the zeal for the rights of people?
4. How does this relate to Hamilton's beliefs concerning the public's opinions?

It is not, however, my design to dwell upon observations of this nature. I am well aware that it would be disingenuous to resolve indiscriminately the opposition of any set of men (merely because their situations might subject them to suspicion) into interested or ambitious views. Candor will oblige us to admit that even such men may be actuated by upright intentions; and it cannot be doubted that much of the opposition which has made its appearance, or may hereafter make its appearance, will spring from sources, blameless at least if not respectable—the honest errors of minds led astray by preconceived jealousies and fears. So numerous indeed and so powerful are the causes which serve to give a false bias to the judgment, that we, upon many occasions, see wise and good men on the wrong as well as on the right side of questions of the first magnitude to society. This circumstance, if duly attended to, would furnish a lesson of moderation to those who are ever so much persuaded of their being in the right in any controversy. And a further reason for caution, in this respect, might be drawn from the reflection that we are not always sure that those who advocate the truth are influenced by purer principles than their antagonists. Ambition, avarice, personal animosity, party opposition, and many other motives not more laudable than these, are apt to operate as well upon those who support as those who oppose the right side of a question. Were there not even inducements to moderation, nothing could be more ill judged than that intolerant spirit which has at all times characterized political parties. For in politics, as in religion, it is equally absurd to aim at making proselytes by fire and sword. Heresies in either can rarely be cured by persecution.

And yet, however just these sentiments must appear to candid men, we have already sufficient indications that it will happen in this as in all former cases of great national discussion. A torrent of angry and malignant passions will be let loose. To judge from the conduct of the opposite parties, we shall be led to conclude that they will mutually hope to evince the justness of their opinions, and to increase the number of their converts by the loudness of their declamations and by the bitterness of their invectives. An enlightened zeal for the energy and efficiency of government will be stigmatized as the offspring of a temper fond of despotic power and hostile to the principles of liberty. An over-scrupulous jealousy of danger to the rights of the people, which is more commonly the fault of the head than of the heart, will be represented as mere pretense and artifice, the stale bait for popularity at the expense of public good. It will be forgotten, on the one hand, that jealousy is the usual concomitant of violent love, and that the noble enthusiasm of liberty is too apt to be infected with a spirit of narrow and illiberal distrust. On the other hand, it will be equally forgotten that the vigor of government is essential to the security of liberty; that, in the contemplation of a sound and well-informed judgment, their interests can never be separated; and that a dangerous ambition more often lurks behind the specious mask of zeal for the rights of the people than under the forbidding appearance of zeal for the firmness and efficiency of government. History will teach us that the former has been found a much more certain road to the introduction of despotism than the latter, and that of those men who have overturned the liberties of republics, the greatest number have begun their career by paying an obsequious court to the people, commencing demagogues and ending tyrants.

Alexander Hamilton
Federalist *Paper 71*
(Excerpt)

DISCUSSION QUESTIONS

1. What is the difference between intending the public good and reasoning correctly about the means of promoting it?
2. What is the role of a politically appointed guardian?
3. What does Hamilton's argument reveal about his views of the people and their opinions?

There are some who would be inclined to regard the servile pliancy of the executive to a prevailing current, either in the community or in the legislature, as its best recommendation. But such men entertain very crude notions, as well of the purposes for which government was instituted, as of the true means by which the public happiness may be promoted. The republican principle demands that the deliberate sense of the community should govern the conduct of those to whom they intrust the management of their affairs; but it does not require an unqualified complaisance to every sudden breeze of passion, or to every transient impulse which the people may receive from the arts of men, who flatter their prejudices to betray their interests. It is a just observation that the people commonly *intend* the PUBLIC GOOD. This often applies to their very errors. But their good sense would despise the adulator who should pretend that they always *reason right* about the *means* of promoting it. They know from experience that they sometimes err; and the wonder is that they so seldom err as they do, beset as they continually are by the wiles of parasites and sycophants, by the snares of the ambitious, the avaricious, the desperate, by the artifices of men who possess their confidence more than they deserve it, and of those who seek to possess rather than to deserve it. When occasions present themselves in which the interests of the people are at variance with their inclinations, it is the duty of the persons whom they have appointed to be the guardians of those interests to withstand the temporary delusion in order to give them time and opportunity for more cool and sedate reflection. Instances might be cited in which a conduct of this kind has saved the people from very fatal consequences of their own mistakes, and has procured lasting monuments of their gratitude to the men who had courage and magnanimity enough to serve them at the peril of their displeasure.

But however inclined we might be to insist upon an unbounded complaisance in the executive to the inclinations of the people, we can with no propriety contend for a like complaisance to the humors of the legislature. The latter may sometimes stand in opposition to the former, and at other times the people may be entirely neutral. In either supposition, it is certainly desirable that the executive should be in a situation to dare to act his own opinion with vigor and decision.

James Madison
Federalist *Paper 45*
(Excerpt)

DISCUSSION QUESTIONS

1. What is the relationship of the sovereignty of the state to the happiness of the people?
2. What is Madison asking of the states?
3. How do you think state sovereignty was related to the opinions of the public?

The adversaries to the plan of the convention, instead of considering in the first place what degree of power was absolutely necessary for the purposes of the federal government, have exhausted themselves in a secondary inquiry into the possible consequences of the proposed degree of power to the governments of the particular States. But if the Union, as has been shown, be essential to the security of the pecple of America against foreign danger; if it be essential to their security against contentions and wars among the different States; if it be essential to guard them against those violent and oppressive factions which embitter the blessings of liberty and against those military establishments which must gradually poison its very fountain; if, in a word, the Union be essential to the happiness of the people of America, is it not preposterous to urge as an objection to a government, without which the objects of the Union cannot be attained, that such a government may derogate from the importance of the governments of the individual States? Was, then, the American Revolution effected, was the American Confederacy formed, was the precious blood of thousands spilt, and the hard-earned substance of millions lavished, not that the people of America should enjoy peace, liberty, and safety, but that the government of the individual States, that particular municipal establishments, might enjoy a certain extent of power and be arrayed with certain dignities and attributes of sovereignty? We have heard of the impious doctrine in the old world, that the people were made for kings, not kings for the people. Is the same doctrine to be revived in the new, in another shape—that the solid happiness of the people is to be sacrificed to the views of political institutions of a different form? It is too early for politicians to presume on our forgetting that the public good, the real welfare of the great body of the people, is the supreme object to be pursued; and that no form of government whatever has any other value than as it may be fitted for the attainment of this object. Were the plan of the convention adverse to the public happiness, my voice would be, Reject the plan. Were the Union itself inconsistent with the public happiness, it would be, Abolish the Union. In like manner, as far as the sovereignty of the States cannot be reconciled to the happiness of the people, the voice of every good citizen must be, Let the former be sacrificed to the latter. How far the sacrifice is necessary has been shown. How far the unsacrificed residue will be endangered is the question before us.

CONTEMPORARY INFLUENCES

Daniel Yankelovich
Coming to Public Judgment: Making Democracy Work in a Complex World
(Excerpts)

DISCUSSION QUESTIONS

1. How do media and public policy experts view public opinion?
2. What are the criteria that political scientists use to assess public opinion?
3. How might the findings of the authors of the *American Voter* reinforce Alexander Hamilton's ideas of public opinion?
4. What are Everett Ladd's arguments concerning public opinion?
5. List some problems with public opinion polling?
6. How were the findings of Yankelovich and Ladd received by mainstream journalists and academics?
7. How might Yankelovich's personal reflections be related to the Antifederalist/Federalist debate on public opinion?
8. Describe the concept of deliberative democracy.
9. What is Yankelovich's vision of a nation giving high priority to public judgment?
10. Does this vision relate more to Federalist, Antifederalist, or Jeffersonian ideas?

There is a missing concept in American democracy, with a mystery attached to it. The mystery is not what the concept is—that is easy to state—but rather, why it is missing. For almost thirty years this question has puzzled me. . . .

The missing concept is a set of terms to describe the *quality* of public opinion and to distinguish "good" public opinion from "bad." Quality judgments are commonplace in our culture. Standards of excellence exist for automobiles, movies, plumbers, surgeons, CEOs, chefs. We know what we mean when we say, "She is a good friend; he is a good neighbor; they are good parents." There are tests and standards, formal and informal, for quality for tangible products and intangible ideas. Its resale value is a good pragmatic test of a car's worth. If the doctor's patient dies, the operation is *not* a success. Good friends are those who stand by you in times of trouble and need. Winning an Oscar for a movie, winning a Pulitzer Prize for a book, winning a Nobel Prize for a scientific achievement—these are society's methods for designating quality and excellence. But when it comes to public opinion, there are no standards for quality.

Students of public opinion have learned that Americans are a highly opinionated people; Americans hold an opinion on almost every subject, whether they

---

Daniel Yankelovich, *Coming to Public Judgment: Making Democracy Work in a Complex World.* Reprinted with the permission of Syracuse University Press, , pp. 15–23, 179–181, 239–241.

know anything about it or not, whether they feel passionately or are indifferent to it. Sometimes the seriousness and generosity of the public's judgments are startling. At other times the public seems mindless and irresponsible. Surely, the reader of public opinion polls must sometimes wonder, "Is this really the public's opinion? How can people be so blind, so foolish, so easily manipulated?" Americans hold strong views on drug abuse, abortion, capital punishment, nuclear power, sex education in the schools, the Strategic Defense Initiative (SDI), protectionism, ethics in government, rising health care costs, acid rain, affirmative action, censorship, and so forth. On some of these issues, the quality of public opinion is amazingly good—on others, abysmally bad.

How does one distinguish "good" from "bad" in a reasonably objective manner? Is public opinion "good" when it agrees with my personal point of view or happens to coincide with the experts' well-informed conclusions or forms part of a coherent political philosophy and "bad" when it fails to meet such criteria? Various influential groups in the society adhere to one or another of these standards of quality, but all are severely flawed.

To begin our search for a viable standard of quality for public opinion, let us briefly glance at how the experts who analyze, measure, and report on public opinion deal with the quality issue.

Media and Public Policy Experts

Many of the most influential observers and analysts of public opinion come from the worlds of journalism and public policy. By inference, they do distinguish good public opinion from bad. Good public opinion is being "well informed"; being poorly informed is synonymous with bad quality.

Journalists, above all others, equate being well informed with high quality. The media are fascinated with opinion polls that show how ignorant the public is. Conduct a poll that reveals that the majority of Americans cannot name a single justice of the Supreme Court, or cannot locate Siberia on a map, and it is sure to get wide TV and newspaper coverage. Journalists hold as an article of faith the traditional belief that a well-informed citizenry is indispensable to the proper functioning of democracy.

It would be perverse to deny that information is relevant to the quality of public opinion. But in a professional lifetime devoted to its study, I have come to the conclusion that equating quality opinion with being well informed is a serious mistake. Obviously, information plays some role in shaping public opinion. But often it is a minor role. To assume that public opinion is invariably improved by inundating people with information grossly distorts the role of information. A society operating on this assumption misconstrues the nature and purpose of public opinion in a democracy.

Admittedly, some experts do harbor misgivings about the relevance of information. Daniel Boorstin, the noted historian, writes, "It is a cliché of our time that what this nation needs is an 'informed citizenry.' By which we mean a citizenry that is up on the latest information, that has not failed to read this week's newsmagazine, today's newspapers, or to watch the seven o'clock news (perhaps also the news at ten o'clock!)—always for more information, always to be better informed." Boorstin adds, "I wonder if that is what we need."[1]

Most experts do not, however, share Boorstin's reservations. They assume that public opinion is of good quality when it agrees with their own views and of poor quality when it does not. The logic is this: they, the experts, are well informed; the public is poorly informed. Give the public more information, and it will agree with them.

But what if even after being better informed, the public still does not agree? Rarely do the experts conclude that the public has a different point of view equally worthy of consideration. They conclude instead that the public is still not sufficiently informed. . . .

Political Scientists

Political scientists have at various times proposed other criteria for judging quality of opinion. There is no need to review their work in detail, but several of their main currents of thought are relevant to our search for a viable definition of quality.

In the 1960s and 1970s, one of the nation's most influential groups of political scientists was associated with the University of Michigan's Survey Research Center. Based on surveys conducted among voters in congressional and presidential elections, they arrived at a severe judgment of the quality of American public opinion. Analyzing the 1956 presidential election, Angus Campbell and his coauthors concluded in their classic work, *The American Voter*, that quality opinion depends on inner coherence—how well a person holding an opinion has developed what coauthor Philip E. Converse called a "political ideology."[2]

By political ideology, the Michigan political scientists meant something different than the customary usage that links ideologies to deeply felt emotional commitments. Their emphasis was wholly cognitive: by ideology they meant a set of broad political principles, carefully thought through and internally consistent, from which one derives one's opinions on particular issues. An ideology, in this sense, is a rationalistic political philosophy that leads to thinking about politics in abstract terms.

The authors of *The American Voter* failed to find many such "ideological" thinkers among the mass of American voters. Even when they stretched the criteria of ideological thinking, they could find only 2.5 percent of the American electorate who could be considered to hold a coherent political ideology. Stretching still further, they added an additional 9 percent whom they categorized as "near Ideologues"—persons who bring some shred of conceptual sophistication to their views.

[1]Daniel J. Boorstin, "Gresham's Law: Knowledge or Information?" remarks at the White House Conference on Library and Information Services, Nov. 19, 1979 (Washington, D.C.: Library of Congress, 1979), 6.

[2]Angus Campbell et al., *The American Voter* (New York: Wiley, 1960).

In an often-quoted article published in 1964, Converse amplified this line of thought.[3] People with well-structured political ideologies should, he maintained, hold predictable views on various issues. If their ideology is liberal and you know their views on one issue, you should be able to predict their position on all the other liberal issues. Similarly, conservative ideologists should also hold readily predictable opinions of a conservative persuasion. Converse reconfirmed the earlier conclusion of the Michigan analysts that average voters do not have well-structured political ideologies: knowing their views on any one issue does not help to predict their views on other issues.

The judgment in *The American Voter* is brutally clear: "Our failure to locate more than a trace of 'ideological' thinking in the protocols of our surveys emphasizes the *general impoverishment of political thought* in a large proportion of the electorate" (emphasis added). Owing to its inadequate level of knowledge about particular policies, "the mass electorate is not able to appraise either its goals or the appropriateness of the means chosen to serve these goals."[4] So much for the ability of Americans to govern themselves!

In subsequent years, other political scientists would seek to soften the harshness of this judgment. In *The Changing American Voter* (1976), Harvard's Sidney Verba, representing another group of political scientists, commented on the earlier studies: "No one expected the average American to be a political philosopher. Yet the gap between the way in which the average citizen thought about political matters and the way in which those matters were conceived by the more politically sophisticated was larger than expected."[5] Reanalyzing the Michigan 1956 and 1958 congressional elections and the presidential elections of 1960, 1964, 1968, and 1972, the new analysis discovered ground for optimism. The authors found the American voter much improved. They concluded that "The proportion of citizens who think in ideologically structured ways about parties and candidates . . . has grown substantially."[6] Using modified measures of ideological sophistication, they arrived at an estimate of 22 percent of voters who bring to bear a modicum of ideological thinking. The authors hastened to add this caveat: "Our category of ideologues is not populated by citizen-philosophers, each with an elaborate and well considered political world view."[7]

The political scientists from Michigan, Harvard, and the other university centers who were engaged in this analysis are scholars of stature: Angus Campbell, Warren Miller, Philip Converse, Sidney Verba, and the others have all done pioneering work in their field. Their empirical analysis shows the average American voter to be minimally involved in politics, inattentive to the issues, poorly informed, pragmatic, inconsistent, and focused on concrete concerns rather than on

---

[3]Philip E. Converse, "The Nature of Belief Systems in Mass Publics," in *Ideology and Discontent*, ed. David Apter (New York: Free Press, 1964), 242.

[4]Campbell et al., 543.

[5]Norman H. Nie, Sidney Verba, and John R. Petrocik, *The Changing American Voter* (Cambridge, Mass.: Harvard Univ. Press, 1976), 18.

[6]Ibid., 116.

[7]Ibid.

general principles. Mountains of subsequent opinion research studies validate this picture: average American voters are *not* intellectuals or ideologists. They are *not* abstract thinkers. They do *not* approach issues or candidates conceptually.

These conclusions have led some social scientists to place their hopes for democracy on a subset of the electorate, usually referred to as the "attentive public." Though the majority may be ill-informed and lack coherence in their thinking, there is an elite minority of the public that is more "with it." They read the *New York Times*, the national news magazines, watch the "MacNeil-Lehrer News Hour" and otherwise fit into the approved model of informed citizen favored by political scientists. Some studies analyze opinions by contrasting the views of this "attentive public"—usually a minority ranging from 5 percent to 25 percent of the population—with those of the "inattentive majority." . . . [8]

In practice, however, the concept of the attentive public is essentially elitist. Elites define quality by their own standards of ideological coherence and being well informed. The concept of the attentive public presupposes this elite definition and seeks to find among the public that minority of people whose thought processes mirror this model most closely. But the public is neither ideological nor well informed. It is pragmatic and usually poorly informed. Does this mean that public opinion is inherently inferior to well-informed expert opinion?

A Different Perspective

Not all political scientists believe that the quality of the public's thought must be inferior to that of experts because the public does not think conceptually and is not well informed. Professor Everett Ladd who heads the Roper Center for Public Opinion Research at Storrs, Connecticut, and is, in his own right, a distinguished political scientist, takes direct issue with the Converse thesis. In a recent textbook on American politics, Ladd discusses it at length. He readily acknowledges that voters are not well informed: "On first review, research seems to raise serious doubts about whether Americans know enough about the various questions of public affairs to play the part democratic theory assigns them. A cursory examination of poll data reveals an extraordinary lack of interest and unawareness, even on basic facts of political life."[9]

He aptly summarizes the canonical thesis:

> An influential study by political scientist Philip E. Converse addressed this subject. Converse concluded that the amount of political information people have goes far toward determining the structure, constraint, and stability of their beliefs. Without much factual information, the beliefs of large segments of the populace bounce around wildly over time. Between 1956 and 1960, the Institute for Social Research at the University of Michigan posed the same questions to the same people on three separate occasions, asking their views on issues such as school desegregation, federal aid to education, foreign aid, and federal housing. Many respondents moved from one side to the other on these ques-

---

[8]For an example of this type of research, see the National Opinion Research Center/Institute for Survey Research at Temple University for the National Science Foundation, Oct. 1979.

[9]Everett Carl Ladd, *The American Polity: The People and Their Government* (New York: Norton, 1985), 315–16.

> tions in successive interviews. After closely examining this pattern, Converse concluded that most of the movement was not true opinion change but rather the result of respondents answering in essentially a random fashion. Only a distinct minority had something close to hard core opinions.[10]

Ladd, however, goes on to cite another body of research that shows the public in a more positive light: "Another type of public opinion research yields conclusions very different from Converse's or even those of his critics. If focuses on the overall patterns of responses Americans give. These turn out to be remarkably stable and predictable."[11]

Ladd is referring here to Gallup poll data, accumulated month by month since the mid-1930s. Ladd finds no inherent contradiction between the Converse image of a poorly informed and unpredictable public and the stable and persisting public suggested by the Gallup data. The two pictures reflect different aspects of the same public: Converse is looking at the coherence with which people hold information; Gallup is reflecting people's underlying values and attitudes. Ladd sums it up cogently:

> Opinion research in the U.S. does reveal a public strikingly inattentive to the details of even the most consequential and controversial policies. This suggests a potential for manipulation. But the research also indicates great stability and coherence in the public's underlying attitudes and values. Americans show themselves perfectly capable of making the distinctions needed to determine what Harwood Childs called "the basic ends of public policy," and of pursuing these logically and clearly. There is a persisting structure to American opinion that belies the picture of a populace helpless before the "engineers of consent."[12]

The two positions lead to radically different conclusions; they concern nothing less than the ability of Americans to govern themselves in keeping with the principles of democracy.

The Polling Profession

When we turn to the professionals who do most of the public opinion polling in America we find yet another set of concerns. Practitioners of public opinion have long been aware of the difficulty of distinguishing good from poor quality. As early as 1947, George Gallup called for a method in opinion research to distinguish between people's "snap judgments" and opinions that have been carefully thought through—an unmistakable dimension of quality.[13]

The technical literature on public opinion surveys from the 1950s to the present shows some modest follow-up on Gallup's proposals, but by and large it moves in other directions. The nation has now had more than one-half century of experi-

---

[10]Ibid., 317–18.

[11]Ibid., 318–19.

[12]Ibid., 350.

[13]George Gallup, "The Quintamensional Plan of Question Design," *Public Opinion Quarterly* 11, no. 3 (Fall 1947): 386.

ence with public opinion polling—from the 1936 presidential election to the present. This experience reveals a mixed picture. On the one hand, opinion polling techniques have proven a cost-effective way to elicit the views of cross sections of the American public. But on the other hand, they have also proven fallible, easy to misinterpret, and subject to abuse. The profession has been preoccupied with improving polling techniques to make them less fallible.

In her presidential address to the American Association of Public Opinion Research (AAPOR) in May 1988, Eleanor Singer inventoried the difficulties that beset the modern public opinion survey, as reflected in the questions raised by scholars and practitioners in the field.[14] The list includes:

- the lack of truthful responses to survey questions;
- the failure to do justice to the richness of people's experience;
- the failure of people to understand certain types of questions that depend on memory or insight into their own feelings;
- the tendency of survey researchers to impose their own framework on the public;
- the fact that certain words in questions mean different things to different people;
- the tendency of people to give an opinion even when they do not have a real point of view on the subject; and,
- the tendency of people to modify their answers to questions when the context shifts or question wording changes.

This is an imposing list. Some of these difficulties are exaggerated; few reflect inherent limitations of the opinion survey method. Most, however, as Singer points out, are solvable through a combination of care, time, and money. In other words, they are practical problems, not conceptual, theoretical, or technical. At the end of her address, Singer quotes Howard Schuman, a past president of AAPOR, who, like herself, has concluded that opinion surveys are beset with difficulties—not so much because of technical or theoretical flaws, but "because human responses are inherently both subtle and complex."[15]

These judgments—that survey methods are potentially capable of giving an accurate picture of public opinion but that to do so they need to be as subtle and complex as public opinion itself—certainly reflect my own experience in conducting public opinion polls. But the conclusion that the difficulties of the polling profession are largely practical does not mean that they are being resolved. Unhappily, the trend is moving in the opposite direction. For subtle and complex human responses, one needs subtle and complex opinion surveys. These demand time, money, and skill. Today, the trend is toward oversimplified, cheap, crude public opinion polls, not subtle and complex ones. This is not because the profession wants it that way: opinion research professionals have never been more alert to the dangers of superficial polls. The villains are the mass media who increasingly commission, pay for, and themselves conduct public opinion polls. The "quickie" opinion polls that make newspaper headlines ("Public Disagrees with High Court

[14]Eleanor Singer, "Presidential Address: Pushing Back the Limits to Surveys," *Public Opinion Quarterly* 52 (1988): 416–26.

[15]Ibid., 424.

on Abortion") or 30-second sound-bites based on simplistic questions are a menace that has grown all too familiar.

Many of these opinion polls are worthless because they ignore every trap and pitfall the profession has uncovered, at great pains and cost, in its more than half century of analyzing poll results. As public opinion polls have grown in popularity and as magazines, newspapers and TV stations have come to believe they must have their own proprietary opinion polls, corners are cut, polls grow shorter and cheaper, and being the first to publish an instant poll is regarded by the press as a desirable coup. Ironically, the more the polling professionals have come to appreciate the subtlety and complexity of human responses, the more the media have worked to oversimplify and falsify that complexity. There are honorable exceptions, like the CBS News/*New York Times* poll and the polls sponsored by the *Los Angeles Times.* But, in general, Gresham's law has prevailed: the bad opinion polls are driving out the good ones. . . .

At the beginning of chapter 1, I referred to a mystery. The mystery concerned the status of concepts described in subsequent chapters. These include: missing standards of quality for public opinion, the peculiar coexistence in the public mind of strands of poor-quality opinion alongside strands of good-quality opinion, the lack of accepted methods for distinguishing one from the other, the complexity of the three-stage process of moving from mass opinion to public judgment, the many potholes that make that road a bumpy one, the inadvertent obstacles thrown up by the mass media as they single-mindedly pursue their task of consciousness raising, the various principles that can, if applied skillfully and in good faith, elevate the quality of public opinion in America, and so on. Why are concepts such as these not a familiar and staple feature of American public life?

For years I have been bewildered about why these ideas are not part of the core vocabulary of democracy along with freedom of opportunity, one person/one vote, the separation of powers, due process, equality before the law, a government of laws not persons, freedom of expression for unpopular ideas, and the other familiar concepts that are the building blocks of our American democracy. Why is there no felt need for such ideas? Why are so few institutions skilled in techniques for enhancing the quality of public opinion and dedicated to doing so? Surely such institutions are as indispensable to the practice of democracy as lawyers and courts and journalists and public interest groups.

These concepts are not particularly subtle or elusive. Indeed, they are as plain as the need for giving greater attention to protecting the environment or taking better care of our nation's children. Why they are neglected and ignored poses a genuine mystery.

When I first began to present these ideas in the mid-1970s, I did so with a mounting sense of discovery, expecting them to be received with enthusiasm and relief. Why enthusiasm? Because theorists of democracy have always recognized that people are not born with a fully developed capacity for self-governance. It is not like walking. It is a high-order skill that must be developed with much nurturing, training, and practice. Many civilizations never develop these skills. Even in our own times, a great civilization like that of China, so gifted in other ways, shows itself pathetically awkward in moving toward genuine democratic institutions. I expected that practitioners like myself who were exploring new ways to enhance public opinion and the capacity for self-governance would be greeted warmly, as bearers of good news. In some circles, that surmise has proven true. There are citizen groups dedicated to enhancing the practice of democracy, as distinct from peddling their pet nostrums to their fellow citizens, and they welcome new approaches.

But not the mainstream. . . . In the abstract, they approve. They see the theoretical point of it. But in the end it turns out to be an unwelcome distraction. They do not know what to do with it. Their heads are somewhere else. Impatiently, they turn back to their own projects and preoccupations.

I had expected these concepts to be welcome news to journalists, academics, and educators who deplore the ignorance of the American public. As Everett Ladd learned from Gallup poll data, the factual ignorance of the public and its fickleness is often counterbalanced by a remarkable stability and sureness of judgment in applying basic values. My own public opinion surveys also show that Americans can form sound judgments on issues without requiring the kind of factual mastery scholars assume to be necessary. It is true that the majority is ignorant of many things. *And* fickle. *And* often inattentive. What a relief, then, to learn that the public has developed compensatory skills that permit people, under proper conditions, to form the kinds of judgments necessary for self-governance.

Here, too, I proved naïve. The optimistic conclusions that Everett Ladd, myself, and other practitioners of public opinion have reached after years of immersion in public opinion surveys make little impression on those who insist on the public's invincible ignorance. Far from being relieved by our conclusions, the journalistic and academic mainstream seem to delight in the idea that the public is ignorant and fickle. They do not want to hear otherwise. They seem committed to the notion that there is only one way to arrive at sound judgments—by experts piling up masses of information—their way. To suggest that the public has another path to sound judgment smacks of sentimentality, mysticism, or just plain nonsense. They will have none of it. Far from being relieved, they are irritated, annoyed. And because they are the gatekeepers of communication, their point of view prevails.

It would be disingenuous to give the impression that I was an innocent and naïve youngster who expected gratitude for goring the experts' oxen. Anyone whose profession consists of conveying bad news much of the time is quickly disabused of naïveté. These days they no longer shoot the messengers bearing the bad news, but neither do they treat them with tender loving care. Many years ago I had ceased to be a stranger to the phenomenon of people's resistance to facts. I had learned that the facts do *not* speak for themselves. If the facts happen to run counter to people's deeply ingrained prejudices or interests or emotional commitments, then so much the worse for the facts. . . .

. . . If America were to give a high priority to public judgment, and the effort were to succeed, what kind of nation would result? In what ways would our society and culture be different than they are today? What vision of the future would we seek to realize?

. . . The essence of democratic dialogue is conveyed in Martin Buber's concept of the "I-thou" relationship. When I and thou engage each other, something deeper than a mere exchange of views is going on. The I-thou interaction implies a genuine receptivity to the other: I do not listen passively to what you are saying; I respond to it with my whole being. I may argue and dispute the correctness of your views, but I "take them in," in the deepest sense of the word. And you do likewise. From the encounter, both I and thou emerge changed. Each of us has internalized the point of view of the other.[16]

Another concept supporting the vision is Habermas's insight that it is disastrous to divorce human reason from the world of ordinary life—the struggle to make a living, raise families, and live peacefully as a community. When experts, influenced by the Culture of Technical Control, conceive reason as something separate and apart from everyday life—the property of a trained class of specialists, scientists, and other elites—then the deepest ideals of the founding fathers of the nation are betrayed. Reason is *not* the exclusive property of a class of experts whose training and credentials certify the possession of a special endowment. Reason is a more humble, more universal, more democratic gift.

To my mind, these are stunning insights. They shape a vision of a democracy that encourages people to listen to each other and to weigh each other's views seriously. It is a vision of a democracy that involves those who wish to be involved and that recognizes that the highest expression of human rationality is not nuclear physics or econometric models but ordinary people speaking and reasoning together on issues of common concern.

It is a vision of what David Mathews calls a *deliberative* democracy, as distinct from a representative or participatory democracy. It is a democracy that revives the notion of thoughtful and active citizenship. Now citizenship is treated like a passive form of consumer behavior. People fail at citizenship not because they are apathetic but because they do not think their actions or views make any real difference. We need to expand the notion of citizen choice now confined to elections to include making choices on the vital issues that confront us every day.

In the 1988 presidential campaign, candidate George Bush promised a "kinder, gentler nation." This appeal struck a responsive chord in the electorate. But after the election, the phrase "kinder and gentler" became a stock laugh line for TV comedians who used it satirically. Why did this happen? It was not because George Bush was hypocritical. There is no reason to question his sincerity. But it did not take long for observers to realize that his invocation of a kinder, gentler America was a mere slogan, empty words devoid of implementation. This well-meant bit of rhetoric added one more stimulus to the growing cynicism of the American public. . . .[17] The vision I have is of an American where average citizens engage in serious dialogue about what would truly make America a "kinder, gentler nation." This is what the public wants for America. But with limited resources

---

[16]See Martin Buber, *I and Thou.* 2d ed., trans. Ronald Gregor Smith (New York: Scribner's, 1958).

[17]See Donald L. Kanter and Philip H. Mirvis, *The Cynical Americans: Living and Working in an Age of Discontent and Disillusion* (San Francisco: Jossey-Bass, 1989).

and conflicting needs, it is difficult to achieve. Slogans and top-down leadership cannot achieve it. It requires serious democratic dialogue to shape a political debate in which the public—the whole public—participates.

As our society is presently organized, few institutions are responsible for the common interest. The theory is that the general interest emerges out of the interplay of special interests. This theory, straight from the textbooks of liberal political philosophy, is today the dominant practice in Washington and the state capitals. It is one of the principal causes of the nation's political gridlock: competing special interests exercise a veto over projects to serve the general interest. The concept of the general interest is, however, an urgent concern for average Americans. As individuals, senior citizens, for example, will give far greater weight to the general interest than will the lobby that represents their special interests.

The vision, then, is of a society in which the general interest is as well represented as special interests and in which average citizens play a decisive role in defining it.

Finally, I see this vision as "actively conservative." It is conservative in the sense of staying true to long-standing American traditions. We need, for example, to recover the public traditions of our political culture, particularly those that understand politics as more than the clash of special interest groups mediated by government. The modern concept of a professional government has no place in it for the public or its citizens. And that concept is at the heart of the resistance to programs for strengthening the public. The public really is not necessary for the prevailing vision of how we govern ourselves. People feel pushed out of this kind of system; they feel incompetent, and so they reject politics.

The vision is active in the sense that staying true to tradition requires a change of direction. The root meaning of conservative is to save, to conserve. Sometimes this translates into protecting the status quo. But sometimes it means transformation. If the tradition is losing its way, then keeping faith with it means finding one's way back to the true path.

A key element of the tradition is captured in the Enlightenment's metaphor of light. Its informing idea was "let in the light." Its faith was that the light of scientific knowledge would banish ignorance and superstition and inequality, conquer poverty and disease, and create freedom with dignity.

As a vision for America we should conserve this heritage—to let in the light of knowledge to elevate the freedom and dignity of people. But in doing so we must also recognize that this means changing our culture and institutions to accommodate a more democratic concept of the light of human reason, one that is not the exclusive property of learned experts but, potentially, of everyone.

7

The United States Congress

The delegates to the Constitutional Convention constructed a House of Representatives and a Senate that would be open to criticisms along a number of fronts. Many different Antifederalist writers expressed similar criticisms of these institutions. It is important to remember that despite these criticisms, Antifederalist writers were not objecting to the establishment of a House of Representatives or a Senate or to the notion of Congress in general. They were perfectly willing to support such institutions. They were, however, objecting to the particular nature of the House and Senate created by the Federalists. What was the nature of the Antifederalist criticisms?

Generally it can be characterized as an effort to ensure greater representation of and participation by the people. Antifederalists objected to the size of the House of Representatives. They reasoned that such a small membership would not and could not adequately represent the multitude of interests and people throughout the nation. The Federal Farmer noted the problem by stating, ". . . It is deceiving a people to tell them they are electors, and can chuse their legislators, if they cannot, in the nature of things, chuse men from among themselves, and genuinely like themselves." Antifederalists would have supported a large-membership House of Representatives, where it would be more likely for various types of people and interests to be represented. Other problems were associated with a small House. It could, for example, lead to corruption via the undue influencing of members by various interests. This would inevitably reduce the public's confidence in the ability of the legislature to govern.

Antifederalists were also concerned with the Senate. All of their criticisms were magnified when they examined the small body of individuals that would function in the Senate. Brutus, in his essay of April 10, 1788, argued that the term for Senators was too long and suggested that a rotation-of-office provision was necessary for the Senate. In this essay Brutus seems to understand the advantages of incumbency that has led, in our modern era, to a reduction in competitive Congressional elections. This is all the more remarkable given his perspective of 1788. The Pennsylvania minority also advocated a rotation-of-office provision for the House based on the one established in their state. Their goal was to rotate these offices and create more opportunity for public service. They believed in tapping the wisdom that they believed was evident in the public.

Federalists did not share these views. In a series of papers, James Madison engages in a systematic attempt to refute the charges of the Antifederalists. He first notes that the small membership in the House will not be permanent because of the provisions for altering its size after the census in three years. The problem of size, he argues, is a temporary thing that will not adversely affect liberty. Besides, the checks and balances between different power centers will prevent the usurpation of government by a few individuals. Madison, in *Federalist* Paper 57, argues that there will be a knowledge of constituents, for each representative will bring with him a knowledge of the member's district. The knowledge of all members from all states will truly be considerable. Madison argues against the possibility of corruption by stating that elected representative government best guards against this possibility. It is the best method for attaining representation by virtuous and wise men. Madison notes, ". . . they [representatives] will enter into public service under circumstances which cannot fail to produce a temporary affection at least to their constituents. There is in every breast a sensibility to marks of honor, of favor, of esteem, and of confidence, which, apart from all other considerations of interests, is some pledge for grateful and benevolent returns." In fact, Madison argues that a multitudinous body may be more susceptible to corruption. Madison, in direct rebuttal to Brutus, champions the longer terms in the Senate. He notes that these terms provide a permanency that the House terms do not and thus add to the stability of the system.

The arguments of the Antifederalists and Federalists live on in the current debate regarding term limits for Congress. Charles R. Kesler argues against these limits, and John H. Fund argues in favor of them. Both arguments are heavily influenced by the founders and their opponents. Antifederalist arguments have influenced our history with regard specifically to the Senate. In 1913 the 17th Amendment was ratified, providing for direct election of the Senate. Antifederalist arguments will continue to influence our politics in the form of the term-limitation debate. As of 1992 state legislative term-limit initiatives succeeded in all 14 states where they were on the ballot. Attempts are underway to extend these limits to the national legislature through legal challenges and formal amendment procedures. One thing is clear: Constitutional debates will continue to live and enrich our political institutions and processes.

THE CONSTITUTION (EXCERPTS)

THE PREAMBLE

We the People of the United States, in Order to form a more perfect Union, establish Justice, insure domestic Tranquility, provide for the common defence, promote the general Welfare, and secure the Blessings of Liberty to ourselves and our Posterity, do ordain and establish this Constitution for the United States of America.

ARTICLE I—THE LEGISLATIVE ARTICLE

Legislative Power

Section 1 All legislative Powers herein granted shall be vested in a Congress of the United States, which shall consist of a Senate and House of Representatives.

House of Representatives: Composition; Qualifications; Apportionment; Impeachment Power

Section 2 The House of Representatives shall be composed of Members chosen every second Year by the People of the several States, and the Electors in each State shall have the Qualifications requisite for Electors of the most numerous Branch of the State Legislature.

No Person shall be a Representative who shall not have attained to the Age of twenty five Years, and been seven Years a Citizen of the United States, and who shall not, when elected, be an Inhabitant of that State in which he shall be chosen.

Representatives and direct Taxes[1] shall be apportioned among the several States which may be included within this Union, according to their respective Numbers, *which shall be determined by adding to the whole Number of free Persons, including those bound to Service for a Term of Years, and excluding Indians not taxed, three fifths of all other Persons.*[2] The actual Enumeration shall be made within three Years after the first Meeting of the Congress of the United States, and within every subsequent Term of ten Years, in such Manner as they shall by Law direct. The Number of Representatives shall not exceed one for every thirty Thousand, but each State shall have at least one Representative; and until each enumeration shall be made, the State of New Hampshire shall be entitled to chuse three, Massachusetts eight, Rhode-Island and Providence Plantations one, Connecticut five, New-York six, New Jersey four, Pennsylvania eight, Delaware one, Maryland six, Virginia ten, North Carolina five, South Carolina five, and Georgia three.

When vacancies happen in the Representation from any State, the Executive Authority thereof shall issue Writs of Election to fill such Vacancies.

The House of Representatives shall chuse their Speaker and other Officers; and shall have the sole Power of Impeachment.

Senate Composition: Qualifications, Impeachment Trials

Section 3 The Senate of the United States shall be composed of two Senators from each State, *chosen by the Legislature thereof,*[3] for six Years; and each Senator shall have one Vote.

Immediately after they shall be assembled in Consequence of the first Election, they shall be divided as equally as may be into three Classes. The Seats of the Senators of the first Class shall be vacated at the Expiration of the second Year, of the second Class at the Expiration of the fourth Year, and of the third Class at the Expiration of the sixth Year, so that one third may be chosen every second Year; *and if Vacancies happen by Resignation, or otherwise, during the Recess of the Legislature of any State, the Executive thereof may make temporary Appointments until the next Meeting of the Legislature, which shall then fill such Vacancies.*[4]

No person shall be a Senator who shall not have attained to the Age of thirty Years, and been nine Years a Citizen of the United States, and who shall

[1]Modified by the 16th Amendment

[2]"Other Persons" refers to black slaves. Replaced by Section 2, 14th Amendment

[3]Repealed by the 17th Amendment

[4]Modified by the 17th Amendment

not, when elected, be an inhabitant of that State for which he shall be chosen.

The Vice President of the United States shall be President of the Senate, but shall have no Vote, unless they be equally divided.

The Senate shall chuse their other Officers, and also a President pro tempore, in the Absence of the Vice President, or when he shall exercise the Office of President of the United States.

The Senate shall have the sole Power to try all Impeachments. When sitting for that Purpose, they shall be on Oath or Affirmation. When the President of the United States is tried, the Chief Justice shall preside: And no Person shall be convicted without the Concurrence of two thirds of the Members present.

Judgment in Cases of Impeachment shall not extend further than to removal from Office, and disqualification to hold and enjoy any Office of honor, Trust or Profit under the United States; but the Party convicted shall nevertheless be liable and subject to Indictment, Trial, Judgment and Punishment, according to law.

Congressional Elections: Times, Places, Manner

Section 4 The Times, Places and Manner of holding Elections for Senators and Representatives, shall be prescribed in each State by the Legislature thereof; but the Congress may at any time by Law make or alter such Regulations, except as to the Places of chusing Senators.

The Congress shall assemble at least once in every Year, *and such Meeting shall be on the first Monday in December, unless they shall by Law appoint a different Day.*[5]

Powers and Duties of the Houses

Section 5 Each House shall be the Judge of the Elections, Returns and Qualifications of its own Members, and a Majority of each shall constitute a Quorum to do Business; but a smaller Number may adjourn from day to day, and may be authorized to compel the Attendance of absent Members, in such Manner, and under the Penalties as each House may provide.

Each House may determine the Rules of its Proceedings, punish its Members for disorderly Behaviour, and, with the Concurrence of two thirds, expel a Member.

Each House shall keep a Journal of its Proceedings, and from time to time publish the same, excepting such Parts as may in their Judgment require Secrecy; and the yeas and Nays of the Members of either House on any question shall, at the Desire of one fifth of those Present, be entered on the Journal.

Neither House, during the Session of Congress, shall, without the Consent of the other, adjourn for more than three days, nor to any other place than that in which the two Houses shall be sitting.

Rights of Members

Section 6 The Senators and Representatives shall receive a Compensation for their Services, to be ascertained by Law, and paid out of the Treasury of the United States. They shall in all Cases, except Treason, Felony and Breach of the Peace, be privileged from Arrest during their Attendance at the Session of their respective Houses, and in going to and returning from the same; and for any Speech or Debate in either House, they shall not be questioned in any other Place.

No Senator or Representative, shall,

[5]Changed by the 20th Amendment.

during the time for which he was elected, be appointed to any civil Office under the authority of the United States, which shall have been created, or the Emoluments whereof shall have been encreased during such time; and no Person holding any Office under the United States, shall be a Member of either House during his Continuance in Office.

Legislative Powers: Bills and Resolutions

Section 7 All Bills for raising Revenue shall originate in the House of Representatives; but the Senate may propose or concur with Amendments as on other Bills.

Every Bill which shall have passed the House of Representatives and the Senate, shall, before it become a Law, be presented to the President of the United States; if he approve he shall sign it, but if not he shall return it, with his Objections to that House in which it shall have originated, who shall enter the Objections at large on their Journal, and proceed to reconsider it. If after such Reconsideration two thirds of that House shall agree to pass the Bill, it shall be sent, together with the Objections, to the other House, by which it shall likewise be reconsidered, and if approved by two thirds of that House, it shall become a Law. But in all such Cases the Votes of both Houses shall be determined by yeas and Nays, and the Names of the Persons voting for and against the Bill shall be entered on the Journal of each House respectively. If any Bill shall not be returned by the President within ten Days (Sundays excepted) after it shall have been presented to him, the Same shall be a Law, in like Manner as if he had signed it, unless the Congress by their Adjournment prevent its Return, in which Case it shall not be a Law.

Every Order, Resolution, or Vote to which the Concurrence of the Senate and House of Representatives may be necessary (except on a question of Adjournment) shall be presented to the President of the United States; and before the Same shall take Effect, shall be approved by him, or being disapproved by him, shall be repassed by two thirds of the Senate and House of Representatives, according to the Rules and Limitations prescribed in the Case of a Bill.

Powers of Congress

Section 8 The Congress shall have Power To lay and collect Taxes, Duties, Imposts and Excises, to pay the Debts and provide for the common Defence and general Welfare of the United States; but all Duties, Imposts and Excises shall be uniform throughout the United States;

To borrow Money on the Credit of the United States;

To regulate Commerce with foreign Nations, and among the several States, and with the Indian Tribes;

To establish an uniform Rule of Naturalization, and uniform Laws on the subject of Bankruptcies throughout the United States;

To coin Money, regulate the Value thereof, and of foreign Coin, and fix the Standard of Weights and Measures;

To provide for the Punishment of counterfeiting the Securities and current Coin of the United States;

To establish Post Offices and post Roads;

To promote the Progress of Science and useful Arts, by securing for limited Times to Authors and Inventors the exclusive Right to their respective Writings and Discoveries,

To constitute Tribunals inferior to the supreme Court,

To define and punish Piracies and Felonies committed on the high Seas, and Offences against the Law of Nations;

To declare War, grant Letters of Marque and Reprisal, and make Rules concerning Captures on Land and Water;

To raise and support Armies, but no Appropriation of Money to that Use shall be for a longer Term than two Years;

To provide and maintain a Navy;

To make Rules for the Government and Regulation of the land and naval Forces;

To provide for calling for the Militia to execute the Laws of the Union, suppress Insurrections and repel Invasions;

To provide for organizing, arming, and disciplining, the Militia, and for governing such Part of them as may be employed in the Service of the United States, reserving to the States respectively, the Appointment of the Officers, and the Authority of training the Militia according to the discipline prescribed by Congress;

To exercise exclusive Legislation in all Cases whatsoever, over such District (not exceeding ten Miles square) as may, by Cession of particular States, and the Acceptance of Congress, become the Seat of the Government of the United States, and to exercise like Authority over all Places purchased by the Consent of the Legislature of the State in which the Same shall be, for the Erection of Forts, Magazines, Arsenals, dock-Yards, and other needful Buildings;—And

To make all Laws which shall be necessary and proper for carrying into Execution the foregoing Powers, and all other Powers vested by this Constitution in the Government of the United States, or in any Department or Officer thereof.

Powers Denied to Congress

Section 9 The Migration or Importation of such Persons as any of the States now existing shall think proper to admit, shall not be prohibited by the Congress prior to the Year one thousand eight hundred and eight, but a Tax or Duty may be imposed on such Importation, not exceeding ten dollars for each Person.

The privilege of the Writ of Habeas Corpus shall not be suspended, unless when in Cases of Rebellion or Invasion the public Safety may require it.

No Bill of Attainder or ex post facto Laws shall be passed.

No Capitation, or other direct, Tax shall be laid, unless in Proportion to the Census or Enumeration herein before directed to be taken.[6]

No Tax or Duty shall be laid on Articles exported from any State.

No Preference shall be given by any Regulation of Commerce or Revenue to the Ports of one State over those of another; nor shall Vessels bound to, or from, one State, be obliged to enter, clear, or pay Duties in another.

No Money shall be drawn from the Treasury, but in Consequence of Appropriations made by Law; and a regular Statement and Account of the Receipts and Expenditures of all public Money shall be published from time to time.

No Title of Nobility shall be granted by the United States; And no Person holding any Office of Profit or Trust under them, shall, without the Consent of the Congress, accept of any present, Emolument, Office, or Title, of any kind whatever, from any King, Prince, or foreign State.

---

[6]Modified by the 16th Amendment

Powers Denied to the States

Section 10 No State shall enter into any Treaty, Alliance, or Confederation; grant Letters of Marque and Reprisal; coin Money; emit Bills of Credit; make any Thing but gold and silver Coin a Tender in Payment of Debts; pass any Bill of Attainder, ex post facto Law, or Law impairing the Obligation of Contracts, or grant any Title of Nobility.

No State shall, without the Consent of the Congress, lay any Imposts or Duties on Imports or Exports, except what may be absolutely necessary for executing it's inspection Laws: and the net Produce of all Duties and Imposts, laid by any State on Imports or Exports, shall be for the Use of the Treasury of the United States; and all such Laws shall be subject to the Revision and Controul of the Congress.

No State shall, without the Consent of Congress, lay any Duty of Tonnage, keep Troops, or Ships of War in time of Peace, enter into any Agreement or Compact with another State, or with a foreign Power, or engage in War, unless actually invaded, or in such imminent Danger as will not admit of Delay.

Amendment 17—Direct Election of Senators

[Ratified April 8, 1913]

The Senate of the United States shall be composed of two Senators from each State, elected by the people thereof, for six years; and each Senator shall have one vote. The electors in each State shall have the qualifications requisite for electors of the most numerous branch of the State legislatures.

When vacancies happen in the representation of any State in the Senate, the executive authority of such State shall issue writs of election to fill such vacancies: *Provided*, That the Legislature of any State may empower the executive thereof to make temporary appointment until the people fill the vacancies by election as the legislature may direct.

This amendment shall not be so construed as to affect the election or term of any Senator chosen before it becomes valid as part of the Constitution.

THE HOUSE OF REPRESENTATIVES: ANTIFEDERALIST ARGUMENTS

"Brutus"
(Probably Robert Yates)
Essay IV
(Excerpts)

DISCUSSION QUESTIONS

1. What are the main points that Brutus makes against a small (in membership) House of Representatives?
2. Why would the public lose confidence in the House of Representatives as conceived under the Constitution?
3. What does Brutus have to say concerning the Congress being authorized under the Constitution to make or alter regulations for elections to the Congress?

The small number which is to compose this legislature, will not only expose it to the danger of that kind of corruption, and undue influence, which will arise from the gift of places of honour and emolument, or the more direct one of bribery, but it will also subject it to another kind of influence no less fatal to the liberties of the people, though it be not so flagrantly repugnant to the principles of rectitude. It is not to be expected that a legislature will be found in any country that will not have some of its members, who will pursue their private ends, and for which they will sacrifice the public good. . . .

The firmest security against this kind of improper and dangerous influence, as well as all other, is a strong and numerous representation: in such a house of assembly, so great a number must be gained over, before the private views of individuals could be gratified that there could be scarce a hope of success. But in the federal assembly, seventeen men are all that is necessary to pass a law. . . .

A farther objection against the feebleness of the representation is, that it will not possess the confidence of the people. The execution of the laws in a free government must rest on this confidence, and this must be founded on the good opinion they entertain of the farmers of the laws. . . .

In order for the people safely to repose themselves on their rulers, they should not only be of their own choice. But it is requisite they should be acquainted with their abilities to manage the public concerns with wisdom. They should be satisfied that those who represent them are men of integrity, who will pursue the good of the community with fidelity; and will not be turned aside from their duty by private interest, or corrupted by undue influence; and that they will have such a zeal for the good of those whom they represent, as to excite them to be diligent in their service; but it is impossible the people of the United States should have sufficient knowledge of their representatives, when the numbers are so few, to acquire any rational satisfaction on either of these points. The people of this state will have very little acquaintance with those who may be chosen to represent them; a great part of them will, probably, not know the characters of their own members, much less that of a majority of those who will compose the federal assembly; they will consist of men, whose names they have never heard, and whose talents and regard for the public good, they are total strangers to; and they will have no persons so immediately of their choice so near them, of their neighbors and of their own rank in life, that they can feel themselves secure in trusting their interests in their hands. The representatives of the people cannot, as they now do, after they have passed laws, mix with the people, and explain to them the motives which induced the adoption of any measure, point out its utility, and remove objections or silence unreasonable clamours against it.—The number will be so small that but a very few of the most sensible and respectable yeomanry of the country can ever have any knowledge of them: being so far removed from the people, their station will be elevated and important, and they will be considered as ambitious and designing. They will not be viewed by the people as part of themselves, but as a body distinct from them, and having separate interests to pursue; the consequence will be, that a perpetual jealousy will exist in the minds of the people against them; their conduct will be narrowly watched; their measures scrutinized; and their laws opposed, evaded, or reluctantly obeyed. This is natural, and exactly corresponds with the conduct of individuals towards those in whose hands they intrust important concerns. If the person confided in, be a neighbour with whom his employer is intimately acquainted, whose talents, he knows, are sufficient to manage the business with which he is charged, his honesty and fidelity unsuspected, and his friendship and zeal for the service of the principal unquestionable, he will commit his affairs into his hands with unreserved confidence, and feel himself secure; all the transactions of the agent will meet with the most favorable construction, and the measures he takes will give satisfaction. But, if the person employed be a stranger, whom he has never seen, and whose character for ability or fidelity he cannot fully learn—If he is constrained to choose him, because it was not in his power to procure one more agreeable to his wishes, he will trust him with caution, and be suspicious of all his conduct. . . .

By section 4, article I, the Congress are authorized, at any time, by law, to make, or alter, regulations respecting the time, place, and manner of holding elections for senators and representatives, except as to the places of choosing senators. By this clause the right of election itself, is, in a great measure, transferred from the people to their rulers.—One would think, that if any thing was necessary to be made a fundamental article of the original compact, it would be, that of fixing the branches of the legislature, so as to put it out of its power to alter itself by modifying the election of its own members at will and pleasure. When a people once resign the privilege of a fair election, they clearly have none left worth contending for. . . .

I know it is said that the dangers apprehended from this clause are merely imaginary, that the proposed general legislature will be disposed to regulate elections upon proper principles, and to use their power with discretion, and to promote the public good. On this, I would observe, that constitutions are not so necessary to regulate the conduct of good rulers as to restrain that of bad ones.—Wise and good men will exercise power so as to promote the public happiness under any form of government. If we are to take it for granted, that those who administer the government under this system, will always pay proper attention to the rights and interests of the people, nothing more was necessary than to say who should be invested with the powers of government, and leave them to exercise it at will and pleasure. Men are apt to be deceived both with respect to their own dispositions and those of others. Though this truth is proved by almost every page of the history of nations, to wit, that power lodged in the hands of rulers to be used at discretion, is almost always exercised to the oppression of the people, and the aggrandizement of themselves; yet most men think if it was lodged in their hands they would not employ it in this manner.

"The Address and Reasons of Dissent of the Minority of the Convention of Pennsylvania to Their Constituents" *December 18, 1787* *(Excerpts)*

DISCUSSION QUESTIONS

1. List the major objections of the Pennsylvania minority to the representation in the House and Senate under the Constitution.
2. What types of people did the Pennsylvania minority believe would be elected to the United States Congress?
3. Has this criticism been justified as our nation evolved? Why or why not?
4. How did the Pennsylvania legislature differ from the one proposed in the Constitution?
5. What was the purpose of a rotation-of-office provision in the Pennsylvania legislature?

The legislature of a free country should be so formed as to have a competent knowledge of its constituents, and enjoy their confidence. To produce these essential requisites, the representation ought to be fair, equal, and sufficiently numerous, to possess the same interests, feelings, opinions, and views, which the people themselves would possess, were they all assembled; and so numerous as to prevent bribery and undue influence, and so responsible to the people, by frequent and fair elections, as to prevent their neglecting or sacrificing the views and interests of their constituents, to their own pursuits.

We will now bring the legislature under this constitution to the test of the foregoing principles, which will demonstrate, that it is deficient in every essential quality of a just and safe representation.

The house of representatives is to consist of 65 members; that is one for about every 50,000 inhabitants, to be chosen every two years. Thirty-three members will form a quorum for doing business; and 17 of these, being the majority, determine the sense of the house.

The senate, the other constituent branch of the legislature, consists of 26 members being *two* from each state, appointed by their legislatures every six years—fourteen senators make a quorum; the majority of whom, eight, determines the sense of that body: except in judging on impeachments, or in making treaties, or in expelling a member, when two thirds of the senators present, must concur.

The president is to have the control over the enacting of laws, so far as to make the concurrence of *two* thirds of the representatives and senators present necessary, if he should object to the laws.

Thus it appears that the liberties, happiness, interests, and great concerns of the whole United States, may be dependent upon the integrity, virtue, wisdom, and knowledge of 25 or 26 men—How inadequate and unsafe a representation! Inadequate, because the sense and views of 3 or 4 millions of people diffused over so extensive a territory comprising such various climates, products, habits, interests, and opinions, cannot be collected in so small a body; and besides, it is not a fair and equal representation of the people even in proportion to its number, for the smallest state has as much weight in the senate as the largest, and from the smallness of the number to be chosen for both branches of the legislature; and from the mode of election and appointment, which is under the control of Congress; and from the nature of the thing, men of the most elevated rank in life, will alone be chosen. The other orders in the society, such as farmers, traders, and mechanics, who all ought to have a competent number of their best informed men in the legislature, will be totally unrepresented.

The representation is unsafe, because in the exercise of such great powers and trusts, it is so exposed to corruption and undue influence, by the gift of the numerous places of honor and emoluments at the disposal of the executive; by the arts and address of the great and designing; and by direct bribery.

The representation is moreover inadequate and unsafe, because of the long terms for which it is appointed, and the mode of its appointment, by which Congress may not only control the choice of the people, but may so manage as to divest the people of this fundamental right, and become self-elected.

. . . In the government of this state, under the old confederation, the members of the legislature are taken from among the people, and their interests and welfare are so inseparably connected with those of their constituents, that they can derive no advantage from oppressive laws and taxes, for they would suffer in common with their fellow citizens; would participate in the burdens they impose on the community, as they must return to the common level, after a short period; and notwithstanding every exertion of influence, every means of corruption, a necessary rotation excludes them from permanency in the legislature.

"The Federal Farmer" (Unknown) Letters, October 9, 1787 and December 31, 1787 (Excerpts)

DISCUSSION QUESTIONS

1. What are the essential parts of a free and good government?
2. How does the Federal Farmer define imperfect representation?
3. Describe the Federal Farmer's ideas on representational balance. What do you think this implies for the legislature?

October 9, 1787

Dear Sir,

The essential parts of a free and good government are a full and equal representation of the people in the legislature, and the jury trial of the vicinage in the administration of justice—a full and equal representation, is that which possesses the same interests, feelings, opinions, and views the people themselves would were they all assembled—a fair representation, therefore, should be so regulated, that every order of men in the community, according to the common course of elections, can have a share in it—in order to allow professional men, merchants, traders, farmers, mechanics, etc. to bring a just proportion of their best informed men respectively into the legislature, the representation must be considerably numerous—We have about 200 state senators in the United States, and a less number than that of federal representatives cannot, clearly, be a full representation of this people, in the affairs of internal taxation and police, were there but one legislature for the whole union. The representation cannot be equal, or the situation of the people proper for one government only—if the extreme parts of the society cannot be represented as fully as the central—It is apparently impracticable that this should be the case in this extensive country—it would be impossible to collect a representation of the parts of the country five, six, and seven hundred miles from the seat of government.

December 31, 1787

Where the people, or their representatives, make the laws, it is probable they will generally be fitted to the national character and circumstances, unless the representation be partial, and the imperfect substitute of the people. However, the people may be electors, if the representation be so formed as to give one or more of the natural classes of men in the society an undue ascendancy over the others, it is imperfect; the former will gradually become masters, and the latter slaves. . . .

It is deceiving a people to tell them they are electors, and can chuse their legislators, if they cannot, in the nature of things, chuse men from among themselves, and genuinely like themselves. . . .

I believe, well founded, that the schools produce but few advocates for republican forms of government; gentlemen of the law, divinity, physic, &c. probably form about a fourth part of the people; yet their political influence, perhaps, is equal to that of all the other descriptions of men; if we may judge from the appointments to Congress, the legal characters will often, in a small representation, be the majority; but the more the representatives are encreased, the more of the farmers, merchants, &c. will be found to be brought into the government.

These general observations will enable you to discern what I intend by different classes, and the general scope of my ideas, when I contend for uniting and balancing their interests, feelings, opinions, and views in the legislature; we may not only so unite and balance these as to prevent a change in the government by the gradual exaltation of one part to the depression of others, but we may derive many other advantages from the combination and full representation; a small representation can never be well informed as to the circumstances of the people, the members of it must be too far removed from the people, in general, to sympathize with them, and too few to communicate with them; a representation must be extremely imperfect where the representatives are not circumstanced to make the proper communications to their constituents, and where the constituents in turn cannot, with tolerable convenience, make known their wants, circumstances, and opinions, to their representatives; where there is but one representative to 30,000 or 40,000 inhabitants, it appears to me, he can only mix, and be acquainted with a few respectable characters among his constituents, even double the federal representation, and then there must be a very great distance between the representatives and the people in general represented.

THE HOUSE OF REPRESENTATIVES: FEDERALIST ARGUMENTS

James Madison
Federalist *Paper 55*
(Excerpts)

DISCUSSION QUESTIONS

1. As documented by James Madison in this paper, what are the charges against the House of Representatives in the Constitution?
2. How does Madison explain the future growth in the membership in the House of Representatives?
3. According to Madison, how does the Constitution protect against the possible corruption of dispensing appointments?

The number of which the House of Representatives is to consist forms another and a very interesting point of view under which this branch of the federal legislature may be contemplated. Scarce any article, indeed, in the whole Constitution seems to be rendered more worthy of attention by the weight of character and the apparent force of argument with which it has been assailed. The charges exhibited against it are, first, that so small a number of representatives will be an unsafe depositary of the public interests; second, that they will not possess a proper knowledge of the local circumstances of their numerous constituents; third, that they will be taken from that class of citizens which will sympathize least with the feelings of the mass of the people and be most likely to aim at a permanent elevation of the few on the depression of the many; fourth, that defective as the number will be in the first instance, it will be more and more disproportionate, by the increase of the people and the obstacles which will prevent a correspondent increase of the representatives.

. . . Let us weigh the objections which have been stated against the number of members proposed for the House of Representatives. It is said, in the first place, that so small a number cannot be safely trusted with so much power.

The number of which this branch of the legislature is to consist, at the outset of the government, will be sixty-five. Within three years a census is to be taken, when the number may be augmented to one for every thirty thousand inhabitants; and within every successive period of ten years the census is to be renewed, and augmentations may continue to be made under the above limitation. It will not be thought an extravagant conjecture that the first census will, at the rate of one for every thirty thousand, raise the number of representatives to at least one hundred. Estimating the Negroes in the proportion of three fifths, it can scarcely be doubted that the population of the United States will by that time, if it does not already, amount to three millions. At the expiration of twenty-five years, according to the computed rate of increase, the number of representatives will amount to two hundred; and of fifty years, to four hundred. This is a number which, I presume, will put an end to all fears arising from the smallness of the body. I take for granted here what I shall, in answering the fourth objection, hereafter show, that the number of representatives will be augmented from time to time in the manner provided by the Constitution. On a contrary supposition, I should admit the objection to have very great weight indeed.

The true question to be decided, then, is whether the smallness of the number, as a temporary regulation, be dangerous to the public liberty? Whether sixty-five members for a few years, and a hundred or two hundred for a few more, be a safe depositary for a limited and well-guarded power of legislating for the United States? I must own that I could not give a negative answer to this question, without first obliterating every impression which I have received with regard to the present genius of the people of America, the spirit which actuates the State legislatures, and the principles which are incorporated with the political character of every class of citizens. . . .

From what quarter can the danger proceed? Are we afraid of foreign gold? If foreign gold could so easily corrupt our federal rulers and enable them to ensnare and betray their constituents, how has it happened that we are at this time a free and independent nation? . . .

Is the danger apprehended from the other branches of the federal government? But where are the means to be found by the President, or the Senate, or both? Their emoluments of office, it is to be presumed, will not, and without a previous corruption of the House of Representatives cannot, more than suffice for very different purposes; their private fortunes, as they must all be American citizens, cannot possibly be sources of danger. The only means, then, which they can possess, will be in the dispensation of appointments. Is it here that suspicion rests her charge? Sometimes we are told that this fund of corruption is to be exhausted by the President in subduing the virtue of the Senate. Now, the fidelity of the other House is to be the victim. The improbability of such a mercenary and perfidious combination of the several members of government, standing on as different foundations as republican principles will well admit, and at the same time accountable to the society over which they are placed, ought alone to quiet this apprehension. But, fortunately, the Constitution has provided a still further safeguard. The members of the Congress are rendered ineligible to any civil offices that may be created, or of which the emoluments may be increased, during the term of their election. No offices therefore can be dealt out to the existing members but such as may become vacant by ordinary casualties: and to suppose that these would be sufficient to purchase the guardians of the people, selected by the people themselves, is to renounce every rule by which events ought to be calculated, and to substitute an indiscriminate and unbounded jealousy, with which all reasoning must be vain.

James Madison
Federalist *Paper 56*
(Excerpts)

DISCUSSION QUESTION

Antifederalists argued that the House of Representatives under the Constitution was too small in membership to possess a due knowledge of the interests of its constituents. How does Madison respond to this charge?

The *second* charge against the House of Representatives is that it will be too small to possess a due knowledge of the interests of its constituents.

. . . The representatives of each State will not only bring with them a considerable knowledge of its laws, and a local knowledge of their respective districts, but will probably in all cases have been members, and may even at the very time be members, of the State legislature, where all the local information and interests of the State are assembled, and from whence they may easily be conveyed by a very few hands into the legislature of the United States.

. . . Taking each State by itself, its laws are the same, and its interests but little diversified. A few men, therefore, will possess all the knowledge requisite for a proper representation of them. Were the interests and affairs of each individual State perfectly simple and uniform, a knowledge of them in one part would involve a knowledge of them in every other, and the whole State might be competently represented by a single member taken from any part of it. On a comparison of the different States together, we find a great dissimilarity in their laws, and in many other circumstances connected with the objects of federal legislation, with all of which the federal representatives ought to have some acquaintance. Whilst a few representatives, therefore, from each State may bring with them a due knowledge of their own State, every representative will have much information to acquire concerning all the other States. The changes of time, as was formerly remarked, on the comparative situation of the different States, will have an assimilating effect.

James Madison
Federalist *Paper 57*
(Excerpt)

DISCUSSION QUESTIONS

1. What is the third Antifederalist charge against the House of Representatives?
2. How does Madison view the ruling class?
3. According to Madison, how do we prevent them from degeneracy in republican governments?
4. Would the Antifederalists have agreed with Madison's arguments concerning the electors of the House of Representatives? Why or why not?

5. Would Antifederalists have agreed with Madison's arguments concerning the "objects of popular choice"?
6. What is Madison's fifth argument in favor of the House of Representatives? Do you agree with his reasoning here? Why or why not?

The *third* charge against the House of Representatives is that it will be taken from that class of citizens which will have least sympathy with the mass of the people, and be most likely to aim at an ambitious sacrifice of the many to the aggrandizement of the few.

Of all the objections which have been framed against the federal Constitution, this is perhaps the most extraordinary. Whilst the objection itself is leveled against a pretended oligarchy, the principle of it strikes at the very root of republican government.

The aim of every political constitution is, or ought to be, first to obtain for rulers men who possess most wisdom to discern, and most virtue to pursue, the common good of the society; and in the next place, to take the most effectual precautions for keeping them virtuous whilst they continue to hold their public trust. The elective mode of obtaining rulers is the characteristic policy of republican government. The means relied on in this form of government for preventing their degeneracy are numerous and various. The most effectual one is such a limitation of the term of appointments as will maintain a proper responsibility to the people.

Let me now ask what circumstance there is in the constitution of the House of Representatives that violates the principles of republican government, or favors the elevation of the few on the ruins of the many? Let me ask whether every circumstance is not, on the contrary, strictly conformable to these principles, and scrupulously impartial to the rights and pretensions of every class and description of citizens?

Who are to be the electors of the federal representatives? Not the rich, more than the poor; not the learned, more than the ignorant; not the haughty heirs of distinguished names, more than the humble sons of obscurity and unpropitious fortune. The electors are to be the great body of the people of the United States. They are to be the same who exercise the right in every State of electing the corresponding branch of the legislature of the State.

Who are to be the objects of popular choice? Every citizen whose merit may recommend him to the esteem and confidence of his country. No qualification of wealth, of birth, of religious faith, or of civil profession is permitted to fetter the judgment or disappoint the inclination of the people.

If we consider the situation of the men on whom the free suffrages of their fellow-citizens may confer the representative trust, we shall find it involving every security which can be devised or desired for their fidelity to their constituents.

In the first place, as they will have been distinguished by the preference of their fellow-citizens, we are to presume that in general they will be somewhat distinguished also by those qualities which entitle them to it, and which promise a sincere and scrupulous regard to the nature of their engagements.

In the second place, they will enter into the public service under circumstances which cannot fail to produce a temporary affection at least to their constituents. There is in every breast a sensibility to marks of honor, of favor, of esteem, and of confidence, which, apart from all considerations of interests, is some pledge for grateful and benevolent returns. Ingratitude is a common topic of declamation against human nature; and it must be confessed that instances of it are but too frequent and flagrant, both in public and in private life. But the universal and extreme indignation which it inspires is itself a proof of the energy and prevalence of the contrary sentiment.

In the third place, those ties which bind the representative to his constituents are strengthened by motives of a more selfish nature. His pride and vanity attach him to a form of government which favors his pretensions and gives him a share in its honors and distinctions. Whatever hopes or projects might be entertained by a few aspiring characters, it must generally happen that a great proportion of the men deriving their advancement from their influence with the people would have more to hope from a preservation of the favor than from innovations in the government subversive of the authority of the people.

All these securities, however, would be found very insufficient without the restraint of frequent elections. Hence, in the fourth place, the House of Representatives is so constituted as to support in the members an habitual recollection of their dependence on the people. Before the sentiments impressed on their minds by the mode of their elevation can be effaced by the exercise of power, they will be compelled to anticipate the moment when their power is to cease, when their exercise of it is to be reviewed, and when they must descend to the level from which they were raised; there forever to remain unless a faithful discharge of their trust shall have established their title to a renewal of it.

I will add, as a fifth circumstance in the situation of the House of Representatives, restraining them from oppressive measures, that they can make no law which will not have its full operation on themselves and their friends, as well as on the great mass of the society. This has always been deemed one of the strongest bonds by which human policy can connect the rulers and the people together. It creates between them that communion of interests and sympathy of sentiments of which few governments have furnished examples; but without which every government degenerates into tyranny. If it be asked, what is to restrain the House of Representatives from making legal discriminations in favor of themselves and a particular class of the society? I answer: the genius of the whole system; the nature of just and constitutional laws; and, above all, the vigilant and manly spirit which actuates the people of America—a spirit which nourishes freedom, and in return is nourished by it.

If this spirit shall ever be so far debased as to tolerate a law not obligatory on the legislature, as well as on the people, the people will be prepared to tolerate anything but liberty.

Such will be the relation between the House of Representatives and their constituents. Duty, gratitude, interest, ambition itself, are the cords by which they will be bound to fidelity and sympathy with the great mass of the people. It is possible that these may all be insufficient to control the caprice and wickedness of men. But are they not all that government will admit, and that human prudence can devise? Are they not the genuine and the characteristic means by which republican government provides for the liberty and happiness of the people? Are they not the identical means on which every State government in the Union relies for the attainment of these important ends? What, then, are we to understand by the objection which this paper has combated? What are we to say to the men who profess the most flaming zeal for republican government, yet boldly impeach the fundamental principle of it; who pretend to be champions for the right and the capacity of the people to choose their own rulers, yet maintain that they will prefer those only who will immediately and infallibly betray the trust truth committed to them?

James Madison
Federalist *Paper 58*
(Excerpts)

DISCUSSION QUESTIONS

1. How does Madison respond to the fifth charge of the Antifederalists against the House of Representatives under the Constitution?
2. What is Madison's argument against the Antifederalist's desire for a larger House of Representatives?
3. What does this argument tell us about Madison's trust of people who are in groups?

The remaining charge against the House of Representatives, which I am to examine, is grounded on a supposition that the number of members will not be augmented from time to time, as the progress of population may demand. . . .

Within every successive term of ten years a census of inhabitants is to be repeated. The unequivocal objects of these regulations are, first, to readjust, from time to time, the apportionment of representatives to the number of inhabitants, under the single exception that each State shall have one representative at least; secondly, to augment the number of representatives at the same periods, under the sole limitation that the whole number shall not exceed one for every thirty thousand inhabitants. If we review the constitutions of the several States we shall find that some of them contain no determinate regulations on this subject, that others correspond pretty much on this point with the federal Constitution, and that the most effectual security in any of them is resolvable into a mere directory provision. . . .

I must be permitted to add on this subject as claiming, in my judgment, a very serious attention. It is that in all legislative assemblies the greater the number composing them may be, the fewer will be the men who will in fact direct their proceedings. In the first place, the more numerous any assembly may be, of whatever characters composed, the greater is known to be the ascendancy of passion over reason. In the next place, the larger the number, the greater will be the proportion of members of limited information and of weak capacities. Now, it is precisely on characters of this description that the eloquence and address of the few are known to act with all their force. In the ancient republics, where the whole body of the people assembled in person, a single orator, or an artful statesman, was generally seen to rule with as complete a sway as if a scepter had been placed in his single hand. On the same principle, the more multitudinous a representative assembly may be rendered, the more it will partake of the infirmities incident to collective meetings of the people. Ignorance will be the dupe of cunning, and passion the slave of sophistry and declamation. The people can never err more than in supposing that by multiplying their representatives beyond a certain limit they strengthen the barrier against the government of a few. Experience will forever admonish them that, on the contrary, *after securing a sufficient number for the purposes of safety, of local information, and of diffusive sympathy with the whole society*, they will counteract their own views by every addition to their representatives. The countenance of the government may become more democratic, but the soul that animates it will be more oligarchic. The machine will be enlarged, but the fewer, and often the more secret, will be the springs by which its motions are directed.

THE SENATE: ANTIFEDERALIST ARGUMENTS

"Brutus"
(Probably Robert Yates)
Essay XVI
(Excerpt)

DISCUSSION QUESTIONS

1. List Brutus' objections to the Senate as configured under the Constitution.
2. Why does Brutus equate the Senate with an aristocracy and the House of Representatives with democracy?
3. Why is a rotation-of-office provision so important to Brutus?
4. Are his observations relevant to our Senate and House today? Why or why not?

The term for which the senate are to be chosen, is in my judgment too long, and no provision being made for a rotation will, I conceive, be of dangerous consequence.

It is difficult to fix the precise period for which the senate should be chosen. It is a matter of opinion, and our sentiments on the matter must be formed, by attending to certain principles. Some of the duties which are to be performed by the senate, seem evidently to point out the propriety of their term of service being extended beyond the period of that of the assembly. Besides as they are designed to represent the aristocracy of the country, it seems fit they should possess more stability, and so continue a longer period than that branch who represent the democracy. The business of making treaties and some other which it will be proper to commit to the senate, requires that they should have experience, and therefore that they should remain some time in office to acquire it.—But still it is of equal importance that they should not be so long in office as to be likely to forget the hand that formed them, or be insensible of their interests. Men long in office are very apt to feel themselves independent and to form and pursue interests separate from those who appointed them. And this is more likely to be the case with the senate, as they will for the most part of the time be absent from the state they represent, and associate with such company as will possess very little of the feelings of the middling class of people. For it is to be remembered that there is to be a *federal city*, and the inhabitants of it will be the great and the mighty of the earth. For these reasons I would shorten the term of their service to four years. Six years is a long period for a man to be absent from his home, it would have a tendency to wean him from his constituents.

A rotation in the senate, would also in my opinion be of great use. It is probable that senators once chosen for a state will, as the system now stands, continue in office for life. The office will be honorable if not lucrative. The persons who occupy it will probably wish to continue in it, and therefore use all their influence and that of their friends to continue in office.—Their friends will be numerous and powerful, for they will have it in their power to confer great favors; besides it will before long be considered as disgraceful not to be re-elected. It will therefore be considered as a matter of delicacy to the character of the senator not to return him again.—Every body acquainted with public affairs knows how difficult it is to remove from office a person who is [has?] long been in it. It is seldom done except in cases of gross misconduct. It is rare that want of competent ability procures it. To prevent this inconvenience I conceive it would be wise to determine, that a senator should not be eligible after he had served for the period assigned by the constitution for a certain number of years; perhaps three would be sufficient. A farther benefit would be derived from such an arrangement; it would give opportunity to bring forward a greater number of men to serve their country, and would return those, who had served, to their state, and afford them the advantage of becoming better acquainted with the condition and politics of their constituents. It farther appears to me proper, that the legislatures should retain the right which they now hold under the confederation, of recalling their members. It seems an evident dictate of reason, that when a person authorises another to do a piece of business for him, he should retain the power to displace him, when he does not conduct according to his pleasure. This power in the state legislatures, under confederation, has not been exercised to the injury of the government, nor do I see any danger of its being so exercised under the new system. It may operate much to the public benefit.

THE SENATE: FEDERALIST ARGUMENTS

James Madison
Federalist *Paper 63*
(Excerpts)

DISCUSSION QUESTIONS

1. According to Madison, what are the problems associated with frequent elections and turnovers in representative bodies?
2. How will the Senate guard against these problems?
3. Antifederalists argued that the Senate would be a dangerous body because it was indirectly elected by the people and for a term of six years. How does Madison respond to this charge?

If I add, as a *sixth* defect, the want, in some important cases, of a due responsibility in the government to the people, arising from that frequency of elections which in other cases produces this responsibility. This remark will, perhaps, appear not only new, but paradoxical. It must nevertheless be acknowledged, when explained, to be as undeniable as it is important.

Responsibility, in order to be reasonable, must be limited to objects within the power of the responsible party, and in order to be effectual, must relate to operations of that power, of which a ready and proper judgment can be formed by the constituents. The objects of government may be divided into two general classes: the one depending on measures which have singly an immediate and sensible operation; the other depending on a succession of well-chosen and well-connected measures, which have a gradual and perhaps unobserved operation. The importance of the latter description to the collective and permanent welfare of every country needs no explanation. And yet it is evident that an assembly elected for so short a term as to be unable to provide more than one or two links in a chain of measures, on which the general welfare may essentially depend, ought not to be answerable for the final result any more than a steward or tenant, engaged for one year, could be justly made to answer for places or improvements which could not be accomplished in less than half a dozen years. Nor is it possible for the people to estimate the *share* of influence which their annual assemblies may respectively have on events resulting from the mixed transactions of several years. It is sufficiently difficult to preserve a personal responsibility in the members of a *numerous* body, for such acts of the body as have an immediate, detached, and palpable operation on its constituents.

The proper remedy for this defect must be an additional body in the legislative department, which, having sufficient permanency to provide for such objects as require a continued attention, and a train of measures, may be justly and effectually answerable for the attainment of those objects. . . .

The jealous adversary of the Constitution will probably content himself with repeating that a senate appointed not immediately by the people, and for the term of six years, must gradually acquire a dangerous pre-eminence in the government and finally transform it into a tyrannical aristocracy.

To this general answer the general reply ought to be sufficient, that liberty may be endangered by the abuses of liberty as well as by the abuses of power; that there are numerous instances of the former as well as of the latter; and that the former, rather than the latter, are apparently most to be apprehended by the United States. That a more particular reply may be given.

Before such a revolution can be effected, the Senate, it is to be observed, must in the first place corrupt itself; must next corrupt the State legislatures, must then corrupt the House of Representatives, and must finally corrupt the people at large. It is evident that the Senate must be first corrupted before it can attempt an establishment of tyranny. Without corrupting the State legislatures it cannot prosecute the attempt because the periodical change of members would otherwise regenerate the whole body. Without exerting the means of corruption with equal success on the House of Representatives, the opposition of that co-equal branch of the government would inevitably defeat the attempt; and without corrupting the people themselves, a succession of new representatives would speedily restore all things to their pristine order. Is there any man who can seriously persuade himself that the proposed Senate can, by any possible means within the compass of human address, arrive at the object of a lawless ambition through all these obstructions? . . .

Besides the conclusive evidence resulting from this assemblage of facts that the federal Senate will never be able to transform itself, by gradual usurpations, into an independent and aristocratic body, we are warranted in believing that if such a revolution should ever happen from causes which the foresight of man cannot guard against, the House of Representatives, with the people on their side, will at all times be able to bring back the Constitution to its primitive form and principles. Against the force of the immediate representatives of the people nothing will be able to maintain even the constitutional authority of the Senate, but such a display of enlightened policy, and attachment to the public good, as will divide with that branch of the legislature the affections and support of the entire body of the people themselves.

CONTEMPORARY INFLUENCES

John H. Fund
"Term Limitation: An Idea Whose Time Has Come"
(Excerpts)

DISCUSSION QUESTIONS

1. What pre-Constitutional evidence do we have that legislative and executive term limits were part of colonial life?
2. Why were mandatory term limits for legislators *not* included in the Constitution?
3. List and discuss the major objections to term limits.
4. What are the author's principal arguments in favor of term limits?

Term limitation is not a new idea, just one that the realities of modern politics have made necessary. Something must be done to help repair the damage caused by the "permanent government" of career politicians that now dominates the U.S. Congress and most state legislatures.

Over the years, term limits for Congress have been endorsed by the likes of Thomas Jefferson, Abraham Lincoln, Harry Truman, Dwight Eisenhower, and John F. Kennedy. Many political scientists have supported the idea since the 1951 constitutional amendment limiting presidents to two terms began creating an imbalance of power in favor of the legislative branch.

The promotion of turnover in the legislative branch predates the Constitution. The Pennsylvania constitution of 1776, the most radical constitution of the revolutionary era, had a strict limit of four years on legislative service. In 1777 the Continental Congress, the direct predecessor of today's Congress, allowed delegates to serve a maximum of three years.[1] The primary motivation was to ensure that legislators reflected the make-up and outlook of the citizenry they claimed to represent.

However, the first attempt to enforce the term limits met with understandable resistance from the incumbent delegates. In 1784 an attempt to deny certain delegates their seats led to a near-rebellion on the floor of the Continental Congress. James Monroe commented, "I never saw more indecent conduct in any assembly before."[2]

When the Constitution was debated in 1787, the sour experience with term limits in the Continental Congress led delegates to hesitate to propose them for the nation's new charter. But there is no doubt that encouraging turnover of legislators was popular at the Constitutional Convention. A proposal by James Madison

---

[1]Edmund C. Burnett, *The Continental Congress.* (New York: Macmillan, 1941), p. 250.

[2]*Ibid.*, p. 605

for three-year elections to the House of Representatives was attacked by Massachusetts delegate Elbridge Gerry as a form of "limited monarchy." Eventually, a proposal for two-year terms was adopted unanimously.[3]

Roger Sherman of Rhode Island summed up the feeling of many delegates when he commented that Congress should be made up of "citizen-legislators" who through the principle of rotation in office would "return home and mix with the people. By remaining at the seat of government, they would acquire the habits of the place, which might differ from those of their constituents."[4]

While mandatory term limits were not included in the final draft of the Constitution, many delegates assumed that voluntary term limits would be the norm. It was never thought that serving in Congress would become a career. And indeed, in the first House election after George Washington was elected president, 40 percent of incumbents [did not return] allaying fears of an entrenched "government of strangers."[5]

Objections to Term Limitation

Opponents of term limits raise several objections, both philosophical and practical, to the idea. Here are the most frequently cited, together with responses.

Won't term limits restrict the voters' choices at the ballot box? That implies that voters now have a choice at the ballot box. Common Cause reports that, as of September 30, of the 405 House incumbents seeking reelection this fall, 78 lack major-party opponents. Another 218 have opponents who have raised less that $25,000, and 86 have opponents who have raised more than $25,000 but less than half the amounts the incumbents have raised. Only 23 races are remotely competitive. People don't vote for someone they've never heard of, and skewed campaign laws mean that almost all the contributions to House races flow to incumbents.

Won't term limits disrupt the way congress works? Yes, and that is one of the best arguments for term limits. Congress has become an ossified structure that accomplishes little of value, wastes much, and impedes progress made by other sectors of society.

Limiting terms would limit abuse of the congressional seniority system by rotating power so it could not remain long enough with any one person for him or her to abuse it. Under the current seniority system, a handful of career-oriented congressmen chair key committees for years and control much of the legislative agenda, often preventing members from even voting on matters of national interest.

Term limitation would create a climate in which talented men and women from businesses and professions would want to run for Congress, since they would know they would reach a position of significant influence in a few short years instead of having to make a career of politics if they wanted to play a major role in congress.

---

[3]Charles O. Jones. *Every Second Year.* (Washington, D.C.: Brookings Institution, 1968), p. 4.

[4]*Ibid.*, p. 4.

[5]George F. Will, "Is 18 Years on the Hill Enough?" *Washington Post,* January 7, 1990, p. B7.

Isn't there a lot of turnover in Congress now? But turnover in Congress should not come chiefly because members choose to leave on their own timetable. In a democratic society, some turnover should be caused at the polls.

The reelection rate for members of the U.S. House seeking new terms, about 90 percent in the generation after World War II, soared closer to 100 percent in the 1980s. In 1988 only 6 of the 405 members lost their reelection bids, and 5 of those were under some sort of ethical cloud.[6]

Won't term limits deprive us of the services of valuable and experienced legislators? Some critics of term limits argue that even 12 years isn't enough time to become an expert legislator. But there are very few jobs that take that long to learn, and representing the public isn't one of them.

Besides, although term limits may shorten the congressional careers of the best members, those people will not have to withdraw from public life. Former congressmen will be available for service in the executive branch, in industry, in think tanks, and in the academy.

And what have our experienced lawmakers brought us? Certainly not innovative and bold public policy. Instead, they have brought us endemic compromise, institutional paralysis, and the Beltway mentality—a narrow, self-contained culture with addictive qualities. . . .

Wouldn't term limits merely shift power to staffers and lobbyists? Of course, any Capitol Hill observer knows that it's the most senior members who are most dependent on staff and lobbyists, not the hot-shot young freshmen. And there is nothing to prevent a reduction in the mushrooming growth of staffers from accompanying term limits [as happened in California . . .].

Critics also say that term limits might increase influence-peddling by putting pressure on members of Congress to curry favor with the interests that might reward them with future employment. But few members are likely to become lobbyists, because the turnover on Capitol Hill will quickly make their contacts obsolete and their influence limited.

The Case for Term Limitation

There are many practical benefits to be gained from imposing a limitation on terms.

Elections would be more competitive. Elections increasingly resemble sullen ratifications of the status quo, rather than competitive contests, and voter turnout is suffering as public interest in politics declines. Voter turnout in 1988 was 50 percent, down 3.4 percent from 1984. Only in Colorado, Nebraska, Nevada, and Utah was turnout up. In the last off-year election, voter turnout was only 37 percent, and it was only 27 percent in states without a contest for governor or U.S. Senator.[7] Voter turnout to select new occupants for open seats for governor, U.S. senator, or U.S.

---

[6]Bill McCollum, speech to the Conservative Political Action Conference, Washington, D.C., March 1, 1990.

[7]Hendrik Hertzberg, "Twelve Is Enough," *New Republic*, May 14, 1990, p. 22.

representative is often much higher than it is for races in which an entrenched incumbent is running.

Term limits would make ability more important than seniority. Term limits will encourage different people to run for office and pave the way for passage of other reforms—including rules to make legislative districts more competitive and reduce incumbent advantages in campaign financing.

Term limits would improve the quality of candidates. One often-overlooked problem with unlimited legislative terms is that they create a situation in which a legislator must remain in office for 15 or 20 years in order to have significant influence. Such a situation attracts those, such as California assemblyman Mike Roos, whose lifelong ambition was to be a politician. Roos, who is in his 13th year as the sole assemblyman for 300,000 citizens, studied public administration in college and never has had to earn a living in the private sector.

Term limits would counter the "culture of ruling." Studies by such respected organizations as the National Taxpayers Union and Citizens for a Sound Economy have found that the longer a legislator is in office, the greater the number of special interests he or she becomes associated with. It is also a common observation that the longer a legislator works in Washington, D.C., or in a state capital, the more self-important that person seems to become. Obviously, that is not always true. But it would defy human nature if it weren't true much of the time. In a capital city one is surrounded by individuals whose daily routine involves setting rules and regulations for the rest of society—a kind of "culture of ruling."

Charles R. Kessler
"Bad Housekeeping: The Case Against Congressional Term Limits"
(Excerpts)

DISCUSSION QUESTIONS

1. How has the modern appeal for Congressional term limits invoked the major themes of the Antifederalists?
2. What are the reasons for the decline of competitive Congressional elections in our modern era?
3. What are the author's arguments against term limits? How do these arguments reflect Federalist thinking?

This is not the first time in American history that a limit on the reeligibility of elected federal officials has been proposed. At the Constitutional Convention in 1787, whether the president ought to be eligible for reelection was extensively de-

Reprinted with permission of *Policy Review* (1990) and the Heritage Foundation.

bated, although always in close connection with the related questions of his term of office and mode of election. With the invention of the electoral college and with his term fixed at four years, it was thought to be productive of good effects and consistent with his independence from the legislature to allow the president to be eligible for reelection indefinitely; and so it remained until the 22nd Amendment was added to the Constitution. But what is less well known is that the Constitutional Convention also considered limitations on the reeligibility of the lower house of the legislature. The so-called Virginia Plan, introduced by Edmund Randolph, would have rendered members of the House ineligible for reelection for an unspecified period after their term's end. The period was never specified because the Convention expunged the limitation less than a month after it had been proposed.

Nevertheless, the question of limiting congressional terms lived on. It was taken up vigorously by the Anti-Federalists, the opponents of the new Constitution, who urged that "rotation in office" be imposed not so much on House members as on senators, whose small numbers, long term of office, and multifaceted powers made them suspiciously undemocratic. The Anti-Federalists built upon the legacy of the Articles of Confederation, which required that members of Congress rotate out after serving three one-year terms within any five-year period.

The current appeal for limits on congressional office-holding echoes the major themes of the Anti-Federalists 200 years ago. One of the most rigorous of the Constitution's critics, the writer who styled himself "The Federal Farmer," put it this way: "[I]n a government consisting of but a few members, elected for long periods, and far removed from the observation of the people, but few changes in the ordinary course of elections take place among the members; they become in some measure a fixed body, and often inattentive to the public good, callous, selfish, and the fountain of corruption." After serving several years in office, he continued, it will be expedient for a man "to return home, mix with the people, and reside some time with them; this will tend to reinstate him in the interests, feelings and views similar to theirs, and thereby confirm in him the essential qualifications of a legislator." Were the people watchful, they could recall him on their own and substitute a new representative at their discretion. But they are not sufficiently vigilant. As Patrick Henry warned at the Virginia ratifying convention, "Virtue will slumber. The wicked will be continually watching: Consequently you will be undone."

The Anti-Federalist arguments were rejected by the advocates of the new Constitution. However, it is only for the presidency that the authors of the most authoritative defense of the Constitution, *The Federalist*, give a detailed refutation of the scheme of rotation in office. In *The Federalist*'s view, there is "an excess of refinement" in the notion of preventing the people from returning to office men who had proved worthy of their confidence. The people are not fools, at least not all of the time, and they can be trusted to keep a reasonably sharp eye on their representatives. So far as history can confirm such a proposition, it seems to pronounce in favor of *The Federalist*. . . .

But . . . today's entrenched Congress is a product of the great changes in American politics that have occurred since the late 19th century, particularly the weakening of political parties and the great increase in the size and scope of the federal government. Serving in Congress has become a profession over the past 100 years.

Since the Second World War, reelection rates have been very high, averaging more than 90 percent; they have risen even further recently, approaching 100 percent in the last few elections. The political scientist David Mayhew identified the key to the incumbency problem as "the vanishing marginals," that is, the decline over the past 40 years in the number of marginal or competitive House districts. (A victory margin of 50 to 55 percent makes a district marginal, that is, capable of being won by a challenger.)

In his arresting book *Congress: Keystone of the Washington Establishment*, the political scientist Morris Fiorina puts his finger on the nub of the problem. During the 1960s, congressmen began to put an unprecedented emphasis on casework or constituent service and pork-barrel activities as a way to ensure their reelection. The new emphasis was made possible precisely by "big government," the federal government's expansion of authority over state and local affairs that began dramatically with the New Deal and accelerated during the Great Society. As the federal bureaucracy expanded, more and more citizens found themselves dealing directly with federal agencies—the Social Security Administration, the Veterans Administration, the Equal Employment Opportunity Commission, the Environmental Protection Agency, and so on. To penetrate the mysteries of the administrative state, to find a friendly face amid the "faceless" bureaucrats and a helping hand among so many seemingly determined to do injustice in particular cases, citizens began increasingly to turn to their congressman for succor.

If this is true, the congressman's expertise is a peculiar sort, involving as it does interceding with civil servants (and appointed officials) in the spirit of personal, particularistic relations, not the spirit of impersonal rule following associated with the civil service. Nonetheless, he is expected to keep benefits and services issuing to the district, just as a nonpartisan city manager is expected to keep the streets clean and the sewers flowing. And to the extent that ombudsmanship is corollary of bureaucracy (as it seems to be, at least in democratic governments), his casework partakes of the spirit of administration rather than of political representation.

Given the . . . nature of the problem with Congress, . . . it is apparent that limiting congressional terms to 12 years will do little or nothing to remedy the situation. Any new faces that are brought to Washington as the result of such an amendment will find themselves up against the same old incentives. They will still be eligible for reelection five times. How will they ensure their continued political prosperity without seeing to constituents' administrative needs? If anything, these new congressmen will find themselves confronting bureaucrats rendered more powerful by the representatives' own ignorance of the bureaucracy; for in the administrative state, knowledge is power. It is likely, therefore, that the new congressmen will initially be at a disadvantage relative to the agencies. To counter this they will seek staff members and advisers who are veterans of the Hill, and perhaps larger and more district-oriented staffs to help ward off challengers who would try to take advantage of their inexperience. Is it wise to increase the already expansive power of bureaucrats and congressional staff for the sake of a new congressman in the district every half-generation or so?

The proposed limitation on congressional terms would also have most of the disadvantages of the old schemes of rotation in office that were criticized by the Federalists. Consider these points made by Alexander Hamilton in *Federalist* No. 72 (concerning rotation in the presidency, but still relevant to rotation in Congress). In the first place, setting a limit on office-holding "would be a diminution of the inducements to good behavior." By allowing indefinite reeligibility, political men will be encouraged to make their interest coincide with their duty, and to undertake "extensive and arduous enterprises for the public benefit" because they will be around to reap the consequences. Second, term limits would be a temptation to "sordid views" and "peculation." As Gouverneur Morris put it at the Constitutional Convention, term limits say to the official, "make hay while the sun shines." Nor does a long term of eligibility (12 years in this case) remove the difficulty. No one will know better than the present incumbent how difficult it will be to defeat the future incumbent. So the limits of his career will always be visible to him, as will the temptation to "make hay" as early as possible.

A third disadvantage of term limits is that they could deprive the country of the experience and wisdom gained by an incumbent, perhaps just when that experience is needed most. This is particularly true for senators, whose terms would be limited even though Senate races are frequently quite competitive (recall 1980 and 1986) and that the Senate was precisely the branch of the legislature in which the Framers sought stability, the child of long service.

8

The Executive Branch

When considering the administrative problems that challenged the framers of the young republic, we are reminded of a particular dilemma that, at least in retrospect, seems to have caught the founding generation, both "Federalist" and "Antifederalist," in a contradiction. Upon achieving victory in the war against the autocracy and perceived tyranny of Crown and Parliament, the first republic established a frame of government which deliberately eschewed institutions that represented centralized power or structural hierarchy. This seemed quite consonant with the ideals of 1776 as announced by Jefferson and Paine and was thereby cast in a fairly democratic hue by the standards of the period. Noticeably absent from the social compact of the first republic, *The Articles of Confederation and Perpetual Union,* is the clear positing of executive authority in a single office or separate branch of government. Nothing like the centralized power of a monarch or duke or the administrative power of certain colonial governors is to be found in the *Articles of Confederation,* and executive authority was treated as an extension of legislative power, such as it was.[1] This was a reflection of the distrust of centralized and hierarchical power stemming from general fears of powerful government experienced by the erstwhile colonists since the mid-1760s and still tangible within their memory. However, as problems of a new and vulnerable nation recently thrust into a world arena populated by fearsome powers without and distracted by confusion and doubts from within, the necessity for more "energetic" and "purposive" government became apparent to at least some of the republic's more notable citizens.

Grappling between the ideal of democratic self-government that had become a part of the pre-revolutionary mind and the perceived necessity for stronger and more efficient governance in order to cope with internal division and the menace of external powers, many of the individuals behind the framing of the "Second American Republic" developed the institution of an independent executive as a necessary element within the Constitutional scheme of dispersed powers. The American Presidency is the result of an attempt to resolve this dilemma. It is the offspring of a union between the understandable fear of absolutism and the equally sobering fear of disorder and vulnerability, and from this issue the American republic has come to know still another paradox of modern democracy.

---

[1]"The united states in congress assembled shall have authority to appoint a committee to sit in the recess of congress, . . . to consist of one delegate from each state; and to . . . appoint one of their number to preside, . . ." *Articles of Confederation,* Article #IX.

Numerous problems of a more fundamental nature concerned the supporters, skeptics, and opponents of the newly proposed Constitution. Ideas and attitudes formed around essential political notions such as individual liberty, political rights, civic virtue, "human nature," national destiny, and the proper scope and function of republican government were the most pressing, provocative, and demanding issues. Questions revolving around the structure and function of the executive branch were usually raised within the larger context of these more essential problems, and thus arguments regarding the executive branch, especially as treated by the opponents of the Constitution, were usually blended with these more fundamental issues. Critics of the Constitution, as in many other instances, did not speak with one voice in response to the executive branch as proposed by the framers and defended by the Federalists, most notably in the Publius articles, more commonly known as the *Federalist* Papers. The *Federalist* Papers provided a much more detailed and cohesive argument in favor of the single, independent executive in contrast to the multivariegated arguments of the scattered opposition.

In the writings of those "Antifederalists" who directly opposed the framers of the new Constitution as well as the authors of the *Federalist* Papers, we find a healthy but often disunited plurality of voices. Some critics of the newly proposed Constitution either accepted the need for an independent executive as conceived by the Philadelphia convention or simply remained silent on the issue. Others accepted the idea of an independent executive but chose to argue against certain details such as term of office or the fear that the President might become a minion of an aristocratic Senate. Still others desired to re-examine the process of selection—some advocating direct election, others favoring investing the power of direct selection in the several states. Suggestions regarding the structure of the executive branch included the idea of a plural executive, usually linked to the notion of sectional representation or a Constitutionally institutionalized "executive council" that would assist a single chief administrator. Edmund Randolph, for example, argued that "unity in the executive" would be the "foetus of monarchy," and he proposed an independent executive consisting of three equal members.[2] This proposition was resisted by James Wilson, who dismissed Randolph's fears as unfounded and advocated a single and independent magistrate.[3] Alexander Hamilton was particularly convinced that the executive should combine both unity and strength, and he devoted a considerable amount of his own energies to forward this notion. Furthermore, although there was opposition to the executive as conceived by Wilson, Hamilton, and James Madison, several other parts of the Constitution drew much more direct, sustained attention and informed criticism. Additionally, the underlying assumption that Washington was to serve as the first President allayed the fears of many skeptics, as Washington enjoyed the respect of many individuals on all sides of the ratification controversy, and the rumor of his participation in the first administration was generally regarded as an encouraging prospect.

Nonetheless, passages in the literature of the Antifederalists excoriate the proposed executive. Some of the more interesting and more prescient criticisms were the products of those who feared the very idea of a powerful and independent executive, detecting the faint odor of absolutism in the air as they scanned problematic passages in the Constitution such as the "presentment clause" (that grants the President the power to approve or disapprove legislation, otherwise known as the "power of the

[2]James Madison, *Notes of Debates in the Federal Convention of 1787* (Athens, Ohio: Ohio State University Press, 1966), p. 46.

[3]Ibid., pp. 45–49.

negative" or "veto") and the "commander-in-chief" clause that attaches a martial property to the executive branch which appears concurrent, and thereby potentially conflictual, with the Congressional authority to "declare" war. Patrick Henry issued a sharp and eloquent warning against this "squinting toward monarchy" and reminded his fellow citizens that the ideals of liberty, understood by many as the animating principle of the revolution, can never be forwarded by governments that seek to become more "energetic" or that invest too much esteem in power and authority at the expense of "milder forms" of governance. Absent the rhetorical flourish of the passionate Henry, the Cato essays are nonetheless particularly valuable, as they are directly related to the arguments of Hamilton (Publius). Essays by "An Old Whig" and "The Impartial Examiner" provide further examples of the concerns that the Antifederalists raised as they extrapolated upon the potential uses and abuses of this new magistracy. The article by Raymond Wrabley both serves as an excellent summary of Antifederalist positions and forms a solid bridge between this earlier challenge to Hamilton's energetic executive and modern criticisms of the expanding Presidency.

Appeals such as these are deflated to an extent by the acts of certain Presidents that actually galvanized the democratic spirit more effectively than their contemporaries in the other two branches. Franklin Roosevelt's economic policies, Truman's desegregation of the armed services, and Lyndon Johnson's pivotal leadership in the struggle for civil rights legislation serve as recent examples of the democratizing potential of Presidential leadership, and any critic of the American Presidency must deal with examples such as these wherein a chief executive did act as first citizen and not as imperator. Owing to examples such as these and against their more "democratic" sensibilities, Americans have indeed become attached to the idea of a strong, active President. The examples of Lincoln, Washington, Jackson, Jefferson, Wilson, and both Roosevelts are often cited by scholars and citizens alike as admirable guides toward democratic leadership. In some instances, such as in the arguments of Hamilton and Fisher Ames, advocates of strength in the executive are driven by a distrust of democratic processes and fears of ochlocracy; in other cases, the office of the President is considered to be the most visible and legitmate forum for the popular "national constituency"—the President as the embodiment of the national will. This was the position advanced by Woodrow Wilson during the early part of this century and carried forward by most of his successors, particularly since Franklin Roosevelt. We can detect the further development and support of this doctrine in the numerous commentaries by Richard Neustadt and most persuasively through the Kennedy campaign speech included in this collection. Clinton Rossiter once referred to the Presidency as an "office of freedom," perhaps one of the more glowing definitions of executive authority.[4] Embraced by autocrats and democrats alike, the American Presidency is often most esteemed when it is strong and forthright in the face of crisis, as demonstrated by the examples of Jefferson (perhaps ironically), Lincoln, Franklin Roosevelt, Truman, and Kennedy himself during the Cuban missile crisis.

All this notwithstanding, the office of the Presidency has in many ways evolved into an institution that often exhibits autocratic dimensions, from the trappings of state authority to the extensive and unforeseen waxing of evolved powers, unforeseen at least by most of the Constitution's advocates, but not by a few Antifederalist champions of the principles of minimal government and republican responsibility who ques-

---

[4]Clinton Rossiter, *The American Presidency* (New York: Harcourt, Brace, Jovanovich, 1956, pp. 138–164.

tioned the creation of a new type of executive power. Although the American Presidency has accumulated in strength and appreciated in value during the course of this century, it has been and still remains a point of some controversy. Nineteenth century critics approached it from a diverse cluster of perspectives, some arguing that it would eventually prove to be the seed of monarchy, as Patrick Henry, Edmund Randolph, and others had presaged. Others, such as James Bryce, claimed that it was a magnet for mediocrity in government, and, when compared with the leadership of the Continent, it was found wanting in both the power of office and the ability to attract talented individuals.[5] Proposals to reform the office are still raised now and again. One of the more interesting comes from John Calhoun, the antebellum Southern champion who was simultaneously driven by a mind inclined toward political inquiry and a passionate, albeit shortsighted, devotion to the interest of a strong, traditional South. Calhoun advocated the institution of a "dual executive," one to represent the interest of the increasingly more powerful North, the other to preserve the parity of the ebbing South. Although this proposal was driven primarily by Calhoun's desire to redistribute influence away from the North and thereby fortifying institutions either based upon or supportive of slavery, the idea is reminiscent of earlier, more "democratic" governmental schemes that included the component of a "plural executive." Calhoun's arguments are not presented here in this collection, but interested students might find his comments on the executive branch provocative and worthy of examination.[6]

Modern critics of the executive branch, while less exotic, are quite capable of answering those supporters who treat the office of the Presidency as the lodestar of American politics and government. This is particularly evident in the tempered criticisms of Theodore Lowi and the more trenchant comments of Francis Hutchins, provided below. Upon reading such modern interpretations of the executive branch, much of what is argued in the Antifederalist contribution to the ratification debate still resonates as we reflect upon the modern political Colossus that is the American Presidency.

THE CONSTITUTION (EXCERPTS)

Art. II

Sec. 1. The executive Power shall be vested in a President of the United States of America. He shall hold his Office during the Term of four Years, and, together with the Vice President, chosen for the same Term, be elected, as follows:

Each State shall appoint, in such Manner as the Legislature thereof may direct, a Number of Electors, equal to the whole Number of Senators and Representatives to which the state may be entitled in the Congress: but no Senator or Representative, or Person holding an Office of Trust or Profit under the United States, shall be appointed an Elector.

The Electors shall meet in their respective States, and vote by Ballot for two Persons, of whom one at least shall not be an Inhabitant of the same State

[5]James Bryce, *The American Commonwealth*, ed. by L. Hacker (New York: G. P. Putnam's Sons, 1959), pp. 27–34.

[6]John C. Calhoun, *A Disquisition on Government and Selections from the Discourse* (New York: Macmillan/American Heritage, 1988),, pp. 100–104.

with themselves. And they shall make a List of all the Persons voted for, and of the Number of Votes for each; which List they shall sign and certify, and transmit sealed to the Seat of the Government of the United States, directed to the President of the Senate. The President of the Senate shall, in the Presence of the Senate and House of Representatives, open all the Certifi-cates, and the Votes shall then be counted. The Person having the greatest Number of Votes shall be the President, if such Number be a Majority of the whole number of Electors appointed; and if there be more than one who have such Majority, and have an equal Number of Votes, then the House of Representatives shall immediately chose by Ballot one of them for President; and if no person have a Majority, then from the five highest on the List the said House shall in like Manner chuse the President. But in chusing the President, the Votes shall be taken by States, the Representation from each state having one Vote; A quorum for this Purpose shall consist of a Member or Members from two thirds of the States, and a Majority of all the States shall be necessary to a Choice. In every Case, after the choice of the President, the Person having the greatest Number of Votes of the electors shall be the Vice President. But if there should remain two or more who have equal Votes, the Senate shall chuse from them by Ballot the Vice President.

The Congress may determine the Time of chusing the Electors, and the Day on which they shall give their Votes; which Day shall be the same throughout the United States.

No Person except a natural born Citizen, or a Citizen of the United States, at the time of the Adoption of this Constitution, shall be eligible to the Office of President; neither shall any Person be eligible to that Office who shall not have attained to the Age of thirty five Years, and been fourteen Years a Resident within the United States.

In Case of the Removal of the President from Office, or of his Death, Resignation, or Inability to discharge the Powers and Duties of the said Office, the Same shall devolve on the Vice President, and the congress may by Law provide for the Case of Removal, Death, Resignation or Inability, both of the President and Vice President, declaring what Officer shall then act as President, and such Officer shall act accordingly, until the Disability be removed, or a President shall be elected.

The President shall, at stated Times, receive for his Services, a Compensation, which shall neither be encreased nor diminished during the Period for which he shall have been elected, and he shall not receive within that Period any other Emolument from the United States, or any of them.

Before he enter on the Execution of his Office, he shall take the following Oath or Affirmation:—"I do solemnly swear (or affirm) that I will faithfully execute the Office of President of the United States, and will to the best of my Ability, preserve, protect and defend the Constitution of the United States."

Sec. 2. The President shall be Commander in Chief of the Army and Navy of the United States, and of the Militia of the several States, when called into the actual Service of the United States; he may require the Opinion, in writing, of the principal Officer in each of the executive Departments, upon any Subject relating to the Duties of their respective Offices, and he shall have Power to grant Reprieves and Pardons for Offences against the United States, except in Cases of Impeachment.

He shall have Power, by and with the

Advice and Consent of the Senate, to make Treaties, provided two thirds of the Senators present concur; and he shall nominate, and by and with the Advice and Consent of the Senate, shall appoint Ambassadors, other public Ministers and Consuls, Judges of the supreme Court, and all other Officers of the United States, whose Appointments are not herein otherwise provided for, and which shall be established by Law: but the Congress may by Law vest the Appointment of such inferior Officers, as they think proper, in the President alone, in the Courts of Law, or in the Heads of Departments.

The President shall have Power to fill up all Vacancies that may happen during the Recess of the Senate, by granting Commissions which shall expire at the End of their next Session.

Sec. 3. He shall from time to time give to the Congress Information of the State of the Union, and recommend to their Consideration such Measures as he shall judge necessary and expedient; he may, on extraordinary Occasions, convene both Houses, or either of them, and in Case of Disagreement between them, with Respect to the Time of Adjournment, he may adjourn them to such Time as he shall think proper; he shall receive Ambassadors and other public Ministers; he shall take Care that the Laws be faithfully executed, and shall Commission all the Officers of the United States.

Sec. 4. The President, Vice President and all civil Officers of the United States, shall be removed from Office on Impeachment for, and conviction of, Treason, Bribery, or other high Crimes and Misdemeanors.

Art. XII

Sept. 25, 1804

The Electors shall meet in their respective states, and vote by ballot for President and Vice-President, one of whom, at least, shall not be an inhabitant of the same state with themselves; they shall name in their ballots the person voted for as President, and in distinct ballots the person voted for as Vice-president, and they shall make distinct lists of all persons voted for as President, and of all persons voted for as vice-President, and of the number of votes for each, which lists they shall sign and certify, and transmit sealed to the seat of the government of the United States, directed to the President of the Senate;—The President of the Senate shall, in the presence of the Senate and House of Representatives, open all the certificates and the votes shall then be counted;–The person having the greatest number of votes for President, shall be the President, if such number be a majority of the whole number of Electors appointed; and if no person have such majority, then from the persons having the highest numbers not exceeding three on the list of those voted for as President, the House of Representatives shall choose immediately, by ballot, the President. But in choosing the President, the votes shall be taken by states, the representation from each state having one vote; a quorum for this purpose shall consist of a member or members from two-thirds of the states, and a majority of all the states shall be necessary to a choice. And if the House of Representatives shall not choose a President whenever the right of choice shall devolve upon them, before the fourth day of March next following, then the Vice-President shall act as President, as in the case of the death or other constitutional disability of the President.—The person having the greatest number of votes as Vice-President, shall be the Vice-President, if such number be a majority of the whole number of Electors appointed, and if no person have a majority, then from the two highest numbers on the list, the Senate shall choose the Vice-President; a quorum for the purpose shall consist of two-thirds of the whole number of Senators, and a majority of the whole number shall be necessary to a choice. But no person constitutionally ineligible to the office of President shall be eligible to that of Vice-President of the United States.

Art. XX

February 6, 1933

Sec. 1. The terms of the President and Vice-President shall end at noon on the twentieth day of January, and the terms of Senators and Representatives at noon on the third day of January, of the years in which such terms would have ended if this article had not been ratified; and the terms of their successors shall then begin.

Sec. 2. The Congress shall assemble at least once in every year, and such meeting shall begin at noon on the third day of January, unless they shall by law appoint a different day.

Sec. 3. If, at the time fixed for the beginning of the term of the President, the President-elect shall have died, the Vice-President-elect shall become President. If a President shall not have been chosen before the time fixed for the beginning of his term, or if the President-elect shall have failed to qualify, then the Vice-President-elect shall act as President until a President shall have qualified; and the Congress may by law provide for the case wherein neither a President-elect nor a Vice-President-elect shall have qualified, declaring who shall then act as President, or the manner in which one who is to act shall be selected, and such person shall act accordingly until a President or Vice-President shall have qualified.

Sec. 4. The Congress may by law provide for the case of the death of any of the persons from whom the House of Representatives may choose a President whenever the right of choice shall have devolved upon them, and for the case of the death of any of the persons from whom the Senate may choose a Vice-President whenever the right of choice shall have devolved upon them.

Sec. 5. Sections 1 and 2 shall take effect on the 15th day of October following the ratification of this article.

Sec. 6. This article shall be inoperative unless it shall have been ratified as an amendment to the Constitution by the legislatures of three-fourths of the several states within seven years from the date of its submission.

Art. XXII

February 26, 1951

Sec. 1. No person shall be elected to the office of the President more than twice, and no person who has held the office of President, or acted as President for more than two years of a term to which some other person was elected President shall be elected to the office of the President more than once. But this Article shall not apply to any person holding the office of President when this Article was proposed by the Congress, and shall not prevent any person who may be holding the office of President, or acting as President, during the term within which this Article becomes operative from holding the office of President or acting as President during the remainder of such term.

Article XXV

February 23, 1967

Sec. 1. In case of the removal of the President from office or his death or resignation, the Vice-President shall become President.

Sec. 2. Whenever there is a vacancy in the office of the Vice-President, the President shall nominate a Vice-President who shall take the office upon confirmation by a majority vote of both houses of Congress.

Sec. 3. Whenever the President transmits to the President pro tempore of the Senate and the Speaker of the House of Representatives his written declaration that he is unable to discharge the powers and duties of his office, and until he transmits to them a written declaration to the contrary, such powers and duties shall be discharged by the Vice-President as Acting President.

Sec. 4. Whenever the Vice-President and a majority of either the principal officers of the executive departments, or of such other body as Congress may by law provide, transmit to the President pro tempore of the Senate and the Speaker of the House of Representatives their written declaration that the President is unable to discharge the powers and duties of his office, the Vice-President shall immediately assume the powers and duties of the office as Acting President.

Thereafter, when the President transmits to the President pro tempore of the Senate and the Speaker of the House of Representatives his written declaration than no inability exists, he shall resume the powers and duties of his office unless the Vice-President and a majority of either the principal officers of the executive department, or of such other body as Congress may by law provide, transmit within four days to the President pro tempore of the Senate and the Speaker of the House of Representatives their written declaration that the President is unable to discharge the powers and duties of his office. Thereupon Congress shall decide the issue, assembling within 48 hours for that purpose if not in session. If the Congress, within 21 days after receipt of the latter written declaration, or, if Congress is not in session, within 21 days after Congress is required to assemble, determines by two-thirds vote of both houses that the President is unable to discharge the powers and duties of his office, the Vice-President shall continue to discharge the same as Acting President; otherwise, the President shall resume the powers and duties of his office.

ANTIFEDERALIST ARGUMENTS

"Cato"
(Probably George Clinton)
Essays IV and V
(Excerpts)

DISCUSSION QUESTION

What are the specific objections to the executive branch raised by Cato in the following excerpts? Upon reading the Constitution as it was initially cast, are his objections valid? Upon examining the Presidency today, are Cato's concerns valid?

IV

To the Citizens of the State of New-York.

Admitting, however, that the vast extent of America, together with the various other reasons which I offered you in my last number, against the practicability of the just exercise of the new government are insufficient to convince you; still it is an undeniable truth, that its several parts are either possessed of principles, which you have heretofore considered as ruinous, and that others are omitted which you have established as fundamental to your political security, and must in their operation, I will venture to assert—fetter your tongues and minds, enchain your bodies, and ultimately extinguish all that is great and noble in man.

In pursuance of my plan, I shall begin with observations on the executive branch of this new system; and though it is not the first in order, as arranged therein, yet being the *chief,* is perhaps entitled by the rules of rank to the first consideration. The executive power as described in the 2d article, consists of a president and vice-president, who are to hold their offices *during* the term of four years; the same article has marked the manner and time of their election, and established the qualifications of the president; it also provides against the removal, death, or inability of the president and vice-president—regulates the salary of the president, delineates his duties and powers; and lastly, declares the causes for which the president and vice-president shall be removed from office.

Notwithstanding the great learning and abilities of the gentlemen who composed the convention, it may be here remarked with deference, that the construction of the first paragraph of the first section of the second article, is vague and inexplicit, and leaves the mind in doubt, as to the election of a president and vice-president, after the expiration of the election for the first term of four years—in every other case, the election of these great officers is expressly provided for; but there is no explicit provision for their election in case of the expiration of their offices, subsequent to the election which is to set this political machine in motion—no certain and express terms as in your state constitution, that *statedly* once in every four years, and as often as these offices shall become vacant, by expiration or otherwise, as is therein expressed, an election shall be held as follows, etc.—this inexplicitness perhaps may lead to an establishment for life.

It is remarked by Montesquieu, in treating of republics, that *in all magistracies, the greatness of the power must be compensated by the brevity of the duration; and that a longer time than a year, would be dangerous.* It is therefore obvious to the least intelligent mind, to account why, great power in the hands of a magistrate, and that power connected, with a considerable duration, may be dangerous to the liberties of a republic—the deposit of vast trusts in the hands of a single magistrate, enables him in their exercise, to create a numerous train of dependants—this tempts his *ambition,* which in a republican magistrate is also remarked, *to be pernicious* and the duration of his office for any considerable time favours his views, gives him the means and time to perfect and execute his designs—*he therefore fancies that he may be great and glorious by oppressing his fellow citizens, and raising himself to permanent grandeur on the ruins of his country.*—And here it may be necessary to compare the vast and important powers of the president, together with his continuance in office with the foregoing doctrine—his eminent magisterial situation will attach many adherents to him, and he will be surrounded by expectants and courtiers—his power of nomination and influence on all appointments—the strong posts in each state comprised within his superintendance, and garrisoned by troops under his direction—his controul over the army, militia, and navy—the unrestrained power of granting pardons for treason, which may be used to screen from punishment, those whom he had secretly instigated to commit the crime, and thereby prevent a discovery of his own guilt—his duration in office for four years: these, and various other principles evidently prove the truth of the position—that if the president is possessed of ambition, he has power and time sufficient to ruin his country.

Though the president, during the sitting of the legislature, is assisted by the senate, yet he is without a constitutional council in their recess—he will therefore be unsupported by proper information and advice, and will generally be directed by minions and favorites, or a council of state will grow out of the principal officers of the great departments, the most dangerous council in a free country.

The ten miles square, which is to become the seat of government, will of course be the place of residence for the president and the great officers of state—the same observations of a great man will apply to the court of a president possessing the powers of a monarch, that is observed of that of a monarch—*ambition with idleness—baseness with pride—the thirst of riches without labour—aversion to truth—flattery—treason—perfidy—violation of engagements—contempt of civil duties—hope from the magistrate's weakness; but above all, the perpetual ridicule of virtue*—these, he remarks, are the characteristics by which the courts in all ages have been distinguished.

The language and the manners of this court will be what distinguishes them from the rest of the community, not what assimilates them to it, and in being remarked for a behaviour that shews they are not *meanly born*, and in adulation to people of fortune and power. . . . Every American whig, not long since, bore his emphatic testimony against a monarchical government, though limited, because of the dangerous inequality that it created among citizens as relative to their rights and property; and wherein does this president, invested with his powers and prerogatives, essentially differ from the king of Great-Britain (save as to name, the creation of nobility and some immaterial incidents, the offspring of absurdity and locality).[T]he direct prerogatives of the president, as springing from his political character, are among the following:—It is necessary, in order to distinguish him from the rest of the community, and enable him to keep, and maintain his court, that the compensation for his services; or in other words, his revenue should be such as to enable him to appear with the splendor of a prince; he has the power of receiving embassadors from, and a great influence on their appointments to foreign courts; as also to make treaties, leagues, and alliances with foreign states, assisted by the senate, which when made, become the supreme law of the land: he is a constituent part of the legislative power; for every bill which shall pass the house of representatives and senate, is to be presented to him for approbation; if he approves of it, he is to sign it, if he disapproves, he is to return it with objections, which in many cases will amount to a compleat negative; and in this view he will have a great share in the power of making peace, coining money, etc. and all the various objects of legislation, expressed or implied in this Constitution: for though it may be asserted that the king of Great-Britain has the express power of making peace or war, yet he never thinks it prudent so to do without the advice of his parliament from whom he is to derive his support, and therefore these powers, in both president and king, are substantially the same: he is the generalissimo of the nation, and of course, has the command and controul of the army, navy and militia; he is the general conservator of the peace of the union—he may pardon all offences, except in cases of impeachment, and the principal fountain of all offices and employments. Will not the exercise of these powers therefore tend either to the establishment of a vile and arbitrary aristocracy, or monarchy? The safety of the people in a republic depends on the share or proportion they have in the government; but experience ought to teach you, that when a man is at the head of an elective government invested with great powers, and interested in his re-election, in what circle appointments will be made; by which means *an imperfect aristocracy* bordering on monarchy may be established.

You must, however, my countrymen, beware, that the advocates of this new system do not deceive you, by a fallacious resemblance between it and your own state government, which you so much prize; and if you examine, you will perceive that the chief magistrate of this state, is your immediate choice, controuled and checked by a just and full representation of the people, divested of the prerogative of influencing war and peace, making treaties, receiving and sending embassies, and commanding standing armies and navies, which belong to the power of the confederation, and will be convinced that this government is no more like a true picture of your own, than an Angel of darkness resembles an Angel of light.

CATO

V

To the Citizens of the State of New-York.

In my last number I endeavored to prove that the language of the article relative to the establishment of the executive of this new government was vague and inexplicit, that the great powers of the President, connected with his duration in office would lead to oppression and ruin. That he would be governed by favorites and flatterers, or that a dangerous council would be collected from the great officers of state;—that the ten miles square, if the remarks of one of the wisest men, drawn from the experience of mankind, may be credited, would be the asylum of the base, idle, avaricious and ambitious, and that the court would possess a language and manners different from yours; that a vice-president is as unnecessary, as he is dangerous in his influence—that the president cannot represent you because he is not of your own immediate choice, that if you adopt this government, you will incline to an arbitrary and odious aristocracy or monarchy—that the president possessed of the power, given him by this frame of government differs but very immaterially from the establishment of monarchy in Great Britain, and I warned you to beware of the fallacious resemblance that is held out to you by the advocates of this new system between it and your own state governments.

And here I cannot help remarking, that inexplicitness seems to pervade this whole political fabric: certainty in political compacts, which Mr. Coke calls *the mother and nurse of repose and quietness*, the want of which induced men to engage in political society, has ever been held by a wise and free people as essential to their security; as, on the one hand it fixes barriers which the ambitious and tyrannically disposed magistrate dare not overleap, and on the other, becomes a wall of safety to the community—otherwise stipulations between the governors and governed are nugatory; and you might as well deposit the important powers of legislation and execution in one or a few and permit them to govern according to their disposition and will; but the world is too full of examples, which prove that *to live by one man's will became the cause of all men's misery*. Before the existence of express political compacts it was reasonably implied that the magistrate should govern with wisdom and justice, but mere implication was too feeble to restrain the unbridled ambition of a bad man, or afford security against negligence, cruelty, or any other defect of mind. It is alledged that the opinions and manners of the people of America, are capable to resist and prevent an extension of prerogative or oppression; but you must recollect that opinion and manners are mutable, and may not always be a permanent obstruction against the encroachments of government; that the progress of a commercial society begets luxury, the parent of inequality, the foe to virtue, and the enemy to restraint; and that ambition and voluptuousness aided by flattery, will teach magistrates, where limits are not explicitly fixed to have separate and distinct interests from the people, besides it will not be denied that government assimilates the manners and opinions of the community to it. Therefore, a general presumption that rulers will govern well is not a sufficient security.— . . .

. . . —It is a duty you owe likewise to your own reputation, for you have a great name to lose; you are characterised as cautious, prudent and jealous in politics; whence is it therefore, that you are about to precipitate yourselves into a sea of uncertainty, and adopt a system so vague, and which has discarded so many of your valuable rights:—Is it because you do not believe that an American can be a tyrant? If this be the case you rest on a weak basis[;] Americans are like other men in similar situations, when the manners and opinions of the community are changed by the causes I mentioned before, and your political compact inexplicit, your posterity will find that great power connected with ambition, luxury, and flattery, will as readily produce a Caesar, Caligula, Nero, and Domitian in America, as the same causes did in the Roman empire.

CATO

Patrick Henry
Speech
June 5 and June 9, 1788
(Excerpts)

DISCUSSION QUESTIONS

1. Why does Henry argue that the Presidency "squints toward monarchy"? Is this conclusion fair?
2. Develop an interpretation of Henry's political philosophy based upon your reading of the excerpt below. From your assessment of Henry, can we say that Henry is a fair representative of the Antifederalist hue? Elaborate.
3. Who is closer to the "Spirit of '76," Henry or Hamilton? (see below)

This Constitution is said to have beautiful features; but when I come to examine these features, Sir, they appear to me horridly frightful: Among other deformities, it has an awful squinting; it squints towards monarchy: And does not this raise indignation in the breast of every American? Your President may easily become King: Your Senate is so imperfectly constructed that your dearest rights may be sacrificed by what may be a small minority; and a very small minority may continue forever unchangeably this Government, although horridly defective: Where are your checks in this Government? Your strong holds will be in the hands of your enemies: It is on a supposition that our American Governors shall be honest, that all the good qualities of this Government are founded: But its defective, and imperfect construction, puts it in their power to perpetrate the worst of mischiefs, should they be bad men: And, Sir, would not all the world, from the Eastern to the Western hemisphere, blame our distracted folly in resting our rights upon the contingency of our rulers being good or bad. Shew me that age and country where the rights and liberties of the people were placed on the sole chance of their rulers being good men, without a consequent loss of liberty? I say that the loss of that dearest privilege has ever followed with absolute certainty, every such mad attempt. If your American chief, be a man of ambition, and abilities, how easy is it for him to render himself absolute: The army is in his hands, and, if he be a man of address, it will be attached to him; and it will be the subject of long meditation with him to seize the first auspicious moment to accomplish his design; and Sir, will the American spirit solely relieve you when this happens? I would rather infinitely, and I am sure most of this Convention are of the same opinion, have a King, Lords, and Commons, than a Government so replete with such insupportable evils. If we make a King, we may prescribe the rules by which he shall rule his people, and interpose such checks as shall prevent him from infringing them: But the President, in the field, at the head of his army, can prescribe the terms on which he shall reign master, so far that it will puzzle any American ever to get his neck from under the galling yoke. I cannot with patience, think of this idea. If ever he violates the laws, one of two things will happen: He shall come to the head of his army to carry every thing before him; or, he will give bail, or do what Mr. Chief Justice will order him.

If he be guilty, will not the recollection of his crimes teach him to make one bold push for the American throne? Will not the immense difference between being master of every thing, and being ignominiously tried and punished, powerfully excite him to make this bold push? But, Sir, where is the existing force to punish him? Can he not at the head of his army beat down every opposition? Away with your President, we shall have a King: The army will salute him Monarch; your militia will leave you and assist in making him King, and fight against you: And what have you to oppose this force? What will then become of you and your rights? Will not absolute despotism ensue? [Here Mr. Henry strongly and pathetically expatiated on the probability of the President's enslaving America and the horrible consequences that must result.]

. . . This Government is so new it wants a name. I wish its other novelties were as harmless as this. He told us, we had an American Dictator in the year 1781—We never had an American President. In making a Dictator, we follow the example of the most glorious, magnanimous and skilful nations. In great dangers this power has been given.—Rome had furnished us with an illustrious example.—America found a person worthy of that trust: She looked to Virginia for him.* We gave a dictatorial power to hands that used it gloriously; and which were rendered more glorious by surrendering it up. Where is there a breed of such Dictators? Shall we find a set of American Presidents of such a breed? Will the American President come and lay prostrate at the feet of Congress his laurels? I fear there are few men who can be trusted on that head. The glorious republic of Holland has erected monuments of her warlike intrepidity and valor: Yet she is now totally ruined by a Stadtholder—a Dutch President. The destructive wars into which that nation has been plunged, has since involved her in ambition. The glorious triumphs of Blenheim and Ramillies were not so conformable to the genius, nor so much to the true interest of the republic, as those numerous and useful canals and dykes, and other objects at which ambition spurns. That republic has, however, by the industry of its inhabitants, and policy of its magistrates, suppressed the ill effects of ambition.—Notwithstanding two of their provinces have paid nothing, yet I hope the example of Holland will tell us, that we can live happily without changing our present despised Government. Cannot people be as happy under a mild, as under an energetic Government? Cannot content and felicity be enjoyed in a republic, as well as in a monarchy, because there are whips, chains and scourges used in the latter? If I am not as rich as my neighbour, if I give my mite—my all—republican forbearance will say, that it is sufficient—So said the honest confederates of Holland.—*You are poor—We are rich.—We will go on and do better, far better, than be under an oppressive Government.*—For better will it be for us to continue as we are, than go under that tight energetic Government .—I am persuaded of what the Honorable Gentleman says, that separate confederacies will ruin us. In my judgment, they are evils never to be thought of till a people are driven by necessity.—When he asks my opinion of consolidation—of one power to reign over America, with a strong hand; I will tell him, I am persuaded,

---

*[*viz.* Washington—Eds.]

of the rectitude of my honorable friend's opinion (Mr. *Mason*) that one Government cannot reign over so extensive a country as this is, without absolute despotism.

"An Old Whig" (Unknown) Essay V (Excerpts)

DISCUSSION QUESTION

Consider the points of comparision drawn by "An Old Whig" between the British monarchy and the proposed American executive. Analyze each point and determine the strengths and weaknesses of the critique. Why does "An Old Whig" consider an "elective monarchy" more pernicious to democracy than the British form?

In the first place the office of President of the United States appears to me to be clothed with such powers as are dangerous. To be the fountain of all honors in the United States, commander in chief of the army, navy and milita, with the power of making treaties and of granting pardons, and to be vested with an authority to put a negative upon all laws, unless two thirds of both houses shall persist in enacting it, and put their names down upon calling the yeas and nays for that purpose, is in reality to be a KING as much *a King as the King of Great-Britain,* and a King too of the worst kind;—an elective King.—If such powers as these are to be trusted in the hands of any man, they ought for the sake of preserving the peace of the community at once to be made hereditary.—Much as I abhor kingly government, yet I venture to pronounce where kings are admitted to rule they should most certainly be vested with hereditary power. The election of a King whether it be in America or Poland, will be a scene of horror and confusion; and I am perfectly serious when I declare that, as a friend to my country, I shall despair of any happiness in the United States until his office is either reduced to a lower pitch of power or made perpetual and hereditary.—When I say that our future President will be as much a king as the king of Great-Britain, I only ask of my readers to look into the constitution of that country, and then tell me what important prerogative the King of Great-Britain is entitled to, which does not also belong to the President during his continuance in office.—The King of Great-Britain it is true can create nobility which our President cannot; but our President will have the power of making all the *great men,* which comes to the same thing.—All the difference is that we shall be embroiled in contention about the choice of the man, whilst they are at peace under the security of an hereditary succession.—To be tumbled headlong from the pinnacle of greatness and be reduced to a shadow of departed royalty is a shock almost too great for human nature to endure. It will cost a man many struggles to resign such eminent powers, and ere long, we shall find, some one who will be very unwilling to part with them.—Let us suppose this man to be a favorite with his army, and that they are unwilling to part with their beloved commander in chief; or to make the thing familiar, let us suppose, a future President and commander in chief adored by his army and the militia to as great a degree as our late illustrious commander in chief; and we have only to suppose one thing more, that this man is without the virtue, the moderation and love of liberty which possessed the mind of our late general, and this country will be involved at once in war and tyranny. So far is it from its being improbable that the man who shall hereafter be in a situation to make the attempt to perpetuate his own power, should want the virtues of General Washington; that it is perhaps a chance of one hundred millions to one that the next age will not furnish an example of so disinterested a use of great power. We may also suppose, without trespassing upon the bounds of probability, that this man may not have the means of supporting in private life the dignity of his former station; that like Caesar, he may be at once ambitious and poor, and deeply involved in debt.—Such a man would die a thousand deaths rather than sink from the heights of splendor and power into obscurity and wretchedness. We are certainly about giving our president too much or too little; and in the course of less than twenty years we shall find that we have given him enough to enable him to take all. It would be infinitely more prudent to give him at once as much as would content him, so that we might be able to retain the rest in peace; for if once power is seized by violence not the least fragment of liberty will survive the shock. I would therefore advise my countrymen seriously to ask themselves this question;—Whether they are prepared TO RECEIVE A KING? If they are[,] to say so at once, and make the kingly office hereditary; to frame a constitution that should set bounds to his power, and, as far as possible secure the liberty of the subject. If we are not prepared to *receive a king*, let us call another convention to revise the proposed constitution, and form it anew on the principles of confederacy of free republics; but by no means, under pretence of a republic, to lay the foundation for a military government, which is the worst of all tyrannies.

Yours, &c.
AN OLD WHIG

"The Impartial Examiner" (Unknown) Essay IV

DISCUSSION QUESTIONS

1. What is the nature of "veto" power? Does the "power of the negative" provide the President with powers beyond the proper role of executive government?
2. What does the "Impartial Examiner" mean by *generalisimo*? Is this description an accurate prophecy? Explain.
3. Consider this question raised by the "Impartial Examiner" below: "Can the different departments be duly balanced when all these high powers cocenter in one branch?" Is this question still relevant today? Explain.

11 June 1788

Although the *senate* and *house of representatives* are to be established, and it seems to be the spirit of the proposed plan of government, that they should be considered as the grand *deputation* of America—the great aggregate *body*, to whom shall be delegated the important trust of *representing* the whole nation—the august, puissant *assembly*, in whom shall reside the full majesty of the people: yet, it seems too, these alone shall not be sufficient to exercise the powers of legislation. It is ordained, as a necessary expedient in the fœderal government, that a *president* of the United States (who is to hold the supreme *executive* power) should also concur in passing every law.

In monarchy, where the established maxim is, that the king should be respected as a great and transcendent personage, who knows no equal—who in his royal political capacity can commit no *wrong*—to whom no evil can be ascribed—in whom exists the height of perfection—who is supreme above all, and accountable to no earthly being, it is consistent with such a maxim, that the *prince* should form a constituent branch of the legislature, and that his power of rejecting whatever has been passed by the other branches should be distinct, and co-extensive with that of either of those branches in rejecting what has been proposed and consented to by the other. It is necessary that the fundamental laws of the realm should ascribe to the king those high and eminent attributes—that he should possess in himself the sovereignty of the nation; and that the regal dignity should distinguish him, as superior to all his subjects, and in his political character endowed with certain inherent qualities, which cannot be supposed to reside in any other individual within the kingdom: otherwise, that constitutional independence, which the laws meant peculiarly to establish in his person, would not be preserved. To this end the king of England is invested with the sole *executive* authority, and a branch of legislative jurisdiction so far as to pass his *negative* on all proceedings of the other two branches, or to confirm them by his *assent.*

This secures to him the intended superiority in the constitution, and gives him the ascendant in government; else his sovereignty would become a shadow—whilst that doctrine, whereby he is declared to be the *head*, the *beginning* and *end* of the great *body politic*, would prove to be nothing more than mere sound. This two-fold jurisdiction established in the British monarch being founded on maxims extremely different from those, which prevail in the American States, the writer hereof is inclined to hope that he will not be thought singular, if he conceives an impropriety in assimilating the component parts of the American government to those of the British: and as the reasons, which to the founders of the British constitution were motives superior to all others to induce them thus to give the *executive* a controul over the *legislative*, are so far from existing in this country, that every principle of that kind is generally, if not universally, exploded; so it should appear that the same *public spirit*, which pervades the nation, would proclaim the doctrine of prerogative and other peculiar properties of the royal character, as incompatible with the view of these states when they are settling the *form of a republican* government. Is it not therefore sufficient that every branch in the proposed system be distinct and independent of each other—that no one branch might receive any accession of power (by taking part of another) which would tend to overturn the balance and thereby endanger the very *being* of the constitution? Whilst the king of England enjoys all the *regalia*, which are annexed to his crown—whilst he exercises a transcendent dominion over his subjects, the existence whereof is coeval with the first rudiments of their constitution—let the free citizens of America, consulting their true national happiness, wish for no innovation, but what is regulated according to the scale of equal liberty, or which may not destroy that liberty by too great a share of power being lodged in any particular hands;—let this collateral jurisdiction, which constitutes the *royal negative*, be held by kings alone, since with kings it first originated:—Let this remain in its native soil, as most congenial to it; there it will cumber less, and be more productive,—here it will be an exotick, and may poison the *stock*, in which it may be engrafted.

It will be said, perhaps, that the power, granted the president, of *approving* or *disapproving* the proceedings, which have passed the senate and house of representatives, will not be so decisive in its nature as the king's *negative*. True it is, this power of rejecting does not extend so far as primarily to produce an entire overthrow of any law, which has passed those *two houses:* but it may be expected that in many instances this *negative* will amount to a final and conclusive rejection. For as a law, which has been once disapproved by the president, cannot be re-passed without the agreement of *two-thirds* of *both houses*, there can be no doubt, it will frequently happen that this concurrence of *two thirds* cannot be obtained. The law must then fall: and thus the president, although he has not the power of *resolving* originally and *enacting* any laws, independent of those two houses, hath nevertheless in the legislative scale of government a weight almost equal to that of two thirds of the whole Congress. If the system proposed had been calculated to extend his authority a little farther, he would preponderate against all—he alone would possess the sovereignty of America. For if the whole executive authority and an absolute, entire *negative* on the legislature should become united in one person, these must, with regard to *that person*, destroy every idea of a subject. Thus circumstanced he cannot be the object of any laws; he will be above all law: as none can be enacted without his consent—he will be elevated to the height of supremacy.—

How near will the *president* approach to this consummate degree of power! The portion allotted him may, however, be amply sufficient to give him the ascendant in the constitution. He must continually acquire great accessions of weight in every scale of government, as *chief magistrate* and *generalissimo* of the United States—at the same time possessing so great a share in the legislature, as a revision of all *bills* and other proceedings which shall have passed the senate and house of representatives with a discretionary right of rejecting them—United with the senate in making treaties, appointing all public ministers, judges, and a train of other officers, who will be necessary for carrying on the business of government; thus dispensing honor and profit throughout America—whilst copious streams of influence must flow from him, as from a source. Can the different departments be duly balanced when all these high powers concenter in one branch? Is it not rather probable that this branch will destroy the balance, and eventually rise to the fulness of dominion?

When the *spirit* of America becomes such, as to ascribe to their president all those extraordinary qualities, which the subjects of kingly governments ascribe to their princes: then, it is presumed, and not till then, he may consistently be invested with a power similar to theirs.

It is remarkable how the president and senate mutually participate in the exercise of a two-fold jurisdiction. How, then, can it be surprising to any one, if some citizens, truly jealous of their liberties, are alarmed with the apprehensions of *aristocracy*? Those, who seriously reflect on the properties of human nature, and who possess republican principles, will suppose they conceive grounds for such apprehensions: those, who have different sentiments, will not care whether there are grounds for such apprehensions, or not.

FEDERALIST ARGUMENTS

Alexander Hamilton
Federalist *Paper 67*
(Excerpts)

DISCUSSION QUESTION

Discuss the main themes as addressed in Cato V and *Federalist Paper* # 67. What are the primary points of disagreement? Which argument is more compelling in itself, based on logical development and political insight? How do these essays relate to the modern Presidency, and what criteria do they help establish for the examination of power?

To the People of the State of New York:

The constitution of the executive department of the proposed government, claims next our attention.

There is hardly any part of the system which could have been attended with greater difficulty in the arrangement of it than this; and there is, perhaps, none which has been inveighed against with less candor or criticised with less judgment.

Here the writers against the Constitution seem to have taken pains to signalize their talent of misrepresentation. Calculating upon the aversion of the people to monarchy, they have endeavored to enlist all their jealousies and apprehensions in opposition to the intended President of the United States; not merely as the embryo, but as the full-grown progeny, of that detested parent. To establish the pretended affinity, they have not scrupled to draw resources even from the regions of fiction. The authorities of a magistrate, in few instances greater, in some instances less, than those of a governor of New York, have been magnified into more than royal prerogatives. He has been decorated with attributes superior in dignity and splendor to those of a king of Great Britain. He has been shown to us with the diadem sparkling on his brow and the imperial purple flowing in his train. He has been seated on a throne surrounded with minions and mistresses, giving audience to the envoys of foreign potentates, in all the supercilious pomp of majesty. The images of Asiatic despotism and voluptuousness have scarcely been wanting to crown the exaggerated scene. We have been taught to tremble at the terrific visages of murdering janizaries, and to blush at the unveiled mysteries of a future seraglio.

Attempts so extravagant as these to disfigure or, it might rather be said, to metamorphose the object, render it necessary to take an accurate view of its real nature and form: in order as well to ascertain its true aspect and genuine appearance, as to unmask the disingenuity and expose the fallacy of the counterfeit resemblances which have been so insidiously, as well as industriously, propagated.

In the execution of this task, there is no man who would not find it an arduous effort either to behold with moderation, or to treat with seriousness, the devices, not less weak than wicked, which have been contrived to pervert the public opinion in relation to the subject. They so far exceed the usual though unjustifiable licenses of party artifice, that even in a disposition the most candid and tolerant, they must force the sentiments which favor an indulgent construction of the conduct of political adversaries to give place to a voluntary and unreserved indignation. It is impossible not to bestow the imputation of deliberate imposture and deception upon the gross pretence of a similitude between a king of Great Britain and a magistrate of the character marked out for that of the President of the United States. It is still more impossible to withhold that imputation from the rash and barefaced expedients which have been employed to give success to the attempted imposition. . . .

This bold experiment upon the discernment of his countrymen has been hazarded by a writer who (whatever may be his real merit) has had no inconsiderable share in the applauses of his party;* and who, upon this false and unfounded suggestion, has built a series of observations equally false and unfounded. Let him now be confronted with the evidence of the fact, and let him, if he be able, justify or extenuate the shameful outrage he has offered to the dictates of truth and to the rules of fair dealing. . . .

[From this point Hamilton addresses what he believes are "misconceptions" advanced by Cato against "the second clause of the second section of the second Article" of the Constitution empowering the president to *"nominate and by and with the advice and consent of the Senate, to appoint ambassadors, other public ministers and consuls, judges of the Supreme Court, and all other officers of the United States whose appointments are not in the Constitution otherwise provided for and which shall be established by law."* Hamilton goes to great lengths to rebuke Cato through a demonstration of the point that the President's appointive powers do not approximate the powers of a king, but are rather shared with the Senate as well as the state legislatures. Hamilton scolds Cato for committing what he claims is a deliberate deception, " . . . too palpable to be obscured by sophistry, too atrocious to be palliated by hypocrisy." Clinton Rossiter has described Cato's complaint as a "frivolous misrepresentation," to which Hamilton felt, nonetheless, "obliged" to refute. —Eds.]

---

*See CATO, No. V.—Publius.

Alexander Hamilton
Federalist *Paper 68*

DISCUSSION QUESTIONS

1. Analyze the following statement: "The process of election affords a moral certainty that the office of Preseident will never fall to the lot of any man who is not in an eminent degree endowed with the requisite qualifications." What does Hamilton mean by "moral certainty"? Why is this passage important, and what does it say about Hamilton's views on the executive?
2. According to Hamilton in *Federalist Paper* #68, what are the strengths of the office of the Presidency? What does Hamilton add regarding the Vice-Presidency?

To the People of the State of New York:

The mode of appointment of the Chief Magistrate of the United States is almost the only part of the system, of any consequence, which has escaped without severe censure, or which has received the slightest mark of approbation from its opponents. The most plausible of these, who has appeared in print, has even deigned to admit that the election of the President is pretty well guarded.* I venture somewhat further, and hesitate not to affirm, that if the manner of it be not perfect, it is at least excellent. It unites in an eminent degree all the advantages, the union of which was to be wished for.

It was desirable that the sense of the people should operate in the choice of the person to whom so important a trust was to be confided. This end will be answered by committing the right of making it, not to any preestablished body, but to men chosen by the people for the special purpose, and at the particular conjuncture.

It was equally desirable, that the immediate election should be made by men most capable of analyzing the qualities adapted to the station, and acting under circumstances favorable to deliberation, and to a judicious combination of all the reasons and inducements which were proper to govern their choice. A small number of persons, selected by their fellow-citizens from the general mass, will be most likely to possess the information and discernment requisite to such complicated investigations.

It was also peculiarly desirable to afford as little opportunity as possible to tumult and disorder. This evil was not least to be dreaded in the election of a magistrate, who was to have so important an agency in the administration of the government as the President of the United States. But the precautions which have been so happily concerted in the system under consideration, promise an effectual security against this mischief. The choice of *several*, to form an intermediate body of electors, will be much less apt to convulse the community with any extraordinary or violent movements, than the choice of *one* who was himself to be the final object of

---

* *Vide Federal Farmer.*—Publius.

the public wishes. And as the electors, chosen in each State, are to assemble and vote in the State in which they are chosen, this detached and divided situation will expose them much less to heats and ferments, which might be communicated from them to the people, than if they were all to be convened at one time, in one place.

Nothing was more to be desired than that every practicable obstacle should be opposed to cabal, intrigue, and corruption. These most deadly adversaries of republican government might naturally have been expected to make their approaches from more than one quarter, but chiefly from the desire in foreign powers to gain an improper ascendant in our councils. How could they better gratify this, than by raising a creature of their own to the chief magistracy of the Union? But the convention have guarded against all danger of this sort, with the most provident and judicious attention. They have not made the appointment of the President to depend on any preexisting bodies of men, who might be tampered with beforehand to prostitute their votes; but they have referred it in the first instance to an immediate act of the people of America, to be exerted in the choice of persons for the temporary and sole purpose of making the appointment. And they have excluded from eligibility to this trust, all those who from situation might be suspected of too great devotion to the President in office. No senator, representative, or other person holding a place of trust or profit under the United States, can be of the numbers of the electors. Thus without corrupting the body of the people, the immediate agents in the election will at least enter upon the task free from any sinister bias. Their transient existence, and their detached situation, already taken notice of, afford a satisfactory prospect of their continuing so, to the conclusion of it. The business of corruption, when it is to embrace so considerable a number of men, requires time as well as means. Nor would it be found easy suddenly to embark them, dispersed as they would be over thirteen States, in any combinations founded upon motives, which though they could not properly be denominated corrupt, might yet be of a nature to mislead them from their duty.

Another and no less important desideratum was, that the Executive should be independent for his continuance in office on all but the people themselves. He might otherwise be tempted to sacrifice his duty to his complaisance for those whose favor was necessary to the duration of his official consequence. This advantage will also be secured, by making his reelection to depend on a special body of representatives, deputed by the society for the single purpose of making the important choice.

All these advantages will happily combine in the plan devised by the convention; which is, that the people of each State shall choose a number of persons as electors, equal to the number of senators and representatives of such State in the national government, who shall assemble within the State, and vote for some fit person as President. Their votes, thus given, are to be transmitted to the seat of the national government, and the person who may happen to have a majority of the whole number of votes will be the President. But as a majority of the votes might not always happen to centre in one man, and as it might be unsafe to permit less than a majority to be conclusive, it is provided that, in such a contingency, the

House of Representatives shall select out of the candidates who shall have the five highest number of votes, the man who in their opinion may be best qualified for the office.

The process of election affords a moral certainty, that the office of President will never fall to the lot of any man who is not in an eminent degree endowed with the requisite qualifications. Talents for low intrigue, and the little arts of popularity, may alone suffice to elevate a man to the first honors in a single State; but it will require other talents, and a different kind of merit, to establish him in the esteem and confidence of the whole Union, or of so considerable a portion of it as would be necessary to make him a successful candidate for the distinguished office of President of the United States. It will not be too strong to say, that there will be a constant probability of seeing the station filled by characters preëminent for ability and virtue. And this will be thought no inconsiderable recommendation of the Constitution, by those who are able to estimate the share which the executive in every government must necessarily have in its good or ill administration. Though we cannot acquiesce in the political heresy of the poet who says:

> For forms of government let fools contest—
> That which is best administered is best—

yet we may safely pronounce, that the true test of a good government is its aptitude and tendency to produce a good administration.

The Vice-President is to be chosen in the same manner with the President; with this difference, that the Senate is to do, in respect to the former, what is to be done by the House of Representatives, in respect to the latter.

The appointment of an extraordinary person, as Vice-President, has been objected to as superfluous, if not mischievous. It has been alleged, that it would have been preferable to have authorized the Senate to elect out of their own body an officer answering that description. But two considerations seem to justify the ideas of the convention in this respect. One is, that to secure at all times the possibility of a definite resolution of the body, it is necessary that the President should have only a casting vote. And to take the senator of any State from his seat as senator, to place him in that of President of the Senate, would be to exchange, in regard to the State from which he came, a constant for a contingent vote. The other consideration is, that as the Vice-President may occasionally become a substitute for the President, in the supreme executive magistracy, all the reasons which recommend the mode of election prescribed for the one, apply with great if not with equal force to the manner of appointing the other. It is remarkable that in this, as in most other instances, the objection which is made would lie against the constitution of this State. We have a Lieutenant-Governor, chosen by the people at large, who presides in the Senate, and is the constitutional substitute for the Governor, in casualties similar to those which would authorize the Vice-President to exercise the authorities and discharge the duties of the President.

PUBLIUS

Alexander Hamilton
Federalist *Paper 70*
(Excerpt)

DISCUSSION QUESTIONS

1. What does Hamilton mean by "energy" in the executive? Why is this important, and how does the Constitution guarantee this? Compare this argument to Patrick Henry's appeal. What problems does Henry anticipate as he examines the lines of authority in the proposed Constitution? What can we say about the democratic impulses of Henry and Hamilton based upon these readings? Who are their ideological heirs?
2. Why is Hamilton so adamant about "unity" and "energy" in the executive? What do these ideas reveal about Hamilton's vision of politics and American destiny? How would Cato respond? Patrick Henry?

To the People of the State of New York:

There is an idea, which is not without its advocates, that a vigorous Executive is inconsistent with the genius of republican government. The enlightened well-wishers to this species of government must at least hope that the supposition is destitute of foundation; since they can never admit its truth, without at the same time admitting the condemnation of their own principles. Energy in the Executive is a leading character in the definition of good government. It is essential to the protection of the community against foreign attacks; it is not less essential to the steady administration of the laws; to the protection of property against those irregular and high-handed combinations which sometimes interrupt the ordinary course of justice; to the security of liberty against the enterprises and assaults of ambition, of faction, and of anarchy. Every man the least conversant in Roman story, knows how often that republic was obliged to take refuge in the absolute power of a single man, under the formidable title of Dictator, as well against the intrigues of ambitious individuals who aspired to the tyranny, and the seditions of whole classes of the community whose conduct threatened the existence of all government, as against the invasions of external enemies who menaced the conquest and destruction of Rome.

There can be no need, however, to multiply arguments or examples on this head. A feeble Executive implies a feeble execution of the government. A feeble execution is but another phrase for a bad execution; and a government ill executed, whatever it may be in theory, must be, in practice, a bad government.

Taking it for granted, therefore, that all men of sense will agree in the necessity of an energetic Executive, it will only remain to inquire, what are the ingredients which constitute this energy? How far can they be combined with those other ingredients which constitute safety in the republican sense? And how far does this combination characterize the plan which has been reported by the convention?

The ingredients which constitute energy in the Executive are, first, unity; secondly, duration; thirdly, an adequate provision for its support; fourthly, competent powers.

The ingredients which constitute safety in the republican sense are, first, a due dependence on the people; secondly, a due responsibility.

Those politicians and statesmen who have been the most celebrated for the soundness of their principles and for the justice of their views, have declared in favor of a single Executive and a numerous legislature. They have, with great propriety, considered energy as the most necessary qualification of the former, and have regarded this as most applicable to power in a single hand; while they have, with equal propriety, considered the latter as best adapted to deliberation and wisdom, and best calculated to conciliate the confidence of the people and to secure their privileges and interests.

That unity is conductive to energy will not be disputed. Decision, activity, secrecy, and despatch will generally characterize the proceedings of one man in a much more eminent degree than the proceedings of any greater number; and in proportion as the number is increased, these qualities will be diminished.

This unity may be destroyed in two ways: either by vesting the power in two or more magistrates of equal dignity and authority; or by vesting it ostensibly in one man, subject, in whole or in part, to the control and cooperation of others, in the capacity of counsellors to him. . . .

Wherever two or more persons are engaged in any common enterprise or pursuit, there is always danger of difference of opinion. If it be a public trust or office, in which they are clothed with equal dignity and authority, there is peculiar danger of personal emulation and even animosity. From either, and especially from all these causes, the most bitter dissensions are apt to spring. Whenever these happen, they lessen the respectability, weaken the authority, and distract the plans and operation of those whom they divide. If they should unfortunately assail the supreme executive magistracy of a country, consisting of a plurality of persons, they might impede or frustrate the most important measures of the government, in the most critical emergencies of the state. And what is still worse, they might split the community into the most violent and irreconcilable factions, adhering differently to the different individuals who composed the magistracy.

Men often oppose a thing, merely because they have had no agency in planning it, or because it may have been planned by those whom they dislike. But if they have been consulted, and have happened to disapprove, opposition then becomes, in their estimation, an indispensable duty of self-love. They seem to think themselves bound in honor, and by all the motives of personal infallibility, to defeat the success of what has been resolved upon contrary to their sentiments. Men of upright, benevolent tempers have too many opportunities of remarking, with horror, to what desperate lengths this disposition is sometimes carried, and how often the great interests of society are sacrificed to the vanity, to the conceit, and to the obstinacy of individuals, who have credit enough to make their passions and their caprices interesting to mankind. Perhaps the question now before the public may, in its consequences, afford melancholy proofs of the effects of this despicable frailty, or rather detestable vice, in the human character.

Upon the principles of a free government, inconveniences from the source just mentioned must necessarily be submitted to in the formation of the legislature; but it is unnecessary, and therefore unwise, to introduce them into the constitution of the Executive. It is here too that they may be most pernicious. In the legislature, promptitude of decision is oftener an evil than a benefit. The differences of opinion, and the jarrings of parties in that department of the government, though they may sometimes obstruct salutary plans, yet often promote deliberation and circumspection, and serve to check excesses in the majority. When a resolution too is once taken, the opposition must be at an end. That resolution is a law, and resistance to it punishable. But no favorable circumstances palliate or atone for the disadvantages of dissension in the executive department. Here, they are pure and unmixed. There is no point at which they cease to operate. They serve to embarrass and weaken the execution of the plan or measure to which they relate, from the first step to the final conclusion of it. They constantly counteract those qualities in the Executive which are the most necessary ingredients in its composition,—vigor and expedition, and this without any counterbalancing good. In the conduct of war, in which the energy of the Executive is the bulwark of the national security, every thing would be to be apprehended from its plurality.

It must be confessed that these observations apply with principal weight to the first case supposed—that is, to a plurality of magistrates of equal dignity and authority, a scheme, the advocates for which are not likely to form a numerous sect; but they apply, though not with equal, yet with considerable weight to the project of a council, whose concurrence is made constitutionally necessary to the operations of the ostensible Executive. An artful cabal in that council would be able to distract and to enervate the whole system of administration. If no such cabal should exist, the mere diversity of views and opinions would alone be sufficient to tincture the exercise of the executive authority with a spirit of habitual feebleness and dilatoriness.

But one of the weightiest objections to a plurality in the Executive, and which lies as much against the last as the first plan, is, that it tends to conceal faults and destroy responsibility. Responsibility is of two kinds—to censure and to punishment. The first is the more important of the two, especially in an elective office. Man, in public trust, will much oftener act in such a manner as to render him unworthy of being any longer trusted, than in such a manner as to make him obnoxious to legal punishment. But the multiplication of the Executive adds to the difficulty of detection in either case. It often becomes impossible, amidst mutual accusations, to determine on whom the blame or the punishment of a pernicious measure, or series of pernicious measures, ought really to fall. It is shifted from one to another with so much dexterity, and under such plausible appearances, that the public opinion is left in suspense about the real author. The circumstances which may have led to any national miscarriage or misfortune are sometimes so complicated that, where there are a number of actors who may have had different degrees and kinds of agency, though we may clearly see upon the whole that there has been mismanagement, yet it may be impracticable to pronounce to whose account the evil which may have been incurred is truly chargeable.

"I was overruled by my council. The council were so divided in their opinions that it was impossible to obtain any better resolution on the point." These and similar pretexts are constantly at hand, whether true or false. And who is there that will either take the trouble or incur the odium, of a strict scrutiny into the secret springs of the transaction? Should there be found a citizen zealous enough to undertake the unpromising task, if there happen to be collusion between the parties concerned, how easy it is to clothe the circumstances with so much ambiguity, as to render it uncertain what was the precise conduct of any of those parties?

In the single instance in which the governor of this State is coupled with a council—that is, in the appointment to offices, we have seen the mischiefs of it in the view now under consideration. Scandalous appointments to important offices have been made. Some cases, indeed, have been so flagrant that ALL PARTIES have agreed in the impropriety of the thing. When inquiry has been made, the blame has been laid by the governor on the members of the council, who, on their part, have charged it upon his nomination; while the people remain altogether at a loss to determine, by whose influence their interests have been committed to hands so unqualified and so manifestly improper. In tenderness to individuals, I forbear to descend to particulars.

It is evident from these considerations, that the plurality of the Executive tends to deprive the people of the two greatest securities they can have for the faithful exercise of any delegated power, *first*, the restraints of public opinion, which lose their efficacy, as well on account of the division of the censure attendant on bad measures among a number, as on account of the uncertainty on whom it ought to fall; and, *secondly*, the opportunity of discovering with facility and clearness the misconduct of the persons they trust, in order either to their removal from office, or to their actual punishment in cases which admit of it.

In England, the king is a perpetual magistrate; and it is a maxim which has obtained for the sake of the public peace, that he is unaccountable for his administration, and his person sacred. Nothing, therefore, can be wiser in that kingdom, than to annex to the king a constitutional council, who may be responsible to the nation for the advice they give. Without this, there would be no responsibility whatever in the executive department—an idea inadmissible in a free government. But even there the king is not bound by the resolutions of his council, though they are answerable for the advice they give. He is the absolute master of his own conduct in the exercise of his office, and may observe or disregard the counsel given to him at his sole discretion.

But in a republic, where every magistrate ought to be personally responsible for his behavior in office, the reason which in the British Constitution dictates the propriety of a council, not only ceases to apply, but turns against the institution. In the monarchy of Great Britain, it furnishes a substitute for the prohibited responsibility of the chief magistrate, which serves in some degree as a hostage to the national justice for his good behavior. In the American republic, it would serve to destroy, or would greatly diminish, the intended and necessary responsibility of the Chief Magistrate himself.

The idea of a council to the Executive, which has so generally obtained in the State constitutions, has been derived from that maxim of republican jealousy which considers power as safer in the hands of a number of men than of a single man. If the maxim should be admitted to be applicable to the case, I should contend that the advantage on that side would not counterbalance the numerous disadvantages on the opposite side. But I do not think the rule at all applicable to the executive power. I clearly concur in opinion, in this particular, with a writer whom the celebrated Junius pronounces to be "deep, solid, and ingenious," that "the executive power is more easily confined when it is ONE";* that it is far more safe there should be a single object for the jealousy and watchfulness of the people; and, in a word, that all multiplication of the Executive is rather dangerous than friendly to liberty.

"Phocian" (Fisher Ames) Essay IV (Excerpts)

DISCUSSION QUESTIONS

1. What does Ames mean by the word "demagogue"? Why is the executive as he understood it a safeguard against demagogues?
2. Hamilton also believed that a strong Presidency can protect the citizenry from attractive demagogues. What kind of demagoguery could Hamilton and his friend Ames be addressing? What are the underlying assumptions of these positions? How would Patrick Henry and Cato respond to this argument?

In democratic states, therefore, public opinion will be impetuous and sudden, and before it can have light it will have authority. Passion will legislate, and those who can kindle it will govern the country. If wise and virtuous men, like Washington, are elected, they will find, as Trinculo says in the play,[1] that they are viceroys by the Constitution. . . .

The *real* people, who consist of householders, solid farmers and mechanics, are content to exercise their right of voting for their rulers, and then they quietly leave the matter to them. Their inaction affords the opportunity for these usurpers to address a *mock* people, as ignorant, as turbulent, as much machines as the lazarroni of Naples, and to overawe and influence the laws and the legislators. . . .

. . . Have not the sober citizens, the householders, the thrifty journeymen, been federal, and have not the body of the clergy, the merchants, the great mass of substantial yeomanry, been supporters of Washington and federalism?

These are facts, and to profit by them we should reason upon their nature and consequences.

*De Lolme

Fisher Ames, *The Works of Fisher Ames*, ed. by W. B. Allen. (Liberty Fund Inc. 8335 Allison Pointe Trail, Suite 300 Indianapolis, Indiana 46250–1687, 1983.) Used by kind permission of the publisher.

Wretched is that country where its mere mob governs. The people, give them time for it, will display good sense, for they are enlightened and honest—and that will, duly formed and maturely considered, will prevail—and it ought to prevail. But no other will ought to prevail. No counterfeit sense of the people expressed in mob meetings, and dictated by the loudest bawls of the man who happens to rise upon a hogshead, ought to control or prevent the measures of the nation and its government. For then the sovereign political power would be placed not where its sense and virtue, and interest be but with its folly, its passion, and its vice. The owners of property would not have the control of it, but the ragged sansculottes, who would exercise their power as their leaders or their necessities would prompt. They would intimidate the owners of property till they ran away. Then they would confiscate it, as the forfeiture of emigration. . . .

. . . In democracies, it is no matter who is chosen to rule. Demagogues, though not chosen, will rule. It is the prettiest thing in the world to say, the whole people have a right to rule, they have the fountain of power, and being intelligent they will exercise it with discretion, and defend it with vigilance. Easy as all this appears in theory, it is found in practice the most difficult of all things, so to model a government, that its sense and virtue, and interest shall govern, and that its vice and passion shall not. All that is vice and passion will be combined and disciplined by the mob leaders to usurp its powers.

A strong executive, with the aid of an independent judiciary, will form some check, and will struggle to maintain it. . . .

An honest and able chief magistrate, will think that he owes it to the *real* people, before described, to maintain the laws and to hold in restraint the turbulence of these usurping demagogues. Such a discharge of duty ought to endear him to the wise and good, but it will invigorate the factious to exclude him at the next election. . . .

The weaker the executive the baser and more corrupt will be the faction opposed to it. The obstacles to the usurpation of the whole power of the office will be few, and when the popular ferment is accidentally or artificially raised, these will disappear. . . .

On the principle of human nature, therefore, that a president had rather govern than be governed, he will try to defend himself by calling on the *real people* to assist him and sustain his authority in doing his duty.

. . . A strong executive, by restraining the turbulence of demagogues, obliges them to moderate their views. They will not struggle for things unattainable. They will content themselves with raising clamors that will delay or modify public measures. Ambition, thus fettered, will seek power, not over the government and the laws, but by taking office under it. There selfishness will look for its rewards. The struggle is no longer so dangerous, not is it for life. Faction sinks into party, which, is a milder form of that evil, which adheres to the very nature of popular liberty. . . .

Let the observers of human nature, the men well read in the history and principles of free commonwealths, reflect on these things. . . .

[1]One of the characters in Shakespeare's *The Tempest.* [Allen.]

CONTEMPORARY INFLUENCES

Richard Neustadt
Presidential Power and the Modern Presidents
(Excerpt)

DISCUSSION QUESTIONS

1. What are the central themes in the Neustadt essay? What sort of attitude regarding Presidential power is indicated in Neustadt's argument? Compare Neustadt to the Federalist and Antifederalist positions, and determine where Neustadt belongs in this debate and why.
2. According to Neustadt, what sort of politician is qualified to assume the Presidential mantle? How would Hamilton respond to this set of criteria? Are Neustadt's assertions compatible with democratic principles? Do they have to be compatible? Explain.
3. Given the complexities of modern government, what is the best way to perform the functions of execution of the laws and administration of the bureaucracy? What kind of leadership can accomplish this? What is the proper role of the President in today's government?

To make the most of power for himself a President must know what it is made of. This book has treated power in the sense of personal influence and influence in the sense of effectiveness prospectively, looking toward tomorrow from today. That look conveys the essence of the task before a man who seeks to maximize his power. If he wants it for the future, he must guard it in the present. He mounts guard, as best he can, when he appraises the effects of present action on the sources of his influence. In making that appraisal he has no one to depend on but himself; his power and its sources are a sphere of expertise reserved to him. But the issues that present themselves for action day by day rarely show his personal risks upon their surface. His expertise must first help him to see beneath the surface if it is to help him weigh what may be there. The President as expert does himself a double service. Without the expertise he cannot do it.

The Presidency, to repeat, is not a place for amateurs. That sort of expertise can hardly be acquired without deep experience in political office. The Presidency is a place for men of politics. But by no means is it a place for every politician.

There is no reason to suppose that politicians, on the average, have the wherewithal to help themselves build presidential power. The men of politics who specialize in organization work and party office scarcely qualify at all; governmental office is the relevant experience. For present purposes we can regard as politicians only those who build careers in public office. Yet skillful use of presidential power does not follow automatically from such experience. No post in government at any level necessarily equips a man to recognize the Presidency's peculiar sources of influ-

---

ence. Those sources have as many parts as a President has constituencies, foreign and domestic; the posts that furnish insights into one part often obscure others. Besides, past officeholding is no guarantee that any man brings with him to the White House the degree and kind of feeling for direction that can help him once he gets there. Former Commerce Secretary Hoover had a sense of purpose so precise as to be stultifying. Former Senator Harding seems to have had none at all. And mere experience, however relevant, is no assurance that a President will find the confidence he needs just when he needs it most. Such confidence requires that his image of himself in office justify an unremitting search for personal power. But it requires, also, that his image of himself allow for failures and frustration in the search.

FDR is said to have remarked that Lincoln "was a sad man because he couldn't get it all at once. And nobody can."[1] If a President is to assist himself through the vicissitudes of four long years or eight, his source of confidence must make him capable of bearing Lincoln's sadness with good grace. The power seeker whose self-confidence requires quick returns and sure success might make a mess of everything including his own power. Grace calls for humor and perspective. Political experience does not assure those qualities. Indeed, it may diminish them in the degree it brings a taste for power. The officeholder who combines them with an insight into presidential influence and hunger for it is no average politician.

Expertise in presidential power seems to be the province not of politicians as a class but of extraordinary politicians. What sets such men apart? Mr. Justice Holmes once characterized Franklin Roosevelt as a "second-class intellect but a first-class temperament." Perhaps this is a necessary combination. The politics of well-established government has rarely been attractive to and rarely has dealt kindly with the men whom intellectuals regard as first-rate intellects. Temperament, at any rate, is the great separator. Experience will leave its mark on expertise; so will a man's ambitions for himself and his constituents. But something like that "first-class" temperament is what turns know-how and desire to his personal account. The necessary confidence is nourished by that temperament. It is a human resource not discovered every day among American politicians.

If skill in maximizing power for himself served purposes no larger than the man's own pride or pleasure, there would be no reason for the rest of us to care whether he were skillful or not. More precisely, there would be no reason except sentiment and partisanship. But a President's success in that endeavor serves objectives far beyond his own and far beyond his party's. For reasons I will come to in a moment, an expert search for presidential influence contributes to the energy of government and to the viability of public policy. Government is energized by a productive tension among its working parts. Policy is kept alive by a sustained transformation of intent into result. Energetic government and viable public policy are at a premium as we begin the seventh decade of the twentieth century. Expertise in presidential power adds to both. A President's constituents, regardless of their party (or their country, for that matter), have a great stake in his search for personal influence.

---

[1]Arthur M. Schlesinger, Jr., *The Age of Roosevelt, Vol. 2, The Coming of the New Deal* (Boston: Houghton-Mifflin, 1959), p. 529.

In the American political system the President sits in a unique seat and works within a unique frame of reference. The things he personally has to do are no respecters of the lines between "civil" and "military," or "foreign" and "domestic," or "legislative" and "executive," or "administrative" and "political." At his desk—and there alone—distinctions of these sorts lose their last shred of meaning. The expectations centered in his person converge upon no other individual; nobody else feels pressure from all five of his constituencies; no one else takes pressure in the consciousness that he has been elected "by the nation." Besides, nobody but the President lives day by day with his responsibility in an atomic age amid Cold War. And he alone can claim unquestionable right to everybody's information on the mysteries of that age and that war. His place and frame of reference are unique. By the same token, though, his power is mercurial. Since no one shares his place, nobody is committed to uphold what he may do there. The consequences are described by every illustration in this book.

The things a President must think about if he would build his influence are not unlike those bearing on the viability of public policy. The correspondence may be inexact, but it is close. The man who thinks about the one can hardly help contributing to the other. A President who senses what his influence is made of and who means to guard his future will approach his present actions with an eye to the reactions of constituents in Washington and out. The very breadth and sweep of his constituencies and of their calls upon him, along with the uncertainty of their response, will make him keen to see and weigh what Arthur Schlesinger has called "the balance of administrative power." This is a balance of political, managerial, psychological, and personal feasibilities. And because the President's own frame of reference is at once so all-encompassing and so political, what he sees as a balance for himself is likely to be close to what is viable in terms of public policy.

What he sees in terms of power gives him clues in terms of policy to help him search beneath the surfaces of issues.

Viability in policy has three ingredients. First is a purpose that moves with the grain of history, a direction consonant with coming needs. Second is an operation that proves manageable to the men who must administer it, acceptable to those who must support it, tolerable to those who must put up with it, in Washington and out. Timing can be crucial for support and acquiescence; proper timing is the third ingredient. The President who sees his power stakes sees something very much like the ingredients that make for viability in policy.

Our system affords nobody a better source of clues. Presidential expertise thus serves effective policy. Deciding what is viable has grown more critical and more complex with almost every turn of world events (and of home politics) since the Second World War. Substantive considerations have become so specialized that experts in one sphere lose touch with expertise in any other. Substantive appraisals have become so tricky that the specialists in every sphere dispute among themselves. In consequence the viability of policy may be the only ground on which a substantive decision can be reached. When that ground is itself inordinately complicated by the tendency of policies to interlock, and overlap, and to leap national boundaries, it becomes a sphere of expertness as specialized as others. In the sphere of viability our system can supply no better expert than a President intent on husbanding his influence—provided that he understands what influence is made of.

The more determinedly a President seeks power, the more he will be likely to bring vigor to his clerkship. As he does so he contributes to the energy of government. In Congress and the agencies and in the national parties, energy is generated by support or opposition. But first there must be something to support or to oppose. Most Washingtonians look to the White House for it. There often is no other place to look. The need of others for a President's initiatives creates dependence on him. Their dependence becomes his advantage. Yet he can only capture the advantage as he meets the need. An energetic clerk will energize all government; the man intent on influence will be that sort of clerk. (So may a man intent on history, provided that he has the heroes of a Harry Truman. But one cannot expect that many men will know their history as well as he, and even those who know it may choose other heroes.)

The contributions that a President can make to government are indispensable. Assuming that he knows what power is and wants it, those contributions cannot help but be forthcoming in some measure as by-products of his search for personal influence. In a relative but real sense one can say of a President what Eisenhower's first secretary of defense once said of General Motors: What is good for the country is good for the President, and vice versa. There is no guarantee, of course, that every President will keep an eye on what is "good" for him; his sense of power and of purpose and the source of his self-confidence may turn his head away. If so, his "contributions" could be lethargy not energy, or policy that moves against, not with, the grain of history. The way he sees his influence and seeks it will affect the rest of us, no matter what becomes of him.

John F. Kennedy
Campaign Speech on the Presidency, 1960
(Excerpts)

DISCUSSION QUESTIONS

1. Why should the "President be at the center of action in our scheme of government," as Kennedy avers? President Kennedy was an open admirer of Thomas Jefferson. Is there anything about his comments on the Presidency that might also indicate a Hamiltonian strain in his political thought? Elaborate.
2. Examine the arguments in the Neustadt and Kennedy pieces. What do these arguments hold in common? How does Kennedy's speech illustrate Neustadt's ideas? How important is the property of "energy" or "vigor" to executive administration in a modern society with democratic aspirations? What are Kennedy's reasons for advocating a vigorous Presidency?

3. Much of the President's power is "evolved"; some of it is delegated by law, some of it is assumed through the principles of inherent power and procedural precedent, and still more is supported by various Supreme Court rulings. Are these evolved powers consonant with the powers explicitly written in the Constitution? Should the President be so deeply immersed in budgetary politics? Why or why not? What other evolved powers should we re-examine? What would Hamilton argue?
4. Machiavelli once argued that a Prince must be concerned with appearance when attending to matters of state and political power. What, if anything, would Neustadt have to add to this argument? What does this reveal about Neustadt's understanding of power? How would Hamilton and Kennedy respond to Neustadt's interpretation of executive power and its link to appearance? Explain.

The modern presidential campaign covers every issue in and out of the platform from cranberries to creation. But the public is rarely alerted to a candidate's views about the central issue on which all the rest turn. That central issue—and the point of my comments this noon—is not the farm problem or defense or India. It is the Presidency itself. Of course a candidate's views on specific policies are important—but Theodore Roosevelt and William Howard Taft shared policy views with entirely different results in the White House. Of course it is important to elect a good man with good intentions—but Woodrow Wilson and Warren G. Harding were both good men of good intentions—so were Lincoln and Buchanan—but there is a Lincoln Room in the White House, and no Buchanan Room. . . .

During the past eight years, we have seen one concept of the Presidency at work. Our needs and hopes have been eloquently stated—but the initiative and follow-through have too often been left to others. And too often his own objectives have been lost by the President's failure to override objections from within his own party, in the Congress or even in his Cabinet.

The American people in 1952 and 1956 may well have preferred this detached, limited concept of the Presidency after twenty years of fast-moving, creative presidential rule. Perhaps historians will regard this as necessarily one of those frequent periods of consolidation, a time to draw breath, to recoup our national energy. To quote the State of the Union Message: "No Congress . . . on surveying the state of the nation, has met with a more pleasing prospect than that which appears at the present time." Unfortunately this is not Mr. Eisenhower's last message to the Congress, but Calvin Coolidge's. He followed to the White House Mr. Harding, whose "sponsor" declared very frankly that the times did not demand a first-rate President. If true, the times and the man met.

But the question is what do the times—and the people—demand for the next four years in the White House?

They demand a vigorous proponent of the national interest—not a passive broker for conflicting private interests. They demand a man capable of acting as the commander in chief of the grand alliance, not merely a bookkeeper who feels that his work is done when the numbers on the balance sheet come out even. They demand that he be the head of a responsible party, not rise so far above politics as to be invisible—a man who will formulate and fight for legislative policies, not be a casual bystander to the legislative process.

Today a restricted concept of the Presidency is not enough. . . .

Whatever the political affiliation of our next President, whatever his views may be on all the issues and problems that rush in upon us, he must above all be the Chief Executive in every sense of the word. He must be prepared to exercise the fullest powers of his office—all that are specified and some that are not. He must master complex problems as well as receive one-page memoranda. He must originate action as well as study groups. He must reopen the channels of communication between the world of thought and the seat of power.

"The President is at liberty, both in law and conscience, to be as big a man as he can." So wrote Professor Woodrow Wilson. But President Woodrow Wilson discovered that to be a big man in the White House inevitably brings cries of dictatorship. So did Lincoln and Jackson and the two Roosevelts. And so may the next occupant of that office, if he is the man the times demand. But how much better it would be. . . . , to have a Roosevelt or a Wilson than to have another James Buchanan, cringing in the White House, afraid to move.

. . . Nor can we afford a Chief Executive who is praised primarily for what he did not do, the disasters he prevented, the bills he vetoed—a President wishing his subordinates would produce more missiles or build more schools. We will need instead what the Constitution envisioned: a Chief Executive who is the vital center of action in our whole scheme of government.

This includes the legislative process as well. The President cannot afford—for the sake of the office as well as the nation—to be another Warren G. Harding, described by one backer as a man who "would, when elected, sign whatever bill the Senate sent him—and not send bills for the Senate to pass." Rather he must know when to lead the Congress, when to consult it and when he should act alone. Having served fourteen years in the Legislative Branch, I would not look with favor upon its domination by the Executive. Under our government of "power as the rival of power," to use Hamilton's phrase, Congress must not surrender its responsibilities. But neither should it dominate. However large its share in the formulation of domestic programs, it is the President alone who must make the major decisions of our foreign policy.

That is what the Constitution wisely commands. And even domestically, the President must initiate policies and devise laws to meet the needs of the nation. And he must be prepared to use all the resources of his office to insure the enactment of that legislation—even when conflict is the result. By the end of his term Theodore Roosevelt was not popular in the Congress—particularly when he criticized an amendment to the Treasury appropriation which forbade the use of Secret Service men to investigate congressmen! And the feeling was mutual, Roosevelt saying: "I do not much admire the Senate, because it is such a helpless body when efficient work is to be done." And Woodrow Wilson was even more bitter after his frustrating quarrels—asked if he might run for the Senate in 1920, he replied: "Outside of the United States, the Senate does not amount to a damn. And inside the United States, the Senate is mostly despised. They haven't had a thought down there in fifty years."

But, however bitter their farewells, the facts of the matter are that Roosevelt and Wilson did get things done—not only through their Executive powers but through the Congress as well. Calvin Coolidge, on the other hand, departed from Washington with cheers of Congress still ringing in his ears. But when his World

Court bill was under fire on Capitol Hill he sent no messages, gave no encouragement to the bill's leaders and paid little or no attention to the whole proceeding—and the cause of world justice was set back. To be sure, Coolidge had held the usual White House breakfasts with congressional leaders—but they were aimed, as he himself said, at "good fellowship," not a discussion of "public business." And at his press conferences, according to press historians, where he preferred to talk about the local flower show and its exhibits, reporters who finally extracted from him a single sentence— "I am against that bill"—would rush to file tongue-in-cheek dispatches, proclaiming that: "President Coolidge, in a fighting mood, today served notice on Congress that he intended to combat, with all the resources at his command, the pending bill. . . ."

But in the coming years, we will need a real fighting mood in the White House—a man who will not retreat in the face of pressure from his congressional leaders—who will not let down those supporting his views on the floor. Divided government over the past six years has only been further confused by this lack of legislative leadership. To restore it next year will help restore purpose to both the Presidency and the Congress.

The facts of the matter are that legislative leadership is not possible without party leadership, in the most political sense— . . . no President, it seems to me, can escape politics. He has not only been chosen by the nation—he has been chosen by his party. And if he insists that he is "President of all the people" and should, therefore, offend none of them—if he blurs the issues and differences between the parties—if he neglects the party machinery and avoids his party's leadership—then he has not only weakened the political party as an instrument of the democratic process—he has dealt a blow to the democratic process itself. I prefer the example of Abe Lincoln, who loved politics with the passion of a born practitioner. For example, he waited up all night in 1863 to get the crucial returns on the Ohio governorship. When the Unionist candidate was elected, Lincoln wired: "Glory to God in the highest! Ohio has saved the nation!"

But the White House is not only the center of political leadership. It must be the center of moral leadership—a "bully pulpit," as Theodore Roosevelt described it. For only the President represents the national interest. And upon him alone converge all the needs and aspirations of all parts of the country, all departments of the government, all nations of the world. It is not enough merely to represent prevailing sentiment—to follow McKinley's practice, as described by Joe Cannon, of "keeping his ear so close to the ground he got it full of grasshoppers." We will need in the Sixties a President who is willing and able to summon his national constituency to its finest hour—to alert the people to our dangers and our opportunities—to demand of them the sacrifices that will be necessary. Despite the increasing evidence of a lost national purpose and a soft national will, F.D.R.'s words in his first inaugural still ring true: "In every dark hour of our national life, a leadership of frankness and vigor has met with that understanding and support of the people themselves which is essential to victory."

Roosevelt fulfilled the role of moral leadership. So did Wilson and Lincoln, Truman and Jackson and Teddy Roosevelt. They led the people as well as the government—they fought for great ideals as well as bills. And the time has come to demand that kind of leadership again. And so, as this vital campaign begins, let us discuss the issues the next President will face—but let us also discuss the powers and tools with which he must face them. For he must endow that office with extraordinary strength and vision. He must act in the image of Abraham Lincoln summoning his wartime Cabinet to a meeting on the Emancipation Proclamation. That Cabinet had been carefully chosen to please and reflect many elements in the country. But "I have gathered you together," Lincoln said, "to hear what I have written down. I do not wish your advice about the main matter—that I have determined for myself." And later when he went to sign it after several hours of exhausting handshaking that had left his arm weak, he said to those present: "If my name goes down in history, it will be for this act. My whole soul is in it. If my hand trembles when I sign this proclamation, all who examine the document hereafter will say: 'He hesitated.'" But Lincoln's hand did not tremble. He did not hesitate. He did not equivocate. For he was the President of the United States. It is in this spirit that we must go forth in the coming months and years.

Raymond Wrabley
"Antifederalism and the Presidency"
(Excerpts)

DISCUSSION QUESTION

Examine the Antifederalist criticisms of the Presidency as discussed in the Wrabley article below and re-evaluate the modern Presidency from the Antifederalist perspective. Were their basic concerns valid and are they still relevant?

In the fall of 1786, Shay's rebellion gave impetus to the calls for a constitutional convention. When debtors and farmers in Massachusetts assembled to disrupt court proceedings against debtors, Massachusetts' Governor Bowdoin turned to the national government for assistance but the lack of a standing army or national revenue to raise one left the government helpless. When Governor Bowdoin called on the Worcester militia to suppress the rebels its members refused. In desperation, Nathaniel Gorham, president of the Confederation Congress, wrote to Prince Henry of Prussia of the "failure of our free institutions" and asked if the Prince would be willing to come to America as King. The Prince declined the offer, writing that "Americans had shown so much determination against their old king that they would not readily submit to a new one."[1] In early 1787, wealthy Boston mer-

Permission granted by the Center for the Study of the Presidency, publisher of *Presidential Studies Quarterly*.

[1]Quoted in Eric Black, "MA revolt was important catalyst for birth of Constitution," *Minneapolis Star-Tribune*, February 3, 1987, p. 8a.

chants pooled their own money to finance an army that defeated Shay's rebels in their attempt to overtake a federal arsenal in Springfield. . . .

With no clear models to copy, the authors of the Constitution invented as they went along, guided by their agreement on general principles. The executive, however, presented special problems. Cognizant of the widespread disdain for monarchy and the emphasis on popular government, they sought to create an executive that had enough power to execute national laws and act in emergencies, yet did not appear too regal. Louis Koenig described the predicament: "The President must be endowed with impressive powers yet must not appear to the people, nor in fact be, another king or incipient tyrant. He must have sufficient but not excessive independence. He must be dependent but not, as state governors commonly were, the mere creature of the legislature.[2]

. . . With regards to the newly created presidency, some of the Antifederalists, especially "Cato," were detailed and severe in their criticisms. On the whole, however, Antifederalist criticisms of the proposed Constitution focused more on the points made above—the creation of an all-powerful national government with no limiting Bill of Rights—and less on the presidency. This is perhaps due to the fact that, as Richard Pious points out, in 18th century experience "president" referred simply to a presiding officer of the legislature. No executive powers as such were attached to the office.[3] Philosophically, the executive was thought best subordinated to the legislature. While the proposed Constitution specifically created an independent executive who would wield executive powers, most of the Constitution's critics focused on the Congress, where the bulk of the national government's new powers were believed to have been vested.

Some of the Antifederalists, however, did view the new presidency as deviating from safe republican principles and as cause for great alarm. Virtually every feature of the proposed presidency generated criticism from at least one Antifederalist writer. The Antifederalists had supported the creation of a plural executive (an executive council), rather than a single executive, and attacked the lack of any type of council to support or check the president, Richard Henry Lee pressed for the addition of a "privy council" to "advise and assist in the arduous business assigned to the executive power."[4] George Mason, echoing an argument made by "Cato" as well as others, called the lack of a council a "fatal defect": "The President of the United States has no constitutional council (a thing unknown in any safe and regular government). He will therefore be unsupported by proper information and advice, and will generally be directed by minions and favorites."[5]

The lack of a council led to another problem for the Antifederalists—"the

[2]Louis W. Koenig, *The Chief Executive*, 5th ed. (New York: Harcourt, Brace, Jovanovich, 1986), p. 24.

[3]Richard Pious, *The American Presidency* (New York: Basic Books, 1979), pp. 21–22.

[4]Richard Henry Lee, in Allen and Lloyd, *The Essential Antifederalist*, p. 26.

[5]George Mason, "Objections to the Constitution of Government Formed by the Convention," in Allen and Lloyd, *The Essential Antifederalist*, p. 12.

alarming dependence and connection between [the legislature] and the supreme executive."[6] The Antifederalists, often quoting Montesquieu on the importance of separating executive and legislative powers, argued that the new Constitution blended executive and legislative branches in ways that were "highly dangerous and oligarchic."[7] The fact that the Senate and the President had to act jointly on appointments and treaties would lead to the emergence of a dangerous "junto" of aristocratic Senators and the executive. Presidential possession of a negative on legislation (the qualified veto) and Congressional possession of impeachment power was also believed to be evidence of inadequate separation of powers.

Several Antifederalist critics also attacked the Constitution's provisions for a 4-year presidential term with indefinite re-eligibility. "Cato," again referring to Montesquieu, argued that "in all magistracies, the greatness of power must be compensated by the brevity of the duration."[8] The Antifederalists adhered to the classical republican belief that, in order for the people to remain sovereign and hold elected representatives responsible, officials must face frequent election, hold short terms, or be subject to rotation in office. The Antifederalists proposed, consistent with most state constitutions, a 1-year term for the executive, rotated among the states. As one Antifederalist wrote about the presidency: "You don't even put the same check on him that you do on your own state governor; a man from and bred among you—a man over whom you have a continual and watchful eye—a man who from the nature of his situation, it is almost impossible can do you any injury; this many you say shall not be elected for more than four years, and yet this mighty—this omnipotent governor general may be elected for years and years."[9] Even Thomas Jefferson, a supporter of the Constitution, said that he strongly disliked the provision for indefinite re-eligibility, arguing that "it will be productive of cruel distress to our country."[10]

The principal Antifederalist criticism of the presidency, however, was that the president was given too much power, with only vague limits. "Philadelphiensis" asserted that the President was "vested with power dangerous to a free people."[11] "Cato" claimed that "the language of the article relative to the establishment of the executive . . . [is] vague and inexplicit . . . [T]he president possessed of the power given him by this frame of government differs but very immaterially from the establishment of monarchy in Great Britain."[12] The Antifederalists were especially concerned that vast but vague executive powers (including the veto, pardon power, and command of the military), combined with a long term in office could

[6]Ibid.

[7]Richard Henry Lee, in Allen and Lloyd, *The Essential Antifederalist*, p. 24.

[8]"Cato," in John D. Lewis, ed. *Anti-Federalists v. Federalists: Selected Documents* (Scranton, PA: Chandler Publishing Company, 1967), p. 193.

[9]Quoted in Jackson Turner Main, *The Anti-federalists* (New York: WW Norton and Company, 1961), pp. 140–141.

[10]Thomas Jefferson, in Allen and Lloyd, *The Essential Antifederalist*, p. 71.

[11]Quoted in Main, *The Anti-federalists*, p. 141.

[12]"Cato," in Allen and Lloyd, *The Essential Antifederalist*, p. 159.

lead to oppressive rule. Again, "Cato" made this argument in the strongest terms: "If the president is possessed of ambition, he has power and time sufficient to ruin his country."[13]

While the Antifederalists generally seemed to respect General George Washington, the presumed heir-apparent to the presidency, they argued that even a good president was not ultimately reassuring, given the "vast and important powers" of the president and the lack of explicit restraints on presidential powers. "A Maryland Farmer" argued: "The chief magistrate is now clothed with full authority to do good. If he does so, he confirms a solid tyranny for his degenerate successors. For if power does not corrupt him it certainly will those that follow. In this view, the best elected magistrates have only entailed misery on mankind . . . [I]n all governments in which there is sown the seeds of the rule of one man, no checks, no bars can prevent its growing into a monarchy or a despotism if the empire is extensive."[14]

This last argument puts the Antifederalist fear of a strong and unified executive into a broader context. The Federalists, especially Alexander Hamilton, fearing legislative power, argued the case for a more energetic executive. The benefits of a strengthened executive were noted, but not much concern for the dangers was expressed. That "energy" had been infused into the new executive office was beyond doubt. It was not as clear, however, how much energy had been invested. The Antifederalists, on the other hand, warned that while greater executive power might have been necessary, vesting that executive power in a single person was dangerous, especially if the powers were vague and the checks apparently few. This was particularly true in the context of stronger national government and the hint of imperial national goals. The threat was apparent even if some individual presidents were trustworthy.

A review of the original Constitutional debate and, especially Antifederalist criticisms helps bring focus to other, less-often discussed issues that may have some bearing on the study of the contemporary presidency. . . .

Today, the presidency is profoundly different than the design, intent, and anticipation of the authors of the Constitution and, in some ways, resembles the expansive institution that the Antifederalists warned of and feared. The modern president has been described as "the central energizer of government policy . . . , the articulator of the national purpose, the principal symbol at home and abroad of the American political system, and the focus of the hopes (and fears) of countless individuals and groups."[15] George Edwards and Stephen Wayne write that, "in the past, the people did not look to the president to solve most national economic, social, and political problems. Today they do."[16] Lowi now describes ours as a "presidential government."

---

[13]"Cato," in Lewis, ed. *Anti-Federalists v. Federalists*, p. 194.

[14]"A Maryland Farmer," in Allen and Lloyd, *The Essential Antifederalist*, p. 260.

[15]Edward Greenberg, *The American Political System*, 4th ed. (Boston: Little, Brown and Company, 1986), p. 220.

[16]George C. Edwards III and Stephen J. Wayne, *Presidential Leadership* (New York: St. Martin's Press, 1985), p. 11.

. . . The consequences and implications for the presidency and democratic government are ones that presidents, scholars, and citizens alike are grappling with today.

Even the titles of recent works on the presidency, such as *The Impossible Presidency: Illusions and Realities of Executive Power and The Dilemmas of Presidential Leadership,* convey the concerns of presidential scholars. After celebrating presidential power in the 1960s as a vehicle for progressive policy change and national leadership, by the 1970s observers issued warnings about the "imperial presidency." By the late 1970s the concern was that the imperial presidency had quickly given way to an "imperiled presidency." Midway through the 1980s, scholars touted the "restored presidency." Today, conflicting analyses and opinions abound. Possibilities and problems—even crises—in the presidency seem to continue.

Theodore Lowi
"Presidential Power: Restoring the Balance"
(Excerpts)

DISCUSSION QUESTIONS

1. What does Lowi mean by "plebiscitary Presidency"? How is this contrasted to the "imperial Presidency"? Why is it important to make this distinction? What would an "imperial Presidency" mean to Patrick Henry and other Antifederalists?
2. Compare Lowi's assessment of "Presidential government" with Kennedy's comments on the role of the chief executive. How do they continue the debate over the executive branch that began during the ratification controversy? Who would be their respective allies?
3. Lowi proposes some changes; what are they? What are the strengths and weaknesses of Lowi's arguments and his suggested reforms? How would the Antifederalists respond to Lowi?

In a single office, the presidency, the great powers of the American people have been invested, making it the most powerful office in the world. Its power is great precisely because it is truly the people's power, in the form of consent regularly granted. But there is great uncertainty about the terms of the social contract. We can know that virtually all power, limited only by the Bill of Rights, has been granted. And we can know that when presidents take the oath of office they accept the power and the conditions for its use: the promise of performance must be met. But we cannot know what is adequate performance. No entrepreneur would ever sign a contract that leaves the conditions of fulfillment to the subjective judgment of the other party. This is precisely what has happened in the new social contract underlying the modern government of the United States.

Ciglar and Loomis, *American Politics* (New York: Houghton-Mifflin). Reprinted with permission from *Political Science Quarterly* 100 (Summer 1985), pp. 185–213.

The system of large positive national government in the United States was a deliberate construction, arising out of the 1930s. The urgency of the times and the poverty of government experience meant that the building was done exuberantly but improvisationally, without much concern for constitutional values or history. The modern presidency is the centerpiece of that construction. Considered by many a triumph of democracy, the modern American presidency is also its victim. . . .

The gains from presidential government were immediate. Presidential government energized the executive; it gave the national government direction; it enhanced the capacity of presidential leadership to build national consensus and to overcome the natural inertia of a highly heterogeneous society. The costs of presidential government were cumulative. Most of the costs result from the fact that the expectations of the masses have grown faster than the capacity of presidential government to meet them. This imbalance has produced a political cycle, running on a regular course from boom to bust and back again. Just when the national government was beginning to develop a capacity to control the extremes of the business cycle, it was foiled by the phenomenon of the political cycle. The potential for political bankruptcy runs high. . . .

The Imperial/Plebiscitary Presidency

Richard Nixon was brought up on the imperial presidency and had no serious misgivings about it. Imperial meant something established, neither extreme nor extraordinary. Schlesinger could conceive of an imperial presidency precisely because it was already a real thing and not a figment of his or of Richard Nixon's imagination. Schlesinger chose the characterization *imperial* because it connotes a strong state with sovereignty and power over foreigners, as well as rank, status, privilege, and authority, and it also connotes the president's power and responsibility to do whatever he judges necessary to maintain the sovereignty of the state and its ability to keep public order, both international and domestic. The imperial presidency turns out on inspection, therefore, to be nothing more nor less than the discretionary presidency grounded in national security rather than domestic government. Characterizing the presidency as plebiscitary is not at all inconsistent; it is an attempt to capture the same factors and at the same time to tie them to the greatest source of everyday pressure on the presidency—not the Soviet Union, not world leadership, but the American people and their expectations. Nixon's understanding of this situation in all its aspects was probably more extensive and complete than that of any other modern president. He understood it to a fault. If so, he was operating logically and sanely under the following assumptions:

The first assumption is that the president and the state are the same thing, that president is state personified. The second is that powers should be commensurate with responsibilities. Since most of the responsibilities of state were intentionally delegated to the president, there is every reason to assume that Congress and the people intended that there be a capacity to carry them out.

The third assumption, intimately related to the second, is that the president should not and cannot be bound by normal legal restrictions. To put this indelicately, the president's actions must be considered above the law or subject to a different kind of law from those of ordinary citizens. While not free to commit any crime merely for the sake of convenience, the president nevertheless cannot be constantly beset by considerations of legality when the state itself is or seems to be at issue.

The first three assumptions head inexorably toward a fourth, which is that any *deliberate* barriers to presidential action must be considered tantamount to disloyalty. Barriers to presidential action can be tolerated up to a point, and it is probable that most presidents, including Richard Nixon, have prided themselves on their uncommon patience with organized protests, well-meaning but embarrassing news leaks, journalistic criticism, and organized political opposition. But there is a point beyond which such barriers cannot be tolerated, and as that point is approached, confidential knowledge of the identities and contentions of the organizers of obstructions must be gathered. When the intentions of these organizers are determined, to the president's satisfaction, to be malicious, it would be foolish for the president to wait until they are fully set in train.

If these assumptions only barely approximate Nixon's understanding of the presidency, then his actions, including his crimes, are entirely consistent and rational, quite possibly motivated by the highest sense of public interest. To reach that conclusion, however, is not to exonerate Nixon but only to bring the system and all its presidents into question. The Gulf of Tonkin incident involved a much greater deceit than Watergate. And Nixon's connection between himself and the state was never so intimate as that made by President Lyndon B. Johnson, who was even able to define the Vietnam War in personal terms: "I won't be the first to lose a war."

"Lying in state" is common practice. Presidents operate on the brink of failure and in ignorance of when, where, and how failure will come. They do not and cannot possibly know about even a small proportion of government activity that bears on their failure. They can only put out fires and smile above the ashes. They don't know what's going on—yet they are responsible for it. And they feed that responsibility every time they take credit for good news not of their own making. The best recent example is President Ronald Reagan's claiming credit for the 1984 rise in average national SAT scores.

"Lying in state" is justifiable when the fundamental interests of the state are in peril: when there exists a palpable threat to public order or to diplomacy in situations where premature popular demands could contribute to war. But modern presidents, among whom Richard Nixon is only one, perceive vital threats to national interests earlier and more often than ever. The threats don't have to be real—and usually aren't. Presidents don't have to believe they are real—and probably don't. Their main obligation is to preserve the myth that they are reserving themselves for the big decisions. This permits them to remain ignorant of most of what is happening; it permits them to leave most of the decisions to staff and most governing to administrators. This is presidential government. *This is presidential government?* It has frequently been observed that one of the main functions of a presidential press conference is the opportunity it provides to brief the president in order to keep him abreast of what is going on. What is presidential government between press conferences?

Presidential Power: If Building It Up Won't Work Try Building It Down

America approaches the end of the twentieth century with an enormous bureaucratized government, a plebiscitary presidency, and apparent faith that the latter can impose on the former an accountability sufficient to meet the rigorous test of democratic theory. Anyone who really shares this faith is living under a happy state of delusion. Anyone who does not believe and argues it nevertheless is engaging in one of Plato's Noble Lies; that is to say, the leaders do not believe it but believe it is in the public interest that the rest of us believe it. Then there are others who don't believe it but would like to make it the truth by giving the president more and more help. Presidents have themselves tried nearly everything to build for themselves a true capacity to govern. Congress, with few exceptions, has cooperated. The Supreme Court . . . has cooperated. The public seems willing to cooperate in making truth out of the noble lie by investing more and more power in the presidency. The intellectuals, perhaps most of all, have cooperated. If that's not enough, then it's possible nothing is enough.

Since building up the presidency has not met the problem of presidential capacity to govern, the time has come to consider building it down. Building down goes against the mentality of American capitalism, whose primary measure of success is buildups. Buildings are so important to American corporate managers that they fake them if necessary, through anything from useless mergers to misrepresentation of profits. Very few leaders have tried to succeed by making a virtue of building down. There was Bismarck, who perceived greater strength in a "smaller Germany." There may be a case or two of weekly magazines whose publishers have sought to strengthen their position by abandoning the struggle for a maximum mass subscription in favor of a smaller and more select but stable readership. But most leaders, in commerce and government, are guilty of what Barry Goldwater popularized in the 1960s, "growthmanship." In many circumstances, building up is an illusory solution, or, at best, a short-term gain.

The most constructive approach to building down the presidency would be the strengthening of political parties. If party organizations returned to the center of presidential selection, they would build down the presidency by making collective responsibility a natural outcome of the selection process rather than an alien intruder. Real parties build down the presidency in constructive ways by making real cabinets possible. The present selection process and the present relationship between the president and public opinion produced the star symbol that renders a president's sharing power almost inconceivable. The selection process with parties involved makes the star system itself hard to conceive of.

A three-party system comes into the picture in at least two ways. First, if a two-party system is indeed an anachronism in modern programmatic governments, a three-party system could be the most reasonable way to make real parties possible. Second, a three-party system might build down the presidency by making it more of a parliamentary office. This development would constitute something of a return to the original intent of the Founders' design, a selection process culminating in the House of Representatives. The French improved upon their system by mixing theirs with ours to create the Fifth Republic. It is time we consider mixing ours with theirs. The Fifth Republic established a better balance than we have by successfully imposing an independently elected president upon a strong parliament, giving the parliament the leadership lacking in the Fourth Republic but keeping the popularly elected president tied closely to it.

The crying need to impose parliamentary responsibility in our independently elected president can be accomplished without formally amending the Constitution. Just as the two-party system transformed the presidential selection system and thereby the presidency, so would a three-party or multiparty system transform the presidency, by bringing Congress back into the selection process. This transformation could, in addition, give Congress incentive to confront the real problems of the presidency. Although I admit that is unlikely, the probability could be improved as more of its members came to realize that Congress's survival as an institution may depend upon depriving the presidency of its claim to represent the Great American Majority. The presidency must be turned into a more parliamentary office.

Presidents who are products of the present system are also unlikely to try to change it—unless they come to recognize its inherent pathologies. The first president to recognize these pathologies will want to build down the presidency, and his or her legacy will be profound and lasting. A president who recognizes the pathology of the plebiscitary presidency will demand changes that will ward off failure and encourage shared responsibility. At a minimum, a rational president would veto congressional enactments delegating powers so broad and so vague that expectations cannot be met. This step in itself would build down the presidency in a very special way: It would incorporate more of Congress into the presidency because the clearer the intentions and the criteria of performance written into a statute, the more responsibility for its outcomes would be shared by the majority in Congress responsible for its passage. Such a way of building down alone would not produce a third party, but it would make the presidency more parliamentary, and thus more accommodating to strong parties and to three parties or more. Put this way, the prospect does not seem so unrealistic. To accomplish it, the president must simply make an analysis of the situation. A president must simply change his point of view.

Institutional reform is desperately needed, but the struggle for reform must be sensitive to the probability that there are no specific and concrete solutions for the problems of the plebiscitary presidency. One of the mischievous consequences of mixing technology and democracy is *belief in solutions*. Solutions are for puzzles. Big government is not a puzzle. The plebiscitary presidency is not a puzzle. Each is a source of important problems because, like all institutions, each is built on some basic contradictions. These contradictions will not go away, because they are the result of mixing highly desirable goals that don't mix well. There is, for example, a contradiction between representation and efficiency. There is a contradiction between the goal of treating everyone equally and the goal of giving special attention to individual variation. There tend to be contradictions wherever demand is intense and supply is limited. Problems in any institution are likely to grow in importance and danger whenever people lose their appreciation for the contradictions inherent in an institution and proceed to maximize one side of a contradiction at the expense of the other. For such contradictions and the problems of balance among desirable but contradictory goals, *coping* is a more realistic goal than *solving*. Successful coping comes mainly from understanding, and the chief barrier to understanding is ideology—the steadfast defense of existing practices and existing distributions of power.

On one point at least there is strong agreement between my argument and Ronald Reagan: his observation that where once government was part of the solution it is now part of the problem. Since I have been arguing the same thing at least since 1969, I celebrate Reagan's recognition of the truth and regret the fact he does not actually believe it. He embraced big government and embraced, nay, enlarged the plebiscitary presidency more than most of his predecessors. Why do all recent presidents and important presidential aspirants look back with such admiration to Harry Truman, a man of such ordinary character and talents? I think they do so because Truman was the last president who was made bigger by the office he occupied. This is not to say that recent presidents have made more mistakes than presidents of the past. It is to say that they have been diminished by having to achieve so much more than past presidents and by having to use so much more deception to compensate for their failures. Modern presidents blame their failures on everything but the presidency, when the fault is the presidency more than anything else. It is there that successful coping must begin, with a change of attitude toward the plebiscitary presidency that will enable presidents and presidential candidates to confront the contradictions in the modern presidency rather than by embracing the office as it is.

George Bernard Shaw put his finger on an essential point in "Don Juan in Hell," the famous interlude in *Man and Superman*:

> *Don Juan:* Señor Commander [The Statue]: You know the way to the frontier of hell and heaven. Be good enough to direct me.
>
> *The Statue:* Oh, the frontier is only the difference between two ways of looking at things. Any road will take you across if you really want to get there.

Real reform in American presidential government will not come until there is real change in the points of view of powerful people. As in psychoanalysis, so in politics, coping is a solution, and it will be found not in techniques but in awareness of the nature of the problem. Techniques will follow.

It is appropriate to end on a psychoanalytic note. And it is not inappropriate to give the last word to a famous fictional psychiatrist, who provided the very last line, freely translated, of [Philip Roth's] *Portnoy's Complaint*: "And now we can begin the analysis."

F. G. Hutchins
"Presidential Autocracy in America"
(Excerpts)

DISCUSSION QUESTIONS

1. What does Hutchins mean by "autocracy"? How is this definition applicable to the executive office? What are Hutchins' complaints about the office of the Presidency? Which thinker from the ratification debate is closest to the attitudes exhibited by Hutchins? What reforms, if any, would you propose?
2. Compare Hutchins to Neustadt and Ames. How do these three thinkers contribute to the debate over Presidential power that began during the ratification controversy?
3. Compare Hutchins' critique with Lowi's. Determine and describe any similarities and differences that you discover in this comparison. Which of these two writers is closer to the spirit of Antifederalism? Why?

The tyranny of the legislature is really the danger most to be feared, and will continue to be so for many years to come. The tyranny of the executive power will come in its turn, but at a more distant period.

—Thomas Jefferson, *letter to James Madison, March 15, 1789.*

The American Presidency has today become the "tyranny" that Jefferson foresaw. The executive branch, the Cinderella of the Constitution of 1789, which fell into such disrepute and inconsequence in the nineteenth century that Lord Bryce felt compelled to explain "Why Great Men are not Elected President," has in the twentieth century come into an inheritance greater than that ever enjoyed by her two sister branches of government.

The triumph of the Presidency was accomplished without constitutional alteration, because the federal government, from the beginning, was a system of separation of power, but fusion of function. Each of the separate branches of government—the Congress, the Presidency, the Court—was assigned legislative, executive, and judicial functions. The "strengthening of the Presidency" has resulted not simply from the growth in the importance of executive authority in an increasingly complex, developed society, but, more importantly, from the fused growth of the legislative, executive, and judicial authority of the Presidency. This has not appeared to involve usurpation of functions from the other two branches, because the constitutional framework did give the Presidency a foothold in all three areas from which to develop. . . .

The legislative, executive, and judicial powers of the President have not only been expanded but also used to justify one another. Enthusiasts stress the representative character of the Presidency; the role of Presidential leadership in foreign

---

Tugwell and Cronin, *The Presidency Re-appraised* (New York: Greenwood/Praeger Publishers, 1974). Reprinted by kind permission of the author.

and domestic affairs; and the judgmental power of the President, who, because of his special representativeness and responsibilities, as well as his special advantages of position and access to advice, is able to arbitrate issues in a uniquely judicious way. The Presidency, in short, is three branches in one. The definition that the Presidency gives to each of these functions is not, however, identical with the definition of these functions traditionally upheld by the other branches. The President's apologists have defined the prime functions associated with the other branches in ways that make it appear that the President is better suited to pursue them than the originally constituted branch.

The most grandiose conception of the President's representativeness was that first articulated by Woodrow Wilson, that the President represents all the people. If the Presidency could be made to seem more truly representative of the "people" than was the Congress, where arguably only "interests" were represented, then the Presidency could, in the name of the people, exercise ultimate power with righteous vigor. . . .

The Wilsonian conception of the Presidency has triumphed far beyond Wilson's wildest imaginings. The President, representing all the people, can act in his executive capacity in response to his representative capacity. He need not think of himself as the executive of the Congress; he is the executive of the people. He does not need a law upon which to base his actions. Actions can be justified by reference to the President's "constitutional powers," which means, in effect, his direct representativeness. In 1973, President Nixon, for example, defended his bombing of Cambodia as an exercise of his "inherent authority" as commander in chief and pointed to his re-election margin of 1972 to refute the apparent constitutional requirement of congressional authorization for military initiatives.

Most recent Presidents have seemed to take literally the Wilsonian aspiration to "represent all of the people all of the time." John Kennedy, however, while still a senator, defended the election of the President by the electoral college against the proposal that the college be abolished in order to ensure a more representative Presidency, on the grounds that the President represented the industrial North to a greater extent than other parts of the country, under the present arrangement, and that this was desirable because other parts of the country were better represented in other parts of the government. Since the Congress was a stronghold of Southern strength, the slight advantage the North had in the contest for the Presidency was important to preserve, in Kennedy's eyes. This argument implied a conception of representation that included the entire government, in which the Presidency was seen as a competing representative institution, representing a part of the whole, while the Congress represented another part.

While few Presidents have advanced such an explicit argument as Kennedy made, all Presidents feel representative of a primary constituency as well as of the people as a whole. One's primary constituency may be only characterized vaguely as "the forgotten man" or "the silent majority," or its existence may be denied altogether. The significant consideration, however, is that the direct, fractional representativeness of the President is not thought to make it impossible for him to be, when necessary, also the representative of all. The President may feel that the better half of the nation that supports him is also more representative of the nation's future, and that, in responding to it, he is thereby responding to the interests of all, properly and prospectively defined. . . .

Montesquieu contended that the governing principle of a constitutional monarchy is honor, whereas that of a republic is virtue. The leader of a republic, Montesquieu suggested, is satisfied with the existence in it of many individually virtuous men. A monarchy, whether elective or hereditary, is concerned with grandeur, with putting all its subjects to tasks of appropriate magnitude, with justifying the awe in which it is held abroad by acting in accordance with the dignity of its power. . . . [1]

Montesquieu was right: If you make a man a King he will begin to think in terms of glory. How could proponents of the enhancement of Presidential power not have anticipated that a great leader armed with great discretion would seek glory rather than goodness? They failed to anticipate this result because they had also written into the drama a role for themselves. The President, subordinating representativeness to the imperatives of executive leadership of a great power, in turn was to subordinate executive leadership to the directives of a "rational" decision-making process. A judicious President, exercising discretion wisely, would be guided at every juncture by the expert advisers at his side.

The original purpose of the Constitution was to give necessary power to officials hamstrung by legal strictures. As Herman Melville put it, "If there are any three things opposed to the genius of the American Constitution, they are these: irresponsibility in a judge, unlimited discretionary authority in an executive, and the union of an irresponsible judge and an unlimited executive in one person." [2] The rule of laws, not men, meant that, though men would rule, they could not rule as idiosyncratically as they would wish. Implicit in the contemporary vision of Presidential government, in contrast, is a vast role for discretion. Centralized action is obviously more efficient; if it can be claimed that it is also more just, then the old fears of the Founding Fathers can be dismissed as out of date.

A judicious President, it is argued, can act with speed, flexibility, and on the basis of expert advice. Is not the President the best-informed person, the best-situated person to make a decision? Actually, the availability of expert advice has served to isolate the President. Whether advised by an elite of independently accomplished men, or by specialists on his own payroll, the President is trapped by those trying to help him. The President may be the worst-informed person in the country if he is systematically shielded from the normal experience and outlook of citizens. Akbar the Great of India and Henry V of England used to disguise themselves as ordinary men and wander freely amongst their subjects to learn what was really going on. Surrounded by sycophants and specialists, these monarchs went to

---

[1]Baron de Montesquieu, *The Spirit of the Laws*, trans. Thomas Nugent (New York: Hafner, 1962).

[2]Herman Melville, *White-Jacket* (New York: Russell and Russell, 1963), p. 178.

their lowly subjects in search of unbiased views on the needs of the kingdom. A President who honors his advisers with the highest possible praise—his trust that their presentation of this country's need makes him well informed—is the most pathetic of captives, a bear on a string.

The myth of the judicious President is not only factually inaccurate, it is deeply destructive of the character of the occupant of the office. The President, we are told, is a different sort of person from the generality of Americans. As he has a special nature, so he has special duties. He alone, for example, can determine when his political opponents are endangering "national security" and giving "comfort to America's enemies." His special duties necessitate his possession of special privileges–picturephones, jet airplanes, summer and winter palaces, and a prescriptive right to impound the consciences of the highest and lowest members of his realm. The Watergate affair demonstrated graphically that a surprising number of Americans of high patriotism felt unable to refuse a request from "the White House" that they break the law of the land.

A structure wrought to ensure rational decision-making has instead hopelessly entangled private whims with national needs. A President, freed to do as he wishes, is expected to be right; in fact, he is permitted no defense against his own fallibility. He is routinely tempted by the logic of false determinism; having made a decision, he is likely to say, and come to believe, that he had "no choice" but to make the decision he did. George Reedy has argued that, with the possible exception of Franklin Roosevelt, recent Presidents have been ordinarily unable to profit from their mistakes. In Reedy's view, a person who enters the Presidency with normal, or even above-normal, intelligence and political sensitivity will soon start making political blunders which would make a ward-heeler blush.[3] Together, the forces around and within the President are likely to destroy even the elementary political sensitivity of men who show enormous subtlety in their march to the throne. . . .

What, finally, can be said of the effect of the myth of the judicious President on the morale of the public at large? The President's superhuman prerogatives ultimately rest on the assumption that it is in the interest of all of us to have a person who is pure and high-minded, and who consequently must be presented publicly as such even if there are good grounds for believing differently. The feeling persists that something dreadful would happen to all of us, and to the entire structure of government from which we benefit so substantially, if anybody acted publicly on the basis of his private knowledge of the personal character of the President. If all avert their eyes, the President will not be in danger of damaging his image by walking around naked. The myth of the Presidency is the creation of people who know better but who are appalled by the prospect of having to consider the alternatives. We cling to the hope that a person, even though an ordinary man to all appearances, when supplied with a magical apparatus, can bring about a complete

---

[3]George Reedy, *The Twilight of the Presidency* (New York: New American Library, 1970). This book provides an excellent insider's account of the "court" atmosphere of the contemporary White House.

change in the entire polity. The irony is, we know that the President's magic is manufactured and maintained by our own efforts and that a man riding on a wish is not really a magician; he is a confidence artist. We supply him with the confidence that makes him look like an artist. You can't fool all the people all the time; but can all the people fool themselves all the time?

9

The Judicial Branch

The Federalist support of the judicial branch as established in the Constitution resulted in a vociferous and antagonistic response from Antifederalist writers. Both the Pennsylvania minority and Brutus (thought to be Robert Yates, a delegate to the Constitutional Convention and a friend of New York Governor George Clinton[1]) reacted strongly to Article III. Antifederalists viewed the judicial branch as the least democratic of the three. They were uncomfortable with the lifetime tenure afforded judges in the Constitution. In addition, the Constitutional provision for the removal of judges was viewed as inadequate. Under this provision a judge could be removed only for "high crimes and misdemeanors," not for improperly adjudicating the law. Antifederalists were concerned that the use of judicial power, especially as proscribed by Hamilton, would impinge upon state legislative and judicial power. From an Antifederalist perspective, there did not seem to be adequate checks upon the judicial branch, particularly by the legislative branch. Antifederalists also complained about the lack of a guarantee for civil jury trials in the Constitution. This, coupled with the insistence of Hamilton on judicial review based upon prior case law precedents, would ultimately assure a legal system populated with professional lawyers and judges complete with its own language. This, the Antifederalists argued, would isolate the common person of moderate to poor means from the law. The cost of litigation would surely and inevitably rise under the Constitution.

To correct this situation, Antifederalists proposed a number of remedies. They desired a guarantee in the Constitution for greater reliance on trials by juries in civil cases. Brutus, in particular, championed the establishment of a tribunal for the purposes of checking and guiding Supreme Court judges when mistakes in the law were made. Antifederalists generally favored temporary commissions or terms for judges and greater ties between the judiciary and the people's legislative branch of government.

Hamilton, in opposition to the Antifederalists, viewed the judicial branch of government as the ". . . least dangerous branch to the political rights in the Constitution." He vigorously defended the separation of powers between the branches. Hamilton argued against a temporary commission for judges and greater ties to the legislative branch of government. He believed that the political expediency of the legislators would affect judicial appointments, and in the final analysis the legislature's knowledge

---

[1]Ralph Ketchum, Ed., *The Anti-Federalist Papers and the Constitutional Convention Debates* (New York: Mentor Books, 1986), p. 269.

of the law is inferior to the knowledge of judges. Hamilton's distrust of the common person runs through his arguments against greater reliance on jury trials in civil cases. He believed that it is easier to corrupt juries than public officials. A type of hierarchy of trust is established in Hamiltonian thought. Judges occupy a pre-eminent and most trustworthy position in society owing to their knowledge of the law, followed by public officials and common people on juries. In *Federalist Paper* #78, Hamilton captures the difference between Federalists and Antifederalists when he states regarding jury trials that, ". . . the former [Federalists] regard it as a valuable safeguard to liberty; the latter [Antifederalists] represent it as the very palladium of free government." Hamilton is wary of the greater participatory democratic notions implied in Antifederalist arguments.

In two modern writings we have the opportunity to judge the lasting effects of this debate. According to Kenneth M. Dolbeare and Linda Medcalf, Hamilton's arguments launched our present legal and economic system. The fears of the Antifederalists have been realized, and the result is a series of problems confronting our nation. Richard A. Brisbin, Jr., traces the conservative ideology of Supreme Court Justice Anton Scalia. As he argues, Scalia's ideology can be associated with the tradition of former Supreme Court Justice Felix Frankfurter. This tradition possesses ties to both Hamilton and Brutus. The ideological mix is not only interesting but again illustrates the enduring effect of the great debate not only upon modern Supreme Court justices but perhaps upon us all.

THE CONSTITUTION (EXCERPTS)

ARTICLE III—THE JUDICIAL ARTICLE

Judicial Power, Courts, Judges

Section 1. The judicial Power of the United States, shall be vested in one supreme Court, and in such inferior Courts as the Congress may from time to time ordain and establish. The Judges, both of the supreme and inferior Courts, shall hold their Offices during good Behaviour, and shall, at stated Times, receive for their Services, a Compensation, which shall not be diminished during their Continuance in Office.

Jurisdiction

Section 2. The judicial Power shall extend to all Cases, in Law and Equity, arising under this Constitution, the Laws of the United States, and Treaties made, or which shall be made, under their Authority; —to all Cases affecting Ambassadors, other public Ministers and Consuls; —to all Cases of admiralty and maritime Jurisdiction; —to Controversies to which the United States shall be a Party; —to Controversies between two or more States; [between a State and Citizens of another State] between Citizens of different States; —between Citizens of the same State claiming Lands under Grants of different States, [and between a State or the Citizens thereof, and foreign States, Citizens or Subjects.][1]

In all Cases affecting Ambassadors, other public Ministers and Consuls, and those in which a State shall be Party, the supreme Court shall have original Jurisdiction. In all the other Cases before mentioned, the supreme Court shall

[1]Modified by the 11th Amendment

have appellate Jurisdiction, both as to Law and Fact, with such Exceptions, and under such Regulations as the Congress shall make.

The Trial of all Crimes, except in Cases of Impeachment, shall be by Jury; and such Trial shall be held in the State where the said Crimes shall have been committed; but when not committed within any State, the Trial shall be at such Place or Places as the Congress may by Law have directed.

Treason

Section 3. Treason against the United States, shall consist only in levying War against them, or in adhering to their Enemies, giving them Aid and Comfort. No Person shall be convicted of Treason unless on the Testimony of two Witnesses to the same overt Act, or on Confession in open Court.

The Congress shall have Power to declare the Punishment of Treason, but no Attainder of Treason shall work Corruption of Blood, or Forfeiture except during the Life of the Person attainted.

Amendment 11

[Ratified February 7, 1795]

The Judicial power of the United States shall not be construed to extend to any suit in law or equity, commenced or prosecuted against one of the United States by Citizens of another State, or by Citizens or Subjects of any Foreign State.

ANTIFEDERALIST ARGUMENTS

"The Address and Reasons of Dissent of the Minority of the Convention of Pennsylvania to Their Constituents" December 18, 1787 (Excerpt)

DISCUSSION QUESTIONS

1. How would you characterize the Pennsylvania minority's criticisms concerning the lack of a guarantee for jury trials in civil cases in the Constitution?
2. What does the minority say about admiralty and maritime jurisdiction?
3. What is the argument of the minority concerning the expense of litigation in civil law courts? How will this impact upon people of poor fortune?
4. How will the appeal process work against the "common people"?
5. As we look at our present system of law, do these Antifederalist criticisms hold any validity today?

We have before noticed the judicial power as it would effect a consolidation of the states into one government; we will now examine it, as it would affect the liberties and welfare of the people, supposing such a government were practicable and proper.

The judicial power, under the proposed constitution, is founded on the well-known principles of the *civil law*, by which the judge determines both on law and fact, and appeals are allowed from the inferior tribunals to the superior, upon the whole question; so that *facts* as well as *law*, would be re-examined, and even new facts brought forward in the court of appeals; and to use the words of a very eminent Civilian— "The cause is many times another thing before the court of appeals, than what it was at the time of the first sentence."

That this mode of proceeding is the one which must be adopted under this constitution, is evident from the following circumstances:—1st. That the trial by jury, which is the grand characteristic of the common law, is secured by the constitution, only in criminal cases.—2d. That the appeal from both *law* and *fact* is expressly established, which is utterly inconsistent with the principles of the common law, and trials by jury. The only mode in which an appeal from law and fact can be established, is, by adopting the principles and practice of the civil law; unless the United States should be drawn into the absurdity of calling and swearing juries, merely for the purpose of contradicting their verdicts, which would render juries contemptible and worse than useless.—3d. That the courts to be established would decide on all cases *of law and equity*, which is a well known characteristic of the civil law, and these courts would have conusance not only of the laws of the United States and of treaties, and of cases affecting ambassadors, but of all cases of *admiralty and maritime jurisdiction*, which last are matters belonging exclusively to the civil law, in every nation in Christendom.

Not to enlarge upon the loss of the invaluable right of trial by an unbiassed jury, so dear to every friend of liberty, the monstrous expence and inconveniences of the mode of proceedings to be adopted, are such as will prove intolerable to the people of this country. The lengthy proceedings of the civil law courts in the chancery of England, and in the courts of Scotland and France, are such that few men of moderate fortune can endure the expence of; the poor man must therefore submit to the wealthy. Length of purse will too often prevail against right and justice. For instance, we are told by the learned judge *Blackstone*, that a question only on the property of an ox, of the value of *three* guineas, originating under the civil law proceedings in Scotland, after many interlocutory orders and sentences below, was carried at length from the court of sessions, the highest court in that part of Great Britain, by way of *appeal* to the house of lords, *where* the question of law and fact was finally determined. He adds, that no pique or spirit could in the court of king's bench or common pleas at Westminster, have given continuance to such a cause for a tenth part of the time, nor have cost a twentieth part of the expence. Yet the costs in the courts of king's bench and common pleas in England, are infinitely greater than those which the people of this country have ever experienced. We abhor the idea of losing the transcendant privilege of trial by jury, with the loss of which, it is remarked by the same learned author, that in Sweden, the liberties of the commons were extinguished by an aristocratic senate: and that *trial by jury* and the liberty of the people went out together. At the same time we regret the intolerable delay, the enormous expences and infinite vexation to which the people of this country will be exposed from the voluminous proceedings of the courts of civil law, and especially from the appellate jurisdiction, by means of which a man may be drawn from the utmost boundaries of this extensive country to the seat of the supreme court of the nation to contend, perhaps with a wealthy and powerful adversary. The consequence of this establishment will be an absolute confirmation of the power of aristocratical influence in the courts of justice: for the common people will not be able to contend or struggle against it.

"Brutus"
(Probably Robert Yates)
Essay XI
(Excerpts)

DISCUSSION QUESTIONS

1. How does Brutus feel about the independent nature of the judicial branch? Why?
2. What does Brutus say about the technical phrases and language of the gentlemen learned in the law?
3. Brutus makes the argument that the Supreme Court will interpret the Constitution ". . . according to what *appears to them*, the *reason* and *spirit* of the Constitution." Why is he uncomfortable with this sentiment? Would the Pennsylvania minority agree? Why or why not?
4. According to Brutus, what effect will judicial power in the Constitution have upon the states?
5. Why does Brutus warn us against the extension of judicial power? In light of such court cases as *Marbury v. Madison* and *McCulloch v. Maryland*, was Brutus correct?

It is, . . . of great importance, to examine with care the nature and extent of the judicial power, because those who are to be vested with it, are to be placed in a situation altogether unprecedented in a free country. They are to be rendered totally independent, both of the people and the legislature, both with respect to their offices and salaries. No errors they may commit can be corrected by any power above them, if any such power there be, nor can they be removed from office for making ever so many erroneous adjudications.

The only causes for which they can be displaced, is, conviction of treason, bribery, and high crimes and misdemeanors.

This part of the plan is so modelled, as to authorise the courts, not only to carry into execution the powers expressly given, but where these are wanting or ambiguously expressed, to supply what is wanting by their own decisions.

That we may be enabled to form a just opinion on this subject, I shall, in considering it,

1st. Examine the nature and extent of the judicial powers—and,

2d. Enquire, whether the courts who are to exercise them, are so constituted as to afford reasonable ground of confidence, that they will exercise them for the general good.

With a regard to the nature and extent of the judicial powers, I have to regret my want of capacity to give that full and minute explanation of them that the subject merits. To be able to do this, a man should be possessed of a degree of law knowledge far beyond what I pretend to. A number of hard words and technical phrases are used in this part of the system, about the meaning of which gentlemen learned in the law differ.

Its advocates know how to avail themselves of these phrases. In a number of instances, where objections are made to the powers given to the judicial, they give such an explanation to the technical terms as to avoid them. . . .

The cases arising under the constitution must be different from those arising under the laws, or else the two clauses mean exactly the same thing.

The cases arising under the constitution must include such, as bring into question its meaning, and will require an explanation of the nature and extent of the powers of the different departments under it.

This article, therefore, vests the judicial with a power to resolve all questions that may arise on any case on the construction of the constitution, either in law or in equity.

1st. They are authorised to determine all questions that may arise upon the meaning of the constitution in law. This article vests the courts with authority to give the constitution a legal construction, or to explain it according to the rules laid down for construing a law.—These rules give a certain degree of latitude of explanation. According to this mode of construction, the courts are to give such meaning to the constitution as comports best with the common, and generally received acceptation of the words in which it is expressed, regarding their ordinary and popular use, rather than their grammatical propriety. Where words are dubious, they will be explained by the context. The end of the clause will be attended to, and the words will be understood, as having a view to it; and the words will not be so understood as to bear no meaning or a very absurd one.

2d. The judicial are not only to decide questions arising upon the meaning of the constitution in law, but also in equity.

By this they are empowered, to explain the constitution according to the reasoning spirit of it, without being confined to the words or letter.

"From this method of interpreting laws," says Blackstone, "by the reason of them, arises what we call equity;" which is thus defined by Grotius, "the correction of that, wherein the law, by reason of its universality, is deficient;" for since in laws all cases cannot be foreseen, or expressed, it is necessary, that when the decrees of the laws cannot be applied to particular cases, there should some where be a power vested of defining those circumstances, which had they been foreseen the legislator would have expressed, and these are the cases, which according to Grotius, "lex non exacte definit, sed arbitrio boni viri permittet."

The same learned author observes, "That equity, thus depending essentially upon each individual case, there can be no established rules and fixed principles of equity laid down, without destroying its very essence, and reducing it to a positive law."

From these remarks, the authority and business of the courts of law, under this clause, may be understood.

They will give the sense of every article of the constitution, that may from time to time come before them. And in their decisions they will not confine themselves to any fixed or established rules, but will determine, according to what appears to them, the reason and spirit of the constitution. The opinions of the supreme court, whatever they may be, will have the force of law; because there is no power provided in the constitution, that can correct their errors, or control their adjudications. From this court there is no appeal. And I conceive the legislature themselves, cannot set aside a judgment of this court, because they are authorised by the constitution to decide in the last resort. The legislature must be controled by the constitution, and not the constitution by them. They have therefore no more right to set aside any judgment pronounced upon the construction of the constitution, than they have to take from the president, the chief command of the army and navy, and commit it to some other person. The reason is plain; the judicial and executive derive their authority from the same source, that the legislature do theirs, and therefore in all cases, where the constitution does not make the one responsible to, or controlable by the other, they are altogether independent of each other.

The judicial power will operate to effect, in the most certain, but yet silent and imperceptible manner, what is evidently the tendency of the constitution—I mean, an entire subversion of the legislative, executive and judicial powers of the individual states. Every adjudication of the supreme court, on any question that may arise upon the nature and extent of the general government, will affect the limits of the state jurisdiction. In proportion as the former enlarge the exercise of their powers, will that of the latter be restricted.

That the judicial power of the United States, will lean strongly in favour of the general government, and will give such an explanation to the constitution, as will favour an extension of its jurisdiction, is very evident from a variety of considerations.

1st. The constitution itself strongly countenances such a mode of construction. Most of the articles in this system, which convey powers of any considerable importance, are conceived in general and indefinite terms, which are either equivocal, ambiguous, or which require long definitions to unfold the extent of their meaning. The two most important powers committed to any government, those of raising money, and of raising and keeping up troops, have already been considered, and shown to be unlimited by any thing but the discretion of the legislature. The clause which vests the power to pass all laws which are proper and necessary, to carry the powers given into execution, it has been shown, leaves the legislature at liberty, to do every thing, which in their judgment is best. It is said, I know, that this clause confers no power on the legislature, which they could not have had without it—though I believe this is not the fact, yet, admitting it to be, it implies that the constitution is not to receive an explanation strictly, according to its letter; but more power is implied than is expressed. And this clause, if it is to be considered, as explanatory of the extent of the powers given, rather than giving a new power, is to be understood as declaring, that in construing any of the articles conveying power, the spirit, intent and design of the clause, should be attended to, as well as the words in their common acceptation. . . .

Every extension of the power of the general legislature, as well as of the judicial powers, will increase the powers of the courts; and the dignity and importance of the judges, will be in proportion to the extent and magnitude of the powers they exercise. I add, it is highly probable the emolument of the judges will be increased, with the increase of the business they will have to transact and its importance. From these considerations the judges will be interested to extend the powers of the courts, and to construe the constitution as much as possible, in such a way as to favour it; and that they will do it, appears probable.

3d. Because they will have precedent to plead, to justify them in it. It is well known, that the courts in England, have by their own authority, extended their jurisdiction far beyond the limits set them in their original institution, and by the laws of the land. . . .

When the courts will have a precedent before them of a court which extended its jurisdiction in opposition to an act of the legislature, is it not to be expected that they will extend theirs, especially when there is nothing in the constitution expressly against it? and they are authorised to construe its meaning, and are not under any control?

This power in the judicial, will enable them to mould the government, into almost any shape they please.—The manner in which this may be effected we will hereafter examine.

BRUTUS

"Brutus"
(Probably Robert Yates)
Essay XII
(Excerpts)

DISCUSSION QUESTION

According to Brutus, how will judicial power extend and encroach upon the authority of the legislative branch of government?

February 7 and 14, 1788

In my last, I showed, that the judicial power of the United States under the first clause of the second section of article eight, would be authorized to explain the constitution, not only according to its letter, but according to its spirit and intention; and having this power, they would strongly incline to give it such a construction as to extend the powers of the general government, as much as possible, to the diminution, and finally to the destruction, of that of the respective states.

I shall now proceed to show how this power will operate in its exercise to effect these purposes. In order to perceive the extent of its influence, I shall consider.

First. How it will tend to extend the legislative authority.

Second. In what manner it will increase the jurisdiction of the courts, and

Third. The way in which it will diminish, and destroy, both the legislative and judicial authority of the United States.

First. Let us enquire how the judicial power will effect an extension of the legislative authority. . . .

It is to be observed, that the supreme court has the power, in the last resort, to determine all questions that may arise in the course of legal discussion, on the meaning and construction of the constitution. This power they will hold under the constitution, and independent of the legislature. The latter can no more deprive the former of this right, than either of them, or both of them together, can take from the president, with the advice of the senate, the power of making treaties, or appointing ambassadors.

In determining these questions, the court must and will assume certain principles, from which they will reason, in forming their decisions. These principles, whatever they may be, when they become fixed, by a course of decisions, will be adopted by the legislature, and will be the rule by which they will explain their own powers. This appears evident from this consideration, that if the legislature pass laws, which, in the judgment of the court, they are not authorised to do by the constitution, the court will not take notice of them; for it will not be denied, that the constitution is the highest or supreme law. And the courts are vested with the supreme and uncontrollable power, to determine, in all cases that come before them, what the constitution means; they cannot, therefore, execute a law, which, in their judgment, opposes the constitution, unless we can suppose they can make a superior law give way to an inferior. The legislature, therefore, will not go over the limits by which the courts may adjudge they are confined. And there is little room to doubt but that they will come up to those bounds, as often as occasion and opportunity may offer, and they may judge it proper to do it. For as on the one hand, they will not readily pass laws which they know the courts will not execute, so on the other, we may be sure they will not scruple to pass such as they know will give effect, as often as they may judge it proper.

From these observations it appears, that the judgment of the judicial, on the constitution, will become the rule to guide the legislature in their construction of their powers.

What the principles are, which the courts will adopt, it is impossible for us to say; but taking up the powers as I have explained them in my last number, which they will possess under this clause, it is not difficult to see, that they may, and probably will, be very liberal ones.

We have seen, that they will be authorized to give the constitution a construction according to its spirit and reason, and not to confine themselves to its letter.

To discover the spirit of the constitution, it is of the first importance to attend to the principal ends and designs it has in view. . . .

The first object declared to be in view is "To form a perfect union." It is to be observed, it is not an union of states or bodies corporate; had this been the case the existence of the state governments, might have been secured. But it is a union of the people of the United States considered as one body, who are to ratify this constitution, if it is adopted. Now to make a union of this kind perfect, it is necessary to abolish all inferior governments, and to give the general one compleat legislative, executive and judicial powers to every purpose. The courts therefore will establish it as a rule in explaining the constitution to give it such a construction as will best tend to perfect the union or take from the state governments every power of either making or executing laws. The second object is "to establish justice." This must include not only the idea of instituting the rule of justice, or of making laws which shall be the measure or rule of right, but also of providing for the application of this rule or of administering justice under it. And under this the courts will in their decisions extend the power of the governments to all cases they possibly can, or otherwise they will be restricted in doing what appears to be the intent of the constitution they should do, to wit, pass laws and provide for the execution of them, for the general distribution of justice between man and man. Another end declared is "to insure domestic tranquility." This comprehends a provision against all private breaches of the peace, as well as against all public commotions or general insurrections; and to attain the object of this clause fully, the government must exercise the power of passing laws on these subjects, as well as of appointing magistrates with authority to execute them. And the courts will adopt these ideas in their expositions. I might proceed to the other clause, in the preamble, and it would appear by a consideration of all of them separately, as it does by taking them together, that if the spirit of this system is to be known from its declared end and design in the preamble, its spirit is to subvert and abolish all the powers of the state government, and to embrace every object to which any government extends.

As it sets out in the preamble with this declared intention, so it proceeds in the different parts with the same idea. Any person, who will peruse the 8th section with attention, in which most of the powers are enumerated, will perceive that they either expressly or by implication extend to almost every thing about which any legislative power can be employed. But if this equitable mode of construction is applied to this part of the constitution; nothing can stand before it.

This will certainly give the first clause in that article a construction which I confess I think the most natural and grammatical one, to authorise the Congress to do any thing which in their judgment will tend to provide for the general welfare, and this amounts to the same thing as general and unlimited powers of legislation in all cases.

"Brutus"
(Probably Robert Yates)
Essay XV
(Excerpts)

DISCUSSION QUESTIONS

1. How does Brutus compare the role and authority of judges under the Constitution with those of the judges in England?
2. What does Brutus have to say about the independence of our judges? (*Note:* He makes three arguments.)
3. According to Brutus, what is the inevitable effect of judicial power on state governments?

I said in my last number, that the supreme court under this constitution would be exalted above all other power in the government, and subject to no control. The business of this paper will be to illustrate this, and to show the danger that will result from it. I question whether the world ever saw, in any period of it, a court of justice invested with such immense powers, and yet placed in a situation so little responsible. Certain it is, that in England, and in the several states, where we have been taught to believe, the courts of law are put upon the most prudent establishment, they are on a very different footing.

The judges in England, it is true, hold their offices during their good behaviour, but then their determinations are subject to correction by the house of lords; and their power is by no means so extensive as that of the proposed supreme court of the union.—I believe they in no instance assume the authority to set aside an act of parliament under the idea that it is inconsistent with their constitution. They consider themselves bound to decide according to the existing laws of the land, and never undertake to control them by adjudging that they are inconsistent with the constitution—much less are they vested with the power of giving an *equitable* construction to the constitution.

The judges in England are under the control of the legislature, for they are bound to determine according to the laws passed by them. But the judges under this constitution will control the legislature, for the supreme court are authorised in the last resort, to determine what is the extent of the powers of the Congress; they are to give the constitution an explanation, and there is no power above them to set aside their judgment. The framers of this constitution appear to have followed that of the British, in rendering the judges independent, by granting them their offices during good behaviour, without following the constitution of England, in instituting a tribunal in which their errors may be corrected; and without averting to this, that the judicial under this system have a power which is above the legislative, and which indeed transcends any power before given to a judicial by any free government under heaven.

I do not object to the judges holding their commissions during good behaviour. I suppose it a proper provision provided they were made properly responsible. But I say, this system has followed the English government in this, while it has departed from almost every other principle of their jurisprudence, under the idea, of rendering the judges independent; which, in the British constitution, means no more than that they hold their places during good behaviour, and have fixed salaries, they have made the judges *independent*, in the fullest sense of the word. There is no power above them, to control any of their decisions. There is no authority that can remove them, and they cannot be controlled by the laws of the legislature. In short, they are independent of the people, of the legislature, and of every power under heaven. Men placed in this situation will generally soon feel themselves independent of heaven itself. Before I proceed to illustrate the truth of these assertions, I beg liberty to make one remark—Though in my opinion the judges ought to hold their offices during good behaviour, yet I think it is clear, that the reasons in favour of this establishment of the judges in England, do by no means apply to this country.

The great reason assigned, why the judges in Britain ought to be commissioned during good behaviour, is this, that they may be placed in a situation, not to be influenced by the crown, to give such decisions, as would tend to increase its powers and prerogatives. . . . But these reasons do not apply to this country, we have no hereditary monarch; those who appoint the judges do not hold their offices for life, nor do they descend to their children. The same arguments, therefore, which will conclude in favor of the tenor of the judge's offices for good behaviour, lose a considerable part of their weight when applied to the state and condition of America. But much less can it be shown, that the nature of our government requires that the courts should be placed beyond all account more independent, so much so as to be above control.

I have said that the judges under this system will be *independent* in the strict sense of the word: To prove this I will show—That there is no power above them that can control their decisions, or correct their errors. There is no authority that can remove them from office for any errors or want of capacity, or lower their salaries, and in many cases their power is superior to that of the legislature.

1st. There is no power above them that can correct their errors or control their decisions—The adjudications of this court are final and irreversible, for there is no court above them to which appeals can lie, either in error or on the merits.—In this respect it differs from the courts in England, for there the house of lords is the highest court, to whom appeals, in error, are carried from the highest of the courts of law.

2d. They cannot be removed from office or suffer a dimunition of their salaries, for any error in judgement or want of capacity.

It is expressly declared by the constitution,—"That they shall at stated times receive a compensation for their services which shall not be diminished during their continuance in office."

The only clause in the constitution which provides for the removal of the judges from office, is that which declares, that "the president, vice-president, and all civil officers of the United States, shall be removed from office, on impeachment for, and conviction of treason, bribery, or other high crimes and misdemeanors." By this paragraph, civil officers, in which the judges are included, are removable only for crimes. Treason and bribery are named, and the rest are included under the general terms of high crimes and misdemeanors.—Errors in judgement, or want of capacity to discharge the duties of the office, can never be supposed to be included in these words, *high crimes and misdemeanors.* A man may mistake a case in giving judgment, or manifest that he is incompetent to the discharge of the duties of a judge, and yet give no evidence of corruption or want of integrity. To support the charge, it will be necessary to give in evidence some facts that will show, that the judges commited the error from wicked and corrupt motives.

3d. The power of this court is in many cases superior to that of the legislature. I have showed, in a former paper, that this court will be authorised to decide upon the meaning of the constitution, and that, not only according to the natural and ob[vious] meaning of the words, but also according to the spirit and intention of it. In the exercise of this power they will not be subordinate to, but above the legislature. For all the departments of this government will receive their powers, so far as they are expressed in the constitution, from the people immediately, who are the source of power. The legislature can only exercise such powers as are given them by the constitution, they cannot assume any of the rights annexed to the judicial, for this plain reason, that the same authority which vested the legislature with their powers, vested the judicial with theirs—both are derived from the same source, both therefore are equally valid, and the judicial hold their powers independently of the legislature, as the legislature do of the judicial.—The supreme court then have a right, independent of the legislature, to give a construction to the constitution and every part of it, and there is no power provided in this system to correct their construction or do it away. If, therefore, the legislature pass any laws, inconsistent with the sense the judges put upon the constitution, they will declare it void; and therefore in this respect their power is superior to that of the legislature. . . .

From the preceding remarks, which have been made on the judicial powers proposed in this system, the policy of it may be fully developed.

I have, in the course of my observation on this constitution, affirmed and endeavored to shew, that it was calculated to abolish entirely the state governments, and to melt down the states into one entire government, for every purpose as well internal and local, as external and national. In this opinion the opposers of the system have generally agreed—and this has been uniformly denied by its advocates in public. Some individuals, indeed, among them, will confess, that it has this tendency, and scruple not to say, it is what they wish; and I will venture to predict, without the spirit of prophecy, that if it is adopted without amendments, or some such precautions as will ensure amendments immediately after its adoption, that the same gentlemen who have employed their talents and abilities with such success to influence the public mind to adopt this plan, will employ the same to persuade the people, that it will be for their good to abolish the state governments as useless and burdensome.

Perhaps nothing could have been better conceived to facilitate the abolition of the state governments than the constitution of the judicial. They will be able to extend the limits of the general government gradually, and by insensible degrees, and to accommodate themselves to the temper of the people. Their decisions on the meaning of the constitution will commonly take place in cases which arise between individuals, with which the public will not be generally acquainted; one adjudication will form a precedent to the next, and this to a following one. These cases will immediately affect individuals only; so that a series of determinations will probably take place before even the people will be informed of them. In the mean time all the art and address of those who wish for the change will be employed to make converts to their opinion. The people will be told, that their state officers, and state legislatures are a burden and expence without affording any solid advantage, for that all the laws passed by them, might be equally well made by the general legislature. If to those who will be interested in the change, be added, those who will be under their influence, and such who will submit to almost any change of government, which they can be persuaded to believe will ease them of taxes, it is easy to see, the party who will favor the abolition of the state governments would be far from being inconsiderable. . . .

Had the construction of the constitution been left with the legislature, they would have explained it at their peril; if they exceed their powers, or sought to find, in the spirit of the constitution, more than was expressed in the letter, the people from whom they derived their power could remove them, and do themselves right; and indeed I can see no other remedy that the people can have against their rulers for encroachments of this nature.

FEDERALIST ARGUMENTS

Alexander Hamilton
Federalist *Paper 83*
(Excerpts)

DISCUSSION QUESTIONS

1. How does Hamilton counter critics of the Constitution who claim that the Constitution is silent on the right to a jury trial in civil cases?
2. What is the distinction that Hamilton makes between friends and adversaries of the Constitution with respect to jury trials?
3. Describe Hamilton's beliefs concerning trial by jury and liberty in civil cases.
4. How might this belief relate to theories of participatory versus representative democracy?
5. How does Hamilton assess trial by jury as a method for diminishing corruption?
6. What does this say about his views toward common people?
7. What two reasons does Hamilton present for the absence of a guarantee for jury trials in civil cases in the Constitution?
8. Describe Hamilton's belief concerning the knowledge of juries, especially with respect to cases involving foreign nations.

The objection to the plan of the convention, which has met with most success in this State, and perhaps in several of the other States, is *that relative to the want of a constitutional provison* for the trial by jury in civil cases.

. . . The mere silence of the Constitution in regard to *civil causes* is represented as an abolition of the trial by jury, and the declamations to which it has afforded a pretext are artfully calculated to induce a persuasion that this pretended abolition is complete and universal, extending not only to every species of civil but even to *criminal causes.* To argue with respect to the latter would, however, be as vain and fruitless as to attempt the serious proof of the *existence* of *matter,* or to demonstrate any of those propositions which, by their own internal evidence, force conviction when expressed in language adapted to convey their meaning.

With regard to civil causes, subtleties almost too contemptible for refutation have been employed to countenance the surmise that a thing which is only *not provided for* is entirely *abolished.* Every man of discernment must at once perceive the wide difference between *silence* and *abolition.* But as the inventors of this fallacy have attempted to support it by certain *legal maxims* of interpretation which they have perverted from their true meaning, it may not be wholly useless to explore the ground they have taken.

The maxims on which they rely are of this nature: "A specification of particulars is an exclusion of generals"; or, "The expression of one thing is the exclusion of another." Hence, say they, as the Constitution has established the trial by jury in criminal cases and is silent in respect to civil, this silence is an implied prohibition of trial by jury in regard to the latter. . . .

A power to constitute courts is a power to prescribe the mode of trial; and consequently, if nothing was said in the Constitution on the subject of juries, the legislature would be at liberty either to adopt that institution or to let it alone. . . .

The pretense, therefore, that the national legislature would not be at full liberty to submit all the civil causes of federal cognizance to the determination of juries is a pretense destitute of all just foundation.

From these observations this conclusion results: that the trial by jury in civil cases would not be abolished; and that the use attempted to be made of the maxims which have been quoted is contrary to reason and common sense, and therefore not admissible. . . .

The friends and adversaries of the plan of the convention, if they agree in nothing else, concur at least in the value they set upon the trial by jury; or if there is any difference between them it consists in this: the former regard it as a valuable safeguard to liberty; the latter represent it as the very palladium of free government. For my own part, the more the operation of the institution had fallen under my observation, the more reason I have discovered for holding it in high estimation; and it would be altogether superfluous to examine to what extent it deserves to be esteemed useful or essential in a representative republic, or how much more merit it may be entitled to as a defense against the oppressions of an hereditary monarch, than as a barrier to the tyranny of popular magistrates in a popular government. Discussions of this kind would be more curious than beneficial, as all are satisfied of the utility of the institution, and of its friendly aspect to liberty. But I must acknowledge that I cannot readily discern the inseparable connection between the existence of liberty and the trial by jury in civil cases. Arbitrary impeachments, arbitrary methods of prosecuting pretended offenses, and arbitrary punishments upon arbitrary convictions have ever appeared to me to be the great engines of judicial despotism; and these have all relation to criminal proceedings. The trial by jury in criminal cases, aided by the *habeas-corpus* act seems therefore to be alone concerned in the question. And both of these are provided for in the most ample manner in the plan of the convention. . . .

The excellence of the trial by jury in civil cases appears to depend on circumstances foreign to the preservation of liberty. The strongest argument in its favor is that it is a security against corruption. As there is always more time and better opportunity to tamper with a standing body of magistrates than with a jury summoned for the occasion, there is room to suppose that a corrupt influence would more easily find its way to the former than to the latter. The force of this consideration is, however, diminished by others. The sheriff, who is the summoner of ordinary juries, and the clerks of courts, who have the nomination of special juries, are themselves standing officers, and, acting individually, may be supposed more accessible to the touch of corruption than the judges, who are a collective body. It is not difficult to see that it would be in the power of those officers to select jurors who would serve the purpose of the party as well as a corrupted bench. In the next place, it may fairly be supposed that there would be less difficulty in gaining some of the jurors promiscuously taken from the public mass, than in gaining men who had been chosen by the government for their probity and good character. But making every deduction for these considerations, the trial by jury must still be a valuable check upon corruption. It greatly multiplies the impediments to its success. As matters now stand, it would be necessary to corrupt both court and jury; for where the jury have gone evidently wrong, the court will generally grant a new trial, and it would be in most cases of little use to practice upon the jury unless the court could be likewise gained. Here then is a double security; and it will readily be perceived that this complicated agency tends to preserve the purity of both institutions. By increasing the obstacles to success, it discourages attempts to seduce the integrity of either. The temptations to prostitution which the judges might have to surmount must certainly be much fewer, while the co-operation of a jury is necessary, than they might be if they had themselves the exclusive determination of all causes.

The great difference between the limits of the jury trial in different States is not generally understood; and as it must have considerable influence on the sentence we ought to pass upon the omission complained of in regard to this point, an explanation of it is necessary. In this State, our judicial establishments resemble, more nearly than in any other, those of Great Britain. . . .

In New Jersey, there is a court of chancery which proceeds like ours, but neither courts of admiralty nor of probates, in the sense in which these last are established with us. In that State the courts of common law have the cognizance of those causes which with us are determinable in the courts of admiralty and of probates, and of course the jury trial is more extensive in New Jersey than in New York. In Pennsylvania, this is perhaps still more the case, for there is no court of chancery in that State, and its common-law courts have equity jurisdiction. It has a court of admiralty, but none of probates, at least on the plan of ours. Delaware has in these respects imitated Pennsylvania. Maryland approaches more nearly to New York, as does also Virginia, except that the latter has a plurality of chancellors.

From this sketch it appears that there is a material diversity, as well in the modification as in the extent of the institution of trial by jury in civil cases, in the several States; and from this fact these obvious reflections flow: first, that no general rule could have been fixed upon by the convention which would have corresponded with the circumstances of all the States; and secondly, that more or at least as much might have been hazarded by taking the system of any one State for a standard, as by omitting a provision altogether and leaving the matter, as has been done, to legislative regulation. . . .

But this is not, in my estimation, the greatest objection. I feel a deep and deliberate conviction that there are many cases in which the trial by jury is an ineligible one. I think it so particularly in cases which concern the public peace with foreign nations—that is, in most cases where the question turns wholly on the laws of nations. Of this nature, among others, are all prize causes. Juries cannot be supposed competent to investigations that require a thorough knowledge of the laws and usages of nations; and they will sometimes be under the influence of impressions which will not suffer them to pay sufficient regard to those considerations of public policy which ought to guide their inquiries. There would of course be always danger that the rights of other nations might be infringed by their decisions so as to afford occasions of reprisal and war. Though the proper province of juries be to determine matters of fact, yet in most cases legal consequences are complicated with fact in such a manner as to render a separation impracticable.

It will add great weight to this remark, in relation to prize causes, to mention that the method of determining them has been thought worthy of particular regulation in various treaties between different powers of Europe, and that, pursuant to such treaties, they are determinable in Great Britain, in the last resort, before the king himself, in his privy council, where the fact, as well as the law, undergoes a re-examination. This alone demonstrates the impolicy of inserting a fundamental provision in the Constitution which would make the State systems a standard for the national government in the article under consideration, and the danger of encumbering the government with any constitutional provisions the propriety of which is not indisputable.

Alexander Hamilton
Federalist *Paper 78*
(Excerpts)

DISCUSSION QUESTIONS

1. How does Hamilton describe the term of judges?
2. According to Hamilton, why is the judiciary the ". . . least dangerous to the political rights of the Constitution"?
3. From where does the right of the courts to void legislative acts originate? How does Hamilton justify this right?
4. How does Hamilton distinguish will from judgment? What does this imply for Hamilton's arguments in favor of permanent tenure for judges?
5. Describe Hamilton's argument against temporary commissions for judges.
6. What is Hamilton's view of precedents and the law? How might this view have contributed to a litigious society? What would be the role of judges and lawyers in such a society?

First. As to the mode of appointing the judges: this is the same with that of appointing the officers of the Union in general and has been so fully discussed in the two last numbers that nothing can be said here which would not be useless repetition.

Second. As to the tenure by which the judges are to hold their places: this chiefly concerns their duration in office, the provisions for their support, the precautions for their responsibility.

According to the plan of the convention, all judges who may be appointed by the United States are to hold their offices *during good behavior;* which is conformable to the most approved of the State constitutions, and among the rest, to that of this State. Its propriety having been drawn into question by the adversaries of that plan is no light symptom of the rage for objection which disorders their imaginations and judgments. The standard of good behavior for the continuance in office of the judicial magistracy is certainly one of the most valuable of the modern improvements in the practice of government. In a monarchy it is an excellent barrier to the despotism of the prince; in a republic it is a no less excellent barrier to the encroachments and oppressions of the representative body. And it is the best expedient which can be devised in any government to secure a steady, upright, and impartial administration of the laws.

Whoever attentively considers the different departments of power must perceive that, in a government in which they are separated from each other, the judiciary, from the nature of its functions, will always be the least dangerous to the political rights of the Constitution; because it will be least in a capacity to annoy or injure them. The executive not only dispenses the honors but holds the sword of the community. The legislature not only commands the purse but prescribes the rules by which the duties and rights of every citizen are to be regulated. The judiciary, on the contrary, has no influence over either the sword or the purse; no direction either of the strength or of the wealth of the society, and can take no active resolution whatever. It may truly be said to have neither FORCE nor WILL but merely judgment; and must ultimately depend upon the aid of the executive arm even for the efficacy of its judgments.

This simple view of the matter suggests several important consequences. It proves incontestably that the judiciary is beyond comparison the weakest of the three departments of power;* that it can never attack with success either of the other two; and that all possible care is requisite to enable it to defend itself against their attacks. It equally proves that though individual oppression may now and then proceed from the courts of justice, the general liberty of the people can never be endangered from that quarter; I mean so long as the judiciary remains truly distinct from both the legislature and the executive. . . .

Some perplexity respecting the rights of the courts to pronounce legislative acts void, because contrary to the Constitution, has arisen from an imagination that the doctrine would imply a superiority of the judiciary to the legislative power. It is urged that the authority which can declare the acts of another void must necessarily be superior to the one whose acts may be declared void. As this doctrine is of great importance in all the American constitutions, a brief discussion of the grounds on which it rests cannot be unacceptable.

There is no position which depends on clearer principles than that every act of a delegated authority, contrary to the tenor of the commission under which it is exercised, is void. No legislative act, therefore, contrary to the Constitution, can be valid. To deny this would be to affirm that the deputy is greater than his principal; that the servant is above his master; that the representatives of the people are superior to the people themselves; that men acting by virtue of powers may do not only what their powers do not authorize, but what they forbid.

If it be said that the legislative body are themselves the constitutional judges of their own powers and that the construction they put upon them is conclusive

---

*The celebrated Montesquieu, speaking of them, says: "Of the three powers above mentioned, the JUDICIARY is next to nothing." —*Spirit of Laws*, Vol. I, page 186.

upon the other departments it may be answered that this cannot be the natural presumption where it is not to be collected from any particular provisions in the Constitution. It is not otherwise to be supposed that the Constitution could intend to enable the representatives of the people to substitute their *will* to that of their constituents. It is far more rational to suppose that the courts were designed to be an intermediate body between the people and the legislature in order, among other things, to keep the latter within the limits assigned to their authority. The interpretation of the laws is the proper and peculiar province of the courts. A constitution is, in fact, and must be regarded by the judges as, a fundamental law. It therefore belongs to them to ascertain its meaning as well as the meaning of any particular act proceeding from the legislative body. If there should happen to be an irreconcilable variance between the two, that which has the superior obligation and validity ought, of course, to be preferred; or, in other words, the Constitution ought to be preferred to the statute, the intention of the people to the intention of their agents.

Nor does this conclusion by any means suppose a superiority of the judicial to the legislative power. It only supposes that the power of the people is superior to both and that where the will of the legislature, declared in its statutes, stands in opposition to that of the people, declared in the Constitution, the judges ought to be governed by the latter rather than the former. They ought to regulate their decisions by the fundamental laws rather than by those which are not fundamental.

This exercise of judicial discretion in determining between two contradictory laws is exemplified in a familiar instance. It not uncommonly happens that there are two statutes existing at one time, clashing in whole or in part with each other and neither of them containing any repealing clause or expression. In such a case, it is the province of the courts to liquidate and fix their meaning and operation. So far as they can, by any fair construction, be reconciled to each other, reason and law conspire to dictate that this should be done; where this is impracticable, it becomes a matter of necessity to give effect to one in exclusion of the other. The rule which has obtained in the courts for determining their relative validity is that the last in order of time shall be preferred to the first. But this is a mere rule of construction, not derived from any positive law but from the nature and reason of the thing. It is a rule not enjoined upon the courts by legislative provision but adopted by themselves, as consonant to truth and propriety, for the direction of their conduct as interpreters of the law. They thought it reasonable that between the interfering acts of an *equal* authority that which was the last indication of its will should have the preference. . . .

It can be of no weight to say that the courts, on the pretense of a repugnancy, may substitute their own pleasure to the constitutional intentions of the legislature. This might as well happen in the case of two contradictory statutes; or it might as well happen in every adjudication upon any single statute. The courts must declare the sense of the law; and if they should be disposed to exercise WILL instead of JUDGMENT, the consequence would equally be the substitution of their pleasure to that of the legislative body. The observation, if it prove anything, would prove that there ought to be no judges distinct from that body.

If, then, the courts of justice are to be considered as the bulwarks of a limited Constitution against legislative encroachments, this consideration will afford a strong argument for the permanent tenure of judicial offices, since nothing will contribute so much as this to that independent spirit in the judges which must be essential to the faithful performance of so arduous a duty.

This independence of the judges is equally requisite to guard the Constitution and the rights of individuals from the effects of those ill humors which the arts of designing men, or the influence of particular conjunctures, sometimes disseminate among the people themselves, and which, though they speedily give place to better information, and more deliberate reflection, have a tendency, in the meantime, to occasion dangerous innovations in the government, and serious oppressions of the minor party in the community. Though I trust the friends of the proposed Constitution will never concur with its enemies* in questioning that fundamental principle of republican government which admits the right of the people to alter or abolish the established Constitution whenever they find it inconsistent with their happiness; yet it is not to be inferred from this principle that the representatives of the people, whenever a momentary inclination happens to lay hold of a majority of their constituents incompatible with the provisions in the existing Constitution would, on that account, be justifiable in a violation of those provisions; or that the courts would be under a greater obligation to connive at infractions in this shape than when they had proceeded wholly from the cabals of the representative body. Until the people have, by some solemn and authoritative act, annulled or changed the established form, it is binding upon themselves collectively, as well as individually; and no presumption, or even knowledge of their sentiments, can warrant their representatives in a departure from it prior to such an act. But it is easy to see that it would require an uncommon portion of fortitude in the judges to do their duty as faithful guardians of the Constitution, where legislative invasions of it had been instigated by the major voice of the community. . . .

That inflexible and uniform adherence to the rights of the Constitution, and of individuals, which we perceive to be indispensable in the courts of justice, can certainly not be expected from judges who hold their offices by a temporary commission. Periodical appointments, however regulated, or by whomsoever made, would, in some way or other, be fatal to their necessary independence. If the power of making them was committed either to the executive or legislature there would be danger of an improper complaisance to the branch which possessed it; if to both, there would be an unwillingness to hazard the displeasure of either; if to the people, or to persons chosen by them for the special purpose, there would be too great a disposition to consult popularity to justify a reliance that nothing would be consulted but the Constitution and the laws.

There is yet a further and a weighty reason for the permanency of the judicial offices which is deducible from the nature of the qualifications they require. It has been frequently remarked with great propriety that a voluminous code of laws is one of the inconveniences necessarily connected with the advantages of a free government. To avoid an arbitrary discretion in the courts, it is indispensable that they should be bound down by strict rules and precedents which serve to define and point out their duty in every particular case that comes before them; and it will readily be conceived from the variety of controversies which grow out of the folly

---

**Vide Protest of the Minority of the Convention of Pennsylvania,* Martin's speech, etc.

and wickedness of mankind that the records of those precedents must unavoidably swell to a very considerable bulk and must demand long and laborious study to acquire a competent knowledge of them. Hence it is that there can be but few men in the society who will have sufficient skill in the laws to qualify them for the stations of judges. And making the proper deductions for the ordinary depravity of human nature, the number must be still smaller of those who unite the requisite integrity with the requisite knowledge. These considerations apprise us that the government can have no great option between fit characters; and that a temporary duration in office which would naturally discourage such characters from quitting a lucrative line of practice to accept a seat on the bench would have a tendency to throw the administration of justice into hands less able and less well qualified to conduct it with utility and dignity. In the present circumstances of this country and in those in which it is likely to be for a long time to come, the disadvantages on this score would be greater than they may at first sight appear; but it must be confessed that they are far inferior to those which present themselves under the other aspects of the subject.

Upon the whole, there can be no room to doubt that the convention acted wisely in copying from the models of those constitutions which have established *good behavior* as the tenure of their judicial offices, in point of duration; and that so far from being blamable on this account, their plan would have been inexcusably defective if it had wanted this important feature of good government. The experience of Great Britain affords an illustrious comment on the excellence of the institution.

PUBLIUS

Alexander Hamilton
Federalist *Paper 81*
(Excerpt)

DISCUSSION QUESTIONS

1. How does Hamilton attack the claim of critics that the judicial branch of government will be uncontrollable by the legislative branch?
2. What is Hamilton's reaction to the claim of the Antifederalists that the judicial branch of government ought to be part of the legislative branch as in England?
3. Describe Hamilton's view of legislative knowledge in comparison to judicial knowledge of the law.

Let us now return to the partition of the judiciary authority between different courts and their relations to each other.

"The judicial power of the United States is" (by the plan of the convention) "to be vested in one Supreme Court, and in such inferior courts as the Congress may, from time to time, ordain and establish."*

*Article 3, Section 1.

That there ought to be one court of supreme and final jurisdiction is a proposition which is not likely to be contested. The reasons for it have been assigned in another place and are too obvious to need repetition. The only question that seems to have been raised concerning it is whether it ought to be a distinct body or a branch of the legislature. The same contradiction is observable in regard to this matter which has been remarked in several other cases. The very men who object to the Senate as a court of impeachments, on the ground of an improper intermixture of powers, advocate, by implication at least, the propriety of vesting the ultimate decision of all causes, in the whole or in a part of the legislative body.

The arguments, or rather suggestions, upon which this charge is founded are to this effect: "The authority of the proposed Supreme Court of the United States, which is to be a separate and independent body, will be superior to that of the legislature. The power of construing the laws according to the *spirit* of the Constitution will enable that court to mould them into whatever shape it may think proper; especially as its decisions will not be in any manner subject to the revision or correction of the legislative body. This is as unprecedented as it is dangerous. In Britain the judicial power, in the last resort; resides in the House of Lords, which is a branch of the legislature; and this part of the British government has been imitated in the State constitutions in general. The Parliament of Great Britain, and the legislatures of the several States, can at any time rectify, by law, the exceptionable decisions of their respective courts. But the errors and usurpations of the Supreme Court of the United States will be uncontrollable and remediless." This, upon examination, will be found to be made up altogether of false reasoning upon misconceived fact.

In the first place, there is not a syllable in the plan under consideration which *directly* empowers the national courts to construe the laws according to the spirit of the Constitution, or which gives them any greater latitude in this respect than may be claimed by the courts of every State. I admit, however, that the Constitution ought to be the standard of construction for the laws, and that wherever there is an evident opposition, the laws ought to give place to the Constitution. But this doctrine is not deducible from any circumstance peculiar to the plan of the convention, but from the general theory of a limited Constitution; and as far as it is true is equally applicable to most if not to all the State governments. There can be no objection, therefore, on this account to the federal judicature which will not lie against the local judicatures in general, and which will not serve to condemn every constitution that attempts to set bounds to legislative discretion.

But perhaps the force of the objection may be thought to consist in the particular organization of the Supreme Court; in its being composed of a distinct body of magistrates, instead of being one of the branches of the legislature, as in the government of Great Britain and that of the State. To insist upon this point, the authors of the objection must renounce the meaning they have labored to annex to the celebrated maxim requiring a separation of the departments of power. It shall, nevertheless, be conceded to them, agreeably to the interpretation given to that maxim in the course of these papers, that it is not violated by vesting the ultimate power of judging in a *part* of the legislative body. But though this be not an absolute violation of that excellent rule, yet it verges so nearly upon it as on this account alone to be less eligible than the mode preferred by the convention. From a body which had even a partial agency in passing bad laws we could rarely expect a disposition to temper and moderate them in the application. The same spirit which had operated in making them would be too apt in interpreting them; still less could it be expected that men who had infringed the Constitution in the character of legislators would be disposed to repair the breach in the character of judges. Nor is this all. Every reason which recommends the tenure of good behavior for judicial offices militates against placing the judiciary power, in the last resort, in a body composed of men chosen for a limited period. There is an absurdity in referring the determination of causes, in the first instance, to judges of permanent standing; in the last, to those of a temporary and mutable constitution. And there is a still greater absurdity in subjecting the decisions of men, selected for their knowledge of the laws, acquired by long and laborious study, to the revision and control of men who, for want of the same advantage, cannot but be deficient in that knowledge. The members of the legislature will rarely be chosen with a view to those qualifications which fit men for the stations of judges; and as, on this account, there will be great reason to apprehend all the ill consequences of defective information, so, on account of the natural propensity of such bodies to party divisions, there will be no less reason to fear that the pestilential breath of faction may poison the fountains of justice. The habit of being continually marshaled on opposite sides will be too apt to stifle the voice both of law and of equity.

These considerations teach us to applaud the wisdom of those States who have committed the judicial power, in the last resort, not to a part of the legislature, but to distinct and independent bodies of men. Contrary to the supposition of those who have represented the plan of the convention, in this respect, as novel and unprecedented, it is but a copy of the constitutions of New Hampshire, Massachusetts, Pennsylvania, Delaware, Maryland, Virginia, North Carolina, South Carolina, and Georgia; and the preference which has been given to those models is highly to be commended.

It is not true, in the second place, that the parliament of Great Britain, or the legislatures of the particular States, can rectify the exceptionable decisions of their respective courts, in any other sense than might be done by a future legislature of the United States. The theory, neither of the British, nor the State constitutions, authorizes the revisal of a judicial sentence by a legislative act. Nor is there anything in the proposed Constitution, more than in either of them, by which it is forbidden. In the former, as well as in the latter, the impropriety of the thing, on the general principles of law and reason, is the sole obstacle. A legislature, without exceeding its province, cannot reverse a determination once made in a particular case; though it may prescribe a new rule for future cases. This is the principle and it applies in all its consequences, exactly in the same manner and extent, to the State governments, as to the national government now under consideration. Not the least difference can be pointed out in any view of the subject.

It may in the last place be observed that the supposed danger of judiciary encroachments on the legislative authority which has been upon many occasions reiterated is in reality a phantom. Particular misconstructions and contraventions of the will of the legislature may now and then happen; but they can never be so extensive as to amount to an inconvenience, or in any sensible degree to affect the order of the political system. This may be inferred with certainty from the general nature of the judicial power, from the objects to which it relates, from the manner in which it is exercised, from its comparative weakness, and from its total incapacity to support its usurpations by force. And the inference is greatly fortified by the consideration of the important constitutional check which the power of instituting impeachments in one part of the legislative body, and of determining upon them in the other, would give to that body upon the members of the judicial department. This is alone a complete security. There never can be danger that the judges, by a series of deliberate usurpations on the authority of the legislature, would hazard the united resentment of the body intrusted with it, while this body was possessed of the means of punishing their presumption by degrading them from their stations. While this ought to remove all apprehensions on the subject it affords, at the same time, a cogent argument for constituting the Senate a court for the trial of impeachments.

Having now examined, and, I trust, removed the objections to the distinct and independent organization of the Supreme Court, I proceed to consider the propriety of the power of constituting inferior courts,* and the relations which will subsist between these and the former.

CONTEMPORARY INFLUENCES

Kenneth M. Dolbeare and Linda Medcalf
"The Dark Side of the Constitution" (Excerpt)

DISCUSSION QUESTIONS

1. According to the authors, what was Hamilton's purpose regarding the establishment of the U.S. legal system?
2. How do the authors describe the emerging legal system?
3. What effect did this have upon juries, lawyers, and the legal profession?
4. Why is Hamilton's *Federalist Paper* #78 so important?
5. How do Hamilton's arguments aid the legal profession?
6. What were the results of Hamilton's arguments on our nation?
7. According to the authors, the United States faces a series of problems. What is the nature of these problems and where did they originate?

---

*This power has been absurdly represented as intended to abolish all the county courts in the several States which are commonly called inferior courts. But the expressions of the Constitution are to constitute "tribunals INFERIOR TO THE SUPREME COURT"; and the evident design of the provision is to enable the institution of local courts, subordinate to the Supreme, either in States or larger districts. It is ridiculous to imagine that county courts were in contemplation.

John F. Manley and Kenneth M. Dolbeare, Eds., *The Case Against the Constitution* (New York: M. E. Sharpe, Inc., 1987), pp. 133–136, 137–38. Reprinted with the permission of M. E. Sharpe Inc. Copyright © 1987.

The *second* means by which Hamilton sought insulation [of the economy] from popular impact was through transferring as much policymaking as possible into the far less visible and apparently neutral and mechanical hands of courts and lawyers. This strategy encompassed not only the usual and often discretionary law-enforcing role of courts, but more significantly a deliberate law-changing function and—most important of all—a major policymaking role for the Supreme Court at least equal to that of the other branches.

We noted earlier that Hamilton gave special emphasis to the principle of having national laws apply directly to individuals without the intermediation of the states or other governments. In this way, assuming as Hamilton did that a federal judiciary would be promptly created (as it was), the national government would have all the legitimacy and effective enforcement potential of the law and the courts behind its enactments. Individuals would be isolated and vulnerable to a variety of court-imposed sanctions.

Hamilton assumed that the federal courts would have common law powers, making them even more effective supplements to the lawmaking and order-maintaining capabilities of the national government, but Jefferson managed to frustrate this goal for some time. The state courts and their uncontested common law powers, however, soon proved more than adequate to the necessity of changing the law, as first Perry Miller and then Morton Horwitz have so well documented.[1]

Let us summarize these developments briefly. At the same time as lawyers were laying exclusive claim to the right to serve as judges, the early nineteenth-century courts were pushing jurors back from their accustomed law-making as well as fact-finding roles. Many of the Antifederalist objections to the ratification arose from what they correctly perceived to be a reduction in the role of juries.[2] Popular participation as judges and jurors, long the established practice, was sharply reduced. Lawyers and judges asserted their expertise as "scientists" to discover the (new, American, common) law governing property and economic transactions generally.

What they discovered in this manner was a new version of the law, complete with new definitions of property and new rules for doing business that were appropriate to the rising capitalist economy. For example, not only did the law of bills and notes and commercial practices have to be changed, but so did established land and water rights have to give way to the need for railroad entrepreneurs and mill owners to be free of liabilities for the (growth-producing) way they used *their* property. Property in the form of real estate had to be converted into a commodity and made subject to ready sale and/or use as security for the credit or loans needed for development. Other kinds of property rights to intangibles had to be created and made enforceable.

Why the law was used in this manner is made very clear by Morton Horwitz:

> Change brought about through technical legal doctrine can more easily disguise underlying political choices.

---

[1]Perry Miller, *The Life of the Mind in America From the Revolution to the Civil War*, Book Two, "The Legal Mentality" (New York: Harcourt, Brace & World, Inc., 1965) and Morton J. Horwitz, *The Transformation of American Law: 1780–1860* (Cambridge, Mass.: Harvard University Press, 1977).

[2]For Example, see Storing, *supra*, Volume 2, pp. 12, 20, 136.

> For the paramount social condition that is necessary for legal formalism to flourish in a society is for the powerful groups in that society to have a great interest in disguising and suppressing the inevitably political and redistributive functions of law.[3]

At the close of his extensive analysis of the extent to which the legal system was used to put the burden of paying for economic development on people other than the entrepreneurs and financiers who were its beneficiaries, he says:

> . . . it does seem fairly clear that the tendency of subsidy through legal change during this period was dramatically to throw the burden of economic development on the weakest and least active elements in the population.[4]

From Horwitz's analysis, it is clear that the purpose of using the increasingly self-conscious and willing legal system and changing the concept of property and the substance of commercial law turn out to be the same.

The key to this governing role for the legal profession, a hallmark of the American system at least since De Tocqueville's famous observations, was Alexander Hamilton. First he created the public image that the Constitution was "law" and therefore properly the province of lawyers, rather than being "values" or "policy" and properly the province of the people or their elected representatives. Then he helped to raise the visibility and potential of the Supreme Court to unprecedented heights, and provided the rationale for Marshall's eventual success in establishing the Court as a co-equal policymaker. Finally, in his private practice after leaving the Cabinet, he made himself a model of what a lawyer could do with a clear sense of policy objectives.

In *Federalist No. 78* and his later opinions, Hamilton seized upon the supremacy clause's declaration that the Constitution is "the "supreme *law* of the land" (emphasis added) to argue that the interpretation of the Constitution's words and phrases was peculiarly the responsibility of lawyers and judges. The issue, of course, turns on the nature of the choice involved in determining what any given provision means.

If (as Hamilton argued) it is a choice of a purely "ministerial" kind involving no discretion—a choice wholly determined by past precedent or rule admitting of a single answer and available to be discovered by appropriate experts—then it might as well belong to lawyers as any other skill group. But if (as Jefferson argued) it is a choice involving values and preferences which might be contested—a choice in which reasonable alternatives are available—it would seem that the people should be involved in some direct way. Needless to say, Hamilton's argument won, and the Constitution is "law," and therefore belongs in an especially proprietary manner to the legal profession.

Federalist No. 78 is also justly famous for its next argument, to the effect that the Supreme Court should have the power to declare when the Congress or the President have exceeded the authority granted them in the Constitution. The

---

[3]Horwitz, *supra*, pp. 101 and 266, respectively.

[4]Horwitz, *supra*, p. 101.

boldness involved in staking this claim so openly in 1788 is not often recognized: not only did this make plain that the Federalists obviously expected the Court to exercise judicial review as well over the acts and decisions of the states, but it also might have jeopardized ratification in the key remaining states. Although the argument was not finally won until *Marbury* and *Dred Scott* were re-validated in the 1890s, the Court reviewed the constitutionality of an act of the Congress as early as 1796 in *Hylton v. U.S*; Hamilton argued the case for the government.

Hamilton insisted that the Constitution was law, and peculiarly the province of courts and lawyers. The Supreme Court had the power of judicial review, he said, but that was a purely neutral and objective decision—"an act of judgment, not of will." Could Alexander Hamilton have been so naive as to believe that the choices judges would make in interpreting the meaning of the Constitution would not involve values and preferences? Or did he know quite well what would be involved, and build a powerful argument for conferring that choice upon the most trustworthy and available skill group he could find? Surely Hamilton was a conscious builder of the legal mystique, and not merely an early victim of the slot-machine theory of law so often articulated at celebratory moments.

In any event, Hamilton's argument applied equally to courts and judges at all levels of the federal and state legal systems. The temptation was far too strong for most judges to resist the opportunity, and lawyers were quick to offer it again and again. In every state, the notion of judicial review by state supreme courts (and therefore by lower courts) became increasingly accepted and its exercise routine. The legal profession had acquired its dominant position as the means of transacting the nation's economic and political affairs by about the 1840s.

The Supreme Court exercised the power of judicial review over acts of the states and state court decisions several times in the early nineteenth century, but did not receive a volume of cases until the Fourteenth Amendment provided what came to be recognized as a broad new channel for reaching the Court. By the 1890s, its frequent use of the power over both states and Congress was widely approved by the business community and thus thoroughly established. In addition, the lower federal courts began to exercise, and the Supreme Court to endorse, just the kind of common law powers that Hamilton had hoped for—particularly in such areas as injunctions on behalf of employers in labor disputes.

But Hamilton's impact was not limited to the power of his *Federalist No. 78* or his later opinions. It owes a great deal to the example he set as a practicing attorney, and to the fervor with which the authors of the two leading Commentaries on American law—James Kent and Joseph Story—endorsed his views of the law.[5] Because for many years there were few ways that an American lawyer could identify authoritative adaptations of the English common law, or locate applicable precedents from the American state or federal legal systems, the Commentaries were

[5]As quoted in Perry Miller, *supra*: "In 1836, when Jackson was President and Kent had delivered another of his panegyrics on Hamilton, Story wrote, 'I always believed that his title to renown was as great as you have portrayed it' " (p. 111). See also James Kent, *Commentaries on American Law* (1st Ed., 4 vols., 1826–1830) and Joseph Story, *Commentaries on Equity Jurisprudence* (1836) and *Commentaries on the Law of Promissory Notes* (1845).

widely used and carried enormous prestige. Both Kent and Story were completely captured by Hamilton as a constitutional thinker and as a courtroom attorney, and they made his view of the law central to their interpretations of the nature of American law on a wide range of subjects.

The effect of Hamilton's various efforts in this area was to raise courts, the law, and the legal profession into a covert policy-making system representing his best hope of protecting the national economy from popular interference. He was apparently willing to pay the price of the law's rigidities and tendency toward backward-looking in order to insulate the economy and its distribution patterns in this way. But the price paid by the people—and ultimately by the constitutional system itself—has yet to be calculated. . . .

Many of the problems of our politics have their origins in the deliberate design of the Constitution, particularly as it was developed by Hamilton. The problems are *real.* The people's response to them is *rational.* What is missing is recognition that the *roots* of the problem lie in Hamilton's very success.

Today's national government is highly centralized, a huge and distant bureaucracy related in a merely episodic manner to gridlocked and unresponsive policy-making institutions. The web of special interests is a pragmatic answer, albeit one that represents only the most powerful few. Media and money call the tune for parties and candidates. People may quite rationally decide not to study issues or to participate in such a system.

What has brought about this set of problems and popular response? One absolutely fundamental cause is Hamilton's successful removal of the substance of policy from popular reach. The major pieces of Hamilton's design—the financial system and the legal system—were put in place in the late 1700s and early 1800s by Hamilton and his followers. They became fully integrated and coherently employed in the Progressive Era, from which the rise of the truly centralized Hamiltonian state can be dated.

Richard A. Brisbin, Jr.
"The Conservatism of Anton Scalia"
(Excerpt)

DISCUSSION QUESTIONS

1. According to Brisbin, what are the underlying concerns that comprise Justice Scalia's democratic vision? Can these views be related to Hamilton, Brutus, or the Pennsylvania minority? If so, how?
2. What is Justice Scalia's attitude toward judicial policy making?
3. List and discuss the seven methods or tactics that Justice Scalia has used to keep courts out of matters that should be assigned to elected leaders.
4. What is Justice Scalia's second standard of Constitutional governance?

Reprinted with permission from *Political Science Quarterly*, Vol. 105, No. 1 (Spring 1990): 6–10, 22–29.

5. Is Justice Scalia a believer in participatory democracy? Why or why not?
6. How do the beliefs of Justice Scalia differ from those espoused during the Warren Court years?
7. Describe how Justice Scalia fits the tradition of Frankfurter, Landis, and Bickel.
8. How might this tradition possess ties to both Hamilton and Brutus?

Judicial Power

. . . Derived from the central proposition of Scalia's democratic vision are a series of standards that define how the Constitution and statutes should be interpreted if his goal of capable leadership of the people is to be achieved. One standard is that the Supreme Court should avoid overseeing or altering the choices of leaders of the other branches of government. In a case challenging the procedures of the Agriculture Department he wrote that "Government mischief whose effects are widely distributed is more readily remedied through the political process, and does not call into play the distinctive function of courts as guardians against the oppression of the few by the many."[1] He believes the idea of separated powers demands that courts are to use the "passive virtues," or adhere to precedent, a "traditional" role, and an undefined methodology of "judicial craftsmanship."[2] In a Court of Appeals case he offered additional confirmation of separated powers as a check on judicial powers, stating that "Such a vision of judicial supremacy, not only in interpreting the Constitution but in controlling every aspect of executive actively bearing upon citizens' constitutional rights, does not comport with our understanding of the separation of powers."[3] Scalia champions the doctrine of standing as a way of restricting "courts to their traditional undemocratic role of protecting individuals and minorities against impositions of the majority" and to exclude "them from the even more undemocratic rule of prescribing how the other two branches should function in order to serve the interest *of the majority itself.*"[4]

Scalia's opinions have applied a specific set of tactics to keep courts out of matters that he would assign to elected leaders. As a first tactic, he provided judicial relief to citizens only when an "injury in fact" was caused by other persons or government.[5] Consequently, he argued against judicial relief for a church and its associated parties subjected to indirect government intelligence-gathering, against agency rules that did not aggrieve or have an impact on the daily affairs of firms, against hearing improperly stated claims, and against hearing a case of indirect re-

---

[1] *Community Nutrition Institute v. Block*, 698 F.2d. 1239, 1256 (D.C. Cir. 1983) (Scalia J., conc. & dissenting).

[2] The concept of passive virtues is defined in Alexander M. Bickel, *The Least Dangerous Branch* (Indianapolis: Bobbs-Merrill, 1962), 111–198; but Scalia establishes its basis in separated powers more than Bickel, who bases it on judicial capabilities. See Antonin Scalia, "The Doctrine of Standing as an Essential Element of the Separation of Powers," *Suffolk University Law Review* 17 (Winter 1983): 881–899. For further insight of the high value he places on established legal rules, see Antonin Scalia, "The Francis Boyer Lecture on Public Policy," The American Enterprise Institute for Public Policy Research, Washington, D.C., C-SPAN, 5 December 1989 (author's notes of the broadcast).

[3] *Ramirez de Arellano v. Weinberger*, 724 F.2d 143, 156 (D.C. Cir. 1983).

[4] Scalia, "Doctrine of Standing," 894. (Emphasis in original.)

[5] *Ibid.*, 894–895. Compare to *Maryland People's Counsel v. FERC*, 760 F.2d 318 (D.C. Cir. 1985).

sponsibility for a crime.[6] He refused to extend the ability of parties to sue government for infringements of civil rights in a case seeking damages for a former serviceman who was given LSD during an experiment while he was on active duty. He also refused relief to the serviceman under the Federal Tort Claims Act.[7]

Scalia, as a second tactic, used separation-of-powers arguments to constrain judicial relief of alleged harms. Relying on a separated powers argument, he denied a court the authority to hire a private attorney to prosecute a contempt against it. He viewed the prosecution of contempt to be an executive task, because it was not afforded to the courts by Congress.[8] Scalia held that a police officer, who conducted a warrantless search while acting in "good faith" that his search was legal, had a qualified executive immunity from suits because of the objective reasonableness in the circumstances confronting him.[9] Scalia also argued that the independent authority of Congress permitted it to restrict judicial review of certain specific provisions of law.[10] He especially objected to judicial ignorance of congressional and court-created rules limiting judicial jurisdiction over disputes.[11]

As a third tactic of passivity, he was cautious in permitting interest groups to challenge governmental actions and agency decisions. For Scalia, group legal action must be reasonable and in accordance with court rules.[12] He narrowly construed the Civil Rights Attorney's Fees Awards Act of 1976 to deny attorney fees to a civil rights litigant who won a favorable interpretation of law from a federal court but who failed to go forward to secure a remedy from the court.[13] As a related means of controlling judicial power, Scalia conceded that legislators can check judicial power by curtailing judicial review of the statutory powers of administrative agencies. Consequently, suits against government by various interest groups or citizens depend on Congress specifically establishing rights or interests that can be subjected to litigation.[14]

---

[6]*United Presbyterian Church in the U.S.A. v. Reagan*, 738 F.2d 455 (D.C. Cir. 1984); *Transwestern Pipeline Co. v. FERC*, 747 F.2d. 784 (D.C. Cir. 1984); *American Trucking Assns. v. ICC*, 747 F.2d 787 (D.C. Cir. 1984); *Carducci v. Regan*, 714 F.2d 171 (D.C. Cir. 1983); *Romero v. National Rifle Assn. of America*, 749 F.2d 77 (D.C. Cir. 1984).

[7]*United States v. Stanley*, 107 S.Ct. 3054 (1987); compare to *Bivens v. Six Unknown Named Agents*, 403 U.S. 443 (1971).

[8]*Young ex rel. United States v. Vuitton et Fils, S.A.*, 107 S.Ct. 2124, 2141–2147 (1987) (Scalia, J., conc.); see also *United States v. Providence Journal*, 108 S.Ct. 1502, 1511 (Scalia, J., conc.).

[9]*Anderson v. Creighton*, 107 S.Ct. 3034 (1987).

[10]*United States v. Fausto*, 108 S.Ct. 396 (1988); *K Mart Corp. v. Cartier, Inc.* (I), 108 S.Ct. 950, 960–2 (1988) (Scalia, J., dissenting).

[11]*Houston v. Lack*, 108 S.Ct. 2379, 2385–9 (1988) (Scalia, J., dissenting); *Torres v. Oakland Scavenger Co.*, 108 S.Ct. 2405, 2409–10 (1988) (Scalia, J., conc.); *Bowen v. Massachusetts*, 108 S.Ct. 2722, 2742–51 (1988) (Scalia, J., dissenting).

[12]*National Black Media Coalition v. FCC*, 760 F.2d 1297 (D.C. Cir. 1985); *Center for Auto Safety v. NHTSA*, 793 F.2d 1322, 1342–1345 (D.C. Cir. 1986) (Scalia, J., dissenting); *Natural Resources Defense Council v. Thomas*, 801 F.2d 457 (D.C. Cir. 1986). See also Richard Nagareda, "The Appellate Jurisprudence of Justice Antonin Scalia," *University of Chicago Law Review* 54 (Spring 1987): 706–715.

[13]*Hewitt v. Helms*, 107 S.Ct. 2672 (1987).

[14]*Sharp v. Weinberger*, 798 F.2d 145 (D.C. Cir. 1986); *ASARCO v. FERC*, 777 F.2d 764 (D.C. Cir) 1985); *Gott v. Walters*, 756 F.2d 902 (D.C. Cir. 1985). Compare *FAIC Securities v. U.S.*, 768 F.2d 352, 356–361 (D.C. Cir. 1985). Scalia also opposes private rights of action that allow private challenges of other private parties who fail to comply with agency rules; *Thompson v. Thompson*, 108 S.Ct. 513 520–523 (1988) (Scalia, J., conc.).

As a fourth tactic, Scalia reluctantly granted preenforcement relief to parties affected by agency rules and regulations. Despite precedents allowing such relief, he afforded it only when there was a strong possibility of irreparable injury.[15] Fifth, he respected the traditional reluctance of courts to consider disputes arising outside the United States, as in a suit by aliens alleging damages because of American violations of international law in Nicaragua.[16] He dissented when the Court of Appeals gave standing to a United States citizen whose property had been damaged during American military maneuvers in Honduras. He deemed the decision to be an "unprecedented" extension of judicial power because of its "elegant agnosticism" in reading a statute on such problems, its "incomprehensible disregard of traditional principles of equitable discretion," its interference with executive policies, an executive agreement, and executive acts of state, and its impugnment of the "integrity and fairness" of the courts of a friendly nation.[17]

As a sixth tactic of passivity, Scalia banned judicial intrusion into the internal conflicts of the Congress. He wrote that courts should not review congressional decisions on the qualifications of its members, the method Congress uses to distribute appropriations to agencies, or member challenges to the rules of the House of Representatives.[18] Seventh, he asserted court rules to prevent frivolous suits, suits on settled matters under a sharper doctrine of finality, moot issues, and actions that resulted in a "squandering of judicial resources."[19]

What kind of conservative is Antonin Scalia? His selection satisfied the desire of an avowed conservative administration that wanted judges supportive of changes in administrative law doctrine and that was inclined to avoid rights controversies and the extension of rights opposing majority values. Thus, Scalia was a conservative in the eyes of most political commentators because of his votes and opinions that contain a repudiation of the political vision of Warren Court liberalism.

Originating in Justice Harlan Stone's *Carolene Products* footnote, this vision suggests that opportunistic or factional politics can be prevented by competition among diverse factions or interests. The vision matured into Earl Warren's proposition that American constitutional politics could continue to exist only if there is cooperation among equals.[20] It is now defended by Justices Brennan and Marshall

---

[15]On preenforcement review, see *South Carolina Gas and Electric Co. v. ICC*, 747 F.2d 1541 (D.C. Cir. 1984); *Air New Zealand v. CAB*, 726 F.2d 832 (D.C. Cir. 1984).

[16]*Sanchez-Espinosa v. Reagan*, 770 F.2d 202, 208 (D.C. Cir. 1985).

[17]*Ramirez de Arellano v. Weinberger*, 747 F.2d 1500, 1555–1564 (D.C. Cir. 1984) (Scalia, J., dissenting). See also *Asociacixxon de Reclamantes v. United Mexican States*, 735 F.2d 1517 (D.C. Cir. 1984); *Beattie v. U.S.*, 756 F.2d 91 (D.C. Cir. 1984) (Scalia, J., dissenting).

[18]*Morgan v. U.S.*, 801 F.2d 445 (D.C. Cir. 1986); *International Union, UAW v. Donovan*, 746 F.2d 855, 861–862 (D.C. Cir. 1984); *Moore v. U.S. House of Representatives*, 733 F.2d 946, 962–965 (D.C. Cir. 1984) (Scalia, J., conc.). See also *National Juvenile Law Center v. Regnery*, 738 F.2d 455 (D.C. Cir. 1984).

[19]*Gulfstream Aerospace Corp. v. Mayacamas Corp.*, 108 S.Ct. 1133, 1144–5 (1988) (Scalia, J., conc.); *Honig v. Doe*, 108 S.Ct. 592, 614 (1988) (Scalia, J., dissenting); *Mathes v. Commissioner of Internal Revenue*, 788 F.2d 33 (D.C. Cir. 1986); *Dozier v. Ford Motor Co.*, 702 F.2d 1189 (D.C. Cir. 1983); Trakas *v. Quality Brands*, 759 F.2d 185 (D.C. Cir. 1985) (Scalia, J., dissenting); *Conafay by Conafay W. Nyeth Laboratories*, 793 F.2d 1322, 1342–1345 (D.C. Cir. 1986) (Scalia, J., dissenting).

[20]*Brown v. Board of Education*, 347 U.S. 483, 494 (1954); *Reynolds v. Sims*, 377 U.S. 533, 565 (1964).

and some legal scholars.[21] This proposition, far different from Scalia's central proposition about the nature of American constitutional government, assumes that political leaders should not adopt policies or practices that fail to treat people with equal dignity and respect or that prevent persons from participating in political decision making.[22] Scalia also differs with the standards of constitutional interpretation supporting the central proposition offered by Warren Court liberalism. Standards he rejects include the belief that the Supreme Court has to foster cooperative relations among equals[23] and that all institutions of government should be open to equal and active public participation and oversight.[24] He rejects the Warren Court liberals' skepticism of markets.[25] Finally, he rejects the Warren Court liberals' belief that government must be neutral in defining rights to choose modes of political, moral, and religious expression. Scalia, in contrast, remains a balancer of community needs for order and political stability against a narrowly defined purpose for rights. Thus he rejects the Warren Court liberal belief that rights serve as a trump card against the efforts of leaders or a majority to enforce a definition of the good life.[26]

If Scalia is not a Warren Court liberal, neither are his values in tune with some of the other brands of conservatism found in the Reagan political coalition. Scalia is not a member of the evangelical religious right whose primary political proposition is that constitutional governance should rest on moral principles identical to those discernible by a literal reading of selected biblical passages. Scalia does not appear to be a devotee of neo-Aristotelian or neo-Thomist natural rights theories. Although these ideas have influenced scholars like Judge John T. Noonan, Jr. of the Ninth Circuit, their language is absent in Scalia's writing. He does not give voice to the belief that constitutional governance should rest on the moral principles of natural

---

[21]Warren Court liberalism is an effort to provide a standard definition of the values of a group of like-minded judges and legal scholars. This theory has distinctive variants, like the natural rights liberalism of Justice William Douglas. It is distinctive from the historical positivism of Justice Hugo Black. See Martin Edelman, *Democratic Theories and the Constitution* (Albany: State University of New York Press, 1984), 121–208, 245–288.

[22]*Miranda v. Arizona*, 384 U.S. 436, 458–466(1966); Ronald Dworkin, *A Matter of Principle* (Cambridge, Mass.: Harvard University Press, 1985), 205–213.

[23]Ronald Dworkin, *Taking Rights Seriously* (Cambridge, Mass.: Harvard University Press, 1978), 131–149; William J. Brennan, Jr., "The Fourteenth Amendment," address to Section on Individual Rights and Responsibilities, American Bar Association, New York University Law School, 8 August 1986, 2, 6–8, 12, 17; Lawrence H. Tribe, *Constitutional Choices* (Cambridge, Mass.: Harvard University Press, 1985), 9–20.

[24]Dworkin, *Matter of Principle*, 211–213; *Greene v. McElroy*, 360 U.S. 474 (1959); *Cafeteria Workers v. McElroy*, 367 U.S. 886, 889–902 (1962) (Brennan, J., dissenting); *Goldberg v. Kelly*, 397 U.S. 254 (1970); *Bishop v. Wood*, 426 U.S. 341, 350–361 (1976) (Brennan, J., dissenting).

[25]Dworkin, *Matter of Principle*, 206–208; Tribe, *Constitutional Choices*, 165–187; Ronald Dworkin, "Is Wealth a Value?" *Journal of Legal Studies* 9 (March 1980): 191–226. See Warren's views in *Fibre-board Paper Products v. NLRB*, 379 U.S. 203 (1964); *NLRB v. Great Dane Trailers*, 388 U.S. 26 (1967); *Brown Shoe Co. v. U.S.*, 370 U.S. 294 (1961); *FTC v. Fred Meyer, Inc.*, 390 U.S. 341 (1968); *U.S. v. du Pont and Co.*, 351 U.S. 377, 414–426 (1956) (Warren, J., dissenting). See also *Dandridge v. Williams*, 397 U.S. 471 (1970) (Marshall, J., dissenting).

[26]Ronald Dworkin, "Liberalism," in Stuart Hampshire, ed., *Public and Private Morality* (Cambridge, England: Cambridge University Press, 1978), 127–136. See also Dworkin, *Taking Rights Seriously*, 266–278; *Cox v. Louisiana*, 379 U.S. 536 (1965); *Abington Township v. Schempp*, 374 U.S. 203 (1963) (Brennan, J., conc.); *Sherbert v. Verner*, 374 U.S. 398 (1963); *Griswold v. Connecticut*, 381 U.S. 479, 487–499 (1965) (Goldberg, J., conc.); *Paul v. Davis*, 424 U.S. 693, 714–735 (1976) (Brennan, J., dissenting).

law or any other abstract moral philosophy.[27] Although Scalia had contact at AEI and the University of Chicago with the proponents of the economic analysis of law, little of their concepts appears in his writings. He makes no reference to their belief that constitutional governance should be based on the maximization of the wealth of individual citizens.[28] Scalia, finally, gives no evidence of supporting the view of Attorney General Edwin Meese III who defends a historical approach to constitutional interpretation based on the belief that constitutional governance rests on loyalty to a literal reading of the original intention of the Constitution and its amendments.[29]

Scalia's political ideas and standards for constitutional interpretation actually modify and extend the propositions about American government propounded by Felix Frankfurter, his former law clerk Alexander Bickel, and his student, James Landis. These scholars believed, like Scalia does, in the central proposition that constitutional government must be directed by expert leaders. Frankfurter expounded on this view, stating: "Our scheme of society is more dependent than any other form of government on knowledge and wisdom and self-discipline for the achievement of its aims."[30] Landis applauded the development of a professional administrative process with the hope "that policies . . . could most adequately be developed by men bred to the facts" rather than the "casual office-seeker."[31] Bickel, fearful of "unvarnished populism" and unrestrained majorities, desired leaders who induce political stability, for "masses of people do not make clear-cut, long-

---

[27]John T. Noonan, Jr., "The Root and Branch of *Roe v. Wade,*" *Nebraska Law Review* 63 (1984): 668–679, effectively summarizes his principles. See also John T. Noonan, Jr., *The Antelope* (Berkeley: University of California Press, 1977), 158–159; John T. Noonan, Jr., *Persons and Masks of the Law* (New York: Farrar, Straus, Giroux, 1976), 152–167, on the natural worth of persons. Compare to Scalia, "Morality, Pragmatism," 123–127.

[28]Richard A. Posner, *The Economics of Justice* (Cambridge, Mass.: Harvard University Press, 1981), 48–115, best states the principle. See also Richard A. Posner, *Economic Analysis of Law,* 2d ed. (Boston: Little, Brown, 1977), 3, 10, 13, 341–359; Richard A. Posner, "Wealth Maximization Revisited," *Journal of Law, Ethics, and Public Policy* 2 (Fall 1985): 85–105; Richard A. Posner, "Free Speech in an Economic Perspective," *Suffolk Law Review* 20 (Spring 1986): 1–54; Richard A. Posner, "Legal Formalism, Legal Realism, and the Interpretation of Statutes and the Constitution," *Case Western Reserve Law Review* 37 (1986–7): 179; Frank H. Easterbrook, "Criminal Procedure as a Market System," *Journal of Legal Studies* 12 (June 1983): 289–332; Frank H. Easterbrook, "Ways of Criticizing the Court," *Harvard Law Review* 95 (February 1981): 802–832. Compare Scalia, "Morality, Pragmatism," 123–127; Scalia, "Economic Affairs," 706. Scalia's one use of economic analysis is an antitrust case, *Business Electronic Corp. v. Sharp Electronics Corp.*, 108 S.Ct. 1515 (1988).

[29]Antonin Scalia, "Originalism: The Lesser Evil," *University of Cincinnati Law Review* 57 (1989): 856–864. Compare Edwin Meese III, "The Battle for the Constitution," *Policy Review* 35 (Winter 1986): 34–35; Edwin Meese III, "Our Constitution's Design," *Marquette Law Review* 70 (Spring 1987): 381; Edwin Meese III, "The Attorney General's View of the Supreme Court," *Public Administration Review* 45 (November 1985): 701; Edwin Meese III, "The Supreme Court of the United States," *South Texas Law Review* 27 (Fall 1986): 455; and Edwin Meese III, "The Law of the Constitution," *Tulane Law Review* 61 (April 1987): 979. Besides not agreeing with Meese, Scalia is not an authoritarian centralist who would deny democratic participation to selected groups and use political institutions to enforce specific patterns of social behavior. Also, his deference to legislative economic policy making and his refusal to adopt a strong protective stance on both economic and personal rights sets him apart from libertarians. Compare Scalia, "Economic Affairs" to Edward H. Crane, "Judicial Activism and Economic Liberty," *Cato Policy Report* 8 (November-December 1986): 2–3; and Steven Macedo, *The New Right and the Constitution* (Washington, D.C.: Cato Institute, 1986); and see the discussion in Richard A. Brisbin, Jr., "Conservation Jurisprudence in the Reagan Era," *Cumberland Law Review* 19 (1988–1989): 497–537.

[30]*Youngstown Sheet and Tube Co. v. Sawyer,* 343 U.S. 579, 593 (1952) (Frankfurter, J., conc.); see also Edelman, *Democratic Theories,* 74–5, 94, 114–20, for an elaboration of this idea.

[31]James M. Landis, *The Administrative Process* (New Haven: Yale University Press, 1938), 154–155.

range decisions. They do not know enough about the issues, about themselves, their needs and wishes, or about what those needs and wishes will appear to them to be two months hence."[32] Landis contended that the administrative process would "fill the need for expertness" that legislatures and courts lacked.[33] These men believed that experts schooled in science and scientific management should set the policy agenda along a single, best course and then implement policy with the discretion to adjust it to new problems.[34] Scalia's policy choices confirm and extend this standard of constitutional interpretation by attempting to free the president from external constraints (as in the special prosecutor case), by affirming presidential direction of agency discretion, and by defending the discretion of the agencies in the interpretation of statutes.

Frankfurter and his associates encouraged judicial restraint in constitutional interpretation. For Frankfurter, checking and balancing of the other branches by the Court was to be confined to rare instances of the breach of specific constitutional rules or clear statutory language[35] and to grievous misconduct that offended the sense of justice embodied in constitutional provisions.[36] He wrote, "Courts are not representative bodies. They are not designed to be a good reflex of a democratic society. Their judgment is best informed, and therefore most defendable, within the narrow limits. Their essential quality is detachment, founded on independence.[37] To insure the courts did not act in a fashion that threatened the policy choices of virtuous leaders, Frankfurter and Bickel proposed that courts rely on the "passive virtues." "Reliance for the most precious interests of civilization . . . must be found outside of their vindication in courts of law. Only a persistent positive translation of the faith of a free society into the convictions and habits and actions of a community is the ultimate reliance against unabated temptations to fetter the human spirit."[38] Scalia is an ardent defender and elaborator of the judicial restraint and passive virtues discussed by Bickel and Frankfurter.

---

[32]Alexander M. Bickel, *The Morality of Consent* (New Haven: Yale University Press, 1975), 16.

[33]Landis, *Administrative Process*, 24, 30–31.

[34]*U.S. v. Morgan*, 313 U.S. 409 (1941); *Scripps Howard Radio v. FCC*, 316 U.S. 4 (1942); *SEC v. Chenery Corp.*, 318 U.S. 80 (1943); *Joint Anti-Fascist Refugee Committee v. McGrath*, 341 U.S. 123, 165–174 (1951) (Frankfurter, J., conc.).

[35]*Youngstown Sheet and Tube Co. v. Sawyer*, 343 U.S. 579, 593–614 (1952) (Frankfurter, J., conc.); *Terry v. Adams*, 345 U.S. 461, 472–477 (1953); *Gomillion v. Lightfoot*, 364 U.S. 334, 346–348 (1960).

[36]*Colegrove v. Green*, 328 U.S. 549, 556 (1946); see also *Rochin v. California*, 342 U.S. 165, 172–173 (1952).

[37]*Dennis v. U.S.*, 342 U.S. 494, 525 (1950) (Frankfurter, J., conc.). Compare *West Virginia State Bd. of Education v. Barnette*, 319 U.S. 624, 651–652 (1943) (Frankfurter, J., dissenting); *Baker v. Carr*, 369 U.S. 186, 280–297 (1962) (Frankfurter, J., dissenting); Alexander M. Bickel, *The Supreme Court and the Idea of Progress* (New York: Harper and Row, 1970), 99, 175.

[38]*West Virginia State Bd. of Education v. Barnette*, 319 U.S. 624, 670–671 (1943) (Frankfurter, J., dissenting). Compare Alexander M. Bickel, *The Least Dangerous Branch* (Indianapolis: Bobbs-Merrill Co., 1962), 111–198; Bickel, *Idea of Progress*, 81–88. See also Frankfurter's support for passivity in, *Coleman v. Miller*, 307 U.S. 433, 460–470 (1939) (opinion of Frankfurter, J.); *Colegrove v. Green*, 328 U.S. 549–556 (1946); *Joint Anti-Fascist Refugee Committee v. McGrath*, 341 U.S. 123, 149–160 (1951) (Frankfurter, J., conc.); *U.S. v. United Auto Workers*, 352 U.S. 567–593 (1957); *Burns v. Ohio*, 360 U.S. 252, 259–263 (1959) (Frankfurter, J., dissenting); *Poe v. Ullman*, 367 U.S. 497–509 (1961); *Baker v. Carr*, 369 U.S. 186, 266–277 (1962) (Frankfurter, J., dissenting); and the discussion in Gary T. Jacobsohn, *Pragmatism, Statesmanship, and the Supreme Court* (Ithaca, N.Y.: Cornell University Press, 1977), 120–121, 131–132.

For the scholars of this tradition of constitutional interpretation, hard policy choices are the province of elected leaders.[39] They did not exclude participation from their vision of the constitutional system, but Frankfurter feared civic lethargy, demagoguery, and corrupting factional interests.[40] Because this tradition holds that the choices of experts and leaders should not be easily challenged by groups or private parties, courts do not need to open administrative actions to participation or legal intervention by groups and private parties.[41] Courts must refrain from permitting interests to question executive policy preferences.[42] Scalia, in his opposition to inquiry into executive actions under the Freedom of Information Act, his opposition to private rights of action, and his reluctance in general to open the courts to claims of individuals alleging harms from agency policies only extends to new topics the legal doctrines supporting this standard of interpretation. His support of exclusive presidential powers and agency discretion in rulemaking also frees leaders for policy action.

In their interpretation of economic liberties, the interpretative standards of Frankfurter and Landis encouraged competitive markets. Like Scalia they wanted to have the policing of markets by expert bodies to ensure that unvirtuous forces did not corrupt the moral teachings of the marketplace.[43] Also, they believed that courts should defer to agency judgments about market policing and that courts should avoid interfering with the market to achieve redistributive policy ends.[44] In his constitutional standards on the topic of federalism, Frankfurter generally assumed, as Scalia now does, the supremacy of national institutions over state and local governments. But, he retained a belief in the benefits of some independence in state policy making, just as Scalia does.[45]

Frankfurter assumed, as Scalia now does, that the good life should be defined by the majority through the political process. The good life is the community's sense of what is virtuous activity, and individual actions should not be allowed to threaten the consensus on the good life.[46] Personal freedom exists "when it is ingrained in a

---

[39]See Bickel, *Idea of Progress*, 175–181; Landis, *Administrative Process*, 68–69.

[40]Jacobsohn, *Pragmatism*, 144–148. See also *SEC v. Chenery Corp.*, 318 U.S. 80, 91–94 (1943); Bickel, *Idea of Progress*, 157; Landis, *Administrative Process*, 75; Felix Frankfurter, *The Public and Its Government* (New Haven: Yale University Press, 1930), 157–163; Sanford V. Levinson, "The Democratic Faith of Felix Frankfurter," *Stanford Law Review* 25 (1973): 438–441.

[41]*U.S. v. Morgan*, 313 U.S. 409, 415–421 (1941); *CBS v. U.S.*, 316 U.S. 407, 429–446 (1942) (Frankfurter, J., dissenting); *Polish National Alliance v. NLRB*, 322 U.S. 643–648 (1944).

[42]*Baker v. Carr*, 369 U.S. 186, 297–302 (1962) (Frankfurter, J., dissenting).

[43]Landis, *Administrative Process*, 154–155; on Frankfurter see *Tigner v. Texas*, 310 U.S. 141–194 (1940); *East New York Savings Bank v. Hahn*, 326 U.S. 230–235 (1945); *American Federation of Labor v. American Sash and Door Co.*, 335 U.S. 538, 545–557 (1949) (Frankfurter, J., conc.).

[44]*Osborn v. Ozlin*, 310 U.S. 53–67 (1940); *Phelps Dodge Corp. v. NLRB*, 313 U.S. 177, 199–200 (1941); *American Federation of Labor v. American Sash and Door Co.*, 335 U.S. 538, 542–557 (1949) (Frankfurter, J., conc.); *Newark Fire Insurance Co. v. State Board*, 307 U.S. 313, 323–324 (1939) (Frankfurter, J.); *Wisconsin v. J.C. Penney Co.*, 311 U.S. 435, 445 (1940) contains Frankfurter's position.

[45]*New York v. U.S.*, 326 U.S. 572 (1946), but note the exception at 582, used to justify the majority position of Court (Rehnquist, J.) in *National League of Cities v. Usery*, 426 U.S. 833 (1976) and the minority positions in *Garcia v. SAMTA*, 469 U.S. 528 (1985). Compare to *Polish National Alliance v. NLRB*, 322 U.S. 643, 649–651 (1944) (Frankfurter, J., dissenting) and *Baker v. Carr*, 369 U.S. 186, 284–285 (1962) (Frankfurter, J., dissenting).

[46]Bickel, *Morality of Consent*, 24, 142; Jacobsohn, *Pragmatism*, 144–148.

people's habits . . . ," or when it is part of the history and common experience of a people.[47] Thus, Frankfurter's constitutional standard was that rights were not a resource to be used to permit diverse theories of the good life to flourish.[48] Instead, they serve as an instrument to control occasional defects in the decisions of elected leaders. In this interpretative tradition there is a recognition of the value of free speech, but free speech that threatens the democratic consensus can be restricted. There is to be criminal due process, but due process should not threaten the majority's sense of what constitutes a secure society.[49] The only times that rights can be used to change the effect of "habits and the feelings they engender. . . . " are when the enforcement of rights teaches the public to respect each other and the community's sense of right or when the enforcement prevents arbitrary actions detrimental to constitutional governance.[50] Thus, rights are to be used by courts to reestablish a community consensus rather than foster diverse values. By his opposition to most rights claims and especially to efforts to promote the equality of individuals, Scalia carries this tradition of interpretation toward a far greater defense of values of the majority. He gives greater weight to majority values on topics like racial equal protection, where Frankfurter voted for minority claimants. Scalia's opinion in *Block v. Meese* permits extensive majority control of publications, his views on religion permit legislative majorities to control religious values in education, his criminal justice case voting record favors the community over the rights of those who may have threatened order in the community, and his equality decisions favor stability over changes in community social and economic relationships beneficial to minorities.

The description of the constitutional values of Frankfurter and his students bears remarkable similarity to the values of Scalia in one additional way. All of these men share a commitment to law as the primary social value. As Bickel states the commitment: "Law is more than just another opinion; not because it embodies all right values, or because the values it does embody tend from time to time to reflect those of a majority or a plurality, but because it is the value of values. Law is the principal institution through which a society can assert its values.[51] Scalia agrees with this proposition, writing, ". . . I have never been able to isolate obligations of justice, except by defining them as those obligations that the law imposes."[52] All of

---

[47] *Minersville School District v. Gobitis*, 310 U.S. 586, 599 (1940). See also *Dennis v. U.S.*, 341 U.S. 494, 555 (1951) (Frankfurter, J., conc.); and Bickel, *Morality of Consent*, 88.

[48] *West Virginia State Bd. of Education v. Barnette*, 319 U.S. 624, 667 (1943) (Frankfurter, J., dissenting); *Milk Wagon Drivers Union v. Meadowmoor Dairies*, 312 U.S. 287, 293–299 (1949); see also Edelman, *Democratic Theories*, 93–114.

[49] On speech, see *Kovacs v. Cooper*, 336 U.S. 77, 89–97 (1949) (Frankfurter, J., conc.); *Dennis v. U.S.*, 341 U.S. 494, 546–556 (1951) (Frankfurter, J., conc.); *Communist Party v. Subversive Activities Control Board*, 367 U.S. 1, 88–105; *Wyman v. Updegraff*, 344 U.S. 183 (1952) (Frankfurter, J., conc.). On criminal due process, see *On Lee v. U.S.*, 343 U.S. 747, 760–762 (Frankfurter, J.); *Adamson v. California*, 332 U.S. 46, 59–68 (Frankfurter, J., conc.).

[50] See Bickel, *Morality of Consent*, 110–111; *Cooper v. Aaron*, 358 U.S. 1, 24–26 (1950) (Frankfurter, J., conc.); *McCollum v. Board of Education*, 333 U.S. 203, 214–220 (1948); *Harris v. U.S.*, 331 U.S. 145, 155–174 (1947) (Frankfurter, J., dissenting); *Haley v. Ohio*, 332 U.S. 596, 601–607 (1947) (Frankfurter, J.); *McNabb v. U.S.*, 318 U.S. 322–347 (1943); and *Niemotko v. Maryland*, 340 U.S. 268, 275–289 (1951) (Frankfurter, J., conc.).

[51] Bickel, *Morality of Consent*, 5.

[52] Scalia, "Morality, Pragmatism, and the Legal Order," 125.

these men are legalists who hold "moral conduct to be a matter of rule following, and moral relationships to consist of duties and rights determined by rules."[53]

Appointed to the Supreme Court because of his record of opinions and publications, his service for and connections to Republican administrations, and his personal character, Antonin Scalia is a typical product of the Reagan administration's judicial selection process. He is a justice who agrees with a majority of the Reagan administration's policy positions in constitutional and statutory litigation. Additionally, Scalia possesses a judicial philosophy and political vision that extend far beyond simple allegiance to a few policy positions. Akin to the tradition of constitutional interpretation of Felix Frankfurter and his students, it is a vision that limits the checking function of the Court in constitutional politics, enhances legislative and executive and agency power, and subjects rights to definition by the majority in control of the government. Finally, it is a majoritarian vision, a vision skeptical of Earl Warren's faith in a people governing themselves through a conflict encouraged by the existence of rights for minorities. In Scalia's democracy, leadership by the virtuous representatives of the majority and policy direction by the state remain the cardinal principles.

Finally, as the bloc analysis has revealed, Scalia's constitutional vision is close to but not identical to the views of the other Reagan administration appointees to the Supreme Court. Despite a few surprise votes or opinions in favor of First Amendment rights claimants, criminal defendants, and minorities, Rehnquist, O'Connor, and Kennedy share Scalia's majoritarian constitutional philosophy. As a group of relatively young justices, they should remain central figures in American constitutional development into the twenty-first century and a barrier for political forces seeking the reinvigoration of Warren Court liberalism.

---

[53]Judith N. Shklar, *Legalism: An Essay on Law, Morals, and Politics* (Cambridge, Mass.: Harvard University Press, 1964), 1.

10

Representation, Participation, and the Future of the Republic

In their classic American government textbook, *Government By The People*, authors James MacGregor Burns, Jack Peltason, and Thomas Cronin distinguish between two diverse and often conflicting visions of American purposes and beliefs. Two different "American dreams" contend for pre-eminence in American praxis (political thought and practice)—the American Way and the American Testament. The American Way reflects American traditional values and practices. It includes such ideas as liberty, freedom, rugged individualism, private property rights, survival of the fittest, success to the best, achievement, merit, excellence, government by the best, and an emphasis on the republic. The American Testament reflects American ideals, hopes, and inspirations. It includes such notions as equality, freedom from discrimination, a sense of commonwealth, community, generosity, fairness, help to those who cannot help themselves, government by the people, and an emphasis on participatory democracy and the common sense of the common people.[1]

The beliefs embodied by the American Way can be directly traced to the Federalist positions during the Constitutional ratification debate. The Federalists were the proponents of rugged individualism and success to the best and the fittest. In their arguments they emphasized that those who represented society's "best," as measured by education and social standing, were also the most fit to serve the public in governmental affairs. James Madison, in *Federalist* Paper 10, makes the classic case for the protection of private property. He equates property with stability and freedom. Indeed, he argues that there can be no freedom when property is in danger of being usurped. *Federalist* Paper 10 remains one of our greatest political tracts not only because it defines the purposes of our political system but because it serves as the basis for American capitalism, the bedrock of our economic system.

Madison and Hamilton were concerned that the American political and economic systems prosper and survive. The true test of a political system was its longevity.

[1]James MacGregor Burns, J. W. Peltason, and Thomas E. Cronin, *Government by the People*, 14th ed. (Englewood Cliffs, N.J.: Prentice-Hall, 1990), p. 163.

Could a political and economic system survive? Would it be stable enough to last? According to Federalist thought, a system could survive and prosper if it was based upon competition, merit, and the freedom guaranteed by the protection of private property. The *Federalist* Papers, contain numerous references to Rome. Rome was considered the ideal political system because it lasted hundreds of years. It exhibited an endurance that Federalists hoped to emulate. Preservation of the republic was foremost in the Federalist mind. One can see this in Madison's dismissal of the arguments for frequent revision of the Constitution and in the general Federalist belief in government by the fittest. Could government be entrusted to common people and still last? Federalists did not believe so.[2]

In contrast, the Antifederalists' thoughts have more in common with the American Testament. They were proponents of government by the people and participatory democracy. As Gordon Wood has observed:

> The Antifederalists emerged as the spokesmen for the growing American antagonism to aristocracy and as the defenders of the most intimate participation in politics of the widest variety of people possible. . . . Whatever else may be said about the Antifederalists, their populism cannot be impugned. They were true champions of the most extreme kind of democratic and egalitarian politics expressed in the Revolutionary era.[3]

Antifederalists championed a larger House of Representatives, where there could be representation by occupation and class. They were also proponents of term limits for national political officeholders. They believed that through rotation of offices and brief terms for governmental service the common sense of common people could best be tapped. Many Antifederalists argued for shorter terms for officeholders in the House of Representatives. They were wary of the lifetime provisions for office guaranteed to members of the Supreme Court in the Constitution.

Although Thomas Jefferson was not considered an Antifederalist, he did share many Antifederalist thoughts. He believed that the earth was for the living and therefore no generation could bind another. Because of this, he championed measures that would make it easier to amend the Constitution. He also believed in reviewing property laws every 19 years or so. Jefferson fervently believed in the right of citizens to participate in the decisions that would affect them. He argued that this could be accomplished via regular meetings in the context of what he termed "ward republics."[4]

Because Antifederalist thought contains such an emphasis on egalitarianism if not outright equality, Federalists viewed these beliefs as threatening to the longevity and stability of a republic. After all, the notion of competition requires a certain amount of inequality, and Madison noted as much in *Federalist* Paper 10 when he implied that movement toward complete equality inevitably leads to the loss of freedom, democracy, and, quite possibly, the republic. Whereas Federalists were concerned with stability, Antifederalists were more concerned with justice. How could a society

---

[2]For an argument that critically discusses Madison's Constitutional equilibric stable system, please see David E. Ingersoll and Richard Matthews, *Liberalism in America* (Englewood Cliffs, N.J.: Prentice-Hall, 1986), pp. 57–89.

[3]Gordon S. Wood, *The Creation of the American Republic, 1776–1787* (New York: W. W. Norton and Company, 1969), p. 516.

[4]For a discussion of Jefferson's beliefs, please see Richard K. Matthews, *The Radical Politics of Thomas Jefferson* (Lawrence: The University of Kansas Press, 1984), *passim*.

achieve justice in its representation if it did not include a greater role for citizens from all walks of life in governmental affairs?

Perhaps Thomas Jefferson serves as a bridge for Antifederalist thoughts influencing our governmental processes. The war of ideas between Antifederalists and Federalists was framed, in large part, by Jefferson's Declaration of Independence. This Declaration emphasized equality as a condition of American rights. It was self-evident that all men are created equal. As Garry Wills notes in *Inventing America,* Jefferson was not an ambiguous thinker in this realm. He had specific ideas of what equality implied.[5] For example, he championed the idea of giving citizens a piece of land, not because he was enamored with property rights, as the majority of Federalists were, but because with property citizens could exercise their rights of franchise and participate in politics. This is the type of equality of participation that Antifederalists also championed. As a result, it is no surprise that the struggle to widen the franchise can be traced back to the ratification period. In fact, a large part of our history includes the struggle to expand the franchise to African Americans, Native Americans, women, and young people.

This struggle is most important because it defines us as a nation. The struggle to widen the franchise is a struggle that indicates the importance of equality in our nation. Without voting rights a people are politically impoverished. The movement to extend voting rights was not solely a struggle of civil rights but also a struggle for participatory rights. Many of the issues that emanated from the struggle for "civil rights" in the 1950s and 1960s were directly or indirectly related to the ability of minority groups, particularly African Americans, to become involved in all aspects of American political and social life as equal citizens, while still preserving an authentic identity and promoting a sense of pride in the role of the descendants of Africa in the American formation. The immediate goals of the civil rights movement were connected to the advancement of electoral power and acceptance into the offices of governance, but the movement was also concerned with the further development of the American democratic spirit as such and the recognition of this spirit as equally the product of both the free and the enslaved, the privileged and the estranged, the great and the humble, the powerful and the oppressed. As our nation struggled with civil rights, women's rights, and the rights of the handicapped, it simultaneously struggled with extending and enlarging democracy. The struggle was initiated with Thomas Jefferson's Declaration of Independence and it was present, in very early form, in the arguments between Antifederalists and Federalists during the Constitutional ratification debate.

During the ratification period, a very radical idea was presented by the Federalists. They believed that democracy could be extended to a large nation. Madison argued for this in *Federalist* Paper 10. Most people, including many Antifederalists, believed that democracy worked only in small geographical areas like the Greek city-states. Any attempt to extend these democratic rights over a large republic would inevitably lead to the loss of democratic freedoms.[6] As it turned out, the Antifederalists were wrong, for democracy could be extended to a large stable republic that would last. Another radical idea was born during the ratification debates—the idea that common people could take part in government decisions and better represent people. This idea implied extending the franchise and ran counter to the aristocratic ideas of many Federalists. This idea would eventually change our nation.

---

[5]Garry Wills, *Inventing America* (New York: Vintage Books, 1978), *passim.*

In fact, it may be impossible to understand our history without understanding that it has been a struggle between the ideas of representative democracy and participatory democracy. The two contending American dreams, the American Way and the American Testament, represent the struggle between representative democracy and participatory democracy. Our history has largely been one of reconciling these two ideas. Thus this philosophical struggle was present at Philadelphia in the late 1700s, at Antietam in the 1860s, in the Progressive Reform Movement and the women's suffrage movement at the turn of the century, in Montgomery Alabama in the 1950s and 1960s, and during the consumer and environmental movements in the 1970s.

One of the abiding characteristics of American politics and the evolution of American democracy is the frequency of paradox resulting from the deeper tensions within the American political culture. Such paradox is noted upon examining the promulgation and implementation of civil rights reforms as they occurred in the late 1950s and early 1960s. Contrary to the predictions of many Antifederalists, the central government actually assumed the mantle of champion of liberties, as it was the federal government that forced recalcitrant state and local governments into compliance with the judicial and legislative commands now issued from the federal level in protection of the rights of oppressed minorities in the states. The federal government did exactly as Madison and Hamilton expected: It protected a minority from the "tyranny of the majority." In this instance it protected a subjugated African American minority from the unjust and unconstitutional practices of legal and state-sponsored segregation. Admittedly, the Federalists were correct in this regard, and even prophetic in their anticipation of such problems. Nonetheless, if one examines the nature of the civil rights movement, one is struck by the manner in which this movement also verifies the concerns of the Antifederalist opposition.

Within the institutions of government proper, the civil rights reforms of the 1950s and 1960s were initiated by the Supreme Court (again, paradoxically, the least democratic entity of the federal system, at least in terms of its relationship with the people), forwarded by two Presidents, and eventually achieved in Congress. The original and most powerful impetus, however, for these reforms was produced by the commitment, energy, and sacrifice of American citizens. Struggling on the local level, African-American leadership, participating in direct democratic action, committed the full force of their being into the construction of a more perfect democratic society. This application of one's whole self—heart, mind, body, and soul—to the perilous fight for freedom represents the purest sense of democratic participation, a participation that Thomas Jefferson demanded of a free citizenry. Eventually joined by compasionate and like-minded freedom-loving allies beyond the African-American community, the civil rights movement, a product of individual courage and communal resolve from the very roots of democracy, confronted the enemies of freedom and forced the central government to respond. Certain institutional structures allowed the eventual support of reform, and in this sense the Federalists' trust in vigorous central government is somewhat vindicated. Simultaneously, and perhaps more importantly, the will of a minority community, exerted at the local level by "ordinary" citizens who battled to dismantle enormous barriers to justice and liberty, prove the proposition, held by Antifederalists, that democracy ultimately is the province and power of the people themselves. Through participatory action, American citizens joined the battle for full democracy. It was a victory for those citizens

---

[6]For a discussion of these beliefs, see Robert A. Dahl, *Democracy And Its Critics* (New Haven: Yale University Press, 1989), pp. 1–37.

when their representative government at last decided to fall into ranks with their constituents, the people, the moving force in any authentically democratic society.

As we have attempted to demonstrate throughout this book, the debates between representative democrats and participatory democrats are as real today as they were during the ratification period. We, as a nation, are still debating the real intrinsic value of voting and the opinion of the public. We still struggle over the role of property in our society and the proper balance of free market capitalism and government intervention in private markets. We are enamored with representation but also believe in the participation of common people with common sense in our political system. Currently, a debate over term limits for representatives to state legislatures appears to be quite similar to portions of the debate heard during the ratification period. Can a proposal for term limits for the national legislature be far behind?

Thomas Jefferson set the parameters of the debate with his Declaration of Independence. He wrote of self-evident truths. Of these truths, equality was mentioned first, quickly followed by life, liberty, and the pursuit of happiness. As Rick Matthews and Garry Wills have argued, happiness was not some euphoric goal or transcendental belief for Jefferson. It was concrete, precise, and real. People could not be happy without the ability to participate in decisions that would affect their lives. A society based upon the notion that people are inherently politically unequal could not and would not be a participatory society. It therefore would not be a society dedicated to the maximum fulfillment of happiness for its citizens.[7] Ever since Jefferson's Declaration, scholars and philosophers have been attempting to reconcile Madison's liberal realism with Jeffersonian idealism, as the two philosophical ideals require different conceptions of justice.[8] For Madison, a just society was a stable one that protected private property from popular insurrection. For Jefferson, a just society was one that ensured the participation of people in governmental affairs. Madison's mind and Jefferson's heart have dominated our history.

Jefferson's ideas, however, were taken seriously only to a point. That point was slavery. Although it is true that some Federalist founders and even Antifederalists opposed the institution of slavery, that institution persisted. It was often referred to as the wart on the American moral conscience. The politics of slavery dominated the early part of our nation's history. In fact, until the Civil War the union of states was a tenuous and fragile one. Philosophically we suffered from conflicting goals—equality and individuality, state's rights and national sovereignty, and stability and justice. The early period of our nation's history was devoted to questions of who we were as a people and what goals we were going collectively to stand for. The Declaration of Independence and the Constitution were fine, but what did they mean? How much power was the federal government going to have? The answer was to be found in two Supreme Court cases, *Marbury v. Madison* and *McCulloch v. Maryland.* What exactly did Jefferson's emphasis upon equality in the Declaration of Independence mean? This question would be answered by a bloody Civil War and ultimately by Lincoln in his Gettysburg Address.

Unlike many politicians and statesmen preceding him, Lincoln took the Jeffersonian goal of equality seriously. Although it is true that, for Lincoln, the Civil War (and even the Emancipation Proclamation) was foremost a struggle to keep the Union intact, by the time of the Gettysburg Address things had changed. It was this address that served to redirect America. It was this address that signaled a "rebirth."

---

[7] Wills, *Inventing America*, pp. 248–255; Matthews, *The Radical Politics of Thomas Jefferson*, pp. 77–96.

It was this address that linked the Declaration of Independence once and for all with the Constitution. After Lincoln's address a fusion of ideas took place: Equality was to be fused with representative government. We have indicated, as did Jefferson, that the emphasis upon equality implies participation, so the fusion was one of representative government with participatory government. This is what Lincoln meant when he uttered the words, "of the people, by the people, for the people." This fusion was paid for in blood. It signaled a beginning, not an end. It signaled a continuing struggle for equality and greater participation in civic affairs among people. It signaled the end of aristocratic and elitist government and the beginning of popular government.

The American founding stretches across a continuum, one that includes the ideas and efforts of both the author of the Declaration of Independence and the framers of the Constitution, as well as the sacrifices of the great champions of freedom who would follow. In the proclamations at Seneca Falls, in Lincoln's declarations at Gettysburg and on the occasion of his second inaugural, in the idealism of Port Huron, and in the martyrdom of Martin Luther King, Jr., that founding act has been repeated and in the process the notion of freedom in America has been renewed. Indeed, one can recall specific moments wherein the spirit of American freedom has become transfigured and the process toward freedom propelled into moments of birth, rebirth, and transformation. The egalitarianism of Jefferson and Lincoln was simultaneously reaffirmed and surpassed as Dr. King confessed his dream for America, a dream wherein the first principles of democratic politics would become finally and irrevocably incarnated in the mundane practices of American political and social reality. Through Dr. King's life and works, the principles that are represented in the notion of "government of the people, by the people, and for the people" were reclaimed for *all* Americans—universally, without exclusion, exception, or stint, and with a limitless faith in the potential of a truly just and democratic polity.

The United States had been heading in this direction since its inception. The widening of the franchise preceded Lincoln, as did the Jacksonian era with its democratization of the common person. But Lincoln, more than any other, understood what his particular moment in time signified. It was a time for a new order. It was a time for a rededication to the principles ensconced in the Declaration of Independence. As one scholar noted, ". . . . Up to the Civil War, 'the United States' was invariably a plural noun: 'The United States are a free government.' After Gettysburg, it became a singular: 'The United States is a free government.'"[9]

The modern civil rights, consumer, environmental, and handicapped rights movements are all a part of this grand rededication that Lincoln launched. None of them would have been successful without the enlargement of the franchise and the increased participation of leaders and members in the movements. No one knows with any certainty the precise events that will shape our nation's future. However, a glance at the arguments made during the ratification debate can assure us of one thing: People will attempt to obtain greater control of their government. This is the lesson of history. It may not mean higher voting percentages in national elections, but it may mean greater attendance at county planning board meetings. It may mean attempts to in-

[8]See, for example, John Rawls, *A Theory of Justice.* (Cambridge: Harvard University Press, 1971), passim; and Michael J. Sandel, *Liberalism and the Limits of Justice.* (Cambridge: Cambridge University Press, 1982); *passim.*

crease the control of the people over their elected representatives. It may mean continuing and intensifying the struggle for gender equality in America. It may mean an emphasis upon new communications technologies to decrease communication gaps between people and elected officials. It may mean greater reliance on interest groups as a means for articulating the desires of the people to their elected representatives. It may also mean a restructuring of political parties to perform this function.

In a way, some scholars and political activists are proposing a quite radical idea. It is just as radical as Madison's extension of representative democracy to a geographically large state during the ratification period. They argue that participatory democracy can indeed be extended to a large nation, that participatory democracy need not be confined to small areas or local governments, that breakthroughs in communications technologies can enhance participatory politics.[10] While scholars and philosophers inevitably argue that representative and participatory politics can never be reconciled, activists continue to try. The reconciliation of the American Way and the American Testament appears to be our future. This reconciliation was framed by Jefferson, argued and debated during the ratification of the Constitution, paid for in blood by the Civil War, and reframed and rededicated by Abraham Lincoln.

> The Gettysburg Address has become an authoritative expression of the American spirit—as authoritative as the Declaration itself, and perhaps even more influential, since it determines how we read the Declaration. For most people now, the Declaration means what Lincoln told us it means, as a way of correcting the Constitution itself without overthrowing it. It is this correction of spirit, this intellectual revolution, that makes attempts to go back beyond Lincoln to some earlier version so feckless. The proponents of states' rights may have arguments, but they have lost their force, in courts as well in the popular mind. By accepting the Gettysburg Address, its concept of a single people dedicated to a proposition, we have been changed. Because of it, we live in a different America.[11]

Freedom and the struggle for equality have been, and will likely always remain, a perpetual endeavor. Our future as a nation has been shaped by our past, and our past has been shaped by Antifederalists, Federalists, Thomas Jefferson, and Abraham Lincoln. Our destiny is one of authentic equality and participation. This destiny will be shaped by fortune. Understanding our past may provide us with some small ability to shape fortune as did Jefferson and Lincoln. We close with a presentation of the Declaration of Independence and the Gettysburg Address.

---

[9]Garry Wills, *Lincoln at Gettysburg: The Words That Remade America* (New York: Simon & Schuster, 1992), 145.

[10]See, for example, Benjamin Barber, *Strong Democracy* (Berkeley: University of California Press, 1984), *passim*; Robert A. Dahl, *Controlling Nuclear Weapons: Democracy Versus Guardianship* (New York: Syracuse University Press, 1985), *passim*; Richard Hollander, *Video Democracy: The Vote from Home Revolution* (Airy: Lomand publications, 1985), *passim*; Robert Fischer, *Let the People Decide: Neighborhood Organizing in America* (Boston: Twayne Publishers, 1984), *passim*.

The Declaration of Independence

July 4, 1776

In Congress, July 4, 1770,

THE UNANIMOUS DECLARATION OF THE THIRTEEN UNITED STATES OF AMERICA,

When in the Course of human events, it becomes necessary for one people to dissolve the political bands which have connected them with another, and to assume among the Powers of the earth, the separate and equal station to which the Laws of Nature and of Nature's God entitle them, a decent respect to the opinions of mankind requires that they should declare the causes which impel them to the separation.

We hold these truths to be self-evident, that all men are created equal, that they are endowed by their Creator with certain unalienable Rights, that among these are Life, Liberty and the pursuit of Happiness. That to secure these rights, Governments are instituted among Men, deriving their just powers from the consent of the governed. That whenever any Form of Government becomes destructive of these ends, it is the Right of the People to alter or to abolish it, and to institute new Government, laying its foundation on such principles and organizing its powers in such form, as to them shall seem most likely to effect their Safety and Happiness. Prudence, indeed, will dictate that Governments long established should not be changed for light and transient causes; and accordingly all experience hath shown, that mankind are more disposed to suffer, while evils are sufferable, than to right themselves by abolishing the forms to which they are accustomed. But when a long train of abuses and usurpations, pursuing invariably the same Object evinces a design to reduce them under absolute Despotism, it is their right, it is their duty, to throw off such Government, and to provide new Guards for their future security.—Such has been the patient sufferance of these Colonies; and such is now the necessity which constrains them to alter their former Systems of Government. The history of the present King of Great Britain is a history of repeated injuries and usurpations, all having in direct object the establishment of an absolute Tyranny over these States. To prove this, let Facts be submitted to a candid world.

He has refused his Assent to Laws, the most wholesome and necessary for the public good.

He has forbidden his Governors to pass Laws of immediate and pressing importance, unless suspended in their operation till his Assent should be obtained; and when so suspended, he has utterly neglected to attend to them.

He has refused to pass other Laws for the accommodation of large districts of people, unless those people would relinquish the right of Representation in the Legislature, a right inestimable to them and formidable to tyrants only.

He has called together legislative bodies at places unusual, uncomfortable, and distant from the depository of their Public Records, for the sole purpose of fatiguing them into compliance with his measures.

---

[11]Garry Wills, *Lincoln at Gettysburg*, pp. 146–147.

He has dissolved Representative Houses repeatedly, for opposing with manly firmness his invasions on the rights of the people.

He has refused for a long time, after such dissolutions, to cause others to be elected; whereby the Legislative Powers, incapable of Annihilation, have returned to the People at large for their exercise; the State remaining in the mean time exposed to all the dangers of invasion from without, and convulsions within.

He has endeavoured to prevent the population of these States; for that purpose obstructing the Laws of Naturalization of Foreigners; refusing to pass others to encourage their migration hither, and raising the conditions of new Appropriations of Lands.

He has obstructed the Administration of Justice, by refusing his Assent to Laws for establishing Judiciary Powers.

He has made Judges dependent on his Will alone, for the tenure of their offices, and the amount and payment of their salaries.

He has erected a multitude of New Offices and sent hither swarms of Officers to harass our People, and eat out their substance.

He has kept among us, in times of peace, Standing Armies without the Consent of our legislature.

He has affected to render the Military independent of and superior to the Civil Power.

He has combined with others to inspect us to a jurisdiction foreign to our constitution, and unacknowledged by our laws; giving his Assent to their acts of pretended legislation:

For quartering large bodies of armed troops among us:

For protecting them, by a mock Trial from Punishment for any Murders which they should commit on the Inhabitants of these States:

For cutting off our Trade with all parts of the world.

For imposing taxes on us without our Consent:

For depriving us in many cases, of the benefits of Trial by Jury:

For transporting us beyond Seas to be tried for pretended offences:

For abolishing the free System of English Laws in a neighbouring Province, establishing therein an Arbitrary government, and enlarging its Boundaries so as to render it at once an example and fit instrument for introducing the same absolute rule into these Colonies:

For taking away our Charters, abolishing our most valuable Laws, and altering fundamentally the Forms of our Governments:

For suspending our own Legislature declaring themselves invested with Power to legislate for us in all cases whatsoever.

He has abdicated Government here, by declaring us out of his Protection and waging war against us.

He has plundered our seas, ravaged our Coasts, burnt our towns, and destroyed the lives of our people.

He is at this time transporting large armies of foreign mercenaries to complete the works of death, desolation and tyranny, already begun with circumstances of cruelty & perfidy scarcely paralleled in the most barbarous ages, and totally unworthy the Head of a civilized nation.

He has constrained our fellow Citizens taken Captive on the high Seas to bear Arms against their Country, to become the executioners of their friends and Brethren, or to fall themselves by their Hands.

He has excited domestic insurrections amongst us, and has endeavoured to bring on the inhabitants of our frontiers, the merciless Indian Savages, whose known rule of warfare, is an undistinguished destruction of all ages, sexes and conditions.

In every stage of these Oppressions We have Petitioned for Redress in the most humble terms: Our repeated Petitions have been answered only by repeated injury. A Prince, whose character is thus marked by every act which may define a Tyrant, is unfit to be the ruler of a free People.

Nor have We been wanting in attention to our Brittish brethren. We have warned them from time to time of attempts by their legislature to extend an unwarrantable jurisdiction over us. We have reminded them of the circumstances of our emigration and settlement here. We have appealed to their native justice and magnanimity, and we have conjured them by the ties of our common kindred to disavow these usurpations, which, would inevitably interrupt our connections and correspondence. They too have been deaf to the voice of justice and of consanguinity. We must, therefore, acquiesce in the necessity, which denounces our Separation, and hold them, as we hold the rest of mankind, Enemies in War, in Peace Friends.

We, therefore, the Representatives of the united States of America, in General Congress, Assembled, appealing to the Supreme Judge of the world for the rectitude of our intentions, do, in the Name, and by Authority of the good People of these Colonies, solemnly publish and declare, That these United Colonies are, and of Right ought to be Free and Independent States; that they are Absolved from all Allegiance to the British Crown, and that all political connection between them and the State of Great Britain, is and ought to be totally dissolved; and that as Free and Independent States, they have full Power to levy War, conclude Peace, contract Alliances, establish Commerce, and to do all other Acts and Things which Independent States may of right do. And for the support of this Declaration, with a firm reliance on the Protection of Divine Providence, we mutually pledge to each other our Lives, our Fortunes and our sacred Honor.

The Gettysburg Address

November 19, 1863

Abraham Lincoln

Four score and seven years ago our fathers brought forth on this continent, a new nation, conceived in Liberty, and dedicated to the proposition that all men are created equal.

Now we are engaged in a great civil war, testing whether that nation or any nation so conceived and so dedicated, can long endure. We are met on a great battle-field of that war. We have come to dedicate a portion of that field, as a final resting place for those who here gave their lives that that nation might live. It is altogether fitting and proper that we should do this.

But, in a larger sense, we can not dedicate—we can not consecrate—we can not hallow—this ground. The brave men, living and dead, who struggled here, have consecrated it, far above our poor power to add or detract. The world will little note, nor long remember what we say here, but it can never forget what they did here. It is for us the living, rather, to be dedicated here to the unfinished work which they who fought here have thus far so nobly advanced. It is rather for us to be here dedicated to the great task remaining before us—that from these honored dead we take increased devotion to that cause for which they gave the last full measure of devotion—that we here highly resolve that these dead shall not have died in vain—that this nation, under God, shall have a new birth of freedom and that government of the people, by the people, for the people, shall not perish from the earth.